THE STREETS OF LONDON
The Booth Notebooks –East

Editors:
Jess Steele
Mike Steele

2018

Deptford Forum Publishing, 2 Osberton Road, London SE12 8AH

The Booth Inquiry archive, of which these notebooks form a part, is held at the British Library of Political and Economic Science at the London School of Economics. The copyright for this edition of the transcribed notebooks is held by Deptford Forum Publishing.

Copyright © Deptford Forum Publishing 2018

Edited by Jess Steele and Mike Steele
Design and layout by Short Run Press
Cover design and title page graphic by Lionel Openshaw
Maps by 6970 Design
Original illustrations by Eve Steele
Printed by Short Run Press, Exeter, Devon

Funded by East London History Society (ELHS)

This is not a facsimile edition. We have tried to reproduce the text in a format that can satisfy both academic and general interest. This has meant making some minor changes for the sake of consistency and readability.

ISBN 978-1-898536-02-4

British Library Cataloguing in Publication Data
A catalogue record for this book is available from the British Library

Contents

Acknowledgements

Producing this book has been a long and arduous task which has involved many people over the years.

Back in the late 1990s Karen Bray began the transcribing which was picked up by Noel and Julia Rooney. Lionel Openshaw and Simon Cowderoy both worked on early designs, Isabel Watson looked up photographs in the Hackney archives. Juliet Desailly and Nigel Thomas, former directors of Deptford Forum Publishing, were a great support. Unfortunately that version of *The Streets of London: East* never materialised, but all that effort has finally found its fruition.

This book would never have happened without Phil Mernick who arranged the funding partnership with the East London History Society.

Indy Bhullar, curator of the Charles Booth archive at LSE Library, helped with the Booth maps. We got help with the photographs from the Museum of London, the Frith Collection, Bilingsgate Institute, and Amir Dotan of Stoke Newington History.

Rosemary O'Day & David Englander wrote the original introduction to the South East volume. Rosemary has helped us to update it for this version and we have included an extract of David's article about Booth's Jews.

We would like to thank Christopher Stephens (Booth's great grandson) for his foreword. Ben Lewis at 6970 Design proved flexible and responsive as always. Mark Couch and Paul Luffman at Short Run Press have been wonderfully patient with us.

Finally, producing this book has been a family affair, with editorial assistance from Sonia Steele, original illustrations by Eve Steele and ongoing support from Ronan Larvor. We take sole responsibility for the errors but we look forward to sharing this book across East London and beyond.

Jess & Mike, June 2018

Foreword

Charles Booth's work has never been more relevant. First, he put his finger on the issue of the day: inequality. Next, he developed a thorough evidence-based methodology, based on quantitative and qualitative research, thus blowing away political beliefs based on false facts. Finally, he paid for nearly 20 years of detailed research with funds generated from his successful Liverpool-based shipping business. He thus gave the lie to the assumption that all business people are narrowly self-interested.

The publication of the next volume of *The Streets of London* edited by Jess and Mike Steele is extremely welcome. Every page contains nuggets of colour about Victorian London. Every page is rich in social comment. In so far as there are obvious parallels with these same streets in 21st century London, they should still stir our consciences.

Christopher Stephens
Great grandson of Charles Booth
12th February 2018

Editors' Preface

Jess first found the Booth Inquiry archive when researching a local history of Deptford in the early 1990s. As she sat in the chilly archive room she found herself writing out in pencil the full text of the walks from the so-called 'police notebooks'. She knew then that she wanted to publish these fascinating snapshots.

There are 392 notebooks in the Booth archive which cover three research collections: Poverty; Industry; and Religious Influences. Around 30 of these are the handwritten notes of 300 walks across the whole of London, while others record over 1,000 interviews with businessmen, workers and trades union representatives, school board visitors, publicans and vicars. The original project had begun by collecting detailed information about individual households. Later they chose to focus on whole streets as it became too time-consuming.

With much help in transcribing, we were pleased to publish the South East volume of walks in 1998 and at that time had high hopes of producing the other volumes in rapid succession. However, constraints of time and money delayed us by a mere 20 years! The breakthrough came when East London History Society agreed to fund this publication.

In the meantime LSE have digitised the original notebooks and made them available at: www.booth.lse.ac.uk. We feel a physical book offers a more useable format. It's certainly much easier to read than Duckworth's longhand and by being organised into chapters from the Thames to 'the far north' in Stoke Newington, it is possible to browse among these neighbourhoods at the end of the 19th century, aided by sketch maps, contemporary photographs and new illustrations, or to use the index to gain a sense of what your street was like 120 years ago.

These neighbourhoods were dynamic "the rich and the poor both leave but the middle class are coming in". Since the research aimed to update their own earlier material these notebooks not only describe the neighbourhoods as they were at the end of the century but also how they had changed in the previous ten years.

Despite the impressive scale and fascinating detail of these walks, it has to be said that Duckworth and his policemen companions are often obnoxious and patronising. They make outrageous assumptions and blatant generalisations which readers may find disturbing. The East London volume, in particular includes innumerable references to Jews. The language used in the notebooks reveals as much about Duckworth and contemporary attitudes as it does about the poor of Stepney or Whitechapel. These views are, of course, not those of ourselves, Deptford Forum Publishing or East London History Society.

This is not the easiest of sources. However, with a little patience you should find yourself happily meandering through the 68 walks in Booth's East London. Through this publication, we hope to contribute to the debates on London's history and its future, its problems and their solutions. We want it to be used in many different ways: as a source for history and the social sciences, as a resource for school projects, as a guide for Sunday strolling, as a spur to comparison and compassion for those who live in London's poverty 120 years after these walks. Most of all we want readers to enjoy the exploration of their own neighbourhoods, whether out on the streets or from the comfort of an armchair.

Jess & Mike Steele, June 2018

Introduction: Police and Social Inquiry In Late-Victorian London

David Englander and Rosemary O'Day 1998
Adapted 2018 for the East London edition

Charles Booth has never wanted for an audience. The 17-volume survey *Life and Labour of the People in London*, which he published between 1889 and 1903, provided the first scientific estimates of poverty and has been the starting point for all serious discussion of the subject ever since. It is rightly regarded as one of the high points in the British tradition of empirical social research. Employing a subsistence definition of poverty Booth found, contrary to his expectations, that nearly 31 per cent of those surveyed were in poverty. His research showed too that, apart from inefficient expenditure, the principal sources of poverty were low wages, unemployment and old age.

Social inquiry, for Booth, was not an academic pursuit but a guide to social action. His suggestions for the creation of an effective policy on employment ranged from the reform and rationalisation of the labour market to the provision of non-contributory old age pensions. His contribution in respect of the latter, first introduced in 1908, was indeed every bit as important as his work on the conceptualisation and measurement of poverty.

Booth's Life and Motivations

Charles James Booth was born in Liverpool on 30th March 1840 into a public-spirited commercial family that was Liberal in politics and Unitarian in religion. Booth was involved in communal controversies from an early age. Earnest, serious and civic-minded, he combined the development of his shipping line with an active commitment to franchise reform, popular education and social betterment. Booth, though, was no ordinary philanthropist. He rejected charity as a cure and Christianity as a creed. Positivism, the Religion of Humanity, presented a more satisfying foundation for a rational faith. Positive Philosophy offered the young, the intellectually curious and those of unsettled faith a humanist religion and a new ethic of personal social obligation. The crisis of authority had a material as well as a spiritual dimension and Positivists were as much preoccupied with the 'social question' as with any other. Booth, like so many of his generation, was repelled by the crass materialism of the age and the selfishness it encouraged. "The race for wealth is run by a few only and the prizes fall to those who are already rich", he wrote.

Positivism had its share of drawing-room radicals, idealists and dreamers. But it also had a hard edge. Booth's close cousin, the able and engaging lawyer Henry Crompton, was among that group of reform-minded intellectuals who enjoyed a special relationship with the trade union movement during the 1860s and '70s. As a large employer of port labour, Booth was hardly unaware of working people and their wants. His attempts to interest trade unionists in arbitration and conciliation procedures, though they proved unavailing, served to enlarge his experience of labour and labour questions, as did the Trades Hall which he helped to found. The sectarianism that destroyed his attempts to introduce free secular education into Liverpool's schools convinced him that Humanity could be better served by means other than politics. The social crisis of the 1880s gave a clear focus to his brooding intellect and expanding moral imagination.

By this time Booth had moved from Liverpool to London where family wealth and connections gave ready access to that band of moralists, philanthropists and members of the professional classes who dominated public debate on the social question. As a Positivist believing that social action should be grounded in the scientific study of the laws of society, Booth found himself both moved and fascinated by the lives of the working poor. The fixing of his interest upon the East End of London, however, may well have reflected the influence of his wife Mary.

Mary Booth was the daughter of Charles Zachary Macaulay, a distinguished public servant. Her mother's father established the Manchester Guardian. It was Mary Booth who, on a visit to the East End in 1878, told her husband that she was stirred "to help in all this misery". Her cousins Kate, Teresa and Beatrice Potter, who were engaged in voluntary social work in Whitechapel, no doubt contributed to that quickening of interest which led Booth to take lodgings in the East End and to invite workmen to his home in the West End in order to extend his knowledge of working class life.

The onset of economic depression, mass unemployment, socialism and social unrest gave these interests a new urgency. Such anxieties as he possessed, however, found release in social inquiry rather than in social work. Impatient with the glacial pace of conventional philanthropy, critical of the *a priori* assumptions of political economy and disturbed by the challenge of socialism, Booth gave primacy to the collection of facts and an accurate description of the condition of the people throughout London as the basis for social diagnosis and public policy. For all the scope, precision and arresting detail of the *Life and Labour Inquiry*, begun in 1886 and completed 17 years later, it was not a simple compendium or statistical cyclopaedia but a major contribution to social economy and social action. The work of a team of researchers who were co-ordinated and financed by Booth himself, it was probably the largest private inquiry ever undertaken.

Life and Labour and the Poverty Maps

Life and Labour of the People in London was divided into three series. The four-volume Poverty Series related degrees of comfort and wellbeing to the ways in which people lived. The Industry Series examined in five volumes how people worked, what they produced and what they received. The remaining seven volumes were devoted to the Religious Influences Series which, in spite of its title, said little about the spiritual life of the people and much about the distinctive character of the religious life and activities in the various districts of London. A striking feature of the project was the inclusion of a series of thematic maps to show the distribution of degrees of comfort and wellbeing and the spatial relationships between the classes. In 1998, when the first Deptford Forum Publishing volume covering South East London was published, these maps had not received the attention they deserve. In the past two decades they have been made fully accessible through the LSE website but it is still useful to be able to look at them alongside the walks.

The extent to which Booth's poverty maps consciously belonged to an existing tradition is uncertain. Social mapping developed during the 19th century in response to commercial and municipal requirements and also to satisfy Victorian concerns about the physical and moral health of the urban masses. Gradation shading, developed by the Belgian statistician Adolphe Quetelet in the 1820s to display the distribution of crimes against people and property, had been translated in 1842, making the technique familiar to an English audience. The Census of Ireland in the previous year had also made innovative use of shaded maps to illustrate population density and certain other social characteristics. Colour-coded maps of social conditions to plot the spread of cholera and insanitary housing likewise gave evidence of the growth of a more sociologically-informed cartography around the mid-century. What Booth knew of all this remains to be established. That he could have worked independently of his predecessors seems improbable but cannot be ruled out. A tendency to reinvent the wheel appears to be a distinctive feature in the history of empirical social research. What is clear is that, from its inception, the diagrammatic representation of poverty was regarded as an integral feature of Booth's inquiry.

Booth's Descriptive Map of Poverty was first presented to the public in the form of a pilot study of East London delivered to the Royal Statistical Society in 1887. An extended version was included with the first two-volume edition of *Life and Labour of the People in London* published in 1889–91. The map represented the predominant social class and character of each of the streets of the Metropolis, classified according to a seven-point colour scheme based largely on the impression of the School Board Visitors (subsequently known as school attendance officers) as told to Booth's research staff. These impressions were then transferred by hand onto a 25-inch base map that was subsequently reduced and reprinted by the celebrated map-maker and publisher Edward Stanford. The maps reproduced here were photographed from the hand-painted 25-inch originals held at BLPES.

The importance of the Descriptive Map of Poverty may be gauged from the considerable resources that Booth invested in its revision in 1897/8 in order to incorporate the changes caused by urban redevelopment and the movement of population in the previous ten years. This time, however, Booth relied upon the impressions of Metropolitan Police officers rather than upon those of the School Board Visitors as his principal source of information. It was a role for which the police were by no means ill prepared.

Police Evidence

Police duties, then as now, extended well beyond the suppression of crime. Britain, though not a police state, often cast the police as a social agency, a kind of substitute civil service, collecting evidence on social problems, asserting a certain expertise in selected areas and offering counsel and advice – sometimes unsolicited – to policy makers. The requirements of public order gave the police considerable latitude in the demarcation of their interests. Questions of poverty, crowding and insanitary conditions, crime, immigration and industrial displacement defined the scope of police observation. Policemen gave evidence to all the principal parliamentary and governmental inquiries of the period: on the housing of the working classes, the sweating system, labour, foreign immigration and the operation of the Sunday Trading laws.

The recognition of police evidence as a significant source of social observation extended beyond the corridors of Whitehall and Westminster. Charles Booth, like Charles Dickens before him, valued the police not only for their protection but also for their opinions and local expertise. With the consent of Police Commissioner Sir Edward Bradford "experienced members of the police force, chosen for their local knowledge" were assigned to the Booth Inquiry in connection with the revision of the Descriptive Map of London Poverty. The Metropolis was parcelled out into a number of beats, each patrolled together by interviewer and policeman. In East London, all of these walks were undertaken by Booth's companionable associate George Herbert Duckworth, the half-brother of Virginia Woolf, who subsequently enjoyed a distinguished career in the public service. Nearly every street in the Metropolitan Police District of London was visited and its social composition recorded. Not only were policemen required to identify the social class and ethnic make-up of individual streets, they also presented much incidental information about the character of the community. "During these walks", wrote Booth, "almost every social influence was discussed, and especially those bearing upon vice and crime, drunkenness and disorder."

How representative are such sources? Bobbies on the beat have left few records. Station records, too, are rare and incomplete. Recent studies of the social composition of the police labour force do, however, suggest that, in terms of class origins, the Metropolitan Police were close to those whom they policed. Policemen were drawn overwhelmingly from the unskilled and semi-skilled working class. With police recruitment (at least up to divisional level) based on a single-tier entry system, lines of authority did not follow social class divisions as in the military. Serving officers had a close understanding of the everyday experiences and practices – legal and otherwise – of the people in London's streets. Booth's investigators, though sceptical of much that was said, had no grounds for thinking that police observation was rank-related or distorted by social class. And neither have we. The information given to the Booth Inquiry is probably as representative of police attitudes and opinion as we are likely to obtain.

The police were asked to accompany the Booth team on their perambulations and give their views on the changes that had taken place on their 'patch' or 'manor' over the course of the previous ten years but the commentaries to the walks are also a prime source for information about the police themselves, their lifestyle and opinions. Such information varies enormously. The policemen themselves seem to leap from the page as Duckworth and his colleagues sum up their appearance and biography.

> Thorpe has been 21 years in the service [and] has been here three years as an Inspector. He is a round podgy man of medium height, moustache, pleasant, good-humoured face and voice.

> Inspector Fitzgerald is a man of medium height, age between 35 and 40. Round faced, rubicund, brown hair, moustache. A bit of a blarney. Has been in the district 3 years but does not know it particularly well. He is an Irishman from somewhere near Dublin. Widower. Wife died 4 weeks ago after an operation. "A beautiful operation, a 40lb tumour was taken away, but she never recovered consciousness." Lives in the Newick Rd at the junction of Upper with Lower Clapton Rd. Is a lodger with a housekeeper to take care of him.

It Takes All Sorts

The types of crime and disorder which characterised each area are summarised in a few words by the policemen.

> Old Ford and Hoxton are the home of housebreakers. Housebreakers seem to be a product of manual skill and liberal ideas. Old Ford also rejoiced in the

possession of Receivers of the stolen goods, known to the police as Fences. One old man they were sure about but never could get enough evidence against. On he went from year to year, At last they obtained enough to 'pinch him', then he went and died and so escaped.

Despite all this incidental detail, the purpose of the walks was not to reveal the attitudes of the police nor yet to inform the reader of their working lives and practices. Rather it was to use the policeman's knowledge of the various districts to facilitate an informed revision of the 1889 maps. How well did the police know the community in which they worked? How did the nature of their work determine the help which they were able to offer Duckworth?

On the face of it, they were very knowledgeable and well able to give the researchers the assistance they needed. There were, however, limits to the police knowledge of the streets and their people. They knew most about the people who caused trouble. This had important implications. If a community did not have a high profile in terms of public disorder or criminality, the police knew relatively little about its life. If a street was well known for charges this was reflected in the police estimate of its colour. Booth and his associates were aiming to use the map to describe the levels of poverty and comfort but they used as guides men for whom criminality and disorder, or their absence, were the defining characteristics of the population.

Bacchus Walk, 2-st, looks clean and is quiet, windows and blinds clean, doors shut, but the home of a fair proportion of criminals, housebreakers, a type of street almost peculiar to Hoxton. Inhabitants neither poor nor rowdy, but sportsmen who break the monotony of their ordinary work by an evening's housebreaking.

Black and Blue

'BLACK' and 'DARK BLUE' became associated less with degrees of poverty than with degrees and kinds of criminality, roughness and disorderliness. In the map key BLACK was defined as 'vicious and semi-criminal'.

The Great Pearl Street district remains as BLACK as it was 10 years ago. As the Dorset Street district belongs to a dweller in it, McCarthy, so this bit belongs to 'Geringer', an inhabitant of Little Pearl Street. The features of both these streets are common lodging houses for men, women and 'doubles' which are little better than brothels. Thieves, bullies and prostitutes are their inhabitants.

Duckworth and the police used the external appearance of buildings, streets and people as the criteria by which they measured the accuracy of the earlier map, so that the reader is often bemused, wondering precisely what was being assessed. The term 'poverty' is not frequently used in the notebooks. Rather the pages are littered with references to 'rough', 'respectable', 'vicious', 'quiet', 'disreputable', 'poor', 'well-to-do' and so on. The BLACK and DARK BLUE areas are defined not by income but by their criminal characteristics.

> Tagg Street, also PURPLE in map, but now as bad as the rest and dark blue at the east end past the turning of Mace St., light blue the west end. Great mess in the street, rough women at the east end, and a thieves' resort. N up Mace Street, better than the rest. The courts out of the west side marked dark blue on the map look better, and not worse than light blue, found a set of boys gambling with cards in one of them, is a great place for Sunday gambling, but the women at the doors of the houses in the courts looked distinctly a class above the Tagg St. set. So did their houses.

Both researcher and policeman would mix obvious signs of poverty and over-crowding with anecdotes of criminal behaviour.

> a cul-de-sac called Barton Court, BLACK in map and still BLACK, 2- and 3-st, windows broken and patched, mess, costers at far end, children several with bad eyes but well fed, gas burning in lamp in centre of court, bird cages hung up outside windows. Overcrowding here. In one house Ryeland found 7 in 2 small rooms on the top floor, 9 persons in 2, on the second floor and 6 in 2 rooms on the ground floor. One man nodded to Ryeland. "He has served several times" said R "but he once saved my life here". Ryeland had been arresting a man in the court when a trolly was dropped from the first floor window on to R's head, he was stunned. This man prevented his fellows from kicking him when down.

Often the rich descriptions were based on Duckworth's impression of a whole scene.

> Then into Carr Street, known to inhabitants as Donkey Row. North end is no longer PURPLE, rather DARK BLUE. Rough, windows broken and dirty, children with unlaced boots playing with the dust heap in the street unnoticed, dirty and ragged, but well-fed looking. Fish curers. Some shops. Many lads loafing. Industries are gasworks, fish curing, costering. Boxing a favourite amusement. 'Is well-known for it, though not quite so well-known as Bermondsey.' The champion boy bruiser was playing pitch and toss as we passed. Houses 2-st, flush with pavement, yellow brick. Rents 8/- to 10/- for 4 rooms. "Very troublesome property." All the streets north of Salmons Lane are variations of

the above, more or less. The whole poorer than it used to be … Think nothing of assaulting the policemen. The corner of Elsa Street and Carr Street is noted for street gambling which nothing seems to stop. Thieves scattered about but not a regular thieves' colony.

After a while the colour scheme became so natural a descriptive method for both researcher and policeman that they would talk of "a RED house" or even "a PINK man".

Changing neighbourhoods

The police knowledge of the various districts led Duckworth to an understanding of the changes going on in the capital's various neighbourhoods. Changes in the physical environment accounted for changes in the population.

> The rich are leaving the district, so are the poor. The first in search of the green fields they used to find here, the second to Walthamstow where houses are cheaper and fares to London by the G.E.R only 2d. Their places are taken by a middle class who, if they have a family rent, a whole house at £30 to £35 and let off some of the rooms.

The physical context of the houses could cause problems with assessing their proper colour.

> It is strange that there should be so much poverty in the neighbourhood of a fine open space like London Fields. The Fields themselves seem to feel the influence of their surroundings and although they have been for some years under the County Council are still rather a dreary waste. The grass is coarse and tussocky. There are no shrubberies, no flowers, the only trees are long lines of aspen poplars. Very few children were playing on them. The lower end has been asphalted but only adds to the general appearance of bareness.

Changes in rents, extensions to the railways and slum clearance of various types resulted in pushing around London the former inhabitants of BLACK and DARK BLUE areas. Often they did not go far.

> Drew spoke of general tendency of Central London to become poorer. The first people to be affected by cheaper locomotion are the richer classes. Life of the poor more sociable and more bound up with places and neighbours than life of the rich. Therefore rich go, poor remain. Therefore a general tendency of the

better streets to become worse, but not of the worst streets to go lower or even to remain as bad because the vicious class is less vicious than formerly.

E into Wilmer Gardens, 3- and 2-st, houses on the south side arranged on the flat system, 3 rooms to a floor, 3 families to a house, rents 6/6 to 7/- per floor, jerry built houses. Street has been built about 15 years. In map it is marked DARK BLUE lined BLACK but is now worse and should be BLACK. Deterioration due to immigration of thieves and housebreakers from Boundary St. area.

The Researchers

We should remember that the records of the East London walks were not kept by the police themselves but by George Duckworth. The views of the police are, therefore, mediated and to them are added those of the researcher. Sometimes there is direct quotation from the police, more often there is a summary of the results of the conversation between the two about the neighbourhood.

Sometimes the researcher would challenge a police description.

Stebondale Street has the (police) character of being the worst street in the Island. Houses with basement floors, 9 feet below high tide, drains that run backwards. Some looked very poor, but by no means all. Had the air of a street that was improving. All the houses looked better than those in Gaverick, Crews and Claude Streets mentioned above. We saw no one dead drunk and insensible as Carter said men become after much opium.

These walks are not a tourist guide to London. There is much here of local interest so that the modern reader can form a picture of the physical environment, even to the extent of the width of the streets, the height of the buildings, and the existence of courts uncharted on any contemporary map. But the perspective of the walks is heavily influenced by the policemen's working environment. As a result one has to accept that the level of detail is variable and the reliability of the information likewise.

Yet for Booth, the police served to underline the purpose of his Inquiry, to describe the lives of Londoners in response to the perceived social crisis of the 1880s. They, like few others, were in a position to pinpoint trouble-spots and trouble-makers. They were prepared to reinforce their assessment of the vicious inhabitants of the Fenian Barracks by a graphic description of hundreds of rats infesting a cargo of fatty ham. They had views, which they readily recounted to the researchers, about the 'problems' of the age – prostitution, gambling, drink, immorality, immigration, marriage, theft, housing, and overcrowding.

The Drama of the Age

Of all the preoccupations of the late-Victorian period, prostitution ranks highly. Vigilance committees were trying to clear out the brothels but many police felt it was "better to have them where you can put your finger on them than in places where you don't know of their existence until they are firmly established."

> Speaking of the suppression of brothels, Superintendent Mulvaney said that if there was a demand for them it was no good suppressing them because they only break out again somewhere else. He himself was all in favour of state inspection and regulation. He said that if women were confined to a known place where would be less temptation than there is at present for the bashful man or boy. "Seeing as I do down here how much illness and trouble is caused by inherited syphilitic tendencies, it is a marvel how anyone can persist in favouring non-regulation."

Prostitution was often associated with the common lodging houses such as those in the Dorset Street area

> The worst street I have seen so far, thieves, prostitutes, bullies. All common lodging houses. Some called 'doubles' with double beds for married couples, but merely another name for brothels. Women, draggled, torn skirts, dirty, unkempt, square Jews standing about in street or on doorsteps. The majority of the houses are owned by Jack McCarthy, keeper of a general shop on the north side of the street.

McCarthy's empire – filled with "ragged women and children. Holey toeless boots. Windows dirty, patched with brown paper and broken. Prostitutes, thieves and ponces" – spread throughout many of the local streets and courts.

Engaging and alarming, inexhaustible and compulsive, these Booth Notebooks present a townscape of crowded streets and bustling thoroughfares, of claustrophobic courts and dark back alleys, a fluid, fast-changing environment in which commerce and people vie for space and amenity, industry and identity. They evoke the sights and sounds, indeed almost the smell, of the congested capital 120 years ago. George Duckworth, with his acute powers of observation and novelist's eye for detail, ushers us into unseemly enclosures and unmapped passageways, through run-down neighbourhoods and the more fashionable quarters, recording land-use changes and population movements with care and precision. Included, too, was much incidental information on house rents and local prices and, where access could be secured, on home work and individual family circumstances.

The streets of London, as presented here, are defined not only by charters and legal regulations, but also by popular culture and popular usage. The information gathered, though selective, is extraordinarily rich. Duckworth was attentive both to the diversity of the built environment and to variations in local architecture. The general condition of the inhabitants, their occupations, dress and bearing were of equal interest. All were captured by his running pen. The modern reader who wishes to understand Victorian London will find Duckworth an indispensable guide. His observations, for all their absorbing and irresistible qualities, however, are not a simple mirror-image of London at its imperial zenith. Perambulations with the police supplied a stock of knowledge that was shot through with a whole range of personal and professional concerns. It embodied the beliefs, attitudes and opinions of policemen, both as public servants and as self-conscious members of the independent working classes.

Apart from the occupational and class biases of police informants, there was the particular viewpoint of the *Life and Labour* Inquiry itself. The observations, recorded in these Booth Notebooks, were passed through an evaluative filter by which the moral and material were recombined to create a body of information that was always something more than a descriptive map of poverty. The colour coding of a particular location was a multiple of discrete assessments based on environment, appearance, spatial relationships, trades, dress, clatter and clamour, ethnicity and crime. It also included a large number of surrogate measures of respectability and deviance ranging from clean curtains and a well-scrubbed doorstep to a neat window-box or strategically-placed flower display. These caveats, though, do not diminish the importance of the Booth Notebooks, either as source or text. These Notebooks not only impress us by their vividness, immediacy and precision, but also by their idiosyncrasy and humanity. As a guide to the preoccupations of the age they have few rivals.

Duckworth and East London Jews

Mike Steele, 2018

The antisemitism on display throughout the notebooks is a shocking reminder of a different time.

As George Duckworth tramped the streets of East London he clearly felt about Jews as Margaret Thatcher did 80 years later when she said Britain might be "swamped" by Black and Asian Commonwealth immigrants. Duckworth used that word slightly differently but with the same perception when he noted "Even in Whitechapel great improvement since the incoming of the Jews. BLACK spots have gone. English remain in small colonies in courts as yet un-swamped by the Jewish tide."

Duckworth's polite distaste was shown in blunt sentences comprising just one or words as in this paragraph:

> W into Rutland Street. 2-st, PURPLE rather than the PINK of the map, "rather better than Bedford Street". Several Jews. N into Newark Street, late New Street, more Jews, PURPLE rather than PINK. The large red-brick church of St Philip is here. "Built by the present rector at a cost of £40,000, but as the parish becomes more Jewish, is less necessary each year, has poor congregation" said Drew. Oxford Street, also PURPLE. Jews. Into Turner Street. 2½-st. Medical students living at north end. PINK as map. Much homework carried out in the houses. Tailoring. Jews. N into Green and Mount Streets. Green Street PURPLE to LIGHT BLUE, not pink. Poor Jews.

In Whitechapel he has five mentions of Jews in 11 lines whereas Wapping was 'peculiar' with 'no Jews'.

Duckworth described the mess of paper etc in some streets but said it "does not mean much in Jewish quarter because Jewish children are always messy." He admitted that Jews "were regular rent payers and respecters of authority but dirty, messy and great cheats; they bring their private quarrels to the police station, each charging the other with crimes. It is impossible to believe either. The Dutch Jew is the lowest and roughest of them. Their work is slop clothes, boots, cigars and fur. They are gradually ousting the Gentile from the better streets. More come every year."

Yet he had to observe that these strange incomers were in many cases much more successful than the other East Londoners among whom they were living.

Grudgingly he came to accept "betterment is noticeable in some of the larger streets such as Hanbury and Church Streets, owing to the incoming of well-to-do Jews, and also in the courts south of Old Montague Street, owing to the displacement of rough English or Irish by poor but quiet Jews."

"Where the races are mixed, neither is pleased and quarrels result", he wrote. In Union Terrace, which was all DARK BLUE to BLACK, "literally covered with old crusts of bread" and the nearby courts where houses were going cheap, Jews were beginning to buy up houses but Duckworth concluded that "they dare not put in any Jewish tenants just yet, they would have too hot a time, they will wait till they have got a whole street, then Jewish tenants will come in en bloc, rents will be raised and the former owners given notice to quit." Nearby Carr Street had a "rough low labouring class" and Duckworth noted the probable invasion of Jews as "the only prospect the district has of ever becoming better than it is." Elsewhere he refers to "the betterment has been due chiefly to the ousting of the rough and vicious by foreign Jews and also to the building of dwellings (Salters Buildings), also tenanted by Jews." Lewis (of Toynbee Hall) spoke of Shepherd Street buildings as an example of a place that had been Jewish but was now Gentile again. "A very rare occurrence. The Jews have been turned out by a set of rough English and Irish."

In Gun Street which he said was "very rough", he came upon a Jewish common lodging known as the poor Jews' home, "where the Jew thieves congregate". This is one of few suggestions that there were thieves among the East London Jews.

Nottingham Place he claims has a "mixture of Jews, Christians and Germans" but does not say what religion the Germans are nor what are the nationalities of the Christians, though soon afterwards he is specific . Going "east down Commercial Road and west along Street "he finds German Jews. He says the trades of this district are "shoes, slippers and tailoring" and notes "absorption of district by Jews, English remain in streets and courts which are wholly English, like Settles Street, Myrtle Street, Charlotte Court. There is a mixture of English and Jews in some streets but friction and quarrels the inevitable result. The repulsion felt of one for the other is mutual. Great mess in Jewish streets. Fishes heads. Paper of all colours. Bread (not a great deal of this), orange peel in abundance."

When Duckworth speaks of other foreigners he is more descriptive and less stereotyping. In Limehouse he found "Great many young French men work here, who live in Acland St and Walker St. They are somewhat loose in their morals." In the north end of Dod Street "live many Germans. Very quiet and respectable people employed for the most part in Hammonds factory." In Gray Street, Whitechapel, he notes a "house on east side is a family of Italian ice-cream makers".

He described the Mildway Medical Mission with several poor Jewesses sitting on steps outside with sick children, waiting for it to open. "Medicine given them with a prayer, only the very poorest go, don't think any are really converted".

"Bow District seems to be the paradise of tally men, in the Campbell Rd they have their dwelling and in the neighbourhood they make their living. Young men, most of them, of a Jewish cast of countenance. There is hardly a thing they won't sell you. Always a bargain but always much dearer than you could buy it for in a shop. They run great risks of bad debts and "the live must pay for the dead." But another concession: "It was almost possible to tell where the Jews were by the houses which had unbroken windows."

Duckworth made no references to Jews in Hoxton nor in Shoreditch. It was in Dalston and Haggerton he found them again in significant numbers. Around St Mark's Road where "Over the walls the back gardens were easily seen. In many of them the weekly wash hung out to dry and slaveys sweeping carpets, in one, a little Jewboy of about 11 years pitching halfpence by himself." Here we have one of the very few examples of Duckworth recognising the humanity of Jewish people but he can't resist referring to the little boy in a way that would be completely unacceptable now.

Only one other individual Jew was mentioned in all the walks: "Round the green was driving a Jew smoking a cigar with his wife by his side, a servant in livery with cockade in his hat behind. Flanagan recognized him as a small tally tailor whom he had known when he was stationed as a constable in the Whitechapel Division … The rest of the district is a noted Jews dwelling place. It is the intermediate stage on their march from Whitechapel to Hampstead. According to Flanagan the Jews are disliked by everybody but can get on in spite of it. Landlords dislike them because they fill every hole and corner of their houses with lodgers, then they are dirty and they take no care of their gardens, added to this they don't seem to patronise the local shopkeepers. Further they stay at home of an evening and don't use the public houses as clubs."

Other traditions could also suffer from the change: "As to pawnbrokers, he said it was not a trade Jews went into because Jews did not patronise the pawn shop. One fact to show the increase of Jews in the subdivision is that a pawnbroker has lately given up because now that there were so many Jews he was unable to make a fair living."

De Beauvoir Town "has seen better days. Small houses and large gardens are its features Generally speaking its inhabitants tend to get poorer as they approach the Ball's Pond Road on the north and the canal on the south. The district is singularly free of Jews. Flanagan said he did not know of any. "The people will not neighbour with Jews and Jews will not intermarry with Christians."

In Boundary Street, Bethnal Green: "No Jews have their foot as yet in this district. 'They would not dare to, they would be so roughly handled'."

In St Thomas' Road "the houses opposite the Park are going up in character. The park is so much better kept now that it is under the LCC that it is more like a garden than a park. Consequently the houses which look on to it have a pleasanter outlook. The Jews have been the first to recognise this and there has been a large influx of them into the neighbourhood." All around the park Duckworth saw the streets "looking decidedly prosperous. All this bit has been going up in character. The map marks St Agnes Terrace and Gore Rd PINK but they are well above this now. Many Jews have come to live in this quarter … The rest of the district has an old fashioned air, easy going and independent. The Jews have taken the best places."

Duckworth's attitude to Jews was not openly hostile but it was never friendly. He noted that in many though not all parts of East London they were living in large and growing numbers.

He did, however, accept that the areas to which they moved would frequently improve as a result though this was not because they integrated. They tended to be more law-abiding than many of the local inhabitants though 'messy'. That seemed to be his main criticism of them. He also accepted that they looked after their children well.

The late David Englander wrote an absorbing article about Charles Booth's attitude to Jews: 'The Presentation of Jews and Judaism in *Life and Labour of the People in London*, [Victorian Studies, Vol. 32, No. 4 (Summer, 1989), pp. 551-571 Published by: Indiana University Press].

David wrote, in part:

At the close of the nineties when research was concluded for what had grown into the multi-volume survey of *Life and Labour of the People in London*, the Jewish population of the metropolis stood at an estimated 140,000 to 150,000 persons. The greater part of this population was still concentrated in Stepney. It would have been unthinkable for Booth and his associates to omit the Jewish community from their survey. The extraordinary emergence of East London Jewry and its influence upon the earnings and occupations of the metropolitan poor directly addressed the central concerns of late-Victorian social investigation.

Apart from D. F. Schloss, who contributed an essay on the trades of East London, none of those connected with Booth's survey were Jews. Booth was a Positivist of sorts; Hubert Llewellyn Smith, who was responsible for the analysis of immigration, came from a Quaker family; Ernest Aves, a resident of Toynbee Hall, was religiously minded as was

Arthur Baxter, his colleague; G. H. Duckworth was an Anglican. Their experience of Jewry, native and foreign, was limited. Beatrice Potter, who came from sturdy Nonconformist stock, was remotely connected through her paternal grandmother, a "tall dark woman of Jewish type" who loved music, read Hebrew, and went mad.

Charles Booth regarded foreign Jews as an unpleasant people next to whom no Gentile could live. Whatever their differing experiences and personal antipathies, all members of the Booth enquiry shared the dominant view of Jews as a peculiar people. Booth, in his preliminary survey of the East End Jewish settlement, had noted and discounted the prospects of political violence from this quarter. "These foreign Jews," he observed, "are straight from the pressure of grinding despotism; some may add nihilism and the bitterest kind of socialistic theories to very filthy habits; but the meek and patient endurance with which they live their hard lives, and their ready obedience to the law, do not suggest any immediate fear of violent revolutionary activity on their part" (Booth, "Conditions and Occupations," p. 48). East Enders themselves sometimes saw the immigrants as dangerous subversives. Police observation, though, tended in general to support Booth's initial assessment. "Polish Jews and Russians who come here are mostly strong socialists," said one informant. "Their first inclination on coming over here and finding their liberty is to break out," but, he added, "they don't do it long" (B350, fol. 45). The Jewish community was said to produce criminals, but no criminal classes. Petty and irksome, Jewish crime was not considered unmanageable. The lodging houses in Gun Street "where the Jew thieves congregate" were all known to the police (B351, fol. 101), as were their gaming houses.

Though aware of its condition, Booth did not find the situation of suburban Jewry engaging. A submissive, sober, industrious community which, its unkempt gardens notwithstanding, posed no threat to property, fell outside the parameters of the Labour Question and so was largely excluded from the portrayal of metropolitan life.

Booth, alas, was not interested in probing the politics of the ghetto. Its interior life formed no part of his picture of the Jewish East End at the close of the Queen's reign. The plurality of approaches to anglicisation he ignored. The conflicts between revolutionary socialist, zionist, and orthodox Jews as analysed by Feldman, or the marvellously evocative studies of W. J. Fishman, find no anticipation in Booth's portrait of metropolitan Jewry. *Life and Labour of the People in London* provides a partial account of Booth's methods of social enquiry. There is an almost total silence about his own role in the selection and interpretation of evidence. The comparative method, as Booth saw it, was a process of bias-elimination that was unaffected by his own arbitrary interventions. In this he was mistaken.

Booth did possess a social theory. First and foremost he was an empiricist confident that in the science of statistics lay the key to social progress. His and Potter's ideas about Jews and Judaism further combined a number of inherited assumptions common to their class and culture with a large dose of an unreflective Lamarckianism that was so signal a feature of Victorian social science. Looking back over four decades, Llewellyn Smith was thus confident that, as a result of the Booth survey, the Polish Jew had been absolved of responsibility for the existence of the sweating system, even if the immigrant presence made it worse. This is pure moonshine. There is in fact little evidence to suggest that attitudes toward Jews, elite or popular, were positively affected by the Booth findings.

In terms of survey research, too, the outcome must be deemed a disappointment. The inclusion of the Jewish community, as noted earlier, was a historical accident due to the coincidence of mass immigration with the genesis of the Booth enquiry rather than any supposed organic relationship with the life of the metropolis. Similarly, its retention among the special studies in the *New Survey of London Life and Labour* forty years later supplied a basis for comparison rather than a pointer toward a sociology of intergroup relations. By then, the concept of the Jewish worker and the intellectual apparatus that accompanied it had disappeared from the language of social investigation. With it, however, had also disappeared all significant interest in the Jewish ethnic minority. Serious survey research had to await the creation of the Research Unit of the Board of Deputies of British Jews in 1965. Metropolitan Jewry deserved better.

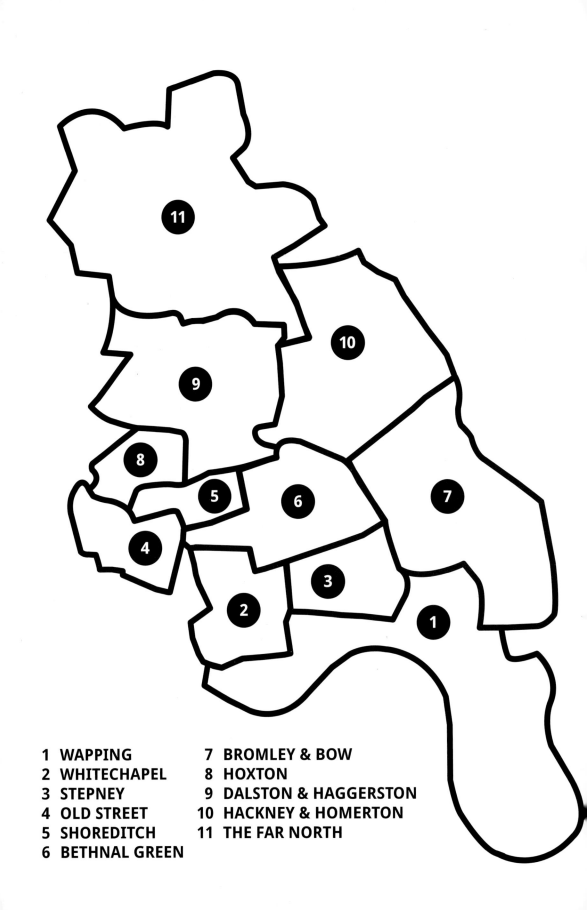

1 WAPPING
2 WHITECHAPEL
3 STEPNEY
4 OLD STREET
5 SHOREDITCH
6 BETHNAL GREEN
7 BROMLEY & BOW
8 HOXTON
9 DALSTON & HAGGERSTON
10 HACKNEY & HOMERTON
11 THE FAR NORTH

WAPPING & LIMEHOUSE

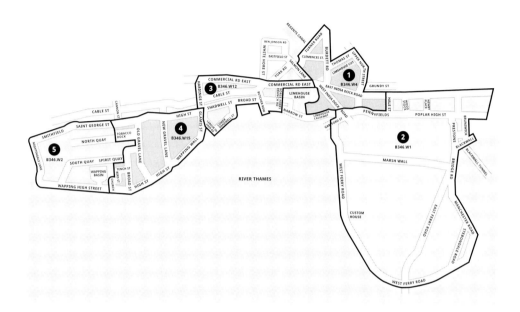

Walk 1

Wednesday 26th May & Saturday 12th June 1897

George Duckworth. This was my first interview and walk with Inspector Caleb Carter.

The Limehouse Police Station is in the West India Dock Rd, next to the Asiatic Home and just opposite Limehouse Causeway.

Speaking generally "Limehouse proper is the same as before". Some streets are worse, but some bad ones are no more. Limehouse proper is the district bounded on the south by the Thames on the east by Garford St, on the north by West India Dock Rd and a little bit of the East India Dock Rd, and on the west by the Limehouse Cut. Official Limehouse extends a long way north of this but local Limehouse doesn't. When people in the neighbourhood speak of going over into Limehouse they mean going over into that bit of it lying between the West India Dock Rd and the river.

Its character is and always has been the same "and probably always will be". Limehouse Causeway is the dwelling place of Japs and Chinamen. Rich Street, Jamaica Place and Gill Street are a nest of brothels frequented by common seamen of every nationality. Up to two years ago 20 houses out of the 24 in Jamaica Place were brothels. The same was the case in Rich St. Ten houses in each street have been prosecuted. Two years ago a vigilance committee was started in the District, with a professed intention of putting a stop to these places. They made it too warm for one or two who had to shut up shop in these streets. But don't suppose they turned good. The only result was that they moved somewhere else and became a centre of contamination for other streets. Better to have them where you can put your finger on them than in places where you don't know of their existence until they are firmly established. Sailors will have somewhere to go to. The charge is 5/- to 10/- and a bed costs 6d or 1/-. The business is a profitable one. Then there is a lot of money made by robbing the sailors. A man very seldom comes out of one of these places with anything in the shape of money or valuables on his person. Sometimes they come and complain to the police but more generally they do not and it is very difficult to get sufficient evidence against these places. The vigilance committee recognised that the fruits of their work were fraught with more harm than good and so voluntarily dissolved. The greatest indirect preventive to spending more money in this way has been the facility now given to sailors to send money home. Before the sailors land, ships are boarded and as the money is paid over much is sent straight away to friends, relations or the savings bank. Money can also be dispatched through the foreign Consuls. Jamaica Street has now been changed to Beccles Street in the hope that a new name may help it in achieving a new character, but it has not done so. Though Beccles St is printed up at the corner of the street, no one knows it by that name.

Note that both Gill St and Rich St are marked far too light in our map. Gill St being PURPLE and Rich St PINK. There must have been a decided worsement going on in these streets during the last 10 years, to be partially explained perhaps by the fact that King John's Court at the west end of Limehouse Causeway has been pulled down. This was a BLACK spot on our map and a row of BLACK houses that backed on the canal down Chusan St have also disappeared. The Contagious Diseases Acts have never been enforced in London as at Portsmouth. The consequence is that this district is a hotbed of venereal disease

Then through Gun Lane and down Three Colt St, more brothels, streets and courts very crowded and narrow. Down Ropemakers Fields past Thomas Rents and Whites Rents, many thieves, to Nightingale Place, a sort of broad paved courtyard into which a street runs, down which you could get a cart without difficulty but though which a cart could not go. This is a noted thieves' resort. Up Nightingale Lane and then W down Globe Alley, some very poor-looking houses, but bits of gardens here and there, then W down Rope Walk and Northey St, marked PINK in our map but now more probably PURPLE or LIGHT BLUE. Then N through Church Row, a much more respectable street, into the West India Dock Rd, crossing the road into a very narrow entrance just past the Burdett Rd. Down a passage called Chusan St and on between factory walls and a very poor set of houses, past the factory gate (Loders Chemical Works), then down a narrow passage which seems to lead to a blank wall only, on reaching the blank wall you turn sharply to the right down another passage and come out in Chusan Place. This is one of the blackest spots in London. "I don't expect you will find it in your map, practically only the police know of its existence" said Carter. But there it is marked BLACK right enough. "By Jove, the chap who coloured up your map must have known London jolly well, I could hardly have believed it." was his next comment.

Chusan Place is better than it was because there is less of it. The houses backing on the Canal have been pulled down so that those that remain have a grand open space in front of them. Each house has a way through into the other. At one end there was a group of children playing at a top window, well fed, bootless, rather dirty but happy looking. At the door, a woman. Well fed but very ill dressed. Her dress is in literal tatters, impossible to understand why it kept on at all. As a contrast at the near end of the court a fairly well-dressed middle aged woman with one of the wickedest of faces. This is a favourite thieves' resort. You are robbed in the West India Dock Rd, off goes the thief down Chusan St, you follow and if you are close enough behind him you manage to land yourself in Chusan Place. There he suddenly disappears. You are glad enough to get out of the place without further mishap. As a rule the thief will have skipped over the wall, on to the towing path and your right course would have been to have turned up the Burdett Rd, down on to the towing path, and he would probably have run into your arms.

Then out into the main road again, down St Anne's St, a very poor street, into the main road, turning NW down Salmons Lane into Galt St. Salmons Lane is a street market out of which there are a number of poor and very poor turnings, which look certainly LIGHT BLUE, probably DARK BLUE.

In Galt St, Henry St, Turner St and Locksley St, there is much greater comfort and respectability. Only one big Public House, fat and comfortable, "Does a big paying jugs trade." This is part of the Cotton Estate. Many have been the applications to open another house. The Landlord or Trustees won't have it, and to all appearances they have been justified by the condition of their estate.

Along the canal is Tomlin Terrace, marked on the map PINK. It looks PURPLE. Between the houses and the canal is a broad road which with the addition of the width of the canal makes a considerable open space. Here the canal, instead of being a sewer running between high walls as it does a little lower down as well as a little higher up and adding to the general baseness of its surroundings, actually increases the amenity of the road. Hence a canal does not necessarily mark out the course of vice, though it seems to to wherever the streets run at right-angles to it and end in a high wall and nothing more.

Then down the Burdett Rd coming out of Clemence St. "The Burdett Rd is very respectable. Mr Wells, the chief of our K division, lives here." Down as far as Thomas St. Up Thomas St past the gold and silver refinery. "Great many young French men work here, who live in Acland St and Walker St. They are somewhat loose in their morals."

Then across Stinkhouse Bridge turning back W again down Cotall St and S down Stainsby Rd. Cotall St and in the streets behind it, Clifton St and Sabbarton St, are the resorts of the prostitutes.

In the north end of the Dod St live many Germans. Very quiet and respectable people employed for the most part in Hammonds factory.

Then E along Canton St past Father Lawless' church. "He is a wonderful man, he can stop a row where we police are of no use at all." Cockney Irish seem to defy all authority except that of the priest. "Once Father Lawless is there the people seem to be ashamed and they slip away one by one and gradually all is quiet. They do not even start it again as soon as his back is turned."

Then S down Upper North St, past Evans St and along Grundy St into Randall's Market. Evans St is now called Pekin St. It is a fairly good respectable street. Many of the police live there.

Randalls's Market is a queer-looking place. Shaped like this [diagram like an ostrich's neck, swallowing an orange]. The stained shops, for the most part furniture shops and mostly belonging to one man. No one there buying and no one there selling. Odd statues running along the roofs of the houses. Carter said the furniture man had a large business and had grown richer and richer. Many prostitutes in the streets round Randall's Market.

Then down Hale St on the west side of which are Rook St and Sophia St, a regular Irish den, situated just at the back of Dr Corner's Garden, the Manor house. All the vices of the Irish rampant, murder, rows, dirt, etc. The Irish have a way of biting both one another and those who interfere with them. However it is not so bad as the Fenian Barracks. Many hatless, bootless and dirty children about and fat, brawny, brawling women, shouting at one another.

Then back down the Poplar High St, through Penny Fields to the Police Station.

Penny Fields has a peculiar character. On the north side which is fairly respectable, there are several little courts, not unrespectable, on the south side there are many boarding houses for foreign seamen and one or two noted brothels. The south side is much worse than the north. We compare them in the map as DARK BLUE is to PURPLE.

General remarks

The Japs and Chinamen are as a rule quiet and easy to deal with. Of the two the Japs are the noisiest. The Chinaman is tame and quiet and once you have made an arrangement with him he keeps to it. Chinese cooks sometimes escape from on board ships and hide in the Limehouse Causeway. But with the help of the chap at the Chinese general shop Carter generally can put his hand on them. That means a sovereign in his pocket. About last Christmas the Japs and the Chinamen found out that their countries had been at war with one another. So they started fighting on their own account, but it wasn't much. The Chinaman has a great respect for authority. The Jap is more like an Englishman. He is a good sailor and more and more are being employed on English ships. He tries to be like an Englishman. When he comes to London he drinks beer, gets drunk and runs after women.

The prices that are being paid for Public Houses now is astounding. Carter knows local men who have taken to dealing in them to their own profit. They buy up small licensed places, they put in a great stock of beer, much more than they can sell, a great deal of it they let drain away into the sewers. Then they come to the Brewers and ask them to buy their houses pointing out the immense amount of beer they have disposed of. The Brewers are only too glad, they have themselves first turned into limited liability companies, they have an enormous capital behind them and they bid amongst themselves with the money of their shareholders for the possession of licensed houses. A new license is very difficult to get so that it is very important to get hold of houses that are already licensed.

£16,000: This sum Carter has on a reliable authority was paid for the Beer house opposite the entrance of the Blackwall Tunnel. This was only two months ago. This house is situated on the west side of the Prestons Road at its junction with the East India Dock Rd. They hoped to get a full license for it and enlarged and rebuilt the house. They have not been successful and he hears that the house is now going for £8,000.

Charringtons is about the best beer in the neighbourhood. But a great deal of filthy stuff is sold. The Brewers put in as managers, men to whom they have advanced large sums. These men must make money. To make money they must adulterate. If they don't they lose and the Brewers foreclose. Some firms are very hard. Perhaps the worst are Brewers on the corner of Dow Rd just before you come to the Stratford Bridge. Their name is Smith & Garratt and Co and the beer they sell is bad. Taylor, Walker in Limehouse used to be large brewers and do a great Indian trade, as well as own the houses in Limehouse. But the India trade has failed them and trade has left Limehouse so they are in a poor way now as compared with former years. At the corner of the Bridge over the Regents Canal entrance there is a house which used to be one of the wealthiest in the town. Big owners used to lunch there regularly. Now no one does. It has failed and though retaining the outward appearance of a pub it is in reality a dingy coffee house. 'To such base uses etc.'.

On Saturday evening June 12th Arthur L Baxter, George Duckworth and Carter went over part of the same district again.
Starting from the Police Station.
SE down West India Dock Rd. Then E down Penny Fields. N into the East India Dock Rd, through North St. W along the East India Dock Rd past the Burdett Rd, into Chusan St, into Chusan Place, out again through St Anne St into the Dock Rd, across the Britannia Bridge. NW through Salmons Lane. N through Carr St. W down Ben Johnson's Rd. S down Whitehorse St. E through Commercial Rd East. S down Horseferry Branch Rd, through Medland St. S again into Narrow St, through Nightingale Place, through a set of courts into Church Row and Three Colt St, through Gun Lane into Jamaica Place. Then S into Limehouse Causeway, so back to the Police Station.

Chusan Place looked more deserted than before. On the way there down Chusan St were many women with babies in their arms, sitting on the doorsteps. The turning into St Ann's Lane, a thieves' resort, was full of children, a group of boys playing pitch and toss with trouser buttons, a girl of about 10 or 12 years also playing the same with two boys, and a group of girls any age from 6 to 12 sitting on the pavement playing knucklebones with square shaped dice-like pieces made of wood or china. Hour: 8.30PM, a fine summer's evening, warm.

Then along Salmon's Lane, a market street, full of booths and shouting butchers, a brisk trade in vegetables, especially tomatoes and lettuces and flowers. Pale pink tomatoes, probably Italian, going for 1d per lb, in good condition. Some big red English ones also, for 6d per lb. The pale pink sort were also on sale in a shop on the Commercial Rd (for 2d and 3d per lb).

Then down Farnham St and across the bridge over the Regents Canal. On the east side of the canal a block of houses reaching down almost to a level with the towing path and entered from the east end of the Bridge. 4-st. Marked apparently PINK in our map, but looked to be DARK BLUE. Shoeless and stockingless children apparently belonging to them were playing along the towing path.

On the west side of the bridge, a spot marked BLACK in our map. A court leading out of a blind alley and rejoining in the name of Johns Gardens. A respectably-dressed woman at one end of it, but a very poor house almost opposite to it. "Seems to have been some improvement here" said Carter. This bit is best seen from the railway train looking out of the left-hand windows going west away from Burdett Rd. After crossing the Regents Canal it is certainly a very DARK BLUE.

Then down Carr St. Just after crossing Repton St is a little blind alley ending in the back entrance into a Public house whose front gives upon Dupont St. A barking black retriever chained up in a kennel gave notice of our approach.

Then down Carr St, DARK BLUE in our map, and out of it on the west side, Maroon St, Eastfield St and North St. (now called Elsa St). Part of Maroon St is PURPLE in our map. Eastfield St is LIGHT BLUE and North St DARK BLUE. The district is all very rough. Nobody calls it Carr St. To the neighbourhood it always is and always has been 'Donkey Row' and any Eastender will tell you where Donkey Row is. "Many of the inhabitants are haddock curers, who can only work when haddocks are cheap. No one will buy them if they are dear." Haddock curing as a staple industry is always a sign of great poverty (in London).

As you go further N there are North St, Manning St, and Halley St where many of those employed in the Commercial gas works close by, live. Gasworkers are rough and drink like fishes. Hard work, i.e. work at very high pressure and great heat and gas fumes, all seem to lead to the bottle.

Then along Ben Jonson Rd passing St John's Church (Rev. Haden, who so far (16. VI.97) has refused to see us), and S down White Horse St. Here the houses are much more respectable, they look out upon the large garden of Stepney Parish Church.

S into the Commercial Rd East and S down Horseferry Branch Rd into Medland St. Hour 9.15. Medland Hall, the Congregational Union Refuge Hall, Rev. Gates, with the notice 'Full' placarded outside. Full means that there are 300 adult men inside. Pipes and cigars relighted before entering and well that they were, otherwise the stench of perspiring humanity would have been over powering. Ranged in bunks along the floor with narrow passages between each row, and in the gallery were 300 men asleep or half-asleep, a few talking. The bunks not unlike coffins and in the dim light the men in them look like corpses arranged for identification after some great disaster. Some were lying dressed, some half-dressed and others naked. Every now and then a pale corpse would rise and flit across the room, silently with bare feet, quite naked in fact. Upstairs there is a room where the more respectable are set apart by themselves. Just now in summertime the galleries are most sought after as being the coolest places. In the evening the men are given a crust of bread and water, they are turned out at 6 in the morning. Only the very poorest are said to come. They have had two tests lately because aspersions have been cast on the character of the institution. On the one occasion the Rev. Gates told the men present that they were said to be able to pay for their own lodgings. They cried, as he had meant them to, 'Search us'. All except two who professed themselves unable to bear the indignity of a search, were searched and 5/2 was the result. On the other occasion a tobacconist was allowed in with half oz packets of tobacco, in two evenings he only disposed of 27 packets. Do they have any place outside where they deposit their money like the workhouse inmates? asked Carter. The Deputy thought not. This evening, the deputy said they had Norwegian carpenters come over in search of jobs on the Jubilee Stands. Each year (?) they emigrate 100 men to the colonies, very seldom have any trouble with them.

Then into Jamaica St passing through Nightingale Place and several small courts, thieves' resorts.

Knocked at the door of No.13 Jamaica St. "Are you at home mother, and may we come in to see you" said Carter. Come in, come in my dear, answered a woman's voice from an inner room. Through a small low room, dark, into another room rather less dark but rather smaller, the greater part of it being taken up by a large square low bed or couch, at the two sides of which were hanging curtains. In the centre of the bed, a tray with a small lamp under a glass shade looking like a nightlight, only the flame was smokeless and clear. Round the lamp 3 or four little boxes or bottles, at the back of the bed 4 small square pillows, and reclining on either side of the lamp a man and a woman, fully dressed, though the man was in his shirt sleeves, and the trousers which he wore hung loosely round his hips and legs showing the outlines of bones and joints which had evidently not been born to wear trousers. The man was an Indian, a Hindoo, and the woman English or perhaps Irish. They were man and wife and kept an opium den.

{Opium pipe can be bought new for 5/- or 6/- but when seasoned is worth £3 to £5} As we entered they were just going to start smoking. Two pipes were reached down from racks on the wall at the back of the bed. The pipes are made of tubes of bamboo wood hollowed, about 2ft long, and about 3/4 of the way down sticks out the bowl of the pipe. The prepared opium which looks like treacle, is taken out of a small bottle hardly larger than a thimble, with a small bone salt or mustard spoon, and put, I think, straight into the bowl of the pipe. Some of it is also stuck round the end of a long knitting needle which is then held over the flame of the lamp and gently roasted. It should not burn during this process and no smoke must get into it, the lamp therefore is fed with the finest colza oil and that is why the flame is so clear and smokeless. Every now and then this knitting needle with the roasted opium is progged down the bowl of the pipe and the two together held over the lamp. Then comes the smoking. The smoke being gulped down as though it were a draught, though after the 3rd or 4th pull it was generally emitted through the mouth and nostrils. About once in every 3 minutes they seemed to be able to get a pull of smoke. To the onlooker the trouble of it seemed to do away with any possible pleasure. On neither of them had it any apparent effect. The smell of the smoke, a cloudy light blue in colour, is nutty and not unpleasant, but one of the most sickly smells when stale, said Carter. That it does have a real effect even on those inured to it is certain because the woman said she could do nothing of a morning without her pipe. "I feel all dribs and drabs and cannot do any of my housework before my smoke in the morning, after it, I am happy and strong and like a lion. It seems to give one heart and courage."

Every now and then the woman spoke as one educated who had seen better things. She spoke of G.A. Sala as her uncle; of having served Lady Burdett in his house; of having to clap on the strait waistcoat when Sala became delirious; of having travelled round with Jan Mace and a circus and acted as property woman, then finally of having had the misfortune to take up with coloured men. "Perhaps that was your luck", remarked her husband deliberately at this point.

Her husband is a Hindoo, a cook, has been employed in the City as curry maker, also at the Indian Exhibition at Earl's Court, now he is out of work and wants something to do badly. ALB [Arthur Baxter] gave him address of Star and Garter Hotel Richmond where Indian guests are staying for the Jubilee. His name is Mr. Khodonabutsch, according to a letter they had had typewritten to send round to various employers of Indian cooks. Carter called her Mrs. Codonabex.

Smoke was offered to the company but we all refused.

Business is very bad, so they said. Their customers, Chinese and Lascars or anyone who comes, don't come. Ships now insist on their crew being aboard by 7PM so smoking is more common in the morning than it used to be and less common at night. No fixed payment is asked. The lid of a tin box is turned upwards and each expected to put something in it as he goes away. We gave between us about 5/- at which they were much pleased.

Mrs K said she was one of the few who really could prepare good opium for smoking. Prussian opium is the best and Persian the worst because it has dirt in it. Raw opium, as far as I could understand, is dark stuff and looks like chocolate or a hard gum. In its raw state it costs 12/- per lb and they buy it from Lacey the Chemists nearly opposite the London Hospital. (The shop has its windows full of patent medicines, it goes a long way back, and has a very queer looking man serving

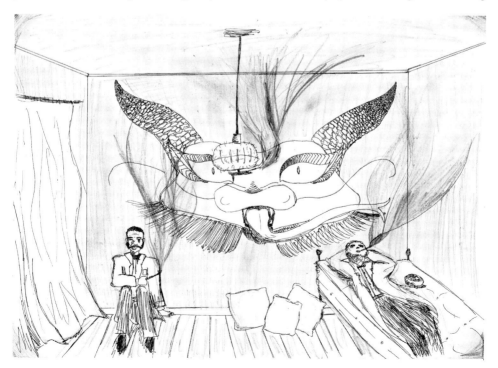

behind the counter). Raw opium is boiled or simmered in a clean copper vessel, then poured off into water, being strained through canvas on its way, then mixed with old opium pipe scraping called neesi or seeni. Then it is ready and looks like treacle. The proper mixing is all important. (NB. this description is probably incorrect). Mrs K smokes about ¼ of ½ an oz of opium daily. 1lb of opium costing 12/-, how much does it cost per day? Answer say 1/-. The Queen's munshi Abdul Karin used to come here to smoke, so did many other Indians whose framed photos she shewed to us.

Then we left. She said we might come again anytime we liked.

Then we walked into Limehouse Causeway, calling in at a Chinese General shop on the west side of the road. Kept by a gay Chinaman. 'Chinamen are very tame but very slippery, tricky and cunning' said Carter. Through the shop and into a back room, about 6ft square. There, a low bed like the other and two Chinamen on it smoking opium. A great ticking of clocks, there were 7 hanging all round the room so that the men may see when to get back to their ships. A very happy jolly looking Chinaman, looked like a Jap, on the bed, face wreathed in smiles who had smoked, and a very sour looking pig-tailed heathen who was just starting his pipe. Business is bad they said here also, in spite of the fact that Foh Sow, this man's rival over the way who had 3 dens is dead and his place turned into a laundry. Nevertheless our man was evidently well off and almost surely a liar. He knew of our coming beforehand. He has several other rooms, I think, for smoking but denied their existence. He does not smoke opium himself. He does all the Chinese business of the quarter, gets together crews for ships and is the adviser of a seaman's general shop in the West India Dock Rd just around the corner.

We saw no one dead drunk and insensible as Carter said men became after much opium.

Then back to the Police Station after a most interesting evening.

Walk 2   B346-1
28th May 1897
George H Duckworth. Perambulation with Mr Carter, local police inspector

Turning S down the Woodstock Road into High Street Poplar
Then W through Penny Fields and back to the police court in the West India Dock Rd. That is part of Limehouse, the whole of the Isle of Dogs, Blackwall, the Orchard House and part of Poplar.

Garford St. Respectful. PINK in colour now as formerly. In it St Peters' Church, Rev. Mr B Alpe "Not much of man, slack, does not seem to take much trouble."

Then on down between high dock walls, road littered with peas that had leaked out from a faulty sack, heavy carts, great noise, echoing walls, wet road. "Traffic always makes much more noise when the roads are wet." Across 'First Bridge' ie. that over Limehouse entrance to the West India Docks, into the West Ferry Rd.

West Ferry Rd. Shops and dwelling houses in the main road. The side nearest the River being as a rule the poorest.

A block of streets bounded on the west by West Ferry Rd, on the north by Cuba St, on the east by Alpha St on the south by Mellish St. Mostly PURPLE in our maps. Comprising Cuba St, Manilla St, Byng St. Labourers, poor but respectable.

Strafford St. Better class. Dock foremen and permanent hands.

Havannah St. Poor in the west end but better class opposite Church on the east end. Tooke St. Labourers. Malabar St (formerly Charles St).

Maria St. Poor street, some Irish. Janet St. Labourers. Mellish St. Set of good labourers.

Alpha Rd bounding these streets on the east, inhabited by dock foremen and permanent hands. Neat fronts, trees, comfortable appearance.

{East of West Ferry Rd, streets marked LIGHT BLUE and PURPLE in our maps. Some eg Strafford St seem to have improved since then, so has Alpha Rd}.

Then down over the 'Second Bridge' over the entrance into the Millwall Docks.

On the west side of West Ferry Rd short streets ending in factory walls. Gaverick St, Crews St, Claude St, low class of laborours, poor aspect. Bearing out dictum that the poorest will always be found nearest the water. LIGHT BLUE in our map, probably now a darker shade of LIGHT BLUE.

Ferry Rd, now called Powis Rd. Cahir St on the north side of West Ferry Rd with a low class of casuals. Chapel House St, Lead St, with a better class.

Then a block of streets bounded on the west by Stebondale St and on the east by Wharf Rd and Manchester Rd.

Stebondale St has the (police) character of being the worst street in the Island. Houses with basement floors, 9 feet below high tide, drains that run backwards. Some looked very poor, but by no means all. Had the air of a street that was improving. All the houses looked better than those in Gaverick, Crews and Claude Streets mentioned above. Marked PURPLE in our maps.

Church St (now Newcastle St) of poorer aspect than Stebondale St, rents of 8/- a week from a notice board at one end. "All houses put in good repair". Newcastle St looked the poorest in this block.

Parsonage St, Billison St, Kingfield St, Seysell St, all of a better class than Newcastle St. Pier St, though marked BLUE, was not given a different character to the foregoing. Then N up the Manchester Rd, a block of streets bounded on the south west by Glengall Rd, on the west south west by East Ferry Rd and on the east by the Manchester Rd, a triangular block. The greater part are occupied by a fair set of permanent hands, the only exception being Marshfield St (PURPLE on our map) out of the Glengall Rd with a low class of labourers and Chipka St also with a low class "but perhaps better than Stebondale St".

Stewart St on the east of the Manchester Rd (PURPLE in map) also very poor looking.

At the corner of the Glengall Rd and the Manchester Rd, a public house, neat and well kept appearance from the outside called 'A cooperative Public House' and run by a cooperative society "The only one I know of in London," said Carter, "and respectably kept".

Then N again towards Blackwall, a poor block of streets between Brunswick St on the east and Prestons Rd on the west. Great changes here owing to the Blackwall tunnel works. Instead of Leicester St (marked DARK BLUE on our maps) a block of County Council dwellings.

Norfolk St (LIGHT BLUE) has been opened up. Of Faselee St only the east side remains standing, the west is down for the tunnel works East side has still a poor appearance but sun and air have done something to make these houses look lighter. Three or four bootless children playing about in the streets. Shows that the inhabitants who remain are still of the poorest.

Further N a block on the west side between Prestage St on the south and Naval Row on the north, all RED in our maps and of the same character now.

Then round into the Orchard St by the South Quay and up into Orchard Place. "Don't have much trouble here, people look rough but don't make much noise, a long way for us to come, we do not often look in here" said Carter.

Some very poor streets or rather courts fronting on the Bow Creek. Very poor. All the evidences of their being of the poorest and roughest. Many bootless children, unwhitened steps, no flowers in the front window etc etc. Three or four Public Houses, all DARK BLUE in character. Evidently official laziness accounts for the fair character given to the place. Carter himself ignorant of the existence of the court fronting on the river.

Then back down Orchard St into East India Dock Rd. A roughish block enclosed by Robin Hood Lane on the east and Cotton St on the west.

Ashton St and Wells St (PURPLE in our map) are the two rough streets of this quarter. Grosvenor Buildings in Manisty St and marking the south side of Wells St look the place of a bad slum. Wells St north side still of rough appearance. In the buildings live a number of prostitutes plying for hire in the East India Dock Rd.

Leading out of Ashton St into East India Dock Rd is Union St with a squalid court known as Osborne Place Court. Providence Place behind the Board School is also very rough.

{22/IX/99. Improvement in both these streets. Ashton St still LIGHT BLUE with a little PINK and some DARK BLUE for the Irish at the north west end. Wells St, north side LIGHT BLUE. South, DARK BLUE}

MUSEUM OF LONDON

Moving W again, a group of respectable streets between Cottage St and the railway.
ie Bow Lane, Montague Place, (now Mountague Place) Newby Place, Grove Villas
On the west side of the railway the Bath Place district lying between the railway and
Woodstock Place, DARK BLUE in our map, a place still with a bad reputation but for
the most part pulled down. The north side of Cottage St is all down. Cottage Row,
the worst street in the block is down altogether, a waste place now. At the south
end of it Finch Court is also shut up. Finch Court consisted of 3 or 4 houses used
together as a cowman lodging house. Tenanted by Mr Muller, a German known
in the neighbourhood as 'Millers' who received the rejections of all the common
lodging houses in the neighbourhood.

Then down along the Poplar High St, the south side of which has a bad reputation.
Brothel at the corner of Simpson's Rd (?), has been one for more than 20 years. Down
Dolphin Lane, formerly a very rough spot, the lower or worst half of which has now
been taken by the parish authorities and used for workhouse (?) buildings. Then

into a little village of small houses occupied by dock employees, each with a little garden known as West India Dock Cottages. The dock company used to support a reading room close by, but it was not sufficiently attended and now belongs to Messers Suffield and Brown, ships coppersmiths.

Up N into the High St and along W the next turning S being Dingle Lane A very low rough place with Hamburg Buildings at one end. Tenanted by Cockney Irish. No English will live near them. This bit has the same character as Sophia St and Rook St.

Then along King St and into West India Dock Rd. A few courts on the north side of King St which are rather better now than they used to be.

General character of the Island

A great many more people work there than live there, though many of those who live there would like to work there. Those who live there seldom leave. From week to week and year to year the men who are islanders remain there. Their women kind are the chief exceptions. On Saturday nights there are special buses to take them to shop in Crisp St. The island itself is very poorly off for shops. No one in the island seems to be rich. Those who are comfortably off are the permanent dock officials. the poorest streets are those nearest the water. These we mark LIGHT BLUE, but half the general tone of the Isle of Dogs is PURPLE.

Of amusements in the island there are practically none. The Millwall Athletic ground football matches attract great crowds and have given the men some interest. Public Houses get up sing songs of an evening, but there are no music halls.

The chief vices of the island are drink, gambling, betting and thievery. There are more juvenile thieves found there than in any other part of the K division. Lots of things to thieve. Old iron, goods from leaky sacks, there is a market for everything. Once anything is found lying about and portable not a boy who would not try to remove it.

Betting largely indulged in. Bookmaker caught last week in the West Ferry Rd betting in the middle of the street. On him they found £40 in gold and £10 in silver, all taken from the natives. At the opening of the Blackwall Tunnel boys came up to thieve among the crowds. One caught with seven empty purses. He was an old hand too. "You can always tell an old hand by his silence when he is pinched". A novice begins to talk and explain. Not so an experienced man.

There are no brothels in the Island. The nearest approach is the presence of a few absent sailors' wives.

A good many Public Houses in the island. Some rough, some respectable. Carter would have the same conditions attached to the holder of a fully licensed house as to the holder of a beer house. A beer house proprietor must live on the premises but the licensee of a fully licensed house may live in Brighton and put in a man to take care of his house in London. that is why the licensees are so difficult to get hold of or to get public opinion to bear upon.

An occasional licence is no longer granted to supply beer on the Athletic ground during football matches. This has diminished drinking on match days as there are many more people who would drink than can be supplied on the premises of the existing Public Houses.

The allotments on the south side of the Glengall Rd have had a quieting effect. Surplus energy worked off there. Leisure time spent there by many instead of at the Public. Holders have arranged among themselves a mutual protection society against outside thieves who steal their flowers etc while they are themselves away at work.

Church work does not seem to have had much influence. Alpe does nothing, but Givan is very active and gets people to listen to him. He is strong, athletic looking, amusing and appeals to his hearers. On Sunday evening crowds go to the public gardens on the north east side to listen to the County Council band. Crowds also wander along the South Quay to the back of the Blackwall Station. This is known in the neighbourhood as 'East End by the Sea', and is recommended by many East End doctors for incipient consumptive patients. You can always get a good healthy blow there.

A great blow dealt to the island by the shutting of Saunders shipping yard. Entirely owing to the action of the trade unions. Carter believes the majority of the men themselves were against the strike. Many of them told him that if a general ballot had been taken, the majority would have been against the strike. They went on because their leaders made them. Now they are sorry for it. Saunders passed through bankrupting court and had to give up the two government ships at which they were at work at the time of the strike.

Men's work has left. Women's work if anything is increasing. Maconochie's jam and tinned provisions factory, Thornton's Jam, give employment to a great number of women.

Note that with perhaps the exception of two or three cul de sacs on the south west of the West Ferry Rd, ie Gaverick St to Crewe St, all the roads in the island have an open airiness very different from the poor streets north and west.

Walk 3   B350-12

Friday 28th and Monday 31st January 1898
George Duckworth with Inspector Drew
Drew does not really know this district well. It is properly under another inspector. Supt Mulvarry however thought that Drew would know it better than the man who

only been there 3 months, so appointed him to go round with me. Drew takes charge of it from time to time but has never spent more than 6 weeks in it.

Starting at Albert Square in the northwest corner.

Not so good as it used to be. 3½-st houses. Lodgers usual – PINK barred rather than RED. Square fairly kept. Supt Mulvarry lives in it, says the place has seen better days. No Jews.

W then S down Havering St. PINK as map, 2½-st, respectable working class. 2 families in each house.

E along Ann St, PURPLE as map, poorer. Carmen. Drink.

Bower Street. 2½-st. One or 2 Jews. Like Havering Street. 1820–1830 houses.

E along Cowan Rd and S down Stepney Causeway. Barnardo's Home takes whole southwest end. At northwest end next beer-house is a rough looking common lodging house. Over and behind a sweetstuff shop and kept by its owner. One barefooted boy in the street.

Hilton St on the east side. Poor. 2-st. LIGHT BLUE, not PINK as map. At the bottom of the Stepney Causeway on the west side is James Place. Entered downstairs, known to the police as Rorke's Drift. DARK BLUE rather than the LIGHT BLUE of map. Very poor. Rough. Narrow with dead wall facing houses about 7 ft from them. Not a hotbed for thieves though there are some of them. 2-st. Windows broken, dirty, children dirty. Two without shoes or stockings; doors open, bare dirty rooms, arms and legs of children unnaturally thin. The first time I have noticed distinct want of food, listless playing.

Half way down the place, the St Ann Public House has a back entrance. Up steps at west end into Devonport Street. E along Brook Street. dark blue as map. Rough poor. Many common lodging houses. No brothels.

E past Friends Meeting House to Cosh's Buildings, which take up the space between School House St and Collingwood St. 4-st, built 1886. Taking up space known as Dunston Place. The centre block is very bad. Shrieks of woman being ill-treated as we walked through, excitement in the court, all women at their windows, one saying "She deserved a good deal but I hope he won't go too far." Ragged, dirty, square-jawed women, some with children. A very rough place. All children booted. On map LIGHT BLUE, but certainly DARK BLUE, even BLACK in centre block. Roughs from neighbouring clearances have come to live here.

Warton Place a cul-de-sac, on west side of School House Lane. 3-st. Rough, dismal, windows broken. Ragged children. One mite of 8 or 9 years scrubbing steps and flag in front of house. On her knees calling "look mother, ain't I getting it clean" and dipping a rag and brush into a pail beside her as if she were at least 15. Only 9 or 10 houses in the street. At the southwest (James Place and Brook St, not shown on map. 8 houses, 2-st) corner to Causeway Court all windows broken. DARK BLUE. Drains stopped. Overflow of everything in to the court. This court is not marked on map. It nearly touches but does not meet 3 Compass Court.

E along Brook St, the first court on the north side is 3 Compass Court. Also DARK BLUE. On south side of Brook St where formerly was Harris Court are the Beachcroft LCC Buildings, ugly but respectable. PURPLE replacing DARK BLUE bit of the map.

N up Caroline St. 2-st. LIGHT BLUE rather than the PURPLE of map. "A little better than Brook St" was all Drew would say of it.

W along Brunswick St. 2-st, rough, DARK BLUE as map, but not much trouble to police. Into Dorset St. 2-st. PURPLE as map. At south end on east side is Susannah Row. Built 1828, poor, rough, LIGHT BLUE rather than DARK BLUE as map, and on west side Elizabeth Place, of same date. LIGHT BLUE not PINK.

Just N of railway arch is Little John St (late Rohley St). 3 cottages. 2-st. LIGHT to DARK BLUE. PURPLE on map.

And N again is Hilton Street (late John St). Poor. LIGHT BLUE not PINK.

N into Commercial Rd, then E to Ratcliffe Square. 2-st. Only poor, LIGHT BLUE, not the DARK BLUE of the map. Wood sawing yard at the southwest side. Just south of the Square are 2 cottages, 2-st and attics.

S down Periwinkle Street, 3- and 2-st. Houses on the northeast side are down. DARK BLUE as map, "very rough coal porters here". On the east side of it is Manor Court. four, 2-st cottages, also DARK BLUE. Giles Place on the west side. DARK BLUE, wash hanging across court.

Into Brook St and eastwards, turning N into Back Ball Court. DARK BLUE as map. There is only one entrance now, the north side has been cleared. The other entrance shut up: remaining houses and inhabitants very poor, very rough. Cistern on small outhouse in court with taps, as the only water supply. Woodchoppers at north end. The wall at north end palisaded off from clearing with wood and barbed wire. Bread lying about. 2 children barefoot. Dirty.

The next court E is Grove Court. Houses have been done up but very poor, chickens, wash. DARK BLUE as map

The next is Balls Buildings. 2-st, rough, DARK BLUE, all doors open.

Then George St. Carmen, coolies. 2-st, PURPLE to LIGHT BLUE (PURPLE in map). There is no court east of George St. This one is shown but not coloured in map.

S down Butcher Row. Carmen, PURPLE as map.

E to Medland Street. Loose women, "sailors' widows" here. DARK BLUE as map. Medland Hall on south side. Being altered or rebuilt. "Brings a number of undesirable loafers to this quarter." The court on the south side of Medland St has been demolished, "has been down 12 or 18 months". It is still an open waste.

N up London St, BLACK as map, very rough, "like Medland St between Horseferry Branch Rd and London St". The court on the east side is closed. A working girls' institute in connection with St James' Ratcliff is at the northwest end. 3 houses below it are shut, two being half down. Old houses at north end. Street well paved, clean, no litter of paper or bread. Children booted but ragged.

E through Rose Lane. One house on south side, fine old house, untenanted and "has been empty for more than a year". S down Horse Ferry Branch Rd, at southwest end a new mortuary and coroners court. W along Narrow St all warehouses with passages across the street, at lower end of London St a large rag and paper warehouse. Working man's club closed, and up for sale as warehouse.

Westwards on the north side is Painters Rents. Houses on the east side only. Seven 3-st houses, very dirty, poor, rough, DARK BLUE as map, "like London St in character". Windows broken, stuffed with rags. No exit at north end.

The Orchard LIGHT BLUE to PURPLE. Respectable. On map DARK BLUE. Houses on west side only. Batgers cooperage on the east, leads to the open space between Crawford and Berc Streets. "A clearance made over 4 years ago by LCC."

S down Spring Gardens, (also LIGHT BLUE. Is DARK BLUE on map, but Drew said it was just like Crawford St) is the name given to what was the continuation of Painters' Alley.

W past board school next to which are the Beachcroft Buildings (PURPLE) which take the place of Harris' Court, marked DARK BLUE in map. Ugly but solid. "Far better than Cosh's Buildings". Only 3 houses are left at the west end of Berc St and two or 3 at the east. Thus a large DARK BLUE patch has been removed. Batgers jam factory takes up the whole of the south side of Berc St with the exception of the open space spoken of above.

N into Brook St. W then S down Collingwood St. Respectable 2-st houses, flush with pavement. Children coming out of school, ragged, fairly clean, very few with hats. At the southeast corner where Collingwood St meets Broad St is a common lodging house, "a regular thieves' den" – BLACK – called Ragcliff Chambers. The first court west of Collingwood St is stable, the second is down.

N up School House Lane. Coopers' Alms Houses on east side (founded 1539, rebuilt 1796). W into Glass House Fields. Moir's Jam Factory. 4 buildings, 2 cottages at southwest end. PURPLE.

N into Brook St, S down Love Lane. Northeast side is a court not marked on map, called Love Lane Square. 3 cottages. LIGHT BLUE. S of Elm Row, Love Lane has a rough character, almost DARK BLUE (on map PURPLE).

W along Elm Row, a few houses, PURPLE (on map LIGHT BLUE). Respectable working class. Leading downhill to large block of Peabody Buildings. Children's Hospital abutting on west end of Elm Row (forming Gars' Alms Houses). S into what was formerly Charles Place (LIGHT BLUE on map) of which only a woodchoppers shed remains. And out into Shadwell High St. All between the Peabody Buildings and the High St is down.

S down Love Lane into Lower Shadwell. Great clearances here owing to fish market. All is down between Love Lane on the east; Lower Shadwell on the south, Labour in Vain on the west and Garth St and Leading St on the north, with the exception of a public house in Lower Shadwell. In the same way the part lying between High St Shadwell and Garth St is also down. In Garth St remain only 2 houses at the west end, and a public house. The covered-in fish market lies between Lower Shadwell and the River and with the Linde refrigerator company, takes up the whole river frontage. In the open space between Garth Street and Lower Shadwell is a long covered corrugated iron shed open on all sides. The triangle south of Leading St has no houses (thus removing a DARK BLUE patch), instead an open waste where boys were playing football. Drew said the fish market was just paying its way.

N up Market Hill (the continuation north of Labour in Vain Street), houses on lower level than road. Poor, 2-st houses, LIGHT BLUE rather than PURPLE.

E along Monmouth St, only 4 houses, clean, LIGHT BLUE as map.

N up Hopes Hill, LIGHT BLUE as map. E along Middle Shadwell. 2-st. LIGHT BLUE as map. Poor. No trouble. Much bread lying about.

S down Spring Gardens, also LIGHT BLUE is DARK BLUE on map but Drew said it was just like the rest. This forms the court of Garth St. (The bit between Middle Shadwell and the High St is nearly all down.)

N across Cable St, respectable working class. Up Hadinge St. 2-st. PURPLE to PINK (in map PINK). Like it is Alfred (late Thyrza) St. On the north side of railway is Newton (late James) St, poorer. Narrow. Stables under railway arches on south side. PURPLE as map. Thomas St. 2-st, built 1849. PURPLE to PINK. Ronald St the same. Steel's Lane. Narrow. South side is PURPLE. North side is being rebuilt. Through north end of Devonport St, PINK as map, and out into the Commercial Rd.

General remarks

Note distinct ill nourishment shown by appearance of children in Rorke's Drift; also the comparatively small numbers who are bootless. Also the rough common lodging houses in Brook St and St George St. District as a whole quieter than it used to be. Fewer sailors. Less money to waste. Fewer prostitutes.

Great clearances at Lower Shadwell.

Met Sir Edward Bradford (*see Notes*) on my way to the station. He on horseback, making one of his surprise visits. He stopped and talked for some time in the street. Said that he hoped I found the police had a good knowledge of the inhabitants in each street "for that I believe is the real way in which they should do their work". He said he tried to impress on them not to ask questions but to observe the comings and goings of all those in their district. In rough streets he liked them to know the names and occupations of every inhabitant. "Then if there is any trouble you can put your finger on it at once and often as not check it before its outbreak by the

Interview with Inspector Drew (Arbour Square Subdivision) and Inspector Derby (Shadewell Subdivision) to check the licensed houses in their respective subdivisions, 9th February 1898

Wapping they spoke as of a quiet shut off place which obtained its roughest labour from Deptford. In consequence the streets are quiet even deserted after 6 PM. The poor, rough quarters in Wapping are Whitethorn Place and Upperwall Street, Lowder Street and the buildings at the corner of Love Lane. These are very poor and very rough, and dangerous places for policemen, to be compared to Donkey Row. (On the mantelpiece of the police station was the battered helmet of a policeman who had been attacked last Saturday in Donkey Row, helmet pulpy and straps wrenched off it, strap also wrenched from the handle of his truncheon.)

They agreed that the "buildings" in Wapping with the exception of those at the corner of Love Lane had taken off the best of the house population. No houses as far as they knew shut before closing time. Women go into all houses, though some are more particularly favoured than others. If they have the money they drink spirits rather than beer.

The effect of closing houses at 10 in Wapping would be to send men home. There might be less drunkenness as consequence but they did not attach much importance to it. "The homes are such very small dark places in Wapping, men want the light and warmth quite as much as the beer." As a general thing they agreed that drinking merely for drinking's sake takes place between 6 and 12.

They deplored the fact that the East End was becoming Jewish. Said that Englishmen were rougher but the Jew more tricky, quoting Judge Montague Williams, "A Jew never tells the truth except by mistake". Endless trouble caused by accusations and counteraccusations. Two window cleaner, one a Jew and the other an Englishman recently came to the station. Each had knocked the other down. The Jew to make his case stronger, pulled his own watch chain to pieces on the road and accused the other man of attempting to steal his watch pointing to the broken chain as evidence. Unfortunately he had been seen breaking his chain, evidence also was given that before starting from the station, he had handed his watch to his servant.

As to changes in the working man, Drew in his 25 years service has not noted any except that holidays are more indulged in than they used to be. He is every bit as rough now as ever he was.

(B350-16)

mere feeling that in some way or other the police do know about all the goings on in a rough district." The difficulty, he said, lay in preventing the people feeling they were watched: for this reason it was always preferable to do too little rather than too much. "But even by standing and watching and remembering, there is a deal you can find out without opening your mouth or being in the least inquisitive." To be always in the background except when there was real need and then to come down like a thunderbolt was, he believed, the real policy of the police. Ending with "Don't you think so?"

Walk 4   B350-15
Monday 7th February 1898
George Duckworth with Inspector Drew

Starting at south end of Glamis Road
Went across the bridge of the Shadwell entrance to the London Docks, along Wapping Wall. 7-st warehouses. St Luke's court on the north side, DARK BLUE and LIGHT BLUE in map, is boarded up.

N up Monza St (late Star St), on map LIGHT BLUE. Some still poor but the rest is PURPLE. Lightermen, etc. with brass plates on their doors. 2-st. Bad smells.

W along the Milk Yard. Messy, vegetable ends, brick bats, old tins, etc, a few houses on the south side, respectable, PURPLE as map.

S down New Gravel Lane. On the east side is Sarah St, a court not coloured on map. 16 2-st cottages, asphalt court. Houses for 2 families. 2 rooms and washhouse downstairs and the same upstairs. 11 ft frontage.

E along Coleman St. 2-st. Poorer. PURPLE to LIGHT BLUE. Clean. Only one house in Fox and Goose Yard at the northeast end.

Back along Coleman St to New Gravel Lane on west side, which is an entry under arch into an unnamed open space – the result of demolitions – leading to Whitethorn Place. DARK BLUE on map. Should be BLACK. Very rough. Most windows broken. Cockney Irish. Women sackmakers. 3 boys barefoot, cries of "here is the School Board" and they promptly disappeared. Children dirty, ragged but well-fed. 3-st houses. "As bad and rough as anything in the subdivision."

N into Prusam St. 2-st. Better, PURPLE to LIGHT BLUE.

N up Malay St, late Gold St. 2-st. Cobble paved. Some bread about. PURPLE as map. Into Agatha Rd, the old schools are now a crèche. Agatha's crèche is 2d per day. The schools now occupy the whole of the triangular piece of ground whose base is opposite the workhouse. Under Father Wainwright, who was crossing the street as we passed, in black cassock and 3-cornered cap – like those worn by RC priests.

SW down Rygate St, LIGHT BLUE as map. 2-st. All doors open, windows clean. "Some rough-uns." Houses outwardly in good repair.

Into Hilliards Court. Rougher. At the corner of Clegg St and Hilliards Court is a very rough house. 3-st. Hardly a pane of glass left. Dirty, DARK BLUE, LIGHT BLUE in map. Hilliards Court narrows as it approaches Gravel Lane but in spite of it, houses get better. PURPLE as map. Entry to Gravel Lane under arch.

E along Cinnamon St, no houses, to Ship St, alongside of gasworks. 2-st, LIGHT BLUE to PURPLE.

W along High St and N into Brewhouse Lane. 5-st. Dwellings belonging to Improved Industrial Dwelling Company. Built 1861. Respectable working class. PURPLE to PINK.

Back into High St, then N along Queens' Head Alley. Rough. Noisy. LIGHT to DARK BLUE.

W into Red Lion St. 3½-st. Older houses with Corinthian capitals to doorposts and panelled doors. Built for a better class. LIGHT BLUE as map. Court on west side with one house into Upperwell Alley. DARK BLUE as map. Very rough – a murder here 18 months ago. 3 st. Grocers Court at northeast end also DARK BLUE. Rough. Five, 2-st cottages.

Into High St westwards, on north side Church Court, 1793. 2-st and attic. Some very poor, PURPLE to LIGHT BLUE.

N up Bird St. 2- and 3½-st, respectable. Improvement here probably owing to demolition of rookery behind and large playground and garden in its place. PURPLE, in map LIGHT BLUE.

E along Tench St. High Dock wall on north side, LCC recreation ground on south.

S down Red Lion St, late Anchor and Hope Alley. Small shops, parts rough, parts respectable. PURPLE as map. At southeast corner of recreation ground is a gymnasium with swings, see-saws, giant stride, etc and covered penthouse with room at one end in which a matron looks after the children.

E along Green Bank. Poor. Better towards Gravel Lane. LIGHT BLUE rather than PINK of map.

N up Gravel Lane, into Love Lane. 4-st buildings at corner. Rough. Dirty, messy backs of houses.

W into Lowder St, late York Place. Newly done up, 3-st houses, very rough. Children hatless but booted and well-fed. Thieves, prostitutes. All doors open. At least DARK BLUE according to police account.

N and W to Watts St, late Calvert St. PURPLE rather than PINK. On the north side where was formerly a church and school are now 4- and 5-st dwellings, respectable, with gravelled garden facing the road.

E into Raymond St. The south end rather rough. 2-st. LIGHT BLUE rather than DARK BLUE. A new casual ward takes up the whole of east side as far as Love Lane. A barefoot girl. North end built 1853.

N up Meeting House Alley. LIGHT BLUE to PURPLE at north end. Chandler St is better. PURPLE to PINK (on map PURPLE.) Bostock St, PINK as map. Has 4 very poor 2-st houses on north side. Rough. DARK BLUE, Drew said, on north. PURPLE on south.

N up Red Lion St, late Broad St. Respectable. PURPLE to PINK. Taylors Rents on the east side. DARK BLUE as map. Sackmakers working at home. Very poor, but clean. Tap in court. Entered under archway.

E along Worcester St. PURPLE rather than PINK. 2 houses at east end, poor, LIGHT BLUE. Broken windows. Worcester Court on south side, old wooden houses. LIGHT BLUE as map.

S down Old Gravel Lane. On the east side are a long block of 4-st red brick mansions called Rainer's Mansions. PINK in character. Better class have moved into them. This may account for apparent worsement in Bostock and Worcester Streets and Green Bank. The DARK BLUE bit at north end has disappeared in consequence of the mansions. On the west side of Gravel Lane just north of Bostock St is Rycrofts Court. Very rough. 6 cottages. Not coloured on map. Barefooted children, windows broken.

N up Gravel Lane across bridge separating the east from the west basin of the London Docks. This and the other bridge in New Gravel Lane are called the Bridge of Sighs because of the numbers of suicides. A policeman is now stationed there between 3 am and 7 am each day as a preventive. There has been a lull in the number the last 2 years but they (suicides) used to be very frequent.

At the northeast end is Starch Yard. Not coloured on map. 3-st houses, one fair but one very poor. LIGHT BLUE. On the northeast side of Gravel Lane the map marks the houses BLACK. Drew said they were only poor, LIGHT BLUE rather than BLACK.

W along Pennington St. Old houses, overhanging red tile roof with ornamental eaves. In map DARK BLUE barred BLACK. No regular brothels. Not notorious in any way, rather rough – perhaps a few unfortunates.

The first court on the north side between Chigwell Hill and Gravel Lane has some rough characters and prostitutes; called Lavender Place.

Chigwell Hill. Poor. Rough. DARK BLUE. Working class. "Better than Whitethorn Place."

E along St George Place. At the corner of Gravel Lane is Star and Garter Yard, on the south side. The vestry stone yard has encroached on the east side of it. Some houses pulled down but still rough and vicious, in the stone yard itself remain 2- or 1-st shanties still inhabited.

Interview with Mr F. Friend, publican, owner of the Lovat Arms Public House in the Burdett Road at the corner of Thomas Street, i.e. just north of the Canal Bridge. On an introduction from Mr Reeve, manager of Truman, Hanbury and Buxtons, 11th February 1898

Mr Friend is tall, dark, strong looking, about 45 years of age. His father took this same house in 1862. On the father's death in 1879, his mother carried it on with him as manager until 1891. Then she died and he has carried it on since.

The neighbourhood is working class and lower middle and middle class. The mainstay of his business in the winter is the jug trade. There is also a regular set from the Whitehead works opposite, and from Thomas Street gold and silver refinery that make use of his house. In sum the proportion of passing trade is much greater.

Burdett Road then becomes crowded with those going up to the Great Eastern Railway station to go to Southend etc, with those going for an airing in Victoria Park, and with those in brakes bound for Epping forest. In winter it is a deserted road.

Children come in great numbers for the dinner and supper beer, sent by their parents, children of all classes. "Even quite well-to-do parents will send their children for beer which does not look if they feared the contamination of the public house." Language is not so bad in the public as in the street, though at times it may be, often not so bad as in their own homes. When a man is talking loud and a child comes in, he hurries it off. "But it does not pay in a large house to allow noisy customers in, they drive away more than they bring." Thinks that the best proof of the little harm children can come by is the fact that parents who might send a servant often send a child. He never remember having seen a child drunk. Does not think there is much in the complaint against children being sent.

He opens at 7.30 AM. One house higher opens at 5 and another lower down at 6. The time of opening depends on the situation. Thinks that more harm is done by early opening than by late closing. Says that the early rum and coffee or rum and hot milk is apt to keep a man away from work altogether, in any case to make him lazy. At present licensed houses must be shut between 12 and 5, thinks that the hour of opening might be extended.

He pays the police regularly 1/- per week to the man on the beat. Thinks that all the houses in the neighbourhood whether beer or public pay the same.

"It's not quite our fault that we pay them, they practically insist on it." Said it was worth being on the right side of the policeman for he could prevent your getting into trouble in several ways. For instance a policeman who is friendly, will tell you a man should not be served when he has seen him come reeling down the street. You would probably have served the man without noticing anything wrong, "for they (i.e. drunken men) have a way of bracing themselves up and in a crowd it is difficult to be sure about their state". If the police is not friendly he lets the man come in and then serves a summons on you as soon as the man comes out. He said there was not much abuse of this sort because the magistrates were severe on policemen who had not a really strong case, but it might be done. Again when there is a row and you want a policeman he is "looking the other way" if you had not given him something. He thought the shilling was well-spent. What he did object to was the general notion of all public servants that they had a right to free drinks from the publican. "About every month the postmen expect something, when the roadsweepers pass they want a drink and are offended if you refuse. They don't go to other shopkeepers but seem to think the publican is fair game."

He said the class of men who became publicans were higher now than formerly and the abuses less than they used to be. For instance, "it is not now the general custom to give beer to the police".

He employs 2 barmen and a housekeeper who has been with them since 1862. Barmen seldom rise to be publicans tho' they have more of a chance now than formerly because of the growth of brewery ownership of public houses and the manager system. He objected to the manager system because he thought there was a much greater temptation to push the sale of drinks when you were a manager than when you were owner and had a personal reputation to maintain.

He does not believe drinking would be increased by the increase in the number of existing houses, but it would decrease the value of present holdings. In the same way he did not think that a decrease in the number would affect the amount drunk.

Beer houses are rather more noisy than publics and appeal generally to a lower class. For instance musicians are allowed to come in and play in the bar and songs are sung. He will not allow this generally because of the annoyance to others but in a Saturday evening he lets those who want to sing go into a special room at the back and drink and sing there. "I'm fond of a song myself and don't see why they should not be allowed it sometimes."

He will be glad to give any further information wanted.

(B350-17)

E along West Gardens. 4-st buildings. Quiet, PURPLE. Along to Elbow Lane. More buildings, with Duke's Court at the extreme east leading up steps into the High St, old fashioned wooden houses. Only one house properly in Duke's Court.

General remarks

The strongest religious forces in Wapping according to Drew are Father Wainwright and Peter Thompson. Father Wainwright has taken off his coat in the street to clothe a beggar. The congregational chapel has not much hold. The industries are dockwork, general waterside labour, soapworkers, gasworkers and, for women, sackmaking. Much drink among the gasworkers. A good number of casuals – poor class. Waiting for jobs at street corners.

More are employed in the district than live in it. Those who come from outside come from Deptford across the river and not from Shadwell.

Wapping is peculiar in that the best of its inhabitants have gone to live in buildings rather than in the small houses. The only rough block of buildings being those at the corner of Gravel Lane and Lowder St. No Jews. Some Cockney Irish. Streets cobble paved. Good deal of mess about especially in the milkyard which should be cleared away. Many women in the public houses especially in that at northeast end of Raymond St. The number of friendly leads and singsongs announced in their windows also remarkable. Houses for the most part small.

Walk 5   B351-2

Tuesday 8ᵗʰ March 1898
George Duckworth with Inspector Joseph Reid

Starting at the north end of Princes Street

PINK as map. Jews in all the houses except one, a Welsh milkman. Church Army Home (lodging houses, beds 6d a night, 3/- a week) at northwest end of the square. Also a "German Oak Club".

Into Princes Square. Old houses. Swedish protestant church in the middle of it, built 1728. Used to be a Swedish colony round about. Now Jew clothiers with workshops at the back. Houses with elaborate doorposts and lintels and panelled doors and passages. In the church cushioned old-fashioned pews. "Sometimes 15 or 20 and sometimes quite full of a Sunday" said a verger. Special pew reserved for the Swedish ambassador. Swedenborg is buried underneath the altar and has a marble commemorative tablet on the south wall of the church. South of the square is Britten's Court. Uncoloured in map. 2-st cottages. Poor on west side. LIGHT BLUE. Jamrach's beast stores on the east side. Up the east side of the square into Cable Street through Mayfield's Buildings. Uncoloured in map but should be BLACK. "The worst place in the subdivision." Not one male in the street above school age that has not been convicted. Thieves. Prostitutes. Rough. Cockney Irish. Broken dirty windows. Bareheaded women. Doors open. Black shiny doorposts. 3-st houses. "Has been the rain of Princes Square, else a quiet country like place."

S down Betts St. Poorer than Princes Square. PURPLE as map. 3-st houses. Nearly half of southwest side is taken up by the Ratcliffe Highbury Mission for fallen women. "Does a lot for women as long as they do not fall again, but will then have nothing to say to them."

By the St George's Public Baths. E along St George St and N up Denmark St Poor cottages. LIGHT BLUE. Southeast end also 2 or 3 courts, uncoloured on map all on east side. Rodgers Court. 2 cottages. 4 rooms. Let for 6/- a week. Is at the end of a narrow passage. Dark, hardly 3 feet between the house windows and the blank wall opposite. The next court northwards is Hope Court. Also LIGHT BLUE. Houses of same class as foregoing but let for 4/6 a week. Not coloured in map.

The east side of Denmark St higher up is factories and warehouses. On the west side Keen's Mustard Factory and the old St George's Watchhouses built 1820. Now tenanted by 2 policemen and families who use the old cells behind as coalholes and washhouses.

W along St George St and S down Virginia Hill. High dock and warehouse walls on either side. E along Pennington St on the north side of which is Breezer's Hill. BLACK in map. Now poor, respectable married people. 2 houses only left in the middle of the east side of the street.

E along Pennington St, on north side a small court. 2 houses, LIGHT BLUE. Cockney Irish. Unnamed and uncoloured on map. Houses in Pennington St poor. Boxmakers. Some old houses with overhanging eaves. Marked DARK BLUE and BLACK in map. Cockney Irish. Rough but better than they were. Some thieves. A good number of prostitutes "but the prostitution is of a sturdy kind and there are no bullies who live off the earnings of the women, it is not like the West End" said Reid.

Artichoke Hill on the north side is BLACK and LIGHT BLUE still as map. Casual labourers. Some prostitutes. Along Pennington St on the north side is a court called Pennington Place. Clean blinds. Children booted, clean, well fed but rather ragged. 5 cottages. Not worse than LIGHT BLUE.

Past Johns Hill. BLACK as map. Much trouble to police. Windows broken, but houses in outwardly good repair. Bread in street. Pitch and toss going on. German prostitutes. Same character as Mayfield St, the worst of this lot of streets. At the southwest corner of Chigwell Hill is a large building to the Dock Company now let out to respectable men. Some city police and docklabourers live here. RED in map, NOW PURPLE.

Past Chigwell Hill. 2 houses only on west side, 4 on east. Court on west side is closed and the northwest end making the corner with St George St is down. Is still a thieves' resort.

Along Pennington St on the north side here is another court. Lavender Place. Not shown on map. Children clean, booted. Docklabourers. Not worse than LIGHT BLUE. Windows and blinds clean, doors shut. The houses in Pennington St should I think be not worse than DARK BLUE. The trouble to the police is from the occasional quarrels in which the people indulge but "for months they are quiet and since dock labour has been more regular the tone and behaviour of the people is quieter than it used to be". There are thieves and prostitutes but no brothels as in Railway Place or Albert St.

Then S down New Gravel Lane. W along Bostock St (one shoeless boy), S down Bird Lane, W along High St and across the Wapping entrance into the London Docks. Houses on either side of the Dock entrance, RED as map, those on the northwest side not quite so good as the others but look better than PINK.

N up Russells Buildings, PINK as map. Respectable dockers. Across Great Hermitage St and N into Cowder St, mixed. LIGHT BLUE and PURPLE. Only ends of houses and dock walls. Past Sampsons Gardens. Old houses with ornamental doorways. 3-st, PINK as map.

At the West End of Redman's Rd at the south side is Mary's Place. Oldish, 1820–1830s houses. Up steps. LIGHT BLUE in map but a rough mixture, perhaps DARK BLUE.

S past Little Hermitage St, shops with old bow windows and small panes of glass. E along Great Hermitage St, built 1726. 3-st houses. PINK as map. The better class of men in Hoave's Brewery live here. In the south side is Barhell St. LIGHT BLUE in map. Now partially rebuilt on west side; then remain only 2 or 3 dwelling houses only half of which can be called LIGHT BLUE, the other two are PURPLE to PINK. On the north side of Great Hermitage St is a long passage, not marked in map, called 29½ Court which used to open into Mary's Place. At the west end of it are 2 respectable cottages. PURPLE. At the east, separated by about 30 yards of stone flagged passage between high walls are 3 or 4 very poor cottages. DARK BLUE. Bread lying about.

Orange Court on the south side of Great Hermitage St is only a passage into the High St. Crown Place has buildings on its east side. PURPLE rather than PINK. On the north side of Great Hermitage St is French Place. 2 cottages overgrown with creepers. Not marked in map. PURPLE. Tap in the court. On the south side the DARK BLUE patch in Plough Alley consists of 4 houses. The lower 2 of which are LIGHT BLUE, the upper are PURPLE. Has been rough but is not now. Globe St further west. 3½-st. PURPLE as map.

S into High St and W on the north side is a cul-de-sac called Wainwrights Place. Paved court. Many houses on either side. Has been rough and noisy. So much so that the landlord has lately given notice to many of his tenants and now nearly the whole of the west side and half the east side is empty. No opening (as map) into

Great Hermitage St. Houses 3-st. Lately done up outside. Looks DARK BLUE.
W along High St, between Crown Place and Bushell St are High Model Dwellings.
PURPLE to LIGHT BLUE, not the PINK of the map. Reid said they were an example
of what dwellings became when the superintendent was slack and compared them
very unfavourably with the Peabody Dwellings.
N up Nightingale Lane and SW down Burr St. PINK as map, 2 PINK houses on west
side, tenanted by Hoaves Brewery men.

General remarks

The respectability of this bit of Wapping is due to the presence of Hoaves Brewery
and to the fact that some of the higher paid dock servants live in it. A very quiet
place on Sundays.
About children fetching beer, Reid said he would not allow any of his own to do so
for fear of what they might hear in the house. Publicans he said generally reserved
a special bar for jugs. He has never seen a child drunk and only very few between
17 and 18. It is after these ages that drunkenness begins. He is afraid that the fact
of going so constantly to public houses in their youth may do a little to encourage
the taste for the smell and company of the place in later life. Said there had been
considerable improvements in the class of people who became publicans especially
in public houses.
As to pawnbrokers, he said it was not a trade Jews went into because Jews did not
patronise the pawn shop. One fact to show the increase of Jews in the subdivision is
that a pawnbroker has lately given up because now that there were so many Jews he
was unable to make a fair living.

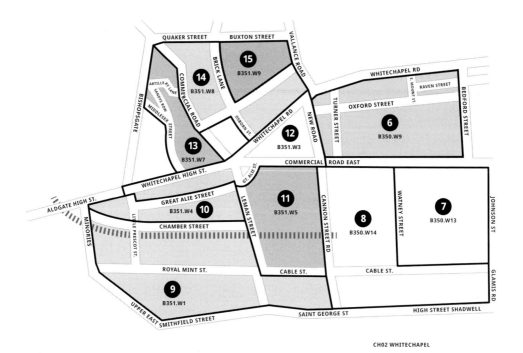

QUAKER STREET BUXTON STREET VALLANCE ROAD WHITECHAPEL RD

15 B351.W9

14 B351.W8

BRICK LANE

ARTILLERY LANE SANDYS ROW COMMERCIAL ROAD MIDDLESEX STREET BISHOPSGATE

OSBORN ST.

13 B351.W7

WHITECHAPEL RD NEW ROAD TURNER STREET OXFORD STREET RAVEN STREET E. MOUNT ST. BEDFORD STREET

12 B351.W3

6 B350.W9

COMMERCIAL ROAD EAST

WHITECHAPEL HIGH ST.

GREAT ALIE STREET GT. ALIE ST. LEMAN STREET CANNON STREET RD WATNEY STREET

ALDGATE HIGH ST. MINORIES

10 B351.W4

11 B351.W5

8 B350.W14

7 B350.W13

JOHNSON ST

LITTLE PRESCOT ST. CHAMBER STREET

ROYAL MINT ST. CABLE ST. CABLE ST. GLAMIS RD

9 B351.W1

UPPER EAST SMITHFIELD STREET SAINT GEORGE ST HIGH STREET SHADWELL

CH02 WHITECHAPEL

Walk 6   B350-9

Tuesday 25th January 1898
George Duckworth with Inspector H. Drew

Starting at Nelson Street

Very poor Jews, 2-st, holey curtain, paper litter, straw in street, doors open. LIGHT BLUE, on map PINK, but worse now. Cameron Place on the north side marked on map LIGHT BLUE, is respectable. 2-st, 11 houses, only on west side of street, trees between wall of the back of Bedford St and the paving in Cameron Place. Should be PURPLE. "Decidedly better than Nelson St."

Into Varden St. Poor Jews. 2-st houses, well-built 1820–1830s type. The road between Turner St and Bedford St is poorer than the bit between, Turner St and New Rd as LIGHT BLUE to PURPLE. Then S down Gray St, west side poorer than east though at bottom (south) house on east side is a family of Italian ice-cream makers.

W into Philpot Rd. A very broad road with the Land Hospital at the north end. PINK as map, some parts better. Hospital nurses in house at corner of Oxford St, northeast end. Into Varden St. Poor Jews "Medicine given them with a prayer, only the very poorest go, don't think any are really converted" said Drew. North end of Philpot St, part of Varden St, is quite PINK-barred in character. Mildmay Medical Mission on east side, large buildings, several poor Jewesses sitting on steps outside with sick children, waiting for it to open.

W into Rutland St. 2-st, PURPLE rather than the PINK of the map, "rather better than Bedford St". Several Jews.

N into Newark St, late New St, more Jews, PURPLE rather than PINK. The large red-brick church of St Philip is here. "Built by the present rector at a cost of £40,000, but as the parish becomes more Jewish, is less necessary each year, has poor congregation" said Drew. Oxford St, also PURPLE. Jews.

Into Turner St. 2½-st. Medical students living at north end. PINK as map. Much homework carried out in the houses. Tailoring. Jews.

N into Green and Mount Streets. Green St PURPLE to LIGHT BLUE. Not PINK. Poor Jews. "Nearly as poor as Bedford St." Mount Street, 3-st and a cellar. "Probably 5 or 6 families in each house, many workrooms. PURPLE to PINK.

E Mount St. 3- and 2-st. Less good north of Raven Row, but PINK lower down as map.

Cotton St behind it hardly looks as poor as LIGHT BLUE. Mixed class. Many Jews. Stables and workshops on the east side, the west end of Raven Row. To the north of it looks poor. LIGHT BLUE rather than PINK of map. Drew said "very poor". Goakleys Buildings on the north side (apparently the servants alms houses marked in the map), built 1804. Inhabitants quiet, poor, children clean though pinafores and clothes rather ragged, all with good boots. 2-st cottages. PURPLE to LIGHT BLUE. Not coloured on map.

The west end of Nelson St, between Turners Rd and the New Rd, is better than the east end. PINK to PURPLE, with the exception of the first house on the northeast side, which is dirty, poor and evil looking.

General remarks

Jews coming in already in most of the streets spoken above. In consequence great difficulty in distinguishing between streets that should be PURPLE and those that should be PINK. Drew said that the better streets had gone down in character in the last 10 years because of the Jewish influx but that none of them were rough. In the Jewish house with its greater crowding there is no china pot with an evergreen plant in the front window on a round table which in North London seemed to be the sure mark of a "PINK" character. Again there is a greater visible dirt in a fairly well-to-do working class Jewish home than in an English one. As far as outward looks are concerned, nearly all the streets belonged to the "PURPLE" category.

No complaints Drew said as to people sleeping in the streets. Jews here are not so poor as those that crowd into the inner circle of Whitechapel. All children seen looked well fed and were well booted.

As to warning publicans not to serve men on the verge of drunkenness, Drew said magistrates now thought it was the police's duty as much to prevent as to detect crime, therefore they had to warn publicans. But he admitted it was a counsel of perfection and in practice was not often carried out.

Walk 7   B350-13

Tuesday 1st February 1898
George Duckworth with Inspector Drew

Starting at Johnson Street in NE corner

Johnson St, a respectable street, like Hardinge, PINK rather than the PURPLE of the map. At northeast end one cottage at end of passage. LIGHT BLUE. A 2-st street, Poonah St, only end of houses.

W into Cable St, looks rather PINK than PURPLE. "No opium dens."

N into Joseph St, which at the north end runs under a railway arch and opens into Lucas St (not shown on map). Now distinctly worse than the PURPLE of map. 2-st, windows broken, children with stockings, toes showing through ends of their boots. Bread lying about, meat at north end, fish heads, paper, etc. Certainly LIGHT BLUE. W into Lucas St. West side nearly all Jews, much shoe and tailoring homework. Street rather poorer north of railway than south of it. 2-st on west side, 3½ on east. 3 and four families in each house. "Is poorer than Johnson St", character PURPLE to PINK.

From Cable St into Cowley St. Entrance same width as rest of street, not narrow as map. Newish, 2-st cottages, built for 2 families, covered with creepers, a cul-de-sac, quiet street, many policemen living in it. Fresh herrings being cried at 4 a 1d (same price as in Watney Street market).

W along Cable St then N up Sutton St East. W into Yule Court (has no opening into Dean St as shown in map). PURPLE in map but now certainly LIGHT to DARK BLUE. All children hatless, one without shoes or stockings. A low class of labourers about, windows broken, a flagged narrow court. Character the same both on north and south sides.

Into Cornwall St, on map LIGHT BLUE, now DARK BLUE, much bread in the street, thieves and prostitutes, not brothels as Railway Place. 2-st houses, 4 rooms for 6/ or 7/. Flush with pavement, like all houses in this block of streets. A few Jews getting into the west end.

Into Station Place, running east and west of Dean St, BLACK in map and still BLACK. Very poor east end, less poor but more vicious west end where loose women are.

The houses have clean blinds, curtains, windows. The east end is crushed in by the railway arches and the whole darkened by them. There is now an opening into Watney St, not shown on map. One shoeless child but several ragged.

S down Dean St. At the southeast end are 6 cottages in a court called Cross Court, which formerly was the continuation of Yule Court. Very poor, Jews, LIGHT BLUE as map. The south end of Dean St is equally rough as Station Place. Ragged children.

On the north side of the railway arch are a block of streets all marked PURPLE on map but all now rough and poor. Probably DARK BLUE. Drew did not know if it was so or not but it is likely that the poor from the Shadwell clearances have moved this way to Martha St, Spencer St, Sheridan St and Tarling St. 2-st, built 1807. Same characteristics about all i.e. bread and mess in street, children with ragged coats and skirts but only one bootless, majority without hats, women sitting on doorsteps with children, doors open. Boards across street doors to keep in small children. Loose women, thieves, but a mixture in every street. Some houses PURPLE. Pots in windows. Clean windows, blinds and curtains, but the majority not. Many broken windows. Character LIGHT to DARK BLUE. All these streets rather better west of Dean St than east of it. Jews beginning to come into Tarling St, they already monopolize the west side of Button St. In the windows of most of the houses, portraits of the two progressive candidates of LCC, C. Balian and C. Barratt. Both shopkeepers in Watney St. Balian is known locally as the 'Toffee Cooler', he is a confectioner. Motto "For progress and the people". Two families in each house, signs that many have been done up, i.e. bricks painted, etc. Costers, carmen, labourers, coalies the inhabitants.

W into Watney St, a crowded street market, an English Wentworth Street, mostly shops of costers i.e. shops have out the barrows in front of their windows. Some prices – 5 lb good turnip tops 2d. Best wheaten bread 4½d per 4 lb loaf. 3 lb fair potatoes 2d. Fair bacon from 3d to 6d per lb. Good pork chops 6d each. Cheese 5d lb. Butter 10d to 1/2 per lb. Margarine 4d to 6d. Sausages 4d, 6d per lb. Meat scraps 2d lb. Fair bits 4d to 6d.

N turning E at Blakesley St. PINK, respectable as map, houses of the 1820–1830s type, 2-st, many Jews. The north ends of Dean St and Sutton St look equally PINK (PURPLE on map). It is as if the few really respectable from Martha St etc. had come to live here.

S down Sutton St. At the northwest end was formerly the primitive Methodist bookstore and chapel. All now shut up. Lower down on the west side the Jews are in. The east side is poorer than the west, especially near Cornwall St. 3-st. Small shops, LIGHT BLUE to PURPLE.

General remarks

Notable decline in character of streets since last survey. 3 or 4 West End ladies about in 'East End' clothes. Many women in the beer-house at the corner of Spencer Street and Watney Street.

Walk 8   B350-14

Wednesday 3rd February 1898
George Duckworth with Inspector Drew

Starting at Winterton Street (late Devonshire Street)

2-st. Rather narrow, smelly, stables at southeast end, brothels, prostitutes and bullies; Jews coming in at north end, very poor.

W into Planet St (late Star St), one or two brothels, several unfortunates besides who work at the Commercial Rd, some Jews but no prostitutes among the Jewesses (Drew only knows of one Jewess prostitute in the subdivision). Christchurch Mission Room on west side, "hardly touches anyone". Some new whitish brick houses with polished yellow bricks making the doorposts (i.e. those parts which become greasiest and dirtiest in poor streets). A rather better street than Winterton St. DARK BLUE as map. At the bottom (south) on the west side are Whites Gardens (PINK in map), now DARK BLUE. Windows broken, is like Planet St.

W along the Commercial Rd. S into Hungerford St. 2-st. More prostitutes, unswept street, cabyard at southeast end. South end lately done up. Broken windows. DARK BLUE as map.

S through Fenton St. LIGHT BLUE to PURPLE as map. Morris St. 2-st. Poor. Rough. LIGHT BLUE rather than PURPLE of map.

W along Tait St. 2-st. LIGHT BLUE to DARK BLUE. Mixed, rough. The DARK BLUE spot shown north and south of Tait St between Tait and Morris Streets is down. The court also on the east of Mary St is boarded up.

N up Mary St. 2- and 3-st. LIGHT BLUE, poor. Like Sheridan St. Into Lower Chapman St. Shops, nearly all Jew. PINK as map.

W into Agra Place which has an outlet in the north side. Into Lower Fenton St. LIGHT BLUE as map. All poor Jews.

S down Tillman, late Ann St. 3-st houses at southeast end, put up by the Chapman Estate. Got a respectable class, PURPLE rather than LIGHT BLUE of map. On southwest side poor 2-st houses, LIGHT BLUE. The PURPLE of the map seems to have moved across the road into the newer houses.

Along Tait St, past Chapman Place. Poor, LIGHT BLUE as map. Flagged passage, doors open. Clean.

S down Anthony St. 3- and 2-st. Poor Jews. Past the west end of Cornwall St.

Not quite so bad as the east, some Jews, bread lying about street, some houses respectable, books, wax flowers and fruits under glass case in front windows, but others very poor, broken windows, holey blinds, black shiny doorposts. 2- and 3-st, many costers. Character LIGHT to DARK BLUE. Map marks this end DARK BLUE and the east end PURPLE.

S down Anthony St and E along Cable St, on south side of which is Prospect Place. Windows clean, only one broken. 16 cottages, 2-st. "But a rough place." LIGHT to DARK BLUE. (LIGHT BLUE in map.)

W along Cable St which looks better than map, 3½-st houses, PINK north and south side in appearance, map gives PURPLE north side and LIGHT BLUE south. All except 2 houses east of the Wesleyan Church up to Dellow St are down. The Board School now coming right up to Cable St.

N up Walburgh Street. Very poor southwest end, 2-st and attic houses. Newish 3-st tenements on southeast side; the greater part of the west side of the street is occupied by Seawards Stables (they are carriers in a large way of business). Walburgh Place. 4 cottages, red tiled, PURPLE. Goodhart Place (late York Place), poor, Jews. LIGHT BLUE. Little Ann St the same, Jews.

Up Anthony St into Lower Fenton St. 2-st. PURPLE to LIGHT BLUE rather than PINK of map. Out of it on north side are Buress St and Fenton St. 3- and 2-st. Very many Jews. Buress rather the better of the two. PURPLE as map.

Into Commercial Rd, then S down Jane St. Nearly all Jews on west side. PURPLE not LIGHT BLUE. The two black bits on the east and west side are pointed wrong way up and should run between the streets – not vicious but very poor indeed, DARK BLUE not BLACK. The passage into Richard St is known as Richard Court. Richard St also PURPLE rather than LIGHT BLUE of map. 3- and 2-st. All doors shut. The only LIGHT BLUE houses are two on the southwest end. West side rather poorer than the east. Whole street is poorer north of the beer-house. Jews.

Into Commercial Rd East to Little Turner St. This is a patch marked BLACK and DARK BLUE on map. Is all much better now. Practically every family is Jewish, poor, foreign. Boot- and shoemakers, many unable to talk English. Children, booted, well fed, fairly clean. Majority hatless.

E along Barrett St, LIGHT BLUE not BLACK, into Kinder St, also LIGHT BLUE. 2-st. Homework: shoes and tailoring. Water that ought to have flowed away lying in a large puddle owing to deficient street-levelling. Like it Sly St on south side of which are tall, 4-st buildings called Salters' Buildings, date 1893. PURPLE in place of DARK BLUE of map, all Jews, windows clean, unbroken.

Into Cannon Street Rd. Well-to-do, 3- and 4-st. All Jews, some shops, much homework and small workshops. S of Cable St, shops on both sides but east side not better than PINK (RED in map) and PURPLE on west side. One or two very old dilapidated-looking houses on southwest side. Servants kept in some houses.

E along St George's St. Formerly the notorious Ratcliff Highway. "But its balmy days are over." Many public houses, many beer houses, many lodging houses of a low class, many courts and remnants of old wooden London are its characteristics. Its shops still redolent of the sea.

On the north side nearly opposite the end of Old Gravel Lane is Harris Terrace. 2-st. LIGHT BLUE as map. The next eastwards is Russell Court. 2-st. Flagged court in good repair. Clean. Ragged boy. LIGHT BLUE as map. Ratcliff St the next leading into St George's churchyard. Respectable, 2 or 3 houses only at northeast and northwest ends. PURPLE to PINK.

N up Dellow St. Great changes here. On the west side of the road is a Board School which has taken the place of some BLACK and BLUE bits. On the east side are tall 4-st and attic LCC buildings, called Dellow and Bewley Buildings, with an asphalt court between them. Road broad and clean. Character of buildings PURPLE. "Have got quite a different class in them to those they turned out." Between the east side of Barley Buildings and Albert St is open space, all houses down, palisaded. A new street to be called Lowood St not yet built on. Whyborrows' Pickle Factory at Cable St end. Albert St is now built on both sides up to Cable St; both sides BLACK in character. 2-st. 3-st in northwest, newer built. Women ragged, several brothels, children dirty, ragged, hatless, one only shoeless. Sage St the next eastwards. Houses on the west side only. Stables on the east, very poor, rough unfortunates, children dirty. 4 cottages called Settles Buildings in a court on southeast side, not shown on map. DARK BLUE. The next street eastwards is Twine Court. At the northwest end of which is a court of 12 1-st cottages with a pump in the middle of it with a tap, called Newton Rents. DARK BLUE. Very poor. A tree in the court, children swinging over dustheap in the corner. Twine Court itself looks outwardly the poorest street I have seen; houses 2-st, built 1887. In good outward repair, but windows broken, children ragged and barefooted, dirty ragged. All doors open, women dirty – women sackmakers, the men ne'er-do-wells. Unadulterated poverty. "Not so vicious as Albert St." DARK BLUE. Notice on houses: "18 houses for sale, let good tenants, bringing in gross rental of £512.4". Has 3 gaslamps and a concrete pavement. There is an entry into Shadwell High St out of the south end of Twine Court.

E along Shadwell High St between Twine Court and Mercers St are a set of rough buildings called Market Buildings, abutting on High St and passage underneath the front leads to another set. "Very rough." Single rooms from 2/- per week, 2 rooms 4/-.

Past Mercers St, 2-st, PINK as map. Down King David Lane. PINK as map. E along High St Shadwell, there is a passage just east of Novvis' Warehouses (couriers), between them and Glamis Rd called Peel Alley. It is a cul-de-sac. (Not open as in map.) Consisting of four 2-st respectable houses. PURPLE as map.

Then N up Glamis Rd (or Labour in Vain Rd). On the west side is a narrow 'carriage way', all stables. Then Juniper St. A street of 4-st industrial dwellings, dismal, ugly, dark, unrelieved, flush with pavement, in a hollow, no colour. Built 1880. At southwest end by the carriage way a single 3-st house built 1845, with a yard to itself, quiet, PINK. The rest PURPLE. Though dismal, the street is respectable.

General remarks

Two great BLACK spots have been removed from this area since our map was compiled. In the northwest corner (Little Turner St) the betterment has been due chiefly to the ousting of the rough and vicious by foreign Jews and also to the building of dwellings (Salters Buildings), also tenanted by Jews. Kinder St and Little Turner St is still very poor but not worse than LIGHT BLUE (was DARK BLUE and BLACK). In the Dellow St area, there has been wholesale clearance followed by the

---

William Hoare. Chairman of the Red Lion Brewery (Hoare and Co.) Lower East Smithfield, 5th October 1897

Went to see him about 1) The class of men put in by them as publicans, 2) The rise in the prices of public houses, 3) Views as to the varying policies of licensing bodies.

Looks rather a weak man. Has no fixed views or policy with regard to any of the above.

The value of the house he said depended on the value of its trade. A trade in spirits is more lucrative than one in beer only. The profit on spirits was about 100%. That on beer only 75%.

Publicans reckon every month as 28 days and every year as consisting of 13 months. Trade is reckoned as so much per month.

All classes of men are put into their houses. There are always a number of applicants 'among our private connection'. Some send their sons to university. The best men are in the largest houses. The worst in the beer houses.

Public Houses cater for a public need. If you did away with them, what would take their place?

Prices have gone up partly because of the immensely greater stability in the trade. Brewers now see they will not be done away with. When he entered the business 30 years ago everyone was afraid of Sir W. Lawson and his followers. Houses were then no assured source of revenue. Now they are to all intents and purposes.

He gave an introduction to one of the publicans. Mr. E.B. Donet of the Hope and Anchor, Hereford Street, Lisson Grove, whom he said would be able to tell most about the relations of police and publican.

(B347-14)

building of high blocks of model dwellings under the LCC. The tenants of the new buildings are of the respectable labouring class. Albert St still remains BLACK.

The third BLACK area in Winterton St remains as it was. Drew was unable to say exactly where the former inhabitants of Dellow St had gone. He has been too short a time in the subdivision. Nor is there any man who has been longer in it than himself.

Judging by appearances alone it seems clear that old Dellow St and perhaps Little Turner St too, has moved into 1) the northwest end of Albert St (BLACK), 2) into Sage St (now DARK BLUE instead of LIGHT BLUE), 3) Twine Court (now DARK BLUE), built in 1887, 4) others have crossed Cable St and turned into Yule Court and Cornwall St (PURPLE in map) or into Martha, Spencer and Sheridan Streets (now DARK BLUE, but formerly PURPLE).

In return it may be that the PURPLE inhabitants of Cornwall, Martha, Spencer and Sheridan Streets have moved into the Dellow St Buildings. In any case the character of Dellow Buildings is PURPLE and of Cornwall St, etc. DARK BLUE. Thus on the face of it there has been merely a change about a general post but it is to be noticed that BLACK Dellow St in the course of it moves to Cornwall St, becomes a shade better i.e. DARK BLUE, so that the net result, if the original supposition be correct, has been a betterment. This betterment is the justification of the LCC policy – nothing very great, but still something.

Walk 9   B351-1

Monday 7th March 1898

George Duckworth with Inspector Joseph Reid

Inspector Reid is a tall man, over 6 ft, fair moustache, energetic. Has been in the subdivision 3 years. Came here from Notting Dale district which he says has rougher streets and more vicious – by reason of the bullies – than anything he has seen down here.

Starting at the police station in Leman Street

S past Chamber St. PURPLE as map. On the east side of Leman St a turning called Mill Yard. BLACK and DARK BLUE on map. Brothel formerly, now shut, houses being rebuilt, newly paved, prosecution at the instance of vestry. Now LIGHT BLUE.

Then W along Royal Mint St. Small shops with 4-st lodging above for carmen, general labourers and dockers, all English. PURPLE to LIGHT BLUE, not marked in map.

S down Glasshouse St. All Peabody Dwellings. "They are very strict and will not allow any noisy family to remain." PURPLE, not marked in map. 20 Jews here. Dwellings 5-st with large asphalt yards. The whole block between Glasshouse St and Cartwright St is a mass of dwellings. All PURPLE. Built either by the Peabody Trust or the Metropolitan Industrial Dwellings Co. 3 rooms from 6/9, 2 rooms from 4/6 and one room from 3/3. Reid said that there were a few thieves in the dwelling. But no known bad characters. Many young girls who work in the city in the single rooms, respectable class. All the dwellings are strictly kept.

Between Glasshouse St and Dock St is Shorters Rents. DARK BLUE on map, poor but no trouble to the police. Rather LIGHT BLUE than DARK BLUE.

S along Glasshouse St on the east side is New Martin St, as map on north side 2-st and attic houses, some very old at the west end but well kept and in good repair. The south side (DARK BLUE on map) is down and now a yard for carts.

S into Royal Mint St, between it and Dock St is Chambers Square, uncoloured on map, consisting of 10 houses. 3-st, fair state, children booted and clean, a very old wooden house at the west side where there is an outlet into Glasshouse Street PURPLE to LIGHT BLUE.

W along Upper East Smithfield St, the next court westwards on the north side of the road is Coopers Row. Now only a smithy. The next is Brown Bear Alley. No houses. The next is Norwich Court, DARK BLUE in map, now two houses (LIGHT BLUE) only remain on the west side, the rest has been demolished. No trouble to police, only very poor, many loose brickbats from the demolished houses. No opening into Loats Buildings which is the next court west. Now no dwellings but a smithy and a cooperage (LIGHT BLUE in map.)

W along Upper East Smithfield, past the Mint into King St and Queen St. PINK and LIGHT BLUE in map. Both have shops underneath. King St as map. Queen St LIGHT BLUE on west side but PURPLE on east. Houses on west side shoved up to prevent their falling. Reid thought the whole were shortly to come down to provide a better approach to the Tower Bridge.

Into Royal Mint St, the whole of the north side with the exception of 4 houses before you come to the railway is down and now used as yards by railway companies.

N up passage formerly called Little Prescot St and Swallow Gardens where one of the Whitechapel murders was committed, under dark railway arch; now all houses down and another piece of DARK BLUE disappears.

Into Chamber St, 3- and 2-st houses on north side only, PURPLE as map. At the west end are Roman Catholic schools. Just east of the schools is a court with part of Cohens Pencil Factory and 2 or 3 houses. PURPLE. West of the schools is another court not marked or coloured on map called Chamber Court. 3-st. 5 houses. Poor, map LIGHT BLUE. Children clean, booted, hatted, well fed, LIGHT BLUE.

S into Royal Mint St. On the south side is Rothschild's Gold Refinery with a little court of houses (probably St Peter's Court on map) for the workmen. All Frenchmen. PINK.

S down Well St and E along Graces Alley. BLACK on map. Now PURPLE to PINK,

Wesleyan East End Mission takes up a large part of the north side. Formerly brothels, now none. It is a clean paved way with shops on either side. One a former restaurant. Into Wellclose Square. The northwest side (DARK BLUE in map) is now taken up by a Roman Catholic Mission to sailors and new warehouses, some still building; PINK now. The western edge, now called Ensign St, was previously called Well St. The southern edge was called Neptune St. On the north side is Graces Alley.

N up Shorter St, the southeast corner of which is down and new warehouses make the southwest side. On the east side is a small court of 2 houses, LIGHT BLUE, not marked on map. The rest of the street is PURPLE to PINK rather than LIGHT BLUE.

Into Cable St, at this point almost completely Jewish. S down North East Passage. BLACK in map, a few sailors' widows still living here. One common lodging house with beds 4d a night on the east side. But the double-bedded common lodging houses next to it are closed. LIGHT BLUE barred BLACK on west side. DARK BLUE on east. At the southeast corner (BLACK in map) is a public house, tap to the brewery next door. The east side of Wellclose Square is made up of the brewery, 2 houses now being pulled down, a doctor's house and a shop.

S down Ship Alley. BLACK in map, now shops and homework. Nearly all Jews, poor, PURPLE to LIGHT BLUE.

Into St George's St and W to Neptune St. The southeast corner of which is now a large public house and higher up is a beer house (all marked BLACK in map) but now rather PINK or RED. The west side (in map DARK BLUE and BLACK) is poor, casual labourers and a few thieves, all children booted, DARK BLUE.

N into the square. At the northeast corner of Neptune St is the old sessions house with dock and judge's chair still remaining, now a secondhand furniture dealer's shop (a Mr Miller, who said he had been about the streets in the city as a boy, matchselling, I think). The southwest side of Wellclose Square are the Grel Emmanuel Almshouses for Jews. The west side of the Square has a court at the lower and above Harad's Place. Not shown in map, with one 3-st wooden house, DARK BLUE, and stables behind. Above it are 4 DARK BLUE houses as map. Rough. One ticket-of-leave, above that is the old fire brigade station with a plaster frieze in relic above the ground floor windows. Now let out as dwellings by the LCC and in character PURPLE.

Harad's Place, at the southwest corner is now PURPLE rather than LIGHT BLUE. Clean doorsteps and windows, doors shut, 2-st houses, no court on the north side.

NE into Cable St, turning S down Pell St (DARK BLUE in map). Several Cockney Irish here, rough, but not of the roughest class. Houses look particularly clean and respectable. Causes trouble to police only during funeral wakes. Built 1774. At the northeast end is Wrights Row. 4 houses, PURPLE. Northwest side is Pell Place. Regular labourers. PURPLE. Lower down in east side is Ludens Place. 8 cottages. PURPLE to LIGHT BLUE. Blinds and windows clean. On the west side are Thomas

Place. LIGHT BLUE. Nothing between it and the block of Wellclose Square. Rougher. But only barely DARK BLUE.

Edwards Place. A little lower down on west side, house empty. On the opposite side is stable yard. In the street some bread about. Reid said the inhabitants were quarrelsome "but they fight it out at home and don't give us trouble". 2 and 3 families to each house. "But no crowding at all like the Jews." And they are getting better.

The court between Pell St and Ship Alley is down and closed so that a large piece of BLACK and DARK BLUE is gone and has helped to the betterment of Pell St.

General remarks

A great betterment noticeable. Fewer sailors, one cause of less vice. Dancing licenses refused. Emigration of roughest class. Greater regularity of Dock labour.

Speaking of the suppression of brothels, Superintendent Mulvaney said that if there was a demand for them it was no good suppressing them because they only break out again somewhere else. He himself was all in favour of state inspection and regulation. He said that if women were confined to a known place there would be less temptation than there is at present for the bashful man or boy. "Seeing as I do down here how much illness and trouble is caused by inherited syphilitic tendencies, it is a marvel how anyone can persist in favouring non-regulation."

Cockney Irish colony in Pell St. Still rough but getting better. Police not many months ago called into a row at a wake where the mourners were drunk and the coffin frills on fire.

The "rough ones" who have left the district have gone, Reid thinks, to Notting Dale (Bangor St is the worst street there), to Bethnal Green and farther east into Stepney.

Walk 10   B351-4

Wednesday 9th March 1898
George Duckworth with Inspector Reid

Starting at the police station in Leman Street

the whole of the southeast side of which below Johnson's Court is taken up by warehouses. E through Johnson's Court. The DARK BLUE on the south side nearest Leman St has given way to Cousin's Wool Warehouse. Opposite are 4-st buildings, PURPLE, making the corner of Leman St and there are two, 3-st houses at the northeast, LIGHT BLUE, where caretakers dwell, windows clean. Used all to be brothels which accounts for the BLACK and DARK BLUE in the map. The southeast corner of Johnson's Court and Rupert St is a public house. Inhabitants not so rough as Pell St.

Into Rupert St. Rough but not so rough as it used to be. Caretakers, cabmen. At the southeast end, not marked on map, are two 4-st houses, PURPLE, belonging to the publican at the corner of Lambeth and Rupert St. The north end of Rupert St is PURPLE to LIGHT BLUE.

N into Alie St, the east end of which is called Goodman's Stile and has houses on the north side belonging to LCC and inhabited by fire brigade men.

S down Lambeth St. On the west side a court called Christopher Court. DARK BLUE on map, now mixed LIGHT BLUE and PURPLE. Not many houses and all but 2 inhabited by Jews. Doors shut. Windows clean. In Lambeth St is the United German Club. At the southwest end are some 4-st very rough houses, windows broken, dirty. Juvenile thieves in them, not marked in map, now DARK BLUE.

W along Great Prescott St. 3- and 4-st houses, PINK as map. Tailors, clothiers, bootmakers, all Jews, old houses many of them red-tiled. A convent and Whitechapel county court on the south side.

S through Magdala Passage, 1 poor house on west side, LIGHT BLUE, unmarked in map. Into Chamber St, the south side is all down at the east end and the extreme east are warehouses. PURPLE as map.

W under railway arches, a V-shaped DARK BLUE bit still standing, now LIGHT BLUE on east side and PURPLE on west side. Jews in now on west side. There used to live a base coiner here. On the east side the windows are broken and dirty, houses cracking from the vibration of the trains passing and the whole will probably soon come down itself.

W into Goodman's Yard and N up Sugarloaf Court. DARK BLUE in map. Dwelling houses on west side only, a cooperage on the east, poor but not worse than LIGHT BLUE. Carmen. "Sometimes rough when in drink" but steps and windows clean, 2-st houses, a flag-paved passage. Griggs Court behind it looks rougher, DARK BLUE as map, but Reid says the class in the houses is the same as those in Sugarloaf Court.

W along Leman St into the Minories, N and E at Haydon St the DARK BLUE bit on the north side has given way to warehouses. N into Church St where is Trinity Church. Small old building. Monuments inside. "Often not more than one or two persons at the Sunday services." Opposite to it in Church St are a few small respectable houses. PURPLE to PINK. Then back again under the railway arches and N into Haydon Square. PURPLE in map. Has only one house now which is a beer house as well as a common lodging house. The rest of the houses are shut up. Has been very rough. There are no houses at the northeast or Mansell St end of Haydon St. The map marks this part DARK BLUE, but opposite are 2 houses to which Reid gave character of poor and quiet and should be now LIGHT BLUE rather than DARK BLUE.

S down Mansell St on the west side between Haydon St and Serum St are two very rough-looking houses, windows dirty, broken, etc. Looks DARK BLUE. W into Swan Street, 3-st houses with shops underneath and owners living above. DARK BLUE in map, now PURPLE to PINK. There is no turning out of Swan St into Haydon St alongside the railway (DARK BLUE in map).

Then E across Mansell St into Great Alie St and south up Tenter St. Down Alie Place on the east side of which is one of the principal manufacturers of Passover Cakes (unleavened, large round flat water biscuits) who has a wine and spirit off-licence which he takes out every year because some of his customers ask for wine when they order their cakes. There is nothing to show outwardly either that he sells wine or has any to sell.

E along Tenter St North, on the north of which is a Jewish slaughterhouse and on the south side making the corner of Tenter St East is a block of 4-st dwelling places. Poor looking. Holey blinds. Boot, shoe and tailoring. Not coloured in map, now PURPLE to PINK. On the east side of Tenter St East is Pott and Hunts Old Gun Factory, now called 'A friend in need', a common lodging house. Lets 1d and 2d per night. Further south is the police section house at the back of Leman St police station. Below that is the poor Jews temporary shelter to which the destitute classes come to from the docks and below that again the East London Shoe Blacks Home.

W along Tenter St South, PURPLE as map. No houses on south side west of St Mark St. Their place taken by Factories' warehouses. In the same way the west side of Tenter St West is all warehouses.

E along Scarborough St. 2-st, PINK as map. N up St Mark St. Better, 3-st, PINK-barred, shops at northeast end.

W along Tenter Street North. The houses on the south side are rather poorer, children booted, hatted. PURPLE rather than PINK of map. Moses' Army Clothing Factory on north side. At the west end is a little court of 4 cottages, poor, LIGHT BLUE rather than PINK of map.

Walk 11 B351-5

Thursday 10th March 1898
George Duckworth with Inspector Reid

Starting at the north end of Gowers Walk

PURPLE as map. At the northeast end is a very large new tobacco factory (Weenen and Cohens). Lower down are houses tenanted by warehousemen and carmen and Jewish tailors. The west side is made by the London and Tilbury Railways Goods Depot, said to be the largest building in London.

Webbs Court on the east side consists of 3 small 2-st houses, windows clean. Doors shut. Poor looking but clean. LIGHT BLUE to PURPLE in character. Quiet. On map DARK BLUE.

E along Commercial Rd and then S down Backchurch Lane. Poor houses. Mostly

Jews. Some shops under houses. But not DARK BLUE now, rather LIGHT BLUE. Built in 1820. Brunswick Place. On west side with Providence Place. Out of it on the north side, dilapidated houses. But all children booted tho' one or two ragged. All Jews. In map DARK BLUE, now LIGHT BLUE.

Further south on the west side of Backchurch Lane is Williams Rents. DARK BLUE in map, now LIGHT BLUE. A few English left but mostly Jews. 17 houses, 2-st. Wash hanging across court. An English woman there, who said she had been in her house 27 years, said there were 4 other families beside herself now English, rest all Jews. She pays 6/6 per week for 2 rooms and washhouse. From opposite the end of Fairclough St to the south (DARK BLUE on map) are now Eagle and Brown's Wool Warehouses. The same firm, said Reid, are covering the whole area between Backchurch Lane and Splidts St with warehouses, with which another BLACK and DARK BLUE piece has disappeared. On the west side of Backchurch Lane, north of Fairclough Street are Batty's Gardens. DARK BLUE in map. Now rebuilt, 2- and 3-st houses. There are houses now on both sides of the Berner St end, the DARK BLUE on the north side of the east end is boarded up. Jews. Homework, mess but quiet. Opposite on the west side of Backchurch Lane is Mundy's Place. DARK BLUE in map. 11 2-st cottages, lately done up. Asphalt court, wash hung across, now PURPLE to LIGHT BLUE in character.

S and E into Pinchin St. N into Splidts St. Narrow houses on the east side only, 2- and 3-st, bread and mess, but children well dressed. A few English still remaining here, now LIGHT BLUE to PURPLE in character, in map PURPLE.

N into Ellen St. 2- and 3-st houses, quite foreign now. Homework, clothing and boots. Foreign Jew costers about, in high boots and fur caps. PURPLE as map.

Ellen Court on the south side uncoloured in map. Three 2-st houses. Very poor, Jews, LIGHT BLUE. Across Philip St. 2- and 3-st. A few English carmen here but mostly Jews, PURPLE as map. Into Ellen Place on the south side. All English here, clean, no mess. Quiet, about 12 2-st houses with flagged pavement in front, built 1822. Look better than the surrounding streets but inhabitants probably poorer than the Jews. LIGHT BLUE as map.

S down Stutfield, late Elizabeth St. PURPLE as map. Houses on both side of street. Queens Place. A court on the east side has four 2-st cottages. Poor but respectable, LIGHT BLUE.

N up Providence Place. 2-st. Better north end than south. Mess, bread, tins, orange peel. PURPLE as map. Into Berner St. Children just coming out of boarding school, Jewish type, all fairly dressed, some very well dressed. All clean, well fed, booted. Large majority with hats, girls and boys. Under gateway on southeast side took place one of the 'Ripper' murders. Houses in street 2-st, PURPLE as map. Mess.

At the north end running west into Backchurch Lane is Sanders St. PURPLE rather than LIGHT BLUE of map. Cleaner than the other streets. St John's Working Men's

Club in the St John's Schools on south side (sublets 2d per week), clean windows and doorsteps. Houses 3-st and attic at northeast end and 3-st at southwest end.

S down Berner St and W through Boyd St. 2-st, all foreign, many cannot speak or understand English. Only trouble to police when ejectments are necessary and neither side can comprehend the other. Children hatless but well fed, crowding, narrow street.

Everard St. Still narrower, 2-st houses, 15 ft frontage, lamps for street lighting on brackets against the house walls. Street full of foreigners. Some rags but all children (crowds of them) are well fed, happy, skipping ropes, hoops, women at doors. Rough cobble roadway, almost blocked by one coster's barrow.

S into Ellen St and E, on the north side is Globe Place. A small English colony of labourers and carmen in eight 2-st houses. Holey blinds. Rows occasionally when men get drunk, otherwise quiet. No Jews here, doors shut, windows clean. Character PURPLE to LIGHT BLUE, in map LIGHT BLUE.

N up Brunswick St. 2-st, Jews, costers going round selling freshwater fish (dace, broach) and beetroot. Into Christian St. A mixture of Christian carmen and Jews. PURPLE as map. Houses down west side below Ellen St as far as Martinean's Sugar Factory. Meredith's and Drew's Biscuit Factory used to be on east side, now dwelling houses. On the east side opposite Ellen St is a passage turning into Grove St, called Turners Buildings. BLACK on map, now PURPLE to LIGHT BLUE. Quiet, poor, Jews, homework tailoring and shoework. Further N are Matilda St and Matilda Place, 2-st. BLACK in map, messy, Jews, poor, now LIGHT BLUE. Further N still on the west side between Christian St and Batty St is Queen's Court. 2-st, very poor but quiet, Jews, LIGHT BLUE.

Batty St. 2-st on the east side, 4-st buildings on the west. Mess, LIGHT BLUE to PURPLE. LIGHT BLUE in map.

N into Commercial Rd then S down Grove St. 2½-st on the east side, 3-st on the west. Sidewalk on west side is below the level of the road. Very thickly populated, mostly Jews, no brothels (Lewis of Toynbee Hall suspects No. 84 but police knew generally of the existence of no such place in Grove St). PURPLE as map. On the west side of Grove St is a court with a long narrow passage running north and south, not marked on map, called Grove Court. Part of it one-storied. Taken up by the Grove St Temperance Club (one of Charringtons of Great Assembly Hall) at the extreme south end are 2 or 3, 2-st houses, occupied by a little English colony.

S down Grove St, past Turner's Buildings. Just before the road narrows on the west side north of the public house (The Mallard Arms) is a court called Meredith Buildings. 8 cottages, 2-st, brickbats and mess about, result of drainage and building operation that have never been taken away. Jews, poor, children well fed, only fairly clean, two with very bad boots, LIGHT BLUE as map.

N into Cable St, then E turning N at Cannon Street Rd, then W into John St. 2-st and attic, old red-tiled houses and 3- and 2-st houses. Mixed English and Jews, mess but not so much as in the other streets. PURPLE to LIGHT BLUE, PURPLE in map.

N up Langdale St, late Marmaduke St. 2- and 3-st, rather poorer, LIGHT BLUE rather than PURPLE of map. Marmaduke Place on the east side, 8 cottages in fair repair, LIGHT BLUE as map.

W along John St, on the north side of which is St George's Court, BLACK in map, used to be very rough. Recently rebuilt and paved, houses all tenanted though not yet quite finished outside. All former pop has disappeared, "out of the district altogether, probably to Bethnal Green or Hoxton or to Notting Dale" said Reid. Now all Jews, character PURPLE to LIGHT BLUE.

The south side of John St is Marmaduke Court. Nearly all English here, very poor, 2-storied houses. Doorposts black and shiny, blinds holey, washhouses and WCs opposite the houses. No mess in street, windows dirty but not broken, looks LIGHT BLUE to DARK BLUE, LIGHT BLUE in map. There is no opening into Grove St at the west end, the only opening is into John St, west of that shown in map, which leads to Wellington Buildings, also shut off by wall from Marmaduke Court. Houses newly done up. All Jews, mess.

Out into John St at the southwest end of Samuel St running parallel with it, though behind it is Waterloo Court. Not coloured on map. 20 houses, inhabited by very poor Jews. Only 3½ feet between the houses. Mess, fishheads at entrance, featherbeds hanging out to air from some of the windows. Women inside houses rocking babies in large wooden cradles. Very close quarters. Quiet. LIGHT BLUE.

N up Samuel St. 2-st, Jews, PURPLE as map. On the north side is one turning called Elijah Cottage and James Place. No trouble to police. Mess, wash, some English living here. 3- and 2-st. LIGHT BLUE as map.

E along James St. 2- and 3-st, some shops, Jews, PURPLE as map.

S down Langdale St. 2-st, PURPLE to LIGHT BLUE, doors open. On the east side are two houses called West Foley standing back at the end of a passage. Very poor, DARK BLUE as map. And the next Langdale Court. Four 2-st cottages, LIGHT BLUE rather than DARK BLUE of map. Wash hanging out, Jews, tap in court.

N into London Terrace. DARK BLUE and BLACK in map. Now all boarded up with the exception of a few houses at the southend side, which are LIGHT BLUE.

N up Morgan St. 2-st, all Jews, poor, mess, LIGHT BLUE to PURPLE. On the west side is Captain Cook Court. 4 houses, 2-st, PURPLE to light blue.

The turning into Umberston St out of the northwest end of Morgan St is Grove St. Jews, LIGHT BLUE to PURPLE, in map DARK BLUE to LIGHT BLUE. Only 4 houses on north side and 2 on the south. Into Umberston St. DARK BLUE in map, now LIGHT BLUE to PURPLE. Quiet. Jews. Behind it on the west side is a passage of 35 houses, 2-st. LIGHT BLUE and BLACK in map, now all LIGHT BLUE. Ground floor shutters up in nearly every house. Fair repair, all doors shut. No broken windows, "shutters up because they are nightwatchmen or single men or women who work away during the day".

General remarks

Great improvement in this district since the incoming of the Jews. BLACK spots have gone. English remain in small colonies in courts as yet unswamped by the Jewish tide. Where the races are mixed, neither is pleased and quarrels result.

Jewish children all look particularly well fed. Reid said it was by reason of the amount of oil they were given as food. Everard St and Boyd St are almost entirely foreign. Many can neither speak nor understand English.

Walk 12   B351-3

Friday 11th March 1898
George Duckworth with Inspector Reid

Starting at the south end of Union Street

PURPLE as map. 3-st houses, Jews, children clean, well dressed.

E into Holloway St and N into Chapel Place. DARK BLUE in map, now PURPLE, though some LIGHT BLUE. 22 2-st houses, in good repair. Mess in street, tailors and bootmakers.

E and N up Mulberry St, DARK BLUE in map, now PURPLE to LIGHT BLUE. 3- and 2-st, mess, fishes heads, paper, orange peel, bread, like all the Jewish streets. Boot and tailors.

Lion Square. All PURPLE. 3-st. A few but very few flower pots on windowsills. DARK BLUE patch has disappeared.

E along Little Holloway St (like the west end of Coke St). Paved passage with shops, Jews.

Coke St. 2- and 3-st, Jews and Germans. These latter are a more burly set than the ordinary Polish or Russian Jew.

N up Plumbers Row. In map PURPLE but more nearly LIGHT BLUE now. Narrow, houses in fair repair but many very poor looking, some women sackmakers. Windows clean, messy street, some rough Germans. Buildings 4-st and attic at northeast end. Inhabited nearly exclusively by Poles, a German keeps the public house at the Coke St corner.

Into Fieldgate St. Shops and 4-st buildings, mantle and corset makers. S down Yalford Street, DARK BLUE in map, now LIGHT BLUE to PURPLE. Street all up for new gas or drainpipes. Reid said the inhabitants were poorer than Plumbers Row. Windows clean, very few broken. Children well fed and well dressed, a few rather ragged but very few. White Hart Court, on the east side leads into Greenfield St and consists of 4 houses, 2½-st with a room underground, "but lived in".

Into Greenfield St 3- and 2-st, PURPLE as map, mess, Germans, furriers. Children in schoolyard at play, skipping, pinafores of girls dirty. All children well fed and clothed, some particularly well dressed. All faces clean except of a few small boys. Notices in one or 2 houses of 'servant wanted'. So here and there the PURPLE verges on PINK.

N into Fieldgate St, on the north side opposite Greenfield St are the Great Eastern Dwellings, 4-st. Court entered by iron gates ("necessary to prevent prostitutes from using the place in the evenings"). Very quiet, all English, belongs to Great Eastern Railway Company in Orange Court. The east side of the buildings all the houses are shut up, back entrance here to 'Wonderland', late the East London Theatre.

E a little, then N to Charlotte Court. Flagged Court, over 30 houses, all English. 3- and 2-st. Respectable working class, PURPLE as map (some LIGHT BLUE).

S down Nottingham Place. Mixture of Jews, Christians and Germans. Good repair, 3½-st houses taken by PINK families in northwest corner, poorer south, on the whole PURPLE as map.

Crossing Fordham St S into Parfelt Place. DARK BLUE in map, now PINK to PURPLE. New houses tenanted by constables, hospital nurses and newspaper reporters. Broad cement-paved court, 3-storied houses. Firmins Court, the BLACK piece behind it is down, the new houses in Parfelt Place are built back so as to take up a good bit of the space formerly covered by Firmins Court, which is itself boarded up.

N into Fordham St. 3- and 2-st, one very poor house at the northwest end. Jews but PURPLE as map. S down Settles St. Well-paved, quiet, 3½- and 2-st, PURPLE to PINK (map PURPLE). St Augustine's Church and Institute, a 4-st red building at the southeast end, "carried on by 3 brothers Wilson, all very hard workers". Nameless court on southwest side, DARK BLUE in map, now PURPLE. 8 houses, 2-st, in good repair, belonging like much of the land about here to the London Hospital. Two respectable women in the court said they rented 2 rooms, a kitchen and washhouse for 7/- a week.

E along Commercial Rd. All the shopkeepers here who have moderate sized shops live above them. N into Myrdle St. Map PURPLE, now PURPLE to PINK. Nearly all English tenants, 2-st houses, mechanics. Into Fordham St, then E and S down Romford St. DARK BLUE in map. Rough, English and Irish costers. 2-st, not much of it remains but what there is, is still DARK BLUE.

S down Fordham St. There are only 2 or 3 houses remaining on the east side and the southwest side has untenanted houses. N of Fordham St the east side of the street for full ¾ of the way up is untenanted.

E into New Rd. Well to do tailors and shops, PINK-barred rather than PINK. 3-st, 'servants wanted' in one or two windows.

N into the Whitechapel Rd, and then W, the first court on the south side is Vine Court. 3- and 2-st, PURPLE as map, windows clean. Karet's tin plate work manufactory and a shoe and slippers factory and also at the east end the Cooperative Civet and Military Clothing Factory. The next court on the south side going westwards is Hampshire Court. Poor, doors shut, children clean, men in employ of vestry, LIGHT BLUE now, was DARK BLUE in map. Little Tongue Yard just west of the theatre is down, right away through to Fieldgate St. Next court is Great Tongue Yard. Small 2-st houses, broken windows, tap in court, LIGHT BLUE now, quiet, DARK BLUE in map. Faces of people and brass candlesticks on chimney pieces showed presence of Jews though Reid said the inhabitants were English.

W along Whitechapel Rd. South at Union St. Buck and Hickman's Great Tool Factory at northeast end.

W into Mountford St. No opening now into John St. 2- and 3-st houses, PINK as map, well paved. Quiet and respectable, China pots in windows, English.

N into Whitechapel Road. W then S down Church Lane and W along Spectacle Alley. Jewish restaurants and shops, PINK as map. Into High St, on the south side is Drum Yard. Not coloured in map. Old red-tiled houses, ten 2- and 3-st houses. All Jews, PURPLE to LIGHT BLUE. There is no passage through from High St to the Commercial Rd as shown in map.

E down Commercial Rd and W along Colchester St (i.e. that part of it on the south side of the Commercial Rd). German Jews, 4- and 3-st houses. PURPLE to PINK.

S down Plough Square. 5-st buildings, rough, DARK BLUE on west side, better LIGHT BLUE on east. The basement of the west side is occupied by the United Brothers Working Men's Club, affiliated to the Club Union, also rather rough looking. Some disorderly German women living above who bring home men.

W along Buckle St the whole of the southeast end is taken up by the Jews infant school. On the southwest side are three 3-st houses, LIGHT BLUE, one of doubtful character. In map LIGHT BLUE.

N up Leman St. W along Whitechapel High St, S at Mansell St (late Somerset St), E along Great Alie St and N under arch into Halfmoon Passage. Hotel largely used for Jewish weddings and feasts at southwest end and Morris' Cigar and Cigarette Works higher up.

E along Duncan St. The house at the west end used to be a brothel, still looks very poor. The whole street is PURPLE, not PINK as map. N up Leman St past Bengle St, late Nelson St which has no turning now into Duncan St.

This walk completes the Leman Street subdivision of the Whitechapel or H. division.

General remarks

Disappearance of BLACK and DARK BLUE spots. Trades of district: shoes, slippers and boots, tailoring. Absorption of district by Jews, English remain in streets and courts which are wholly English, like Settles St, Myrtle St, Charlotte Court. There is a mixture of English and Jews in some streets but friction and quarrels the inevitable result. The repulsion felt of one for the other is mutual.

Great mess in Jewish streets. Fishes heads. Paper of all colours. Bread (not a great deal of this), orange peel in abundance.

The constant whirr of the sewing machine or tap of the hammer as you pass through the streets. Women with dark abundant hair, olive complexions, no hats but shawls. Children well fed and dressed. Dark beards, fur caps and long boots of men. The feeling as of being in a foreign town.

Walk 13   B351-7

Thursday 17th March 1898

George Duckworth with Sergeant French of the Commercial Street subdivision of the Whitechapel or H Police division.

Sergeant French has been 13 years in the service. He started in this division as a constable, he has been here 5 years as a sergeant, coming here from Westminster. Middle height, sturdy, moustache, rather heavy face; very willing.

Starting at the Police Court in Commercial Street

W down Fleur-de-Lis St, RED in map, now not so good. Formerly inhabited by weavers, houses 3½-st, 3 families in each. Jews beginning to come in. Respectable market porters and labourers, get drunk on Saturdays. Not better than PURPLE.

S down Blossom St, PINK in map. Warehouses on west side. 3-st tenements and houses on the east side, rough, Cockney Irish. Now DARK BLUE. Blossom Place on the west side, 11 houses, 2- and 3-st. Jew tailors and bootmakers. Quiet. PURPLE, on map PINK. Blossom Passage on east side, 4 houses, 2- and 3-st, Irish, rough. DARK BLUE, PINK in map.

E along White Lion St, RED as map. Respectable tradesmen, Jews principally. Respectable, 2- and 3-st houses. To Elder St. 3½- and 4-st, old Queen Anne houses with ornamented porches, workshops, furriers, Jews, RED as map. At the corner of White Lion St (north side) and Commercial St is a block of Peabody dwellings. PURPLE, in map RED.

S down Wheeler St, in map PURPLE, now DARK BLUE, rough. Several ticket-of-leave men living here, mess in street, bread, old boots, paper, windows dirty and broken. Irish, thieves. Like it Chapel St, DARK BLUE as map. Houses 4-st with long weavers room, windows at the top.

W into Church Passage which has a court out of it on the west side, not coloured in map. Clean and quiet. Four 2-st houses, PURPLE, called Chapel Place.

Into White Lion St and W, then S down Spital Square. 4-st, all Jews, RED rather than

PINK of map. Cigarette factory. Well-to-do, better than White Lion Street. German Synagogue on east side and the Central Foundation Schools at the south side.

W to Norton Folgate passing Spital Yards on the south side, mostly backs of warehouses in the main road, but 3 houses in which working class live on west side and one on the east. PURPLE rather than PINK of map.

E along Lamb St to Spitalfields market. Flowers, fruits, vegetables. Lamb St is PINK rather than RED, small shops, owners living above, also market salesmen. On the north side is a rough court called Lamb Court. Irish, one barefoot boy, bullies or ponces, DARK BLUE rather than PURPLE of map.

S down Crispin St which bounds the west side of the market, like Lamb St. PINK rather than PURPLE of map. Market shops to Brushfields St which bounds the south side. PINK as map.

W along Brushfields St, N up Gun St. Very rough. Mixture of dwelling houses and factories. 3-st and attic houses. A Jewish common lodging at the northwest end where the Jew thieves congregate. It is called the "poor Jews' home" on the board outside.

S of Brushfields St Gun St is rougher than the north end. Street narrow, 18 ft across from wall to wall. Old boots and mess in street, 4½-st houses. A lodging house at southeast end, dilapidated looking. Ticket-of-leave men living here. At least DARK BLUE, on map PURPLE. "But it is not a street particularly noted for prostitutes." At the north end is Fort St. Fairly well-to-do. PINK rather than PURPLE of map. Jew middlemen live here. Like it is Stewards St. 4-st. Windows dirty but PINK. On map PURPLE.

Duke St has houses on the east side, the west side is all factories and warehouses. Character DARK BLUE to LIGHT BLUE. In map PURPLE. "The coster flower and fruit sellers in Liverpool St come from here." Inhabitants are a mixture of Jews and Irish.

S into Artillery Lane. 3-st. Synagogue on west side, dwelling houses on the east side. PURPLE to PINK. W along Artillery Passage. All Jews, rather narrow passage with shops on either side. PINK as map, on the north side of it is a passage leading to Artillery Lane called Artillery Court. Not coloured on map, ragged children, fish curers, rough, DARK BLUE.

E along Artillery Lane, past the Roman Catholic dormitory at the corner of Bell Lane. The hour was only 1 PM but there was already a crowd of 30 men and 2 women waiting to be taken in, though the doors do not open till 4. French said they were a set of scoundrels but they did not look as if they belonged to the worst class, all fairly clothed, one or two old cripples.

Into Dorset St. BLACK in map. Still BLACK. The worst street I have seen so far, thieves, prostitutes, bullies. All common lodging houses. Some called 'doubles' with double beds for married couples, but merely another name for brothels. Women, draggled, torn skirts, dirty, unkempt, square jaws standing about in street or on doorsteps. The majority of the houses are owned by Jack McCarthy, keeper of a general shop on the north side of the street. Several courts on the north side of the street and New Court. 3-st houses. Also BLACK. Further east Dorset Court. The backrooms of a common lodging house for men and women come through into the court from the front of the street. Open basins and taps on the west side of the court for washing purposes. The next east is Old Dorset Court. Has been done up, Irish, a Negro at the washtub, windows dirty and broken, narrow. 2-st houses. Also BLACK.

At the west end of Dorset St leading into Brushfields St is Little Paternoster Row. BLACK on both sides, in map on east side only. 2- and 3-st common lodging houses. Ragged women and children. Holey toeless boots. Windows dirty, patched with brown paper and broken. Prostitutes, thieves and ponces. Buildings owned by the notorious Jack McCarthy of Dorset St.

S down Crispin St and E into Whites Row. PURPLE in map but now BLACK on both sides as far as the building. Called a Catholic Chapel in the map (now a lodging house) then come shops on the south side and street improves to PURPLE till the southwest corner is reached where by reason of thieves and bullies, it becomes BLACK again.

S under an archway into the Tenter district. Two very rough houses at northeast end, "really part of Whites Row". Tenter St. 3-st, all Jews, poor, fairly quiet, "though rowdy for Jews". PURPLE not PINK. On the east side are Butler St, barrows belonging to Petticoat Lane costers in the street. PURPLE to LIGHT BLUE. Not PINK. Out of it on the north side, west end, is Emery's Place. LIGHT BLUE. Freeman Street. 3-st, PURPLE to LIGHT BLUE, not PINK. Palmer St and Tilley St, both 3-st. PURPLE not PINK. On the west side of Tenter St is Tenter Court. Not shown in map, 3 cottages, 2-st, very narrow, being rebuilt. At the southwest end of Tenter St is an entry past a dairy and cow keepers into Bell Lane – not shown in map. At the east end of Tilley St is another passage, past another dairy into Wentworth St.

N up Shepherd St. At the northwest end are rough buildings. DARK BLUE. Irish. At the northwest end corner of Butler St is a public house. Rough, frequented by the loose characters in Whites Row, Dorset St. The Christ Church Mission Hall is at the northwest end also. "They moved here from Dorset Street, finding it too rough there."

S down Commercial St and W into Wentworth St, at the southeast end the Victoria Home, a lodging house. Rough character, DARK BLUE. Wentworth St itself thronged every day by stalls, both buyers and sellers nearly but not altogether Jews. Women bareheaded, bewigged, coarse woollen shawls over shoulders, more like a foreign market scene than anything English. Small shops and houses on north side, shops below buildings on south side. "No poor here except in the courts."

Going westwards on the north side are Ann's Place, 3-st, LIGHT BLUE, Wentworth

Court East, poor, rather quarrelsome, windows broken. 10 houses, tap in court, LIGHT BLUE to DARK BLUE. Wentworth Court West, 10 houses, a crockery dealer uses the whole of ground floor of house at southeast corner as a storeroom, LIGHT BLUE. Katharine Terrace. 4 houses, 3-st, better, doors open, PURPLE to PINK. Eastmans Court. 7 houses, 2-st, PURPLE. (None of the foregoing are marked or coloured in the map.)

N up Bell Lane on the west side is Coburg Court. Three 2-st houses, PURPLE to LIGHT BLUE. W down Montague St, which has houses on south side only with the exception of one at the Bale Lane end north side. Small shops Into Short St, 2-st, poor, messy, houses on west side only, LIGHT BLUE to PURPLE. On map PINK. To Cobbs Yard. 2-st, narrow, poor Jews, LIGHT BLUE to PURPLE. E into Cox Square. Rough Jews. Cellars used for fruit, cases of oranges, lemons stacked in the square, also a cart of vegetables. Square used as a feeding ground for the stalls in Wentworth St. Bundles of umbrellas, etc. Some windows broken, PURPLE as map.

E into Bell Lane. Small shops on east side only, narrow street, PURPLE to PINK as map. On the east side is a poor court called Bell Court. Not marked in map. 2-st, LIGHT BLUE to PURPLE. Windows clean but broken.

N past the Jews Free School and W along Frying Pan Alley, houses on the north side, narrow, poor, LIGHT BLUE. (In map west end only coloured PURPLE). Into Sandy's Row, which, in the north end of Middlesex St, changes here. High LCC, 4-st dwellings on east side, courts have been shaved off to make room for street improvements. The Petticoat Lane poultry market is held on the east side along pavement and in what was formerly Cobb Court, now demolished. Crates of live fowls every day but more especially on Thursday and Friday mornings (before the Sabbath feast); fowls bought alive and then carried by the legs to the kosher butcher by the buyers.

E into Tewson's Court. Partially down, 2-st, LIGHT BLUE. S along Diners Buildings. 12 2-st houses, very narrow, 6 ft between house and house, LIGHT BLUE. W along Lardners Buildings. Litter of old fish and orange boxes, 2-st, LIGHT BLUE. Into Fisher Alley, a court off Lardners Buildings. 2-st, mess, garbage being picked over by sandy, cats. LIGHT BLUE. Into Cobbs Yard. 2-st, LIGHT BLUE. Through Corea Place, late New Court, 2-st, cleaner but poor looking.

W through Bull Court to Middlesex St. 3-st, houses at Middlesex St end shoved up with beams, crates of chickens, looks rather rougher than the rest. Windows broken, LIGHT BLUE.

S down New Coulston St. Models on either side of the road. All Jews, journeymen. Built 1895. PURPLE as map. Down Coulston St, all 6-st buildings. German Church on the west side and baths on the east.

Into Whitechapel High St. E, N under arch into Castle Alley. No houses, factories on either side. Two of the Whitechapel Murders were committed at the south end. The street is quiet and used as a place of resort by the dwellers in the Whitechapel Common Lodging Houses. By custom women sit on the west side of the pavement, men on the east. There were a number of each class there today. The north end, east side is PURPLE not PINK. Holey blinds, dirty windows. 3-st.

E along Old Castle Place. 3-st. PURPLE rather than PINK of map. S down Newcastle Place. Shut off, quiet, all Jews, 26 houses, "like the Tenter Ground". Many clothiers living here. The houses look better than the Tenter Ground. PURPLE to PINK, in map PINK. Into Newcastle St. 3-st, same as foregoing.

General remarks
Again difficulty of telling by appearances whether some of the small Jew streets should be PINK, PURPLE or LIGHT BLUE. For vice it would be difficult to find anywhere a worse street than Dorset St, Paternoster Row and Whites Row. No sign of improvement nor prospects of it. Juvenile thieves a feature of the neighbourhood. "Taught in the kitchens of common lodging houses."

Lewis (of Toynbee Hall) says that the Tenter Ground should not be better than PURPLE being a mixture of costers and cigar makers, some poor, others fairly well-off. Shepherd St buildings he spoke of as a sample of a place that had been Jewish but was now Gentile again. A very rare occurrence. The Jews have been turned out by a set of rough English and Irish. Character DARK BLUE.

Walk 14   B351-8

Friday 18th March 1898
George Duckworth with Sergeant French

Starting at the police station in Commercial Street

E past St Stephen's church into Quaker Street. 3-st. Rough. Irish. Brothels on south side past the court called New Square. Also a Salvation Army "Lighthouse", which encourages the disrespectable to come this way. The railway has now absorbed all the houses on the north side as far as opposite Pool Square. DARK BLUE rather than the PURPLE of map. Wheeler St on the south side, also rough. Irish. 2- and 3-st houses, does not look bad, shops underneath, but French said rough and DARK BLUE rather than PURPLE of map. On the south side going eastwards are Wheeler Court (Wheeler Court is out of the east side of Wheeler St and divided by a paling from Popeshead Court). Three 2 st houses, rough, Irish, DARK BLUE. Popeshead Court, lately done up and repaired. A new class in them since the repairs, now poor not rough, LIGHT BLUE, not DARK BLUE of map. One or 2 old houses still remaining with long weavers windows in the higher stories.

New Square. 2-st, rough. One 1-st house, dogs chained to each garden, thieves, LIGHT BLUE barred.

Pool Square. 3-st houses, rough women about, Irish, one house with a wooden top storey. Windows broken, DARK BLUE instead of LIGHT BLUE of map.

This is the last of an Irish colony, the Jews begin to predominate when Grey Eagle St is reached. These courts belong to small owners who generally themselves occupy one of the houses in the courts themselves.

Past Grey Eagle St. 3- and 2-st. Jews on east side, poor, LIGHT BLUE. Gentiles, rough, on west side DARK BLUE. Mixture of criminals, men on street, looks very poor, even the Jewish side, but children booted, fairly clean, well clothed and well fed. Map gives both sides PURPLE.

E to Wilkes St. Tramans Bray along the east side. Houses 4-st, roadway 18 ft and sidewalk 4½ ft on either side, a road of average width. All Jews, tailors, boot makers, working class. PURPLE as map. Into Hanbury Street, 4-st, Jews. Shops. PINK rather than PURPLE of map.

W towards Grey Eagle St there are two courts on the north side of Hanbury St. Bennets Place. Five 2-st houses, poor looking but not rough, LIGHT BLUE. Lotus

Court. Ten 2 st houses, windows clean but broken, with a rough character. LIGHT BLUE to DARK BLUE, neither coloured on map.

N up Grey Eagle St to Corbets Court. 2-st, rough, Irish, brothels on either side of north end. Children booted but some with very bad boots, "by no manner of means respectable". On map PURPLE now DARK BLUE to BLACK.

N up Grey Eagle St to Great Pearl St. Common lodging houses with double beds, thieves, bullies, prostitutes, like Dorset St. 3-st houses. Badly paved, cobbles, not much mess in street. BLACK as map. Courts on the north side are: Wilkes Court, 2-st also BLACK as map, Pearl Court, with one house and a wood yard, BLACK as map.

S down Little Pearl St, late Vine Court. 3-st, BLACK as map. Old houses with long, small-paned weavers windows to top stories. Some boarded up in the middle. A few Jews. On the west side lives F. Geringer ("Barrows to let"), the owner of all these houses. On the west side is Vine Court. Broad, cement court, well done up. WCs at the west end away from houses. Perhaps a little better than rest and DARK BLUE rather than BLACK. On the east side of the street is Crown Court. 2-st. Men packing up sacks of parsley. Owner lives in one house, DARK BLUE in map "but it should be as BLACK as you can make it".

Out into Commercial St, brothels on southeast side of Little Pearl St. BLACK as map. A thoroughly vicious quarter. The presence of Cambridge Music Hall in Commercial St makes it a focusing point for prostitutes.

S down Commercial St, past Puma Court, late Red Lion Court. A passage, shops. PINK as map on south side, PURPLE on north side, east of Alms Houses.

S to Fournier St, late Church St. 3-st houses, well-to-do Jews, keep servants, one family to each house, said French. RED rather than PINK of map.

N up Wilkes St, late Wood St. On east side is a lodging house frequented by ex-convicts. "Six or seven old lags living there now." No shame about having been in prison here, one came across street to ask whether his licence had come up yet.

E along Rincelet, late Princes St. 3-st, Jews. PINK as map, excluding at the corners of Brick Lane at its east end. Here are 2 common lodging houses, 4d a night, 2-/ a week. Thieves, prostitutes, bullies. "One of Cooney's houses." Cooney has many common lodgings of doubtful reputation in the neighbourhood. Marie Lloyd, the singer, is a relation and often comes down visiting here in a smart brougham.

Into Brick Lane. Jews. Shops. Mixture of good, bad and indifferent. At the southeast end are brothels. The common lodging houses also have a bad name. On map it is marked PINK. The large Wesleyan Chapel at the end of Fournier St is now being converted into a synagogue. The best part of Brick Lane, said French, is the centre, both ends are bad.

W along Fashion St. Union Court on the north side (DARK BLUE in map) is down. 3-st and attic buildings with shops underneath has taken its place. PINK. South side is PURPLE as map. Out of the south side are several courts, going westwards.

Rosemary Court. 8 2-st houses, Jews, LIGHT BLUE to PURPLE. Fashion Court. 12 2-st houses, clean, PURPLE. New Court. 15 houses, 2-st, LIGHT BLUE to PURPLE. A synagogue in this court, fairly clean and well kept. On the north side of Fashion St is Harriet's Place. 8 2-st houses, 2 rooms in each house, letting at 6/- per house. All Jews in this street and courts.

S and E into Flower and Dean St. BLACK in map, now PURPLE. Tall, 6-st buildings on either side, belonging to the Rothschilds. Street 27 ft across. 4½ ft of area to each block. Mess, bits of fish. The east end of the street some way past George St narrows to 15 ft and has common lodging houses. "As BLACK here as you like."

Down Brick Lane. W along Thrawl St on the north side are 5-st redbrick buildings. PURPLE. Brick Lane end on the south side is one of McCarthy's lodging houses. "Filled with thieves."

S down Lolesworth St, late George St. Buildings on west side. The east side is BLACK as map. Brothels, thieves, prostitutes, ponces. Into Wentworth St buildings, west end. East end on the north side are cocoa works. On the south side Brick Lane end is one of the largest common lodging houses in London. "Holds about 800 persons." Called Wildermuth's, built 1893. BLACK rather than DARK BLUE of map.

S down George Yard. On west side of it is George Place. Houses, backing on Toynbee Hall. Respectable, poor, PURPLE. On the east side are common lodging houses, 'doubles', a brothel, situated just below the dust destructor of the Whitechapel board of works. BLACK as map. Angel Alley, DARK BLUE in map, is closed.

S down Osborn St. Shops. PINK. A coffee house on the west side and a lodging house on the east. Both reputed brothels.

N and E along Old Montague St. Narrow, long, 3-st houses, shops, owners living above. PURPLE to PINK, on map PURPLE. Many courts out of the south side. All Jews. Going eastwards. Green Dragon Place. Poor Jews, used to be rough, now LIGHT BLUE rather than DARK BLUE of map, to turning on the east side. Montague Place. 4 houses only, 2-st, homework, cement paved, clean, LIGHT BLUE to PURPLE. DARK BLUE in map. Easington Buildings. 15 2-st houses, narrower and poorer looking, dirty children, LIGHT BLUE, DARK BLUE in map. Kings Arms Court. DARK BLUE in map, now no dwelling houses, great mess, old boots, tins, orange peel, onion skins, paper. Black Lion Yard. Still DARK BLUE as map, mixture of Irish and Jews. Rough. Houses 4-, 3-, 2-st, small shops.

Across Great Garden St, the east corner of which both on the north and south sides are brothels, thieves, prostitutes and bullies. In map PURPLE.

S down St Mary St, on the west side 12 houses, called Moss Buildings. In map PINK but of mixed working class, not better than PURPLE. On the east side is a synagogue. The DARK BLUE on either side is gone, the LIGHT BLUE on the west side remains. There are no houses on the east side.

N up into Montague St then E. On the south side are more courts. All DARK BLUE in map. Going eastwards the first is Princes Place. 6 3-st houses, rough, many windows broken, English occupiers, as map. John's Place. 8 2-st houses, children dirty, Jews, LIGHT BLUE to DARK BLUE. Green's Place. 8 2-st houses, better, Jews, LIGHT BLUE. Eagle Place. 12 houses, 2-st, newish houses, LIGHT BLUE. The old Coroners Court and mortuary were formerly here. Regal Place. 12 2-st houses, better than the rest. "Sheenies." PURPLE.

General remarks

The Great Pearl Street district remains as BLACK as it was 10 years ago. As the Dorset St district belongs to a dweller in it, McCarthy, so this bit belongs to 'Geringer', an inhabitant of Little Pearl St. The features of both these streets are common lodging houses for men, women and 'doubles' which are little better than brothels. Thieves, bullies and prostitutes are their inhabitants. The only BLACK piece that has disappeared is that on the north side of Flower and Dean St which has had to make way for the Rothschilds' dwellings. Union Court, at the back of Fashion St which was DARK BLUE, has been demolished. Those who have been displaced, said French, have crowded into Bethnal Green or Walthamstow.

Betterment is noticeable in some of the larger streets such as Hanbury and Church Streets, owing to the incoming of well-to-do Jews, and also in the courts south of Old Montague St, owing to the displacement of rough English or Irish by poor but quiet Jews.

The alteration of the Wesleyan Chapel to suit the requirements of a Jewish synagogue is characteristic of the change that has taken place in the neighbourhood.

Streets on the whole well paved, except Great Pearl St. All with cobbles. Houses in very fair repair and in many cases better than their inhabitants. Here as elsewhere it looks as if the landlords had had their attention effectually called to the state of their property especially the DARK BLUE streets.

Common lodging houses also a feature. A great number of them. But not one that French spoke of as having decent inhabitants.

Invasion of Jews. Small English colonies dotted about. Friction where the two live together in one street. The roughest public houses are that at the corner of Commercial St and Wentworth St, the George belonging to Truman Hamburg and Buxton, the beer house at the end of Dorset St, and the Public at the corner of Shepherd and Butler Streets.

Industries: market porters, hawkers among the English. Cigar and tobacco making, tailoring and boot making among the Jews.

French said that he hardly knew whether he ought to have an opinion about public houses but he thought that in the interests of sobriety there should be a greater number than there are. For he said, you got drunkenness and rows where there was a crowd. If there were more houses there would be less crowding at the bars, it would be easier to refuse to serve those who had already had too much. As to children fetching beer, he disapproved of their doing it but thought it was better for them than for their mothers to fetch it. "Mothers stay but children come away at once."

Walk 15 B351-9

Monday 21st March 1898
George Duckworth with Sergeant Charles Horatio French

Starting at the west end of Buxton Street

S down Brick Lane, E along Carter St. Truman's Brewery on north side and stables on south, except for 2 or 3 houses at southeast end. LIGHT BLUE as map, only less of it. Into Spital St. 3-st, rough, working class, mixed Jews and English. Doors open, 24 ft across road, house to house. Doors open, great mess in street, LIGHT BLUE rather than PURPLE of the map.

E along Pelham St. 3- and 4-st, all Jews. Vegetable ends, orange peel, paper, etc, litter over the street. Overcrowding. Chiefly tailors, but not very poor. Character PURPLE to LIGHT BLUE, on map PURPLE.

S into Hanbury St. 4-st, one lodging house for single men, "the most respectable in the district", a small one, small shops. Character PURPLE to PINK, on map PURPLE.

N up Spital St, on the east side of which is Spital Court. Three 3-st houses with weavers windows, PURPLE in character.

E along Buxton St, S down Hunt St. Awful smell from drain being repaired, street up. On the east side is Hunt Court, 2 houses only, poor Jews, LIGHT BLUE and another court of 5 houses, 3-st, all Jews. PURPLE to LIGHT BLUE. On the east side of the street are sets of 3-st buildings running east out of Hunt St, having a balcony above the first storey, cement court, messy, called Davis' Buildings. Davis, the owner, is supposed to be an illegitimate son of Lord Rothschild, according to French. Character of buildings PURPLE.

Further south leading to the R.C. chapel is Davis Place, late Hunt Court. No opening into Underwood St and on the same side still further south is Orange Mews. Stables. No dwellings. Hunt St is quiet, character PURPLE to LIGHT BLUE, in map PURPLE.

E along Pelham St, on the north side of which are some 4-st building models. English inhabitants, doubtful character. French called them "a bit dissipated".

E across the north end of Spelman St. 2- and 3-st, Jews, PURPLE as map. Across Lombard Street. 3-st and attic, looks better than the others, tho' French said it was the same. PURPLE to PINK, in map PINK. The court east of it on the south side of Pelham St is Hobson's Place. 2 st, newish, PURPLE to LIGHT BLUE, in map LIGHT BLUE. Next to it is Hobson's Court. 14 2-st houses, also PURPLE to LIGHT BLUE, in map LIGHT BLUE. Pelham St opposite these courts is 2-st and PINK in character.

China flowerpots. Across Deal St, 2-st, Jews, PURPLE rather than PINK of map. E along Pelham St, on the north side are 2-st houses and on the south are Pelham Buildings. "Hardworking English labourers", both PURPLE, neither coloured on map.

W then N up Albert St. On the west side of which are 16 2-st cottages, 2 families, clean, small gardens with flowers in front. PURPLE now, in map LIGHT BLUE, called Albert Cottages. On the east side corresponding to them are 14 2-st houses called Victoria Cottages. Also PURPLE, unmarked on map. N up Albert St on the east side are Howard Buildings and the Metropolitan Buildings. 4½-st. "Brewery draymen living here." PURPLE, in map LIGHT BLUE.

W along Underwood St, 2-st, broader, 40 ft from house to house. Jews in the west end, PURPLE, in map LIGHT BLUE. Further E are new red brick 3-st houses, also Jews, some poor English. E of Buttress St, LIGHT BLUE as map. N into North Place. English, cleaner, 2-st, 28 houses, respectable working class. PURPLE to PINK, in map PINK. E past Buttress St. 2-st, LIGHT BLUE as map.

E into Vallance Rd, S to Hanbury St, then W past Queen St. Rough, Irish, cab yard and iron foundry northwest end and at northeast end Tingle Jacobs Yard (carriers) and a large fish curing place. Windows dirty, some broken, children well fed, some rags, rather dirty. On the whole not worse than LIGHT BLUE, in map PURPLE.

S down Queen St, W along Old Montague St. N up King Edward St. 3-st, Irish, vestry scavengers, rough. LIGHT BLUE to DARK BLUE. On the east side is Spring Gardens. 2-st, poor mixture of Jews and Irish. "A rough place for the police." Windows broken, patched and dirty, narrow, flagged, houses on both sides, DARK BLUE, in map PURPLE. The next court north is Eale St. 2-st, all Jews, costers, very poor but quiet, great mess, LIGHT BLUE to DARK BLUE. Johnson St, the court north of it is only warehouses. W along Chicksand Street. 3-st, Jews, tailors, clean windows, PURPLE as map. N and S of it runs Dink St, built 1766. 3-st, Jews, synagogue on west side. PURPLE as map, north of Chicksand St, LIGHT BLUE south of it.

W along Chicksand St. On the south side between Great Garden St and Casson St are 2 courts. Garden Place about 14 2-st houses, very poor, quiet, Jews, wash hanging out. Children well fed and clean faces, crowded. Looks DARK BLUE as map but probably not worse than LIGHT BLUE. Out of one house came a very respectably-dressed sheeny clerk, black coat, good hat and boots. W of it is Chicksand Court. 8 2-st houses, Jews, LIGHT BLUE, in map DARK BLUE.

S down Great Garden St, 2- and 3-st, some shops, PURPLE as map. Out of the southwest end is Garden Court. Jews, 8 cottages, separated from Garden Place by a wall. LIGHT BLUE, not marked in map. At the east corner of Old Montague St in Garden St is one of Cooney's lodging houses, 'doubles', a brothel, rough. N up Casson St. 2-st, PURPLE to PINK, in map PURPLE. On the east side of it is George Court. Five 2-st houses, poor Jews, 2-roomed houses letting at 5/-. No washhouse, LIGHT BLUE. Not coloured in map. At the northeast corner of Casson St is Ramar Place. Entered down steps. 2-st houses, tap in court, quiet, very messy. Well-dressed girl in spectacles came out of one house, LIGHT BLUE, in map DARK BLUE. W along Heneage St. Jews, PURPLE, in map PINK. N up Spelman St. PURPLE to PINK, in map PURPLE. Furriers. On the east side are 2 courts. Specks Fields, warehouses, and further north Spelman Court. In map DARK BLUE, Three 2-st houses, poor and very dirty, brickbats, orange peel and general mess, Jews, quiet. LIGHT BLUE now. Children well dressed and booted.

W along Booth St. 3-st, Jews, tailors, shoe makers, PURPLE as map. On the south side are Booth St Buildings. 4-st, look very rough and are very poor, all Jews. Broken windows stuffed with rags, dirty, no curtains or blinds to windows, only a bit of stuff drawn across lower half. Ragged dirty children, no trouble to the police "because the Jews are not men enough to be rough". Corners of the yard used as urinals, "stench in hot weather", "there is a superintendent but he never looks after anything". Some prostitutes living here, DARK BLUE as map.

S down Brick Lane, E along Heneage St, PINK in map, now PURPLE. One of Cooney's

Interview with Superintendent Mulvaney, head of the H or Whitechapel Division of Police. Headquarters Leman Street East, 7th January 1898

Superintendent Mulvaney is a man rather over 50, blackish beard, medium height, inclined to drop his aitches tho' not so much as Superintendent Weston, spits frequently. Very friendly and anxious to do anything in his power to help. Had never before seen this map showing the streets coloured according to character and was very much struck by it.

He said that his district was a hybrid one and therefore very peculiar. A large number cannot speak English. On the whole, law abiding. Not brought towards the police. They knife one another but not those in authority. Stabbing cases fairly frequent in the foreign streets.

Polish Jews and Russians who come over are mostly strong socialists. Their first inclination in coming over here, finding their liberty is to break out, but they don't do it long. They are great spirit drinkers. Those who come from Russia can stand more raw spirit than an Englishman. The other day 3 men went into a house and ordered 2 pints of neat whiskey in a can. The publican gave it to them, never dreaming that they would be likely to try to drink it at a draught. One did for a wager, he fell down insensible, was taken home, left to recover but found dead the next morning.

He deplored the cheap spirit sold by some of the 'cutting' houses. Said that even a small quantity had an extraordinary effect on women. He had seen them brought in after drinking a small glass, when they got outside the public house, they had dropped down unconscious and so been taken off by the policeman. He would like to see a law that spirits might not be sold under a certain maturity.

Women, he said, drink more than they used to. He thought there were more cases of drunkenness among women than among men, even though many of the men in the district were sailors.

But London is ceasing to be a port. In consequence, fewer sailors, less drunkenness, less prostitution, greater difficulty of publicans in making a living than formerly. Jews and foreigners drink more than the Englishmen but get less drunk upon it.

In this district publicans are not unwilling to give up 2 or 3 licences in favour of a new licence being granted in a more paying district. The result may be that more is drunk in the new house than in the 3 old ones put together but he still thinks it a good policy on the part of the Justices to allow this practice because you are less likely to get malpractices in a house that pays by honest trade than in one that will not pay with honest trade. Said that the publican was "squeezed" by the broker and the brewer, more especially gentlemen's servants. "It is a curious thing how old servants, coachmen and butlers think it the proper thing to become a publican once they have saved £300 or £400." Often he has wished to warn them but knows he would be prosecuted for libel if he did so.

Sleeping out of doors is one of the features of Whitechapel. It is a centre for common lodging houses and shelters. Destitutes from all sides drawn here. Many would rather sleep out of doors than indoors. They are covered with vermin. If they are without visible means of subsistence, the police can charge them. If they have a few pence "and they generally have", they can only move them on from door to door. Finally they won't move any further. Police dislike touching the class who do this because they are covered with vermin and won't come to the station without considerable handling. Result, they are left sleeping on the doorsteps. The real sleep of this class is in the day on the seats round Spitalfields church in the afternoon.

Loafers he would have if possible cared for by the state, "in some large Broadmoor". As they are, they do no good to themselves, only harm to others. There was no hope, he said, of their ever becoming any better, the only chance lay in preventing their making other people worse.

Then he took me through Wentworth St to see the Jews marketing for their Sabbath. Very little crowd. Then into Dorset St (BLACK on the map), still BLACK. "3 stabbing cases and one murder from this street in the last 3 months." Common lodging houses for both sexes, "where they do not ask for your marriage certificate". One very fat lady at a window. "She has sat there for years. She is now too fat to get out of the door."

He favours fixed points, not on any principle but merely because he has always had them.

(B350-4)

lodging houses at southwest end, DARK BLUE, very rough. The rest of Heneage St is
3½-st, messy, Jews, PURPLE not PINK.

S down Spelman St, on the east side is John's Court, 14 houses, 2-st, Jews, LIGHT
BLUE to PURPLE. Not coloured in map and just south of it is Boundry Court. Four
2-st houses, Jews, LIGHT BLUE to DARK BLUE. At the corner of Chicksand St and
Spelman St is Little Halifax St. LIGHT BLUE in map, now better, PURPLE. Clean
windows, all doors shut. 16 2-st houses, quiet, respectable, paved passage.

E down Frick St, 2-st, Jews, PURPLE as map. On the south side is Hope St. 3- and
2-st, Jews, quiet, like French St, PURPLE not DARK BLUE. On the north side Ely Place,
2-st, very poor, quiet, all Jews, children well fed, some rags, LIGHT BLUE, in map
DARK BLUE. W along Chicksand St, PURPLE as map. All Jews, principally tailors and
machinists, building with workshops at the top and motto on the outside, "Work,
wait, win". 3- and 4-st, mess in street. On the south side next to Board School is
Luntley Place. DARK BLUE in map, now LIGHT BLUE. Jews, houses 2-st, in good
repair. The east end of Chicksand St is called Osborn Place. 2 of Cooney's lodging
houses on the north side, brothels, BLACK, in map PURPLE. 3-st. Notice up: 8, 9, 10,
11 Osborn Place. Let for 70 years from 1874, at £208. Holey boots and clothes but
well-fed children. LIGHT BLUE, in map DARK BLUE. "4 Osborn Court, let at £57.4."

S down Brick Lane and E into Finch St, the northwest end of which is rough, DARK
BLUE, windows broken, in map PURPLE. Like it is Frostic Place, 2-st, Jews, trouble to
police, DARK BLUE as map.

Back into Brick Lane, the houses on the east side between Finch St and Old Montague
St are all brothels with shops underneath.

General remarks

The same difficulty here as in the Leman Street subdivision as to determining
whether a street should be PURPLE or LIGHT BLUE. Seemingly a greater mixture of
well-to-do, poor and very poor in adjacent houses or even in the same house, among
Jews than among Gentiles. Mess in every street, "not the fault of the vestry who do
their best to clear it away".

The children's games in vogue now (March) are marbles and tipcat. Marbles coming
in with warmer weather. Industries of the district: fur dressing, tailoring and shoe
making.

Note how the height of the houses gradually increases as Whitechapel is approached
and tendency in Jewish districts to increase the accommodation both extensively by
occupying other streets and intensively by building higher houses.

As to call-money, French said the police still got some money in this way but
less than formerly. He did not know of payments made by publicans in place of
the beer which they used to get during his 4½ years in the division. He has not known
of a case of a constable receiving money from publicans to come up before him.

3
STEPNEY

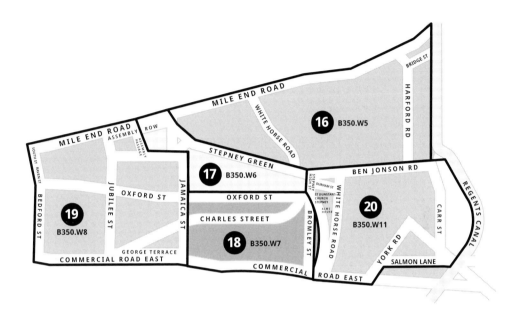

Walk 16

B350-5

Tuesday 18th January 1898
George Duckworth with Inspector Drew

Starting at SW corner of Stepney Green

Houses old, dated 1839. 2½- and 3½-st, some servants kept. A few old wooden houses half way up east side. Also 6-st and 2 attics model dwellings almost entirely tenanted by poor Jews. Backs are worse than their fronts. 3 rooms for 7/6. Montague House, also on the east side "let out and used for Jewish weddings". Large mews with a house and some workshops as well as stables also on east side. At the northeast end a poorer block of buildings called Paragon Mansions, 4-st and attics with a synagogue called an orthodox synagogue at one corner. Windows broken, inhabitants very poor.

Character of Stepney Green as a whole, PINK as map, but many houses are better and Paragon Mansions worse. Green well kept by LCC. Behind it is Rectory Square. 2-st 6-roomed houses letting for £28 to £30, tenanted by small business men. Small gardens, PINK to PINK-barred (on map PINK).

Northeast end of Stepney Green a turning without a name, PURPLE as map. "Very poor labourers, not vicious" said Drew. Windows broken and litter of paper, but children booted and clean.

Into the Mile End Road and eastwards, the first court on the south side clean, PURPLE in character, carmen its inhabitants, 2-st and one house 1-st. The second court has 2 houses only. PURPLE.

S down Beaumont St. 2½-st. PINK as map. On the west side Louisa St, 2-st, 2 families to each house. Mixture of Jews and English, "pretty quiet labouring class" said Drew. PINK to PURPLE (on map PINK).

Into Beaumont Square. 3-st, PINK-barred on north, west and east sides (map PINK), south side not so good, PURPLE as map. "Great influx of Jews here, who are gradually driving out the Gentiles." Mess of paper, etc on streets. "Does not mean much in Jewish quarter because Jewish children are always messy." Much housework done in the neighbourhood. Square well kept by LCC.

Maria Terrace. On map PURPLE, is better than Louisa St, should be PINK.

E along Shandy St. 2-st, some new houses. Into Whitehorse Lane. Mixture of shops and dwelling houses. Children coming out of school. All well dressed, fairly clean, hatted and booted.

Trafalgar Square on the east side of Whitehorse Lane is less good now than the PINK of the map. There is an entrance at the southeast corner into the poor rough quarter of Ocean St, Knolt St, etc. Houses now tenanted by poor Jews and labourers, not better than PURPLE. "Same class as at the bottom end of Beaumont Square" said Drew. 3-st.

N up Whitehorse Lane and E along the Mile End Rd. On the south side Floriston Rd, PINK on map. Now undoubtedly worse. East side LIGHT BLUE, west rather better, PURPLE. Bricks of houses worn light by constant rubbing, holes in the plaster, doors open, 2-st, poor but not rough.

S into Ely Place. Very narrow here and rather rough. Not coloured on map. "Maybe there are one or two respectable families living here" said Drew. Jews getting in, rough Dutch Jews. Better the west than the east end.

Running N out of Ely Place at the back of Floriston Rd is Eaton Place. 2-st. Well paved. Houses on the east side only. Wash hung across street. Poor. BLUE to PURPLE.

Along Ely Terrace into Calverly St, rather better than Floriston St. PINK in map but looks no better than PURPLE. Litter in street, doors open, 2-st, windows dirty. The next street eastwards is a cul-de-sac. Formerly Crown Place, now Jewel St. Quiet, respectable working-class and one or 2 clerks, 2 families to each house, 2-st houses, trees in little railinged fronts. PURPLE to PINK as map.

Into Mile End Rd, an unnamed turning, west of Harford St, leads south to a Mission Room, with an open space, litter, old cans, bricks, remains of a demolished shed, etc, on the west side of which is a double-fronted cottage.

Harford St. 2-st. PINK instead of PURPLE at the northeast end, new shops.

The next turning eastwards out of the Mile End Rd is Wade's Place. Very poor, 2-st, LIGHT BLUE as map, windows broken and patched, street narrow. No pavement, just room for cart, leads to a cooperage and stables, and wood and tub dealer's yard, very muddy.

Then up to the Canal. A beer house on the south side. Advertises "Bread, cheese, pickles and glass of ale for 2½d". Across the Canal and southwest along Bridge St, respectable mechanics, 2-st houses, mess in the street. PURPLE rather than LIGHT BLUE. Out of it on the north side is Single Gardens. Cottages done up last year and outhouses built on to their fronts, "rather a poorer class than Bridge St, mostly carmen" said Drew. LIGHT BLUE as map.

Into the east end of Ely Terrace, rougher here than the west end. 2-st. Some new cottages at the north side. Along Ernest St, PINK on map but now much worse, 2-st houses, rough class. Several unfortunates and criminals living in the street, should be DARK BLUE to BLACK. Dirty children at play. Litter in street, pieces of bread, etc. Children setting fire to paper, one little girl crying for no apparent reason, till its mother found its petticoats smouldering. Some houses 3-st. "As bad as Donkey Row" said Drew.

Skidmore St. 2-st. Rather better than Ernest St, but not much. The middle part opposite the public house is as bad as it can be, but other houses in the street quite respectable. East end PURPLE. Costers and carmen. Many bare-armed and bare-headed women in groups round open doors. At the east end of Skidmore Street is Emmott St. Allan's large chocolate and cocoa manufactory at north end, employing many of the girls of the district. PURPLE as map. 2-st.

S along Harford St, past Commodore, PURPLE as map. Monsey, and Emmott Streets. All 2-st. Working class. On map PINK but not better than PURPLE. Out of Cologne Street are Louvain, Bonn and Bale Streets. None PINK now (as map). Louvain PURPLE. Bonn PURPLE to LIGHT BLUE, and Bale LIGHT BLUE. Gasworkers living here. 2-st houses. Dainty ragged children but not dirty, holey stockings and shoes, some prostitutes, doors open and groups of women.

S of Bale St are some new 2-st streets which have taken off the cream of the district and account for discrepancy between map and present time. Dongola, Monteagle, Essian Streets all PURPLE to PINK, 2-st, 6-roomed houses letting at 12/- to 13/- per week.

Then W into Duckett St (formerly Edward St) into a rough neighbourhood. Thieves, a few prostitutes, ticket-of-leave men; in appearance and character like the Donkey Row district. LIGHT to DARK BLUE. Mary St. 3- and 2-st. Passage under house on south side called Lonas Buildings, leading to Ben Johnson Rd. Like it Master's St (late Chambers St) with a passage leading out of its west end into Trafalgar Square). Cadiz St. 2-st. Ocean St. 2- and 3-st. Knolt St. 2-st, with no outlet at its southern end. All LIGHT to DARK BLUE. Costers, thieves. Good for nothing unfortunates.

Hatless girls and women, doors open, bread about, rough. The map only marks Knolt St DARK BLUE but there is little difference, said Drew, between this and any of the rest though he was inclined to say that Knolt St was still the worst of the lot. At the southwest end of Ocean Street are some more respectable houses with gardens in front of them. No Jews in these streets, whose worsement must be due to the overflow consequent on natural increase of population in the neighbourhooding Donkey Row district.

General remark

As to drink, Drew pointed to a slight decrease among men and an increase among women. "Not due here to grocers or off-licences because we have so few of them." Less shame now in entering public houses but he could not say why. Sweet-giving has been stopped by order but it makes no difference to the number of children sent to fetch beer. He wishes they could be prevented, saying that children though they did not become drunk yet acquired a taste for both the beer and its smell by being sent to public houses to fetch it. As life becomes less interesting the child turns to drink for excitement.

About half the population in his subdivision are Jews, who are regular rent payers and respecters of authority but dirty, messy and great cheats; they bring their private quarrels to the police station, each charging the other with crimes. It is impossible to believe either. The Dutch Jew is the lowest and roughest of them. Their work is slop clothes, boots, cigars and fur. They are gradually ousting the Gentile from the better streets. More come every year. Immigration has increased rather than decreased.

There are a great many beer houses in the district. "Hard put to it for an honest living."

Subdivisional Inspector Henry Drew has been 3 years in this district, coming from Deptford. He is of medium height, reddish beard and whiskers, turning grey, reddish face. Silent and cautious, never volunteering any information. Has been 25 years in the service.

Walk 17   B350-6

Thursday 20th January 1898
George Duckworth with subdivisional Inspector H. Drew

Starting at Wellesley Street, a turning northwards out of Oxford Street

2½-st. Has been better than it is. Some broken windows but inhabited by a quiet and respectable working class. Jews beginning to come in. PURPLE as map.

W along Clive St, formerly George St, into Silver St. Well paved, clean, poor, quiet,

2- to 3-st houses, flush with the pavement. London City Mission Hall at north end. Carmen and costers. The 3-st are only one room thick. PURPLE to LIGHT BLUE (PURPLE in map.) Like it are Gold St, Hare St and Brilliant St. PURPLE as map, a little broader than Silver St. Some bread lying about in all these streets.

W into Jamaica St. 2-st. PINK as map. Much broader street. Jews getting in; very fair gardens. Out of the east side is a turning to a mews used by Seaward Bros. Carmen – evidently cut off from the gardens at the back of Silver Street, which in consequence have nothing but small yards behind.

W along Redman's Rd, small shops, 2-st. On the south side is a cul-de-sac between Jamaica St and Silver St called Pearl Place. Poor, quiet, 10 cottages, windows and women clean, one said her house had 2 rooms and a kitchen and she paid 5/- a week for it. LIGHT BLUE to PURPLE (on map LIGHT BLUE.)

W into Hannibal Rd. Many poor Jews coming in – poorer than map. Door posts dirty, windows broken, PURPLE rather than PINK, some LIGHT BLUE. On the west side is a court, LIGHT BLUE as map. 2 cottages there, 1-st.

S along Stepney Green. Houses at northeast end dated 1845, those on the southwest side are older, red tiled. S along Cressy Place – Cressy Buildings. 4-st, red brick, belonging to the East End Dwellings Society, here taken up the whole of the triangle made by Daniels Row, Hannibal Rd and Cressy Place. A very mixed class in the buildings. A curate – lady worker, a County Council architect (Mr Fleming) as well as artisans, 2 doctors from the London Hospital. None there for doing work in the Buildings but simply for their own convenience. 111 lettings in the buildings, 2/- for 1 room, 6/- for 2 rooms. Only four 4-roomed holdings, there used to be more but they have been divided as the demand is for 2-roomed holdings. No restriction as to the number allowed in a room though caretaker has to see that are not too many allowed in. Washhouse in a low building in the court; everything clean looking. The poorest live in the rooms facing Hannibal Rd, the richest in those facing Daniels Row of which only 2 cottages remain on the east side, nothing on the west side. Only 2 or 3 families in the buildings are Jews.

The next turning SW out of Stepney Green has six 2-st cottages, quiet, clean, PURPLE. S into a block of working class, 2-st streets. Each house with 2 families. Oley St and Diggons St are the best of them and PINK as map. Pole Street, Copley St, Latimer Street are rather poorer, not better than PURPLE, Copley Street being the best of these three, windows and blinds clean, doors shut, houses in fair condition, not worse than LIGHT BLUE. The second court with only 3 cottages.

King John St. Very respectable, PINK rather than PURPLE of map. Many police living there. 2-st houses.

S down High St and into Oxford St, on the south side is Bromley St. Older houses. 1827. 2-st, 3 rooms upstairs and 3 downstairs and 1 washhouse, letting for 15/- to 17/- per week, on quarterly, and some on 3 yearly agreements. Railings in front and fair gardens behind. Drew lives in one of these himself. Many small tradesmen, a few keep a servant.

W along Oxford St. Small shops and public houses, used to be many brothels here; dispersed by the efforts of Charington but have re-established themselves in Shadwell.

N into George Place and George St. Quiet, rather poor, well paved, PURPLE to LIGHT BLUE (PURPLE in map).

General remarks

The Arbour Square subdivision of the Whitechapel Police is bounded on the north by the south side of the Mile End Rd, on the east by the west side of the Regents' Canal, on the south by the north side of the Commercial Rd and on the west by the east side of the New Rd.

The police staff of the subdivision is 111 of whom about 95 are constables (he was not sure that he ought to give this information and is going to ask the superintendent, who said he was not to give it).

The beer houses are small and medium-sized in this subdivision, there is nothing very large. There is nothing worth more than £2,000 and the lowest would fetch about £300. Publicans would have to be the possessors of at least £200 before entry.

Betting on the increase: has been driven from the streets but goes on nevertheless. Drew thinks newspapers are the principal cause of its increase. Does not see how it can be stopped. Jews gamble rather than bet. Has 3 clubs in the subdivision, gambling goes on in them (this he said with much hesitation). Card playing, music at home and at the music hall are the chief amusements of the Jews.

Spoke of general tendency of Central London to become poorer. The first people to be affected by cheaper locomotion are the richer classes. Life of the poor more sociable and more bound up with places and neighbours than life of the rich. Therefore rich go, poor remain. Therefore a general tendency of the better streets to become worse, but not of the worst streets to go lower or even to remain as bad because the vicious class is less vicious than formerly.

Doubts as to the expediency of routing out brothels unless you can undertake the care of the women who use them as their homes. Thinks there are just as many prostitutes now in the subdivision as there were before the Charrington crusade; while the number of brothels in Shadwell has increased. Prostitutes are equally Jewesses and Gentiles.

A good many juvenile thieves – not so many perhaps as in Whitechapel but still a number. All are taught by the "old hands". Knows of no regular school for them. "The kitchens of low lodging houses are about the most demoralising place a boy can enter."

As to the police accepting money from publicans or anyone else: he would hardly admit it but said it might be done in some cases. "Call money", he said, was "a thing of the past. But police are human as most men."

The shopping streets are Commercial Rd for the better class and Whitehorse Rd for the poorer. As to buildings. Drew said their character depended mainly upon the character of the superintendent. A strong man could keep out or turn out bad characters, a weak one could not. For their inhabitants they are an education either for better or for worse. For better if discipline is maintained and cleanliness insisted on and for worse if it is neglected because one bad family can more easily affect a large number in a building than in a house.

Walk 18   B350-7

Friday 21st January 1898
George Duckworth with Inspector Drew

Starting at the police station in Arbour Street East

N into Charles St. Small shops, 2-st. PINK as map. E and S down Fair St. 2-st. 6 rooms and a scullery. Houses built 1854. Working class, 2 families to each. PURPLE to PINK.

Like it Diggons St, built 1866, and Senrab St, formerly Alton Gardens. New, built within last 6 years. Rents 7/- for ½ a house. 2-st houses containing 6 rooms and a scullery; respectable working class and several policemen.

Heath St west of it is older, 2-st, narrow, "not a den of thieves, but there are thieves living there". Houses mixed in character, costers, fish curers, and respectable artisans, as a whole rough and noisy. Middle part the worst, dirty children and women, many house-workers. Character LIGHT to DARK BLUE (on map PURPLE). South end is still PURPLE in appearance.

Like it is the next street, Old Church Rd. 2-st and attic houses, newer. Large cowsheds at southeast end. Mixed class here also, but as a whole LIGHT BLUE. "Rough." Back entrance out of it into the public house in Heath St. At the north end is Church Passage, paved with flags, called Charles St on map, poor courts on either side, curers. 2-st, LIGHT BLUE as map. The easterly court is called Eltham Place, built 1849. Windows clean in all these streets.

E and S down Grosvenor St, PURPLE as map, better than either Heath St or Old Church Rd. Walter St. 2-st, better, PINK as map. Venetian blinds, flowers in china pots, better curtains, etc. Like it are Portland and Albany Streets, PINK as map.

Down Belgrave St. Poorer north end than south as PURPLE to PINK. Southwest end PINK-barred, one or 2 keep servants. 2- and 2½-st, a cellar making the half storey. Sometimes used as a living room, but more often as a cellar, seen under grating, forming part of the pavement. At the back occupying the space between the back

gardens south of Belgrave St and Bromley St is a rope walk (Good's) running to the whole length of the street down to the Commercial Rd.

Into Commercial Rd, westwards. N into Heath St which has a turning into Senrab St, south end, which has a turning into Fair St, neither shown on map. At the bottom of Senrab St is the wall of the large garden to a house in Commercial Rd, belonging to Dr Cunningham. (Not correctly shown on map.)

Into Arbour Square. Indifferently kept. Belongs to Mercer's Company. Was done up 2 years ago, but has since been allowed to go to waste, no one allowed to use it, is now being tidied up, houses round occupied by mixed class. Jews coming in.

Northern, southern, and western sides better than eastern. Houses 3½-st with fair gardens. Most take in lodgers. PINK as map. West side inclined to PURPLE.

E into Jamaica St. 2-st, a few small shops, 2 builders-, fish-, sweets-, paper-shops. Jews getting in at top, better north end than south. A PURPLY PINK in character.

E along Bermuda St and into Perth St. LIGHT BLUE as map. Rough. Poor. Bread in street, but well-paved with imitation granite cubes with level edges. No thieves.

N up Paterson St. PURPLY PINK. "Not poorer than Jamaica St". On map PURPLE, respectable working class.

E along Oxford St and S down Apsley St (one end formerly called Anne St). Houses done up not long ago. PURPLE rather than LIGHT BLUE of map. Not near so poor as Heath St. Built 1854.

General remarks

The above a district of small beer houses, and small public houses. Majority of family houses 2-st, flush with pavement; roads fairly clean. The poorer ones lately paved with hard imitation granite cubes, easily washed down and apparently wearing well. Some of the houses eg. southwest end of Heath St, only one room thick, though with a back scullery on ground floor.

Drew spoke of the great difficulty of finding small houses and the demand for them. "They are generally let before they are empty." The consequence very little migration from street to street. "People dare not move."

Noticed many books on the tables in the windows of houses even in small streets. Not school prizes, odd volumes of novels, 'good words', illustrated papers. All children booted, but many ragged and hatless, not very dirty and all looking well-fed and healthy; a few very young mothers at the doors in Heath St.

Not many pawnbrokers in the subdivision. "Only 3 big ones" said Drew. Only one Jewee pawnbroker among them all. Good many stolen goods disposed of here. Thieves work the strand; do not confine their efforts to the east end.

Walk 19   B350-8

Monday 24th January 1898
George Duckworth with Inspector Drew

Starting at the police station in Arbour Street East

Crowd of loafers, out of works, hanging round the Thames Police Court (next door to station), a few young women, all of casual class. "Generally from 60 to 100 charge at the police court every Monday morning." Drawn from the whole of the police court district – drunkenness, disorder, felony, larceny. All sorts of misdemeanour. No one is a particular feature of the court.

W along Charles St and S down Exmouth St. PINK as map. 2-st. Out of it on the west side Exmouth Court (DARK BLUE on map) has all been balled down and rebuilt. 4 cottages, artistic, red brick and stucco with diamond glass windows, one occupied, others still being built. Now respectable, well built, concrete passage between houses, narrow. "There will be no difficulty in finding tenants, the demand is for such houses as these."

N up Dempsey St and across Clark St. 2-st. Both PINK as map. Houses of the 1820–1830s type. Well built. Flowers in china pots on round tables in front windows, clean curtains, windows doorsteps, sometimes books. Built of a reddish-yellow brick. "Nos. 5, 7, 9, 11 and 17 of Dempsey St, 23 Charles St, 69 and 73 Clark Street let for £209. Tenants paying rates and taxes; Dempsey St held for 76¾ years from June 1824 at £34 a year. 17 Dempsey St 65¾ years, from 1835 at £4 a year. 23 Charles St 76½ years at £4. 69 Clark St 72 years from 1828 at £4. To be sold." Property about here all belongs to the Mercers Company. On the southwest side at back is a long line of stables, cowsheds, etc. Otherwise very fair gardens at backs of houses, none of which has been turned into workshops like those in the north of London. Quiet, broad streets, fairly kept. Like it is Smith St.

N up Jamaica St and W along Redmans Rd. On the south side opposite Hannibal Rd is a cul-de-sac with houses on the east side only not on the west side as on map, slips of gardens with iron railings in front. LIGHT BLUE rather than the PURPLE of the map. "Very poor but not rough."

Redmans Rd 3½- and 2½-st. Small shops, many Jews. On north side is Assembly Place leading to Mile End Rd. Only five 2-st dwelling houses, respectable at northwest end. The other side is all mews and workshops, tin plate factory, etc, called Winter Buildings. Built 1879.

W along Mile End Rd. S down Jubilee St. Shops at northwest end. On the northeast side is a small court, now shut up, one lodging house remaining at the end of passage. Very poor. Doubtful reputation. Called Hewitts Court.

W along Mile End Rd. On the south side are Leslie St, 2-st and cellar, poor, Jews, PURPLE; used to be respectable English and PINK as map. "The streets west of Jubilee St are all being absorbed by the Jews, English are moving out to Plaistow." Drew spoke of the district as "a great garden". Like it is Cecil St and Greenwood St. A court (unnamed) between Harlow and Greenwood Streets, contains one very poor house and a wholesale boot factory. "No trouble to police." LIGHT BLUE, BLACK on map. Harlow St. 2-st. Poor. Jews. LIGHT BLUE to PURPLE. Gateshead Place. Also poor but well-paved and clean. LIGHT BLUE to PURPLE.

Then S down Bedford St, the name now given to what were formerly called South St and Raven St. E into Raven Row. On the north side is a court with 2-st cottages. Respectable. Well-dressed child. No trouble to police. Look PURPLE but BLACK on map. On the south side two courts, one known as Lewins Buildings. BLACK on map but now LIGHT BLUE. Poor Jews, boot factories. 4 clean and fairly dressed children playing in front of one house. "Not rough or in any way criminal." Next to it down another passage are Dorset Buildings, only very poor. LIGHT BLUE. Jews. No trouble. Between Gateshead Place and Sidney St on the north side of Adelina Grove are five 2-st cottages without a name, PURPLE in character.

Along Adelina Grove. Used to be Lady Lakes' Grove. There is still a rough common lodging house on the south side but no brothel, inhabited largely by costers who have barrows in Petticoat Lane. Where the BLACK is shown on map, there are now poor Jews. Character LIGHT BLUE to PURPLE. E across Jubilee St, north end shops, lower end 2-st and cellar houses, PINK to PURPLE (map PINK).

W into Lindley St, a cab yard and poor Jews LIGHT BLUE to PURPLE. On map PURPLE. Hawkins St. 2-st. Jews getting in, PURPLE to PINK (map PURPLE).

Richardson St down the centre of these 2 streets, PURPLE, Jews, children clean and tidy, no LIGHT BLUE now. Houses lately done up. A blackmasters stables under arch on east side.

Wolsey St. PURPLE, but southeast end near Jubilee St very poor. LIGHT BLUE. Rag-sorters.

W along Newark St (late New St), the BLACK spot between Newark and Oxford St no longer there, now poor Jews, LIGHT BLUE.

S down Bedford St which is the boundary between Whitechapel and M.E.O.T.* Poor Jews. LIGHT BLUE, southeast end PURPLE to LIGHT BLUE.

Past Ford Square (late Bedford Square), a rough field uncared for. Shut and entirely neglected. All Jews living round the square, 3-st houses, 3 to four families in each house, character PINK to PURPLE.

E along Rutland St (2- and 3-st) to Sidney Square. Equally uncared for. Better class of inhabitants on east side then west, some servants kept on east side.

S down Jubilee St, small shops at south end and small beer house (porter, 3d per pot).

W into Commercial Rd and N into Bromehead Rd, leading into a quiet set of streets, shut off from the rest of the world. All PINK in map but looking poorer now. Streets little used by cart traffic, but wanting mending badly. Bromehead St is poor, quiet, messy, bread and paper, outside leaves of cabbages lying about, LIGHT BLUE rather than PINK. A few Jews.

Newbold St, more bread, 2-st, PURPLE. Gardom St also PURPLE as is the piece behind it, working class, poor, narrow backs, children clean. Bromehead St is better, policemen living here, PURPLE to PINK.

Out into Commercial Rd, N up Sidney St, W along Nelson St. LIGHT BLUE rather than PINK of map, very poor Jews. On the north side of it is the BLACK spot (in

*Note: MEOT is an ancient name for Mile End Old Town.

map) called John's Place. Known to police, as Jack's hole. Better now than it used to be. Well paved. More respectable than unrespectable families, though still 1 or 2 rough families. All houses done up, parish shut up one or two houses which were unsanitary or brothel. Some unfortunates living here. LIGHT TO DARK BLUE.

Baker St, a little further west. Very poor, one or 2 shady houses with prostitutes and thieves. LIGHT TO DARK BLUE, on map PURPLE.

Into Bedford St of which the southeast end is rough. Buildings 4-st. Jewish. All very poor costers, Russian, Polish Jews. Very quarrelsome. No physical trouble to police but a great deal of bother. Each accuses the other and neither can be believed. A quarrel in progress as we passed. Final adjournment of the parties to the police station, where they all spoke at once.

Walk 20   B350-11
Thursday 27 January 1898
George Duckworth with Inspector Drew

Starting at Durham Row in the northwest corner
Respectable 2- and 3-st houses, shops, frequented passenger way, at sort of St Paul's churchyard of the east end, St Paul's being St Dunstan's. On the north side of it Ashfield Place, BLACK in map, has been closed by vestry and is boarded up.

Market St. DARK BLUE on map, is not worse than PURPLE to LIGHT BLUE. "Not rough", a few shops, 2-st.

Whitehorse St. No row, a market street not for costers but the shops all have barrows on the pavement. Eastwards the first court on the south side of Ben Jonson's Rd (not coloured on map) is rough, 2-st, doors open, windows broken, called Hope Place. Should be DARK BLUE. The next is Taylors Place, also DARK BLUE as map. "Rough set of men here and all round, working in gasworks in winter, brickfields in summer." Ben Jonson's Rd. Here PURPLE as map.

S along Carr St and W into Halley St, which Drew spoke of as being about the best of all the streets in the Donkey Row area. On map LIGHT BLUE, is now perhaps PURPLE. Has 2 courts. That on the north side called Providence Place, leading to some 2-st cottages. Clean windows, respectable looking "but it is a rare place for Sunday gambling". That on the south side to the backs of the Manning Street houses is called Piron. The street itself is of concrete, and clean.

Then into Carr St, known to inhabitants as Donkey Row. North end is no longer PURPLE, rather DARK BLUE. Rough, windows broken and dirty, children with unlaced boots playing with the dust heap in the street unnoticed, dirty and ragged, but well-fed looking. Fish curers. Some shops. Many lads loafing. Industries are gasworks, fish curing, costering. Boxing a favourite amusement. "Is well-known for it, though not quite so well-known as Bermondsey." The champion boy bruiser was playing pitch and toss as we passed. Houses 2-st, flush with pavement, yellow brick. Rents 8/- to 10/- for 4 rooms. "Very troublesome property." All the streets north of Salmons Lane are variations of the above, more or less. The whole poorer than it used to be. Drew spoke of it as as bad as Notting Dale, where he once was quartered; people quite as rough but Notting Dale more vicious, because of the numbers of low prostitutes which are absent here. Think nothing of assaulting the policemen. The corner of Elsa St and Carr St is noted for street gambling which nothing seems to stop. Thieves scattered about but not a regular thieves colony.

Elsa St, late North St, narrower, 2-st, DARK BLUE. That part of it east of Carr St is full of fish curers, cartloads of fresh haddock standing at doors, also sacks of sawdust used for the curing, stables at northeast end with respectable traps. These curers make good money when fish is plentiful and cheap, their customers are shops both in city and West End; fish done up in neat parcels and driven off in the morning. "You would never imagine they came out of such dirty holes."

Eastfield St, LIGHT BLUE in map, is the same and should be DARK BLUE. Met children coming out of school. Rather ragged, all booted. Minority wearing hats. All looking as if they had enough to eat.

On south side of street the first court after crossing Carr St is May's Place. 12 cottages, one room thick, most windows broken, "two now doing time from this court, 'regular tigers' they were". Union Terrace, the next court is like it, so is Beard's Place. At the back was a penthouse literally covered with old crusts of bread. All DARK BLUE to BLACK. Like it is Reform House, which make up the 4 courts out of the south side of Eastfield St. Houses going cheap here. Jews are beginning to buy some up but they dare not put in any Jewish tenants just yet, they would have too hot a time, they will wait till they have got a whole street, then Jewish tenants will come in en bloc, rents will be raised and the former owners given notice to quit.

Maroon St. 2- and 3-st, west end PURPLE on map but is LIGHT BLUE. Past Samuel St going east. Out of it on the south side beginning at east end are: Dupont St at northeast end, 6 new 2-st cottages built 1897. Better than rest i.e. LIGHT BLUE, the rest as map DARK BLUE. "It's more the people than the houses that are rough."

Blumont St. 2-st. PURPLE to LIGHT BLUE. Not quite so rough as rest.

Brenton St, poor looking. Class like Perth St (out of Charles St near Arbour Square). LIGHT BLUE, not PURPLE. Samuel St, same. Conder St, same. 3- and 2-st, ten courts at northwest end.

York Place. On the north side of Maroon St, opposite the north end of Samuel St is a court of dwellings. Entered through an iron gate, 3-st, built 1882, very rough, DARK BLUE.

Aston St, south of Cagley St better than north of it but more PURPLE than PINK.

E along Repton St just across Carr St on the east side of the railway is a small court not shown on map, called John's Gardens. 2 cottages only, very poor indeed, DARK BLUE. Small child crying for another slice of bread but not looking ill fed. Water supply from tap in middle of court. Further south is Regents' Court. BLACK in map, "rough but not worse than the others". Very poor, one child boot and stockingless. Some Irish here, but DARK BLUE.

S into Salmons Lane and westwards. 2½-st, rather better west than east end, some carmen; PINK to PURPLE.

N up Aston St into Matlock St (late Wilson St). PINK as map. 2-st and cellared houses. S down Barnes St, the name given to York St West. Rather poorer northeast than south end, PURPLE to PINK. Jews coming in.

E along Chaseley St, late Henry St, respectable PURPLE to PINK. Across York Square and York Rd (late York St East). Houses 2-st and attic and cellar, letting for 17/- per week. Square fairly kept by the residents.

N up Raby St, poor, LIGHT BLUE rather than PINK of the map. E under railway bridge. The DARK BLUE piece of the south side is called Wrights Buildings. 2- and 3-st houses with palinged gardens in front. Some very rough. DARK BLUE as map.

S along Railway Place (late York Rd). Houses on the east side poor, but not worse than LIGHT BLUE. On west side are railway arches and often a house at the far end of the arch, tenanted by small carters and contractors, trucks to be let out at 2d per hour, costers barrows at 3d a day. (A truck is a two wheel high cart with a handle to push with.)

Bruntons Cottages on the east side of Railway Place. LIGHT not DARK BLUE, only poor. Bruntons Place is rough. DARK BLUE as map, very poor dingy looking but not much trouble to the police. 2-st and attic.

Then out into the Commercial Rd, under the railway bridge and N up York Rd are 2 houses known as Devonshire Cottages, which have seen better days. Are still respectable, PURPLE to PINK (not coloured on map), light cut off at gardens by the railway.

General remarks

The whole of the Carr St area dates between 1820 and 1830. Rough low labouring class. Interesting to note probable invasion of Jews, "the only prospect the district has of ever becoming better than it is". The amusements of the district are boxing, friendly leads and bird singing contests. "But" said Drew "it is nothing compared to Bethnal Green for bird fancying."

The worst bits Drew said were: the whole of Elsa St, Eastfield St and Carr St, the east end of Maroon St and Regent's Court.

Public houses and beer houses small. "Each with its own special clientele."

The street game everywhere for girls was battledore and shuttlecock.

4
OLD STREET

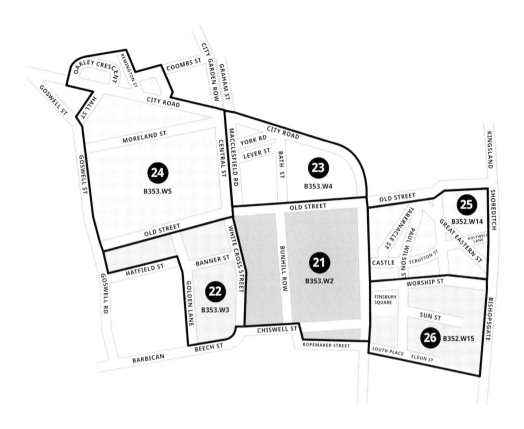

Walk 21

B353-2

Thursday 2nd June 1898
George Duckworth with PC R. Machell

Starting at the corner of Bunhill Row and Old Street
Along Old St, on the south side of which are Martha's Buildings, all factories, no dwellings. S down the City Rd. W along Featherstone St. The north side is now all 4-st factories (LIGHT BLUE in map). On the south side are Featherstone Buildings, 4-st, poor, windows broken, patched and dirty. Look rough but 'no trouble' to the police. LIGHT BLUE as map. Court behind the buildings with a glass blowers factory leading to another court which has two houses. Comfortable, respectable, PINK, not coloured in map. Industries of the street are, box and show card making, umbrella and stick making, etc.

E again to City Rd, S, W along Chiswell St. 4-st, shops, and warehouses, mixed, wood paved. The Churchill home for the better class of City factory girl is here (meals etc.)

S down City Rd and W along Ropemaker St, asphalt, all warehouses, 4-st.

N up Finsbury St, cobbles, 5-st warehouses.

W to Moor Lane, on the west side of which is Sun Court, the boundary between the Metropolitan and City Police. Moor Lane is all factories and dining rooms. All public houses about have bills of fare in their windows. Above Crown Court are Broad Arrow Court and Type Court, all warehouses. Into Chiswell St then W to Milton St whose west side is made up of the walls of Whitbread's brewery, 4-st warehouses on the east side.

N up Bunhill Row, whose south west end is now all warehouses and factories. W along Cherry Tree Alley to Lambs Buildings, which has a few dwelling houses on its east and west sides, a Roman Catholic priest living in one on the west, the rest inhabited by warehousemen. PURPLE rather than the LIGHT BLUE of map.

W to Lambs Passage. The LIGHT BLUE houses of the map have now given way to an extension of Whitbread's Brewery. E again into Bunhill Row. N past De La Rue's card and stamp factory on the west side. The northern end of the street is all factories (PINK-barred in map). On the east side is Dr. Tibble's Vi-Cocoa, on the west, new buildings in course of erection for Bovril.

W along Banner St. Houses on north side, now all factories, warehouses or institution, one of which is the Houseless Poor Asylum, founded 1819, open in winter only. On the south side is the Loyal United Friends Inst. and Lecture Hall, and some houses, PURPLE as map.

S down Baird St (one house on east side), to Roscoe St, all warehouses. Thence S to Dufferin St, between Baird St and Whitecross St. Making the west ends of Banner, Roscoe, Chequer and Dufferin Streets are great blocks of Peabody dwellings. 5- and 6-st, prison looking, but always full "generally a waiting list as well".

In Dufferin St on the south side, east of the Peabody Dwellings is a block of costers' dwellings with sheds in the yard for their barrows, tenanted by costers only, noisy but not rough.

S into Errol St, at the southeast end is the Leysian Mission House. Whitbread's Brewery is being extended north up to Errol St.

S in to Belward Avenue, DARK BLUE in map, used to be rough, now untenanted and coming down to make way for more Brewery extension.

W into Whitecross St, a market street, meat scraps 2d per lb, good meat between 3d and 6d per lb. Strawberries 4d and 5d per lb. (Strawberries of the same class were selling this day in the Grays Inn Rd at 6d and 8d per lb and in Oxford St at 10d and 1/-.) Large cucumbers 2½d and 3d each. Spring cabbages 4lb for 2d, good bacon 5d, lettuces (fair) 4 and 6 a penny, bread 6½d for 4lb (West End price 7.5 and 8d). Street full of young men and boys out during dinner, lounging, curious, not buying as far as I could see, almost complete absence of women or girls.

Going S down Whitecross St on the east side is Blyth Yard, 2 houses, 2- and 3-st, poor costers, LIGHT BLUE, not coloured in map, and Three King Court, 1 house, mess, windows broken, DARK BLUE, probably soon to come down for Brewery extension.

North up Whitecross St. N of Banner St on the east side is Elizabeth Place, 9 houses, old, date 1741, 2-st, 3-roomed houses for 9/-, belong to butcher at the entry, costers, poor, old tenants, one woman said she had been in the same house 24 years. LIGHT BLUE as map. N of it is Withers Place, 10 houses, 2-st, costers, rougher a good deal, windows broken, flowers and birds, DARK BLUE rather than LIGHT BLUE of map, like the Vinegar Ground.

N into Old St and E, on the south side is Royley St, 2½-st, asphalt paved, 16 houses, working class, no poor, PURPLE to PINK, in map PURPLE. Further E is Beckford Square, 14 houses, very rough, "like Withers Place and the Vinegar Ground". Old red-tiled houses, none on the south side. Steep wooden staircases, wash hanging across the court, windows broken, dirty, DARK BLUE as map. E of it is Tilney Court, not coloured in map, 4 houses closed and condemned on the east side, 4 houses, 2-st tenanted on the west. Should be DARK BLUE.

General remarks

Note the encroachment of warehouses and factories upon the dwelling houses. The 3 rough bits in this walk are Withers Place in the northeast end of Whitecross St and Beckford Square and Tilney Place on the south side of Old St.

As to policemen's duties, Machell thinks that fixed point duty and night duty are the two most disagreeable in a policeman's lot. Regulation of traffic, though tiring, is interesting and your attention always has something to distract it.

Hours of duty are:

6AM to 10AM & 2PM to 6PM for one set. 10AM to 2PM & 6PM to 10PM for another. (These two sets for day duty). 5PM to 1AM for night patrols.

For point duty the hours are 1PM to 5PM & 5PM to 9PM for Early Points. 1PM to 5PM & 9PM to 1AM for Late Points.

There are 168 policemen in the Subdivision. Night duty is irksome because of the sharpness of the air and the weight of the lamp that he carries in his waist. He said it weighed 1½lb.

Machell himself was a bookbinder before he became a policeman. As policeman he began at 23 years of age, he is now 35½ years old, 12½ years in this Subdivision and never in any other. The limits of age for a policeman to enter the service are between 20 and 27.

Walk 22

Friday 3rd June 1898
George Duckworth with Police Constable R. Machell

Starting at the corner of Golden Lane and Old Street

Great changes, width of street trebled. Now factories and warehouses on either side of street, many firms in dry goods line. Street used to be the same width as Central St on the north side of Old St. is at present. E along Old St. On the south side is Young's Buildings, not coloured in map, houses on west side only, seven in number, 2-st, 3 rooms to a house, no washhouse, rent 7/- (information given by one of the tenants). A narrow, smelly, flagged alley, passage only 6ft across, rough and semi-criminal inhabitants, dirty broken windows. Should be DARK BLUE lined BLACK. A forge on the east side.

E then S down Whitecross St (hour 11.15), street full of women marketing, crowd, sombre, black hats or bonnets and shawls or capes, a few dull blues or red shawls the only colour apart from the green and yellow of the divided spring cabbage and the raw meat of the butchers shops. Houses 3-st, shops below, stalls next the pavement in the street. New potatoes 1d and 1½d per lb. Spring cabbage 4lb for 2d at the north end of the street, and 3lb for 1d at the south end, identical in appearance.

On the west side are Whites Yard, stables, no dwellings, in map PINK.

S and W at Banner St, Peabody Buildings, 6-st, on the south side, factories (Brown's boot polish) on the north side. Clearance at the northwest end. One old house remaining at the corner of what was Bull Court, very poor and rough, most windows broken, DARK BLUE.

S to Roscoe St. Peabody Buildings, like the rest, forbidding and prison like, colourless, but windows fairly clean and unbroken, PURPLE as map.

S down Whitecross St. On the west side is Warwick Place leading to mortuary and stables. No habitations. The next on the west side of Whitecross St going south is Playhouse Yard. Factories on north side and warehouses, on the south side are a few 3- and 4-st old houses inhabited by a very poor class, but not rough. LIGHT BLUE, not marked in map. Further S past a common lodging house, criminal, thieves resort, beds 5d a night, 2/6 per week.

{This lodging house is S of Shrewsbury Court and is called Whitecross St Chambers} Shrewsbury Court, 2 dwelling houses only, dirty children, and holey boots, costers, looks DARK BLUE. S of it is Red Lion Market, marked DARK BLUE lined in map, now the only part of this character is the north side of the southeast end, leading back to Whitecross St. The rest is either down or warehouses. On the north side is Sutton's carriers yard, on the south a timber yard and some half-dismantled houses.

S into Beech St, W, then N up Golden Lane. This part is in the City police district. On the west side of the street is the Lansdown Building of the Cripplegate Institute.

On the east side of Golden Lane are Angel and Porter Yard, all warehouses. North of it is Lensden Place, late George Yard. White faced china glazed brick warehouses and factories, box, straw hats, braces and belts, children millinery and pipes. Past Playhouse Yard, factories on either side and no court behind on the south side, so that a large piece of DARK BLUE disappears. past Rose Court, a passage leading down from Golden Lane to Roscoe St. North of Banner St on the east side (PURPLE in map) are all factories, no dwellings. The west side is equally factories and warehouses as far orth as the Board School.

W along Baltic St. Asphalt paved, messy, mixture of criminals and costers, 3-st, ragged children, rather better east than west end, as DARK BLUE to LIGHT BLUE, in map PURPLE. (But better than it used to be, said Machell.) On the north side is Honduras St, 4-st, cobble paved, bread and mess in street, children well fed but dirty, women ragged, windows broken and patched. "Like Baltic St." No prostitutes but thieves, DARK BLUE lined rather than DARK BLUE of map. W of it is Norway St, 3-st, much better, doors shut, windows clean, PURPLE as map. W again is Domingo Street, rather poorer but quiet, LIGHT BLUE rather than DARK BLUE of map.

W along Memel St, houses on south side only. North side all factories, so a streak of DARK BLUE has disappeared. Windows broken and patched but not rough, according to Machell, and therefore LIGHT BLUE rather than DARK BLUE of map.

N into Middle Row, all factories on north side. South side has two common lodging houses, with 'Beds for travellers', frequented by prostitutes and thieves, BLACK. Further west are small shops and PURPLE in character. On north side, running to Old St is Sycamore St, all factories.

E along Thomas Place, 3- and 2-st, children very dirty, three of them insufficiently fed, houses both sides, thieves, squalid, ill-kept. Mess in street, smells, very rough, DARK BLUE lined rather than DARK BLUE and PURPLE of map. Facing the east end of Thomas Place are two courts (south of the beer house) called Baltic Place and Court. {New Court, 7 2-st houses on south side only, two-roomed, rent 5/-, labourers, narrow, dirty children, LIGHT BLUE to DARK BLUE, in map PURPLE. Is the court that makes the continuation westwards of Baltic St. but is walled off from it}.

Baltic Place, 4 houses only, 2-st, poor, 2-roomed and basement, rent 5/6. Baltic Court, 8 houses, 2-st, costers, looks rough, some thieves, both DARK BLUE as map, many children about with sore eyes.

S into Hatfield St, 3- and 2-st, west end leads out under an arch into Goswell Rd, narrow, asphalt paved, many dirty children, cricket being played actively in middle of street. Airless, not quite so bad as it was, bird cages at windows, in and out of pocket handkerchiefs, perhaps DARK BLUE rather than DARK BLUE lined. The east end at the Golden Lane end is all factories. Behind it on the south side, not marked or coloured in map, is a court called Deans Court, of about 7 houses. One woman in the largest of them said that the whole house was let for 6/6 a week, and sublet to her and another. She paid 5/- for kitchen and first floor room, the other tenant paying 3/- for the remaining room.

The great BLACK patch south of Hatfield St is now all down and replaced by factories. The present streets being called French Alley and Bayer St. In Bayer St which was formerly Bell Alley there is still one house (DARK BLUE) tenanted on the south side. The rest are closed or down.

The west end of Great Arthur St is New Court, 6 houses on the south side, all workshops except two. On north side of east end are 5 houses, 2- and 3-st, inhabited by costers, "drunken poor, not criminal". Character LIGHT BLUE to DARK BLUE, in map LIGHT BLUE. Along Little Arthur St, asphalt paved, cooler, south side all factories. Four houses on north side, LIGHT BLUE to DARK BLUE, in map LIGHT BLUE.

E past mission room to Osmans Place, cul-de-sac court. Six 3-st houses, better than the rest. Quiet, poor, warehousemen, some windows broken but clean, character PURPLE to LIGHT BLUE, in map DARK BLUE. E along continuation of Great Arthur St. The Rev. May's Mission occupies spot marked BLACK on south side. Opposite, on the north side, are four 3-st houses, rough, costers, mess, DARK BLUE rather than BLACK of map. S into Fann St. City boundary runs through here. Factories. Hot Water Court, on the north side of Fann St running between Fann St and Great Arthur St is boarded up on the west side. Factories on the east, 4-st. The south side of Fann St is in the 'City'. Saddlers Buildings on north side, only a box makers factory.

General remarks

Much has been cleared in the DARK BLUE and BLACK portion that lies between Golden Lane and Aldersgate, but a good deal still remains. An airless, poverty-stricken and vicious-looking neighbourhood. The growth of high factories all round it prevent a draught and on a hot day such as this, the smells are very bad. Better than it used to because there is less of it.

Walk 23   B353-4

Tuesday 7th June 1898.
Walk with Police Constable Richard Machell

E along Old St then N up Central Street

2-st and attic, and 3-st houses, narrow, asphalt paved, gets poorer as it nears Old St. The south end is rough, small shops with owners living above and taking in lodgers, PURPLE as map. On the east side is Whitby Court, 3 houses only, 3 rooms each, very poor, not rough nor crowded, LIGHT BLUE as map.

E along Mitchell St, broader, 3-st houses, doors shut and windows clean, police live here, rather messy, bread, paper, fish heads. Some china flower pots in windows, PURPLE to PINK, in map PURPLE. Lewins Court on the north side, rent for 2 rooms and wash-house, 8/6. Possibly a little better than Mitchell St but the same class of people, property belongs to the Ironmongers Co. The almshouses at the north end are now let as habitations like the rest, character PURPLE to PINK, in map PINK.

N up Norman Buildings, date on houses 1761. Ironmongers Co. alms, factories on east side, poorer at north east end, PURPLE to PINK, in map PURPLE. S past Paton St, 2-st, some noisy, looks poorer than other streets, but PURPLE as map. W along Langton St, with Langton Avenue on north side, 2½-st houses, newly done up. 'Lodgings for single men.' Windows clean but children dirty, both PURPLE, map gives LIGHT BLUE to the avenue.

N up Central St. On the east side is Clarence Place, 2-st, asphalt, mess, rough, poor, men are labourers and the women box makers, many windows broken and dirty, 2 rooms and wash-house 7/-. DARK BLUE rather than LIGHT BLUE of map. North of it is Garden Row, 2-st, poor, with a streak of criminals, thieves and housebreakers. "Like all the streets round about here." Rent for 3 rooms and kitchen is 7/-. The east end turns south and is quieter than the rest, it looks very poor. "Used to be very rough." 2 rooms here for 5/6. Those details as to rents obtained in each case from women who happen to be standing at their doors as we pass. DARK BLUE as map.

N across Lever St and up Clarence St, pickpockets and burglars working out of the district, similar character but rather better dressed than those in the Vinegar Ground. A poor class of women about with holey black shawls round their shoulders, straw hats trimmed with faded finery, skirts frayed at the hem, but lifted off the ground. "No prostitutes." DARK BLUE lined BLACK or LIGHT BLUE lined BLACK. Uncertain earnings because of the uncertainty of the hauls and the varying length of the terms of imprisonment. Back into Lever Street, which is better west than east of Central St. "Not so good as Central St." A thieves' resort, cobble paved, receivers. Machell pointed out a sweet stuff shop keeper on the south side who had just served his time for one offence and whom he thought was still at the old business, i.e. 'fencing'. On the north side is a coffee shop 'Slopers', where thieves are allowed food on credit and pay money or kind. The PURPLE of Lever St east of Central St should have a line of BLACK. On the north side of the road is Hulls Place. "Very bad, rough, criminal." 2-st houses, windows dirty, broken etc., bird cages. Doors open, children dirty, all to be sold on June 28th and pulled down for the erection of model dwellings. Hulls Place in map DARK BLUE, should have a line of BLACK added. Europa Place on the south side, is a shade better, but rough and poor, 3-st, a few criminals, children dirty with holey boots and sore eyes, asphalt paved, DARK BLUE as map. Wellington Place, 3 houses only, like Europa Place, houses on west side only, not shown in map. It is between Europa and John's Place. DARK BLUE.

John's Place, 9 houses, 2-st, 2 rooms, 5/6. One old lady who said she had been there 24 years only pays 4/6. Says her rent is not raised because she is so old a tenant. Quiet, LIGHT BLUE, not shown in map. One barefoot child.

N up Hulls Street, on the east side of which is Charles Court, 6 houses, 3-st, rough, criminal. Boy with toes out of boots, and many children about who ought to have been in school. DARK BLUE lined BLACK, rather than DARK BLUE of map. N of it is Garden Court, same as Charles Court, criminal, flagged court. "But it's not so bad as Moneyer St (in the Nile St area) where they'd knock your head off for 2d" said Machell.

Into the York Rd, rough, DARK BLUE as map. The north side is all Pickfords the carriers offices, stables, granaries etc. Westwards, on the north side is Macclesfield Place, 17 2-st houses, noisy, Machell said "Very similar" but, with flowers and books in many of the front windows, it looks better than the rest. In map DARK BLUE.

W into Central St. On the east side of Central St, between York Rd and Lever St, is York Place. Three 2-st houses, quiet, poor, LIGHT BLUE, not shown in map. N up Central St, the north end, both sides alike, PURPLE, map makes west side PINK. E along President St, this end not so good as the part west of Central St, though some windows show china pots in front windows. This end PURPLE rather than PINK of map.

N up Macclesfield St which is LIGHT BLUE at the south end but DARK BLUE and BLACK at the north. Rough, "like the York Rd". Two 3-st houses on the west side are common lodging houses, frequented by prostitutes. The east side are all timber merchants etc.

S across York Rd and down Ironmonger Row. 2- and 3-st, working class, poor end to end, PURPLE as map. E along Lever St. On the north side is George Row, four poor, quiet houses at the south west end. The rest of the street are factories, furniture, box makers etc. At the southeast corner of Lever St and George Row is a poor class of buildings, 4-st, LIGHT BLUE, in map PURPLE.

E past Waterloo St, 2- and 3-st, mixed class, some respectable, others 'West' men, i.e. burglars whose business is done in the West End. Fry's cocoa works has taken all the east side, LIGHT BLUE lined BLACK on west side rather than DARK BLUE of map. On north side of Lever St is Nelson Street 3-st, built for a better class than is now in them. Police live here, very few poor. Rents 7/6 and 8/- for 2 rooms, tenements, PURPLE rather than LIGHT BLUE of map. On south side of Lever St is Murton St, DARK BLUE lined BLACK in map, now better than it was. "Not so bad as Hulls Place, more like Hull St." 3- and 4-st, houses on east side only. Frys cocoa works have all the west side. Rough, DARK BLUE.

E along Lever St past Ratcliffe Grove, which has poor, quiet houses on its west side. The east side is made up of high 5-st and attic, red brick Guinness Buildings, LIGHT BLUE. On the north side of Lever St are St Clement's Buildings, 6-st, tenements, 4/6 to 7/-, respectable poor, children booted, well fed and fairly clean, PURPLE. Behind the Guinness Buildings, between two blocks is a cement playing ground for children with a raised covered seat at the east end, airless, dark, a well, but many children playing, mostly hatted, clean pinafores.

E into the City Rd. Between Bath St and Nelson St on the south side are the Eagle Dwellings with shops on the ground floor facing the main street. PURPLE to PINK. E of Bath St is a set of 3-st houses, RED in map, now not so good, PURPLE to PINK. Cayton St is all Liptons new offices which run nearly to Peerless St.

S past Peerless and Roby Streets, past two short turnings, of which the northernmost is all furniture factories and houses being pulled down. The southernmost is called Lewington's Buildings. 2-st, used to be brothels and is still rough, DARK BLUE as map.

W along Old St and N up Bath St, 3-st, fairly well-to-do, shops, crowds of men and women moving northwards for their dinners. Women with hats but no jackets, who mean to dine near their work in a coffeeshop, and with jackets going home.

E along Baldwin St, late Roby St. 3-st, majority of inhabitants rough, some criminal, many thieves, very badly cobble paved. Coffee shop on the north side at the east or City Rd end used as a brothel. Character LIGHT BLUE barred BLACK rather than LIGHT BLUE of map.

S down Bath Buildings, LIGHT BLUE as map. The Finsbury Radical Club on the west side, "a rough, low class drinking club" said Machell, "very noisy on Saturdays and Sundays, no respectable man would belong to it".

N up Radsworth St, quieter, better, LIGHT BLUE.

N up City Rd and W along Peerless St. On the north side is a new wing of the Eye Hospital. "Like Baldwin St, rough." 3-st houses, working class, thieves, girls generally at work. Some poor, LIGHT BLUE-barred, in map LIGHT BLUE. Buildings on the north side at west end hold a better class, PURPLE as map.

Across Bath St N, then W along Galway St, 3- and 2-st, old houses, mess in street, not so bad as Peerless St but some thieves, fairly quiet, LIGHT BLUE as map. Like it is Gastigny Place on the south side, 3-st and basement. Property all round here belongs to St Bartholomew's Hospital. W along Radnor St, like Galway St. 3-st, LIGHT BLUE as map. Some small shops. S down Lizard St, LIGHT BLUE as map, past Ironmonger St, 3-st, doors shut, better than the rest, newly cobble paved in appearance but work badly done. PURPLE to PINK, in map PINK. Ironmonger Passage behind it on the south side has poor, 2-st, LIGHT BLUE houses at the east and west ends and workshops in the centre, in map it is all PURPLE.

S into Richmond St, "like Radnor and Galway Streets", 2- and 3-st, LIGHT BLUE as map. On the south side is Bartholomew Square, 3-st, asphalt playground in centre, on one bench, Machell pointed out a fairly respectably-dressed middle aged lady, eating her dinner out of a newspaper, who had been in prison "nearly as often as Jane

Cakebread". Houses being done up, used to be a rough spot, LIGHT BLUE as map. At the southeast end of the square is King St, 3-st, rather better than Bartholomew Square, but not as good as Ironmonger St. Some thieves, inhabitants are labourers, packers, warehousemen. PURPLE rather than PINK of map.

W along Old St. N up New St, 2-st, houses being done up, "better than Lizard St". PURPLE rather than LIGHT BLUE. W along Mitchell St, late Richmond St. 3-st, noisy, this is the worst end of it "compares with Peerless St" and should have a line of BLACK added to the LIGHT BLUE of map.

N then W. Church Row. 3-st, respectable, working class, "a good deal of homework about here." Poor, houses east side only. It runs north out of Norman St. LIGHT BLUE as map. Norman St, LIGHT BLUE in appearance, 3-st, like Church Row. S down Helmet Row, better, PINK rather than PURPLE of map, when south of Mitchell St.

S into Old St then W. On the north side are Anchor Yard, 2-st houses, rough, 2-roomed houses, no washhouse, rent 7/-, DARK BLUE as map. Roby St, late Baldwin St, 5-roomed, 2-st and basement houses. One house only on the east side, LIGHT BLUE as map. Richards Place, box factory, tenements, narrow, dark, 6/- for 2 rooms, dwelling houses at north end, very poor, in map LIGHT BLUE, now DARK BLUE. George Yard, 2-st and attic, better, flowers in window boxes, doors open, woman sitting on a doorstep, PURPLE to LIGHT BLUE, in map LIGHT BLUE.

General remarks

A very poor neighbourhood with a large proportion of thieves and housebreakers. Has probably suffered from the demolitions in the Nile St area and Banner St. Streets badly cleaned and badly paved, a contrast in this respect to Shoreditch.

It is probable that much of the worst will come down when Hulls St area is sold on June 28th and the intention is to replace it by model dwellings. The high Guinness type of buildings with their dark airless wells, called playgrounds, can hardly be much of an improvement. Although Machell said "we very rarely get any of the criminal class from model dwellings."

The 4lb loaf of bread was this day selling for 7½d in Central St and 6½d in Lever St.

The poor are caught as if in a trap here between the City Road and Old Street.

Walk 24   B353-5

Thursday 9th June 1898
George Duckworth with PC Richard Machell

Starting at the south end of the Goswell Road.

On the east side is Ludlow St, late Willow Row. Houses on north side only, rough labourers and thieves, "van-draggers who pinch parcels from vans", a rough class of thief. Houses 2- and 3-st, all doors open, windows broken and dirty, children dirty, narrow passage only 6½ft across from wall of factories to housewalls. Rough women with bare arms standing at doors, a drinking set, but "women who keep to their husbands and have to work hard". DARK BLUE lined, rather than LIGHT BLUE of map.

N into Gee St, better class on the south side west of Ludlow St, than in the rest of the street. Houses 3-st and basement, many noisy charges from this street. In character like Bastwick St. Some fair-looking houses, a mixture of poor quiet and poor rough in appearance. Children very dirty, playing with horse dung in the street, mess. 'Our Own' Mission room at the west end of street. DARK BLUE rather than LIGHT BLUE of map.

N to Bastwick St, one barefoot child. 4-st tenements on south side, 3-st on north, Children nearly all hatless, ragged, holey boots, sizes too large, out and over trodden. A narrow street, 18ft across, windows broken, dirty and patched with paper, all doors open, some flowers on window ledges and in boxes, creeping jenny the favourite, here and there a geranium. Bread, mess, stagnant water and chickens in the street. DARK BLUE as map.

N to Peartree St, 3-st, quiet, poor, not many living houses. Houses south side only. Carter Paterson's yard at east end on north side, character PURPLE to LIGHT BLUE, in map PURPLE.

N to Seward St. On the north side is the Parcels post yard, which has caused the disappearance of two courts marked LIGHT BLUE in map. On the south side are 6-st model dwellings, poor, rough, a few thieves, noisy. The eastern blocks are rougher than the western, as DARK BLUE to LIGHT BLUE, in map all LIGHT BLUE. Many windows broken, children dirty, well fed, cement yards between the blocks (5 blocks I think), only 24ft across. Inhabitants are labourers, warehousemen, packing case makers. At the extreme west end is an asphalt space belonging to the buildings, used as a playing ground by its inhabitants.

W into Goswell Rd, here on the west side are the Compton Buildings, 5- and 6-st and attic, shops on a level with the street, let to a good class, PINK as map. N to Lever St, 3-st, respectable, old houses, working class, a few poor, PURPLE to PINK, in map PURPLE.

N up Telfer St. On a lamp in the middle of the street is a notice 'Standing for 6 hackney carriages', a reminder of the past respectability of the district. Into King Square, 3½-st, PINK-barred as map. Home for St Bartholomew's Hospital probationers at southeast end. In the middle a good square belonging to inhabitants and not open to the public. Would be an advantage to the neighbourhood if it were, though not to the square. Powell St at south east end, 3-st, old houses, great many watch and jewel makers plates. PINK rather than PINK barred of map. President St at north east end is like it, neither so good as the Square.

N up Leverington St, PINK as map, cobble paved, 3-st houses. Into Rahere St, 3-st, poorer, brass plates on most doors, morocco case makers, Fusee chain makers (*see notes*) etc. PURPLE as map. On the south side at the east end is Presidents Place, DARK BLUE in map, only three houses on the west side. One man from one of them now doing 10 years for 'fencing'. None poor. On the east side is a beer engine factory, PINK or PURPLE barred BLACK would seem the proper colour.

N up Central St and W along Masons Place. The north side is all down and has been a desert of brick bats for the last 3 years. Houses on the south side are 2-st and 2-roomed, rough labouring class with a dash of thieves. Some doors open, right into living rooms, very messy "like Bastwick St" DARK BLUE lined BLACK as map.

N to Moreland St, 3½-st, cobble paved. On the north side is the large factory of the Vulcanised India Rubber works, with gas lamps outside each window for lighting purposes. Process too inflammable to have them inside, said Machell. Character PURPLE to PINK, in map PURPLE. N up Goswell Rd, past Goswell Mews, now dwelling houses, back of India Rubber factory, to Hall St. Very respectable, 2½-st, PINK as map. Like it is New Charles St, as map. James St, leading to Charles St is poorer, "like Rahere and Moreland Streets". PURPLE rather than PINK of map.

S down Cottage Lane, 2-st, poor, quiet on east side, with well cared for front gardens, LIGHT BLUE as map. West side is better and PURPLE, in map LIGHT BLUE. At the south end is Parkinson's Gas meter factory, "Employs about 200 men."

N across the City Rd to Oakley Crescent, 3½-st, quiet, singlemen lodgers, PINK-barred rather than red. E to Remington St, 2½-st, not quite so good as Hall and Charles Streets, clean windows, PURPLE to PINK, in map PINK. Coombs and Haverstock Streets are like it, in map PINK.

E to City Garden Row, which is better north of Nelson Place than south of it. The map reverses this. Palmerston Buildings on the west side of the southern end are 6-st, PINK as map. Many police living in them. Below the buildings are Vertues the publishers store rooms.

E to Graham St, 3-st, like the east side of City Garden Row. Windows dirty, doors open, LIGHT BLUE as map. Electric light station at southeast end and 3 poor dwelling houses only on east side. S across Pickard St, 3½-st, dull respectability, fish heads and mess in street.

General remarks

Clerkenwell, said Machell, is the house of engineering, jewellery and watch trades. It also harbours many thieves, both pick-pockets and burglars. 'Tea-leaf' is the slang police word for a pick-pocket, but he does not know the origin of it. So is 'Buster' for the burglar. On the other hand, thieves speak of the police as 'Rozzers'. 'Copper' is the name given them by the respectable poor.

Very little call money is now paid. The riots of 1887 gave it a death blow. The publican as far as he knows, pays nothing. "They are too poor about here to be able to give away their money".

Two respectable-looking men in the Goswell Rd with black tail coats, bowler hats, good boots, white shirts and collars, shaven except for a moustache, he pointed out as well known 'busters'.

The district was at one time more prosperous than it is now. The decline of the watch trade has made some difference. But to judge from the small brass plates on most doors, there must be a good deal of watch and jewellery work still done in Clerkenwell. Streets messy.

Walk 25   B352-14

Friday 20th May 1898
George Duckworth with PC W. Ryeland

Starting at the junction of Old Street and Shoreditch

S down Shoreditch High St. Shops of a good class "and getting better every year", the demand from the inhabitants of part of the rebuilt Boundary St area responsible for part of this improvement. On the west side is Rivington St, only one or two living houses, the rest workshops on ground floor, living rooms above. Rents "not under 16/-" per week. PINK as map. Pleasant Place to the east of it is now taken up by an Iron Foundry. Elizabeth Place, west of it, is all factories.

W into Curtain Rd, the great dealing place for the cabinet trade. The shops are shops of dealers and warehousemen rather than of manufacturers. Curtain Rd is the warehouse and mart, the side streets, the factory of the furniture trade.

S then E into Norfolk Gardens. The north side is all factories, but the south side is rough as before. 4-st dwellings, drunk, rowdy, criminal, the west end better than the east or the back in appearance. Back of the block and the east end, very bad, broken and patched windows, dirty, ragged children talking, leaning out through the paneless window frames. Pools of stagnant, dirty water on a piece of ground opposite the 3-st houses, which Ryeland said was private ground. A general shop, thieves, like Wilmer Gardens, DARK BLUE lined rather than DARK BLUE of map.

E along New Norfolk St, asphalted, houses down and opened up since map. What remain, DARK BLUE lined, in map DARK BLUE. E along French Alley, now all workshops and widened. In map DARK BLUE.

E along French Alley to Shoreditch. On the east side of the road is the London Marie Hall, "very respectable". W along Bateman Row, mostly cabinet factories. On the north side are 5 houses, poor, quiet, hemmed in on either side by factories. LIGHT BLUE as map (only much less of it). On the south side is Anning St (called after

local Bank Manager who is active on the Vestry), late Spencer St. It is all factories, with passages across the street from the upper storeys. W along Bateman Row. On the north side nearly opposite New Inn Broadway is Margaret's Place, 6 houses, 2-st. windows broken and patched, "a little better than Norfolk Buildings", cement paved. Irish cockneys here. DARK BLUE, in map LIGHT BLUE.

S down New Inn Broadway, 3-st, poor, rough, noisy, not criminal. Factories on the west side where the road gets broader. DARK BLUE as map. On the east side is a turning called Socrates Place, date 1787. Looks poor but not rough. Ryeland said, "Irish cockney, very noisy of a Saturday". LIGHT BLUE to DARK BLUE, in map LIGHT BLUE. At the east end of it is a passage under a house leading to a place without a name. And so to Bateman Row. Old, well built, 2-st and attic, houses on west side only. East side demolished up to railway arches, LIGHT BLUE as map.

E along Bateman Row. S down Spencer St. W along New Inn Yard. 3-st, small shops and factories, very few inhabitants, PINK as map. N into New Inn Square, on south side of Bateman Row. Poor, noisy, 3-st, Irish, windows broken, used to be quiet but not so now, DARK BLUE, in map LIGHT BLUE.

S into Wood's Buildings, 4 houses, 3-st, poor, quiet, houses on south side only, LIGHT BLUE as map. SE into King John Court. 3 houses only on north side, very respectable, PURPLE, one a packing case maker, the two others being carmen.

Into Holywell Lane. Shops, Jewish element beginning to come in. Holywell Place on the north side, just east of the railway, 5 houses, 3-st, poor, quiet, tailoresses. Homeworkers living here. Doors shut, windows clean though some broken, LIGHT BLUE, not coloured in map.

E into Shoreditch, past the Standard Theatre (a beer house and two public houses almost next to one another here). W along George Street to Great Eastern St. 4-st warehouses on south side and the back of the Theatre on the north.

W along Great Eastern St, at the southeast corner west of the railway bridge are a block of dwellings, Hamilton Buildings. Rents 9/- to 12/- for 3 and 4 rooms and scullery. Good class, tenanted by fairly well-to-do artisans. 3 staircases, 5½-st and very quiet. PURPLE to PINK, not marked in map. Great Eastern St is a great centre of the bicycle trade, there are 12 houses for them at the east end.

S down Curtain Rd, on the west side of which are Gatesborough St (late Thomas St). 2 houses at south west end, homeworking polishers, PURPLE, otherwise all factories. S of it is Luke St, late Charles St. 4-st factories (feathers, chair, couch, billiard seat, bedroom suites). Motley St also factories.

W into Phipp St, also factories, large wireworkers on east side. S down Phipp St. W along Scrutton St, PURPLE as map. N into New North Place, poor, 2-st, houses on west side, LIGHT BLUE. Small workshops on the 'flat' principle on the east side. W and N into Providence Place, 2- and 3-st, principally carmen, poor, quiet, LIGHT BLUE as map. W then N up Clifton St, 3-st and basement, artisans, better than Scrutton St. PINK as map.

W then N up Clifton Place, 1824, 3-st, better than Providence Place, artisans, PURPLE rather than LIGHT BLUE of map. W to Paul St, all factories and business houses. E along Luke St, on the north side are 5-st buildings called Victoria Chambers. Rents 7/6 to 10/6 for 3 and 4 rooms and scullery. All PURPLE, in map half LIGHT BLUE and half PURPLE. On the south side is another great block of buildings called Granville Buildings. Rents 6/- to 8/6, poorer, LIGHT BLUE rather than PURPLE of map. They look poorer.

N up Ravey St (late Cross St) past Mark St whose south side is all the Victoria Chambers, past St Michael's Church (High Church, one in which Mr Kensit made a fuss a few Sundays ago). Into Leonard St, on the north side of which at the Great Eastern St end is a large block of buildings called Albert Buildings. 6½-st, rents

9/- to 12/- "like Hamilton Buildings". Artisans with good ordinary earnings, PINK, not coloured in map. On the south side from Ravey St to Paul St are more buildings called Allen Buildings, built 1870. No poor, PURPLE to PINK, not coloured in map.

S down Whitefield St, all warehouses, into Paradise St (the same). Platina St, taken up by Bell Punch Co. Castle St, Waterlows printing factory.

W into City Rd, then N to Welsh Weslyan Chapel, which has behind it a set of buildings let for the profit of the Chapel. Artisans, PURPLE to PINK.

N into Old St, then E and S down Singer St late Wood St. On the east side forming the south side of Great Eastern St are 5-st buildings, PINK. Glover St running east is all workshops on its south side.

{Gladstone Buildings, 6½-st. First set built by Sir Sidney Waterlow in 1869, many police from G, H and City divisions. Rents lower than Chichester and Hamilton Buildings, Character PURPLE to PINK.}

S down Paul St and E into Willow St, Gladstone Buildings on south side, St Agatha's Buildings on north. Respectable artisans, PINK. Little Leonard St, south of it, has the back of Gladstone Buildings on its north side and warehouses on its south. The DARK BLUE patch on the west side of Paul St is all factories.

N across Great Eastern St, E along Rivington St and N to Bath Place. Carlyle working men's club on the west side. On the east, 2 turnings marked DARK BLUE in map, now all factories.

S to Garden Walk, down Charlotte St, a few small masters in 2-st houses working in their downstairs rooms on the east side (about 5 houses). The rest factories, character PURPLE to LIGHT BLUE, in map LIGHT BLUE.

{All north side out except small patch at east. West end, south side, goes.

Mills Court, between Curtain Rd and Charlotte St has 3 very poor, 2-st houses at the north end. The rest is factories, DARK BLUE as map.}

W along Rivington St and S down Garden Walk, composed of workshops and the Great Eastern Buildings on the west side, 6-st, and Derby Buildings on the east. Poor, respectable. 2 rooms for 6/- and 4 rooms for 9/-. Character PURPLE to LIGHT BLUE, not marked in map.

General remarks

Ryeland at first said he would rather not speak about the relations of police and publicans though he said "they are any how better now than they used to be". Later he complained of the great pressure put upon the police by publicans, also the pressure by the police on the police not to give up a lucrative source of revenue. Very little beer is now given and, as far as I could make out, money payments have taken its place. Improvement has also come by the recent practice of giving over to the steadiest man in the station the induction of new hands to their beats. Before it was chance whether a good or indifferent man did this, and "so much depends upon the beginning".

Betting is increasing, mostly in tobacco shops and barbers, a little in public houses. Also pitch and toss. Education in Ryeland's opinion had made good people better, but bad ones worse.

Short beats he favoured in preference to fixed points as less tiring for the man and enabling to get rid of talkers and would-be friends.

He said the practice of Building Section houses both for married and single was increasing. "You save a little money because rent is less, but there is always the chance of being routed up at any hour, and I'd rather not."

{News clipping: The landlord of the British Lion public-house, Shoreditch, was fined this week for supplying liquor to two constables on duty. Two constables were seen by an inspector standing outside the public-house, and the potman was observed to supply them with beer. Publicans have no business to supply constables on duty with liquor; but it was not clearly shown in this case whether the landlord was aware the men were on duty or not. It is a great temptation for a landlord to supply constables with beer, and, if they do not ask for a drink, we are pretty certain that the landlord would not offer. Any punishment which should follow should be inflicted on the constables, and not on the landlord.}

Walk 26   B352-15

Monday 23rd May 1898

George Duckworth with police constable W.R. Ryeland, Hoxton Subdivision of the G division of the Metropolitan Police (private address, 49 Ormsby St Shoreditch)

Starting at the junction of Holywell Row and Worship Street

Some dwelling houses at the east end, PINK as map, rest warehouses and factories. Worship St Police court here. W then N up Paul St. 4-st warehouses, mixed with small tailors, haircutters and grocers shops on the west side.

W along Hill St. North side, Waterlow warehouses, Johnsons Distillery and MacNamara's stables. On the south side are eight 3-st dwelling houses, poor, respectable, PURPLE to LIGHT BLUE, in map LIGHT BLUE. And at the back of them, 9 houses, Irish cockneys, tailors, "remnants of the old time when the tailoring trade was Irish and had not been absorbed by the Jews" said Ryeland. Windows broken and patched, noisy, rowdy, poor, DARK BLUE rather than LIGHT BLUE of map.

N up Tabernacle St, warehouses.

W into City Rd, then S to Finsbury Square. 4½-st houses used as residences and offices. Large, well-kept square in centre, used only by the residents. Should be converted into open space, much wanted here. Many German hotels. (Note that all hotels that have a bar and a full license are marked as a public house on the map. Seyds hotel at the southeast corner is much used for Jewish weddings and dances.

S along Finsbury Pavement, 4- and 5-st. Banks and offices on east side, shops on the west, RED as map.

S past Cross St, all warehouses. E along South Place, running north out of which is South Street, all hotels and offices "with a few policemen caretakers". E past Wilson St, warehouses. Along Eldon St, shops.

N up Finsbury Avenue, on the west side is Queens Square, only one inhabited house at the west end,. The north side as far as White Cross St is now covered by an extension of the NW Railways Goods station. Thus Horseshoe Alley. marked PURPLE in map, has disappeared. "Used to be a little 'Ell'" said Ryeland.

W along White Cross Place, flag paved. On the south side are model dwellings, on the north side a succession of small courts. "A rough criminal spot in the midst of most valuable property". "A dangerous place for policemen. On a Saturday night, about closing time, each man on the beat looks to his neighbour so that help may be at hand if needed" said Ryeland. He knows of 8 or 9 men from this street doing long terms now. The buildings on the south side are 5-st, and on a board was "One, two and 3 rooms from 3/6 to 7/6 per week." Inhabitants Irish cockneys. Character DARK BLUE lined BLACK rather than PURPLE of map. "Colour it the same as Wilmer Gardens." On the north side going east to west are Lees Buildings. Built 1829, ten 2-st houses, poor, flower pots on window ledges, children dirty, well fed. Railway porters living here. Character PURPLE as map. West of it is another court leading past a small cabinetmakers shop, called Bond's Court. One house, 3-st and attic, old, Irish cockney, windows broken and patched, rough, DARK BLUE lined, in map PURPLE. West of it again and divided from it by a wall only is Masham's Court. One house only, let out in single rooms, horse collar maker on the west side of passage leading to it. W again is Renous Court, 2-st houses on both east and west sides, 7 houses, criminal, "perhaps the worst of the lot". BLACK, in map LIGHT BLUE. Windows broken, dirty, all doors open, rough women, but clean, well-dressed children at one door. Awkward place to deal with, entered under arches from the north side of White Cross Place.

N up Clifton St, small shops on east side, habitation on west. This, and Sun St, is a centre for the saddlery and horseclothing trade. On the east side is a court. Brown's Buildings, 8 houses, 2-st, tenanted by butchers market porters, poor, quiet, birds at windows, looks respectable, LIGHT BLUE to PURPLE, in map LIGHT BLUE.

W along Earl St, the southeast end is taken up by an extension of Waterlows printing works, as is also the opposite side. N to Finsbury Market, now covered by Waterlows factory. "Great fuss when this was given over", used to be right of way through the middle, as the inhabitants have forgotten about it Waterlow put up gates, which for some time he kept open, now he shuts them and no one can walk through. Finsbury

Market was a good general market, Ryeland can remember going to it as a boy. Its day was Friday. The shops round are PINK rather than PURPLE of the map.

W along Market St, which is now carried right through into Appold St (late Long Alley). On the north side are Mary Ann Place, poor, quiet, 2-st, PURPLE as map, and east of it Johns Place. Houses both sides, better, PURPLE to PINK, not coloured in map. And then at the corner of Market St and Appold St, a block of good class buildings, 5-st, called Alabaster Buildings, PINK, not coloured in map. All this piece belongs to Mr Alabaster, JP, an active member of the Vestry who was himself in the act of collecting his rents as we passed. Mr A. is director of the firm of Battys Ginger Beer.

N up Appold Street, late Long Alley. No courts on the west side, but warehouses, coal sidings on the east. Across Worship St north, on the east side is Hearn Street, DARK BLUE in map, now only two dwelling houses left on the north side. Rough and DARK BLUE. Further west is a great waste space formerly occupied by Hearn's Soap and fat boilers. At the end of the street at the northeast corner are the warehouses of Osmond and Matthews, Italian Warehousemen. South side of Hearn St are coal wharves.

N up Curtain Rd and E along Hewett St, 3-st, poor, LIGHT BLUE as map at the west end south side, workshops further east. On the north side are 4-st buildings, respectable PURPLE rather than PINK of map, and at the extreme northeast are Hamilton Buildings, PINK, entered from Great Eastern St.

N up Curtain Rd, then SE down Great Eastern St under railway bridge, across George St (on the south side of Great Eastern St). At the east side, running nearly to Shoreditch are 5-st buildings, working class, like Gladstone and Derby Buildings in Garden Walk. PURPLE, not coloured in map.

S down Shoreditch past Plough Yard, on the west side, stabling and tent works.

S into Norton Folgate, cobble paved, fair class shops. City boundary. On west side are public houses of all kinds, small with green wooden pails of water outside on the pavement. The haunt of carmen, "good pull-ups" and large modern with grill room and luncheon room for the City man and clerk.

Note the encroachment of factories upon spaces formerly occupied by dwelling houses. 5- and 6-st model dwellings are with a few exceptions the only habitation of artisans in the district. These exceptions are a few courts in the neighbourhood of Sun St occupied by a rough criminal class. The sooner they are cleared away the better.

The trades of the district are saddlery, printing and a small amount of cabinetmaking and tailoring. In addition there is a vast amount of warehousing of all kinds.

As to the amount spent by working men in drink, Ryeland had no certain idea. He thought that a temperance man earning 25/- a week would give 23/- to his wife for general household expenses, and that a moderate drinker would give 20/-

The trade that drinks most, "there is not a shadow of doubt about it", are the French polishers. Ryeland was on duty during their strike last month. "They make 9d an hour and have regular work if they like. It was not about their money but about the refusal of one master to allow beer to be brought in to his works, that they struck." The strike is now at an end. New hands have been engaged, "but no foreigners".

All the furniture trade keeps Saint Monday and "work a ghost" on Friday night to make it possible. His two sons come home constantly of a Monday early, saying they are tired of being alone in the shop.

5
SHOREDITCH

Walk 27

B351-10

Tuesday 22nd March 1898
George Duckworth with Sergeant French

Starting at W end of Sclater Street

DARK BLUE in map and still DARK BLUE. Known in the locality as Club Row. 3- and 4-st houses, shops underneath, centre for bird fanciers, larks, thrushes, canaries, parrots, rabbits, etc, in cages. Small square cages wrapped up in pocket handkerchief, outside windows "for new birds to pick up the right note from their fellows". Long weavers windows in top storeys; no weavers now, nor prostitutes, simply rough class. "All thieves or receivers of stolen goods. They go out 'dipping' on Sunday morning, what we call larceny from the person" said French. At the corner of Brick Lane an elaborate stone shield in a red brick niche. 'This is Sclater St'. 1778.

S into St John St (late King St), not coloured on map. 3-st, rough, broken patched windows. Jews beginning to come in. Their first step into an otherwise typically rough English district, said French. It was almost possible to tell where the Jews were by the houses which had unbroken windows. LIGHT BLUE to DARK BLUE. Better at the corner turning into Sclater St, LIGHT BLUE to PURPLE, houses on the west side only.

E along Hare St, DARK BLUE as map. Some Jews, shops underneath, the rest rough, thieves.

S down 3 Colt Corner. BLACK in map, now DARK BLUE on west side only. The east side is a factory. It leads to a bridge across the Great Eastern Railway main line. To Pedley St, out of which on the south side is Brably St. 2-st, rather rough, poor, drunken, some Irish, but not so notoriously bad as Sclater St or Busby St. In map LIGHT BLUE, now LIGHT BLUE to DARK BLUE.

E along Pedley St. French knew no reason for the BLACK at the east corner, it looks like the rest, poor, rough, LIGHT BLUE to DARK BLUE. Into Weaver St. 2-st, narrow, only 15 ft between house and house, some Jews, others thieves. Poor. "Not so good as Underwood St, a different class altogether" said French. Underwood St is marked LIGHT BLUE in map. The west end past Fleet St is better than the rest and PURPLE as map, the rest being LIGHT BLUE to DARK BLUE. Fleet St, LIGHT BLUE to DARK BLUE, on map LIGHT BLUE. 2-st, a child here with only one shoe, all children very dirty.

N up New Church St, which looks rather better but French said was the same as Weaver St. Into Pedley St, some thieves and prostitutes from Boundary St area, cab yard. LIGHT BLUE to DARK BLUE. On the south side going west is Eckersley St, a paved 2-st passage. Jews, broken and patched windows. Run right through into Buxton Street, LIGHT BLUE to DARK BLUE, in map LIGHT BLUE.

Colliers' Court, west of it, stops short, does not run through as map. 2-st, 4-roomed houses, letting for 12/- a week, messy, LIGHT BLUE to DARK BLUE.

S down Code St. 6 new 3-st houses on west side. Jews, LIGHT BLUE to PURPLE, in map DARK BLUE. At the east side of the road is Whites Court. Eight 2 st houses, with weavers windows, looks poorer but is of the same class as Pedley St. Very messy, tap in court. DARK BLUE as map. Butlers' Buildings south of it, about 13, 2-st houses, Jews, children ragged but well fed. Shoe makers, messy. LIGHT BLUE to DARK BLUE, in map BLACK.

W along Buxton St. Rough. Across Brick Lane, on the north side is Sheba St, late Queen St. 4-st, Davis' Buildings, poor Jews. LIGHT BLUE to PURPLE. The west side of Sheba St to the east side of Wilkes St (late Hope St) are buildings put up by the Great Eastern Railway in which some of their employees live. PURPLE as map on east side, LIGHT BLUE to DARK BLUE on west side. 3-st houses, broken windows, rough.

W to the end of Grey Eagle St 1 house on the west side, on the east side 3-st, poor Jews, costers. LIGHT BLUE, furniture factory on west side. Just here Quaker St on the north side is rough. DARK BLUE, in map PURPLE.

E along Buxton St to Vallance Rd (late Bakers Row), N to Selby St. Broader street, more air, working English labourers, houses 2-st, 4 rooms, 12/- per week. Doors open, bare-armed women at doors, a few but very few windows broken and patched. PURPLE to LIGHT BLUE, in map PURPLE. Macadam road instead of the usual cobbles. Like it are Anglesey, Clarence and Artillery Streets and Nottingham St, now called Vallance Rd. All PURPLE to LIGHT BLUE, a few thieves, no prostitutes.

N up Vallance Rd into Winchester St. 2- and 3-st small shops, Great Eastern Railway building on south side. LIGHT BLUE to PURPLE as map. On the north side, not marked or coloured, is a small court. DARK BLUE on west side and LIGHT BLUE on east, rough. On the south side is Carlisle Street, a short street ending in the railway. No way through, G.E.R. stables on east side, 2-st houses on west side, PURPLE as map. The court west of it, in map DARK BLUE, also been swallowed up by G.E.R. stables. This court still exists, entered through wooden lattice gate. 8 houses (4 each side), LIGHT BLUE to DARK BLUE, in map DARK BLUE.

W along Hare St, DARK BLUE as map, by French's account, tho' it looks better. On the south side is Hare Marsh. Houses on the west side only, LIGHT BLUE rather than DARK BLUE of map.

N up Church Row. 2½- and 3-st. PURPLE to LIGHT BLUE. On map PURPLE on south end. W into Wood Row. PURPLE as map, S down Wood St. 2-, 3-, and 4-st, doors open, windows dirty, broken. PURPLE to LIGHT BLUE, on map PURPLE.

E past the south end of Hereford St, a court just on the north side not marked in map, just east of Hereford St called Hereford Buildings. 2-st, poor, weavers windows, ragged children, LIGHT BLUE. N up Hereford St, the south end of which is LIGHT BLUE rather than PURPLE of map. North end better, PURPLE, doors open, built 1844. E to Sale St, 2-st, not better than PURPLE, in map PINK. "All these streets are rather poor and a bit rough, some queer customers in all of them" said French. On the south side is Ramsey St. 3-st, messy, PURPLE in map PINK.

N up Tavistock St into Derbyshire St. 2-st, poor, in map LIGHT BLUE, worse east side than west, broken, patched windows. DARK BLUE east side, LIGHT BLUE west. Into Derbyshire St, PURPLE as map. 3- and 2-st. S down Abbey St. 2-st, mess, LIGHT BLUE between Derbyshire and Sale Streets on the east side. Very poor looking this bit, the rest PURPLE not PINK.

E to Vallance Rd, late Whites Row. 2-st, PURPLE rather than PINK of map. N into Bethnal Green Rd, on the west side is Granby Row. Marked BLACK in map, new houses, dwelling houses at east and west ends only, stables in middle and all along south side. Poor, not worse than LIGHT BLUE.

W along Busby St, into the DARK BLUE patch shown in map. No part of the triangle formed by Bethnal Green Rd on the north, Fullers Rd on the east, Sclater St on the south, is now PURPLE. All a rough class of costers, thieves, prostitutes, bird fanciers mixed with here and there a chair or cabinet factory. All a sporting set of men "who bear no ill-will to the police as long as we take them fairly". Streets look very rough, no Jews, yet much life in the street, several boys boxing with gloves on, only a few

Talk with Mr Reeve, manager of Truman, Hanbury and Buxton's Brewery at Brick Lane, 22nd October 1897

People generally drink more beer now than ever they did but the proportion of alcohol consumed is not any greater. Statistics of all countries show this, even in spirit-drinking countries, i.e. that the amount of alcohol consumed per head is a steady quantity. The beer brewed now is much lighter than the beer of former days. Men will have beer. Coal heavers and all who want a quantity of drink, don't care for water but on the other hand they don't want to get drunk, they are insisting more and more on light beer. Brewers are now recognising this demand. The great bulk of the beer drunk is 'Four Ale'. Those higher in the social scale who have extraordinary thirst to quench prefer something heavier. They drink less in quantity but as far as alcohol is concerned there is not much to choose between the two.

The profit on spirit is more than on beer but it is always the more important item. In not one per cent of their houses is a larger sum paid for spirit than for beer. In a fair house the payment to the brewers per month should be £50 for spirit and £100 for beer.

The price of houses has gone up enormously. Only yesterday a man came to him. A speculator who had bought three 'untied' Public Houses and had paid £300,000 for them. One of them being a good deal more valuable than either of the other two. There is a great deal of speculation. Men buy houses without any intention of keeping them, do them up, then resell them. They have thought for many years that top prices had been reached but they still moved upwards. (Noel Buxton said that at present prices they did just pay. The lowest price for a beer house in London would be £500. "But anything worth so little as that would not be worth it at all.")

With regard to the policies of licensing magistrates they have no policy. If you gradually increased the numbers of licensed houses, he did not think it would increase the amount of drunkenness or make people drink more but it would "give the rowdy ones greater opportunities, you would probably have more noise and cost of supervision would be greater". What you want is just to keep abreast of demand. If you stint it there will be a natural resort to illegal practises, if you give much greater latitude, you will be providing a greater number of places to which noisy fellows will be able to resort.

The system of putting in managers answers very well. The supervision is much greater. They have men constantly going round to see that their beer is not adulterated. Salaries of managers vary from 30/- per week to £500 a year in a very large house; the ordinary rate for a man working with the help of his wife and a potman is 50/- or 60/- per week. A bonus on profits is sometimes given. "All the police are paid or given drinks, with Inspectors it takes the form of a testimonial when they are leaving the district." It is more of a bribe to them to do their duty than to neglect it. A policeman will come at once when called if he gets something. He will keep loafers from the door, he will take less notice of a drunken man ("it may not be the publicans' fault that a man has been served"). It is a trade custom to tip him. Buxton said this payment went under the guise of service rendered in calling the publican in the morning.

Mr Reeve promised an introduction to a friend of his, the clerk to the Tower Hamlets Licensing Justices and also to some publicans, both managers and force men. Himself he has risen to the position of manager of the brewery from being an office boy in it. He is now about 60 years old and his father was a poor dissenting minister.

Trumans regularly use the map of London Poverty before buying any new house in London as a check on the would-be vendor's statements as to the character of the neighbourhood round his home.

(B348-6)

onlookers. The triangle lives together as a happy family. When any of them gets into trouble there is at once a whip around for money for bail or defence and it is always forecoming. A great part of the old Boundary St has come here but has not been bettered by its move in the same way as those in the Dellow St area. Most of it was DARK BLUE before. Now it is all DARK BLUE with some additional BLACK. Children all looked sturdy ruffians, well fed.

Fuller St as map, PURPLE to the north and BLACK on either side at the south end where are very rough buildings ("3 rooms 7/6"). Busby St, rough, criminal, the DARK BLUE should have a line of BLACK. Kerbela St, late Edward St, DARK BLUE, in map PURPLE. 3-st. Out of the southwest end is a court called Edwards Place. Not in map, very poor, very rough, like Dorset St. Five 3-st houses, BLACK.

N up Kerbela St, W along Granby St. 3- and 2-st, houses look better at northwest end but French gave them all the same character. S down Granby Court. 2-st, houses on the east side only. Weavers windows, DARK BLUE as map. Opposite the south end of it are two courts, Busby Square, 2-st, vicious, children all clean and with good boots, windows broken. DARK BLUE to BLACK, BLACK in map. Byders Buildings, four 2-st houses, DARK BLUE, in map BLACK. Into Bacon St. 3-st and 4-st buildings. Thieves, prostitutes, mess, ragged children, between Chilton St and Brick Lane, Bacon Street may be fairly coloured BLACK, in map DARK BLUE. Into Chilton St. No part worse than the other, all DARK BLUE. 3- and 4-st houses, the BLACK between Busby St and Bacon St on the east side has disappeared.

S into Hare St and W. Just before coming to Brick Lane is a small unnamed court of five 3-st houses. Rough, vicious, BLACK, not in map. Across Brick Lane. A very busy market here. Shops with stalls in front, strings of shoes and clothes over poles sticking out from shop walls across sidewalk, as in pictures of old London, much life and good humour. South under the railway bridge are more shops and restaurants, in one on the west side took place the Brick Lane tragedy of which French has charge. W along Sclater St, N up Cygnet St, late known Swan St, a great market for goats on Sunday.

W across Bethnal Green Rd and down Church St. 4-st, PINK in map, now DARK BLUE and BLACK. Some shops, thieves, prostitutes, "inhabitants from Old Nichols St have come here". S down Club Row, which gives its name to the whole of Sclater St locally, W into York Row. No dwelling houses till west of Chance St, then all BLACK. Thieves, etc, rough looking, in map PURPLE.

N up Chance Row, also BLACK, at the corner of which and York Row on the east side is a public house, The Blue Anchor. "The most noted thieves' resort in London", "we could but we do not often betake them there". Every Sunday they congregate here from all parts of London.

W along Church Rd. "The shops on either side are receivers", French pointed out, especially a fish shop on the south side and a furniture shop on the north. At the corner of Ebor St was a quiet sad-looking man with a grey moustache, black bowler hat, brown coat, dark trousers, good boots, well brushed and gentlemanly looking, "a well-known thieves' tutor".

Then S down Ebor St, all thieves. 3-st, BLACK rather than the PURPLE of the map. There is no court now (PURPLE in map) between Ebor St and Shoreditch on the south side of Church Rd.

General remarks

General worsement noticeable, owing apparently to rough immigrants from Whitechapel and other parts of Bethnal Green, especially the Boundary St area.

The Sclater St area is a remnant of Old London with ante Board School traditions and habits. French said the majority of them would not know how to write their own names. In this bit the change of locality has had no visible influence for the better on those who have moved. The men have not the wastrel good-for-nothing look of the loafers in Commercial St and the women more of the flower-girl roughness, feathers, horseplay, etc, than the absolute vicious degradation of the Dorset St inhabitant.

He again said that publicans did not now offer either drinks or money to constables. "They do not like us enough for that, we summon them too often." But I think it was only true for himself.

Walk 28   B351-11

Thursday 24th March 1898
George Duckworth with Sergeant French

Starting at the south end of Shoreditch

going NE along Boundary Passage, which opens into the end of Old Nichol St, costers, 3-st, LIGHT BLUE to DARK BLUE. N of it Hare Alley, a little worse, much ventilation, very poor, rough costers, DARK BLUE. N of it Jane Shore Court, houses empty, all coming down to make way for an extension of the London Music Hall. None of the above coloured in map.

N past Calvert St, the St Leonards Church Yard has been extended to the road and planted with shrubs, houses demolished, part of Boundary St improvement. On the south side are high, red-brick LCC, 5-st Buildings with shops underneath, tenanted by clerks and mechanics "whose work is in or near the city and have come in from outside districts as the opportunity of good house room offered", in character PINK. Calvert St has been carried east directly, ending in Mount St.

N round St Leonards Church into Austin St, 3-st wooden top storeys, old houses with weavers windows, shops, PURPLE to LIGHT BLUE. On the south side is Victoria Place, 3-st, costers, PURPLE to LIGHT BLUE.

S into Boundary St, on the west side of which near Calvert St is a block of old buildings, LCC, entered under arch, called Kossuth's Buildings, a colony of rough, poor Irish, ragged and dirty children, rough-looking women, LIGHT BLUE to DARK BLUE.

Great changes here owing to County Council Boundary Area Improvement Scheme. Blocks of dwelling houses have been built up with an elevated pyramidal garden as a common centre on the top of which a band plays in summer. These dwellings reach as far south as Half Nichols St, south of which on the east side is a Board School and more dwellings. The space between Half Nichols St on the north, Boundary St on the west, Old Nichols St on the south and the street behind Mount St i.e. Turnville St on the east, is not yet built upon.

S down Turnville St into Church Rd, turning N at Mount St, BLACK in map, now the LCC dwellings on the west side are PURPLE and the 3-st houses on the east side DARK BLUE rather than BLACK, a rough lot said French. Into Virginia Rd, DARK BLUE as map, 3-st, furniture makers, rough, thieves.

E to Brick Lane, 3- and 2-st houses, small shops, very rough, some of old Boundary

St have come here, thieves, prostitutes, bullies, windows broken, DARK BLUE to BLACK from Virginia Rd to Ducal St, between Ducal St and Princes St it improves and looks PURPLE as map on both sides of the road.

W into Boreham St, 2-st, French said rough but looks no worse than poor, "worse than what it used to be". A small boy with a couple of gross of match boxes done up in a blue cloth on his head, poor, LIGHT BLUE to DARK BLUE, in map LIGHT BLUE.

S into Peter St, 3-st, windows broken, DARK BLUE as map.

E along Shacklewell St, the south side of which is all Buildings, 4-st, LIGHT BLUE to PURPLE. The north side is 2-st, rough, poor, DARK BLUE as map. At the extreme east end the road turns sharply south then east with two 2-st, PURPLE houses on its north side, meeting the Bethnal Green Rd at Gibraltar Walk.

N up Gibraltar Walk, "the beginning of a hotbed of thieves". At the south end on the west side is a mission hall and a house with a good garden behind. "An old lady lived in it", now untenanted, little shops on the west side, in map PURPLE now DARK BLUE. W along Princes Court. Houses all down on the south side except 3 at the Brick Lane end. In map DARK BLUE, now BLACK. Thieves, prostitutes, bullies, mess in street, windows, bird cages and flower pots on window ledges, dirty ragged children, hatless, but all with boots and shoes, though holey ones.

N up Brick Lane, then E along Ducal St, on the north side, a rough spot, Albion Place (DARK BLUE in map), has been replaced by new workshops, the rest of the street DARK BLUE as map. N up Newling St, 2-st and attic. On the east side, new houses, on the west side, 2-st, in good repair, very rough, thieves and prostitutes. The Nichol gang have come into here and into Chambord St. Behind, DARK BLUE to BLACK, in map LIGHT BLUE. N to Gosset St, 2-st houses, and 4-st buildings, PURPLE in map, but now DARK BLUE. N up Princes Place, which has buildings on its east side only, DARK BLUE to BLACK, in map DARK BLUE. "Oh its a sweet place this" said French.

E along Virginia Rd then S down Chambord St, old 2-st houses on the east side, new buildings on west side of the same kind as in Newling St. Looks rougher than Newling St, more windows broken, women apronless, ragged, bird cages wrapped up in black stuff on window ledges, windows dirty and blinds and curtains holey. French gave it the same character as Newling St, DARK BLUE to BLACK.

Into Gilbraltar Walk, which is more respectable this end, PURPLE as map. E along Wellington Rd, which is PURPLE to PINK, in map PINK. S down Orange St, LIGHT BLUE in map but looks better now. 2-st houses, some windows broken but coloured china pots in others, "better than either Gosset St or Gibraltar Walk" said French. East side below Gosset St is coming down for a new Board School, and houses are untenanted. Now PURPLE. At the southeast corner is Orange Court, 4 houses, very poor, 2-st, one window piled with cardboard boxes, LIGHT BLUE to DARK BLUE, not marked in map. The end of Orange St is called Satchwell Rents, same character as rest. On west side is a court of 4 houses and cabinet factory and back entrance to northeast district post office, in map DARK BLUE, look LIGHT BLUE to DARK BLUE. Into Bethnal Green Rd and W, turning N at Gilbraltar Gardens, "another crib". A paved passage with 2-st houses on either side with small gardens in front, not coloured in map until the north end is reached, should be DARK BLUE to BLACK, the north end turns to the right (i.e. eastwards). 3 tall 3-st houses, cul-de-sac, a blank factory wall on the north side, mess, windows dirty and broken, one filled with coloured air balls, this bit looks worse and is BLACK as map. There is a passage at the west end into Gibralter Walk, "used by thieves to escape by after snatching watches in the main road".

Back into the Bethnal Green Rd and N up Turin St, rough working class, bricklayers etc not skilled mechanics, rather better than the side streets off it but not more than PURPLE, in map PINK. On the southwest side is Thorold Passage, newish 3-st houses, formerly Thorold St, now runs right through into Gibraltar Walk. Rough, mixed class, thieves, a few decent, but "like Bacon St, of the same order if not quite so bad", nearly all doors open, windows broken and patched, is a broad flagged passage, DARK BLUE, in map PURPLE. On the east side of Turin St is Tyrell St, 2-st, used to be better than it is, but rough now, like Thorold Passage though it looks quieter, windows broken, messy, LIGHT BLUE to DARK BLUE, in map LIGHT BLUE. Dirty ragged children. North of it, on the west side of Turin St is Satchwell St, LIGHT BLUE to PURPLE, 2- and 3-st, narrow. Some windows broken, as map LIGHT BLUE. North of it New Tysson St, 3- and 2-st, LIGHT BLUE as map, bread about. There is a turning on the north side called Rapely St, leading to Daniel St, workshops of sideboard, dining table and cabinet manufacturers. Daniel St, rather better on the east than on the west side, but dirty broken windows, "same as the others", LIGHT BLUE as map.

On the east side of Turin St are Charlotte St, 36 houses, cul-de-sac, 2-st, street 21ft broad, quieter but poor, LIGHT BLUE as map. Cymon St, 2-st, poor, LIGHT BLUE not PINK as map though at southwest end one or 2 houses have china flower pots, one of the badges of PINKness. N into Gosset St, 2-st, PURPLE as map here. N up Delta St, LIGHT BLUE as map (late Cross St) to Wellington Row, PURPLE to PINK, in map PINK, 2-st.

E then S down Barnet Grove, late Harts Lane, more respectable than Wellington Row. Mechanics, PINK to PURPLE, in map PURPLE. On the east side Brady's Buildings, 11 houses, 2-st, 4 rooms 10/6, PINK to PURPLE, not coloured in map.

E along Gosset St to Squirries St, 2- and 3-st, not so good as Barnet Grove, PURPLE as map. Running out of it on the west side is Florida St, 2-st, PURPLE rather than LIGHT BLUE of map. Robert St, poorer, LIGHT BLUE as map, 2-st. Ivimey St, 2-st, PURPLE, in map LIGHT BLUE.

N up Warner Place, 2-st, respectable, quiet, china pots, clean steps, curtains, windows, PINK as map. Into Hackney Rd turning S into Ion Square. Well kept square, should be PINK but "a bad lot here", prostitutes, windows broken, 2-st houses, LIGHT BLUE lined BLACK, in map LIGHT BLUE. "They tried to improve it by doing up the square, putting in benches but nothing has come of it".

Then SW down Columbia Rd, late Bird Cage Walk, Guiness Trust Buildings, 1892, 6-st on south side, LIGHT BLUE, because they will only take the very poor. Windows clean, look well kept. "Policemen here tried to lodge there but they will not have them, say they are too well off."

E along Baxendale St, respectable, 2-st, PURPLE not LIGHT BLUE. Durant St, rather better, PINK as map. W along Winbolt St, 2-st, like Baxendale St, PURPLE not LIGHT BLUE. S down Barnet Grove, PINK as map, W along Quilter St, 2- st, 6-roomed, 14/-, PURPLE to PINK and Elwin St, like it, PURPLE to PINK.

General remarks

The Boundary St area is better because the old class has left and a new more respectable one has come in. But the streets immediately east of it are worse than they used to be. French said that all between Virginia Rd on the north, Chambord St and Gibraltar Walk on the east, Bethnal Green Rd on the south and Brick Lane on the west, were in character DARK BLUE and BLACK. Much of this was DARK BLUE before but it is worse now by reason of the immigration of the worst characters from Boundary St. "Thieves, prostitutes and bullies, especially thieves". Here and there parties of 3 to 6 lads gossiping. French called them Bethnal Green 'nibs' and said they were all thieves.

No Jews have their foot as yet in this district. "They would not dare to, they would be so roughly handled." Columbia Rd in spring and summer is one of the great flower markets of London. Flowers even now conspicuous in windows of poor streets.

The Commercial St subdivision has 100 men all told of whom 10 are sergeants and 5 inspectors. French said the difference between the duties of a policeman here and in the West End was that here they had to deal with a rough class and little property or traffic, whereas in the West End there was much traffic, much property and a quiet set of people.

The main industry of the district is cabinet making and the scream of the circular saw takes the place of the whir of the Jewish sewing machine. Legs of tables, unfinished chair backs etc, in evidence. Of the poorest classes, the men and boys are costers, flower sellers in Columbia Rd, and hawkers and the women cardboard box-makers.

Walk 29   B351-12

Saturday 26th March 1898
George Duckworth with Sergeant French

Starting at the southwest corner along Austin Street

3-st, mixed, some houses very rough, others well-to-do, shops, on the whole PURPLE as map. On the north side at the angle made by Austin St and Virginia Rd is Sweet Apple Court, 8 houses, 2-st, cement pavement, houses new, rather poor and some rough, houses on east side only. It looks PURPLE to LIGHT BLUE, in map LIGHT BLUE. The west side is taken up by the Mildmay Hospital as is also the court marked in map DARK BLUE to the west of it. Further east is Bakers Court, four 3-st houses, DARK BLUE as map, mangle in one house, a pile of small tot horses and carts at the far end, a 'gun' at one house talking to 2 youths, i.e. a "flash pick-pocket", long black coat and bowler hat.

N up Gasgoigne Place, newish, 3-st houses on the east side, PURPLE, in map LIGHT BLUE. On the west side is a turning with rough houses, "extreme depravity, all brothels" said French. Houses belong to Geringer of Great Pearl St notoriety, called Margeret Place. Houses 3- and 2-st, doors open, broken windows and general bareness and dirtiness, dirty and very ragged children, on the north side is a depot for piano organs.

W along Coopers Gardens, new houses on south side only, north side are workshops, 2-st, concrete paved, poor, some rough, LIGHT BLUE to DARK BLUE, in map PURPLE. At the east end are older houses (1837) and the Coopers Gardens Technical Schools (Baroness Burdett Coutts). N into Victoria St, the houses on the east side going north are poorer then the rest, DARK BLUE as map, Victoria St is like Coopers Gardens, houses south side only, LIGHT BLUE as map.

N up Hackney Rd, on the east side are Bakers Rents, 2-st, poor, not marked in map, LIGHT BLUE, houses on west side only, a better class living on the ground floor than upstairs. E along Columbia Rd, on the south side of which are Leopold Buildings, 5-st PURPLE to PINK, very respectable, a better class than live in the Burdett Coutts Columbia Buildings.

S down Brick Lane. Not shown on map the north end of Brick Lane has been continued right away to the Columbia Rd, 3-st, cabinetmakers living above their shops, PURPLE to PINK. A court behind the present Brick Lane and Gascoigne Place called Ewans Yard, has only cabinetmakers workshops.

E along Virginia Rd between Brick Lane and Fountain St is Inkhorn Yard, only workshops. N up Fountain St, no turnings now on either side of it, workshops upon west side, PURPLE on east.

On the north side of Columbia Rd is Columbia Square, blocks of Burdett Coutts 5-st

With Noel Buxton to see 3 of their managers in Red Lion Street, Holborn, Clerkenwell, corner of Chapel St and Liverpool Rd in Islington, 22nd October 1897

The first had been in the place a year. He is now doing a business of £50-60 a month (13 month to a year). Before he took it, the house only did £42 and was very rough in character. He determined to get rid of the rough ones. Refused to sell to noisy customers. Got the policemen on his side. Gives him about 6d per week so that he should always be there when wanted and more important than that should clear the neighbourhood of his door of hungers and rough characters.

He now does a good spirit trade. Two thirds spirit to one of beer. Gets the 'legal gentlemen' from the Sheriffs Court and Bedford Row close by. Opens at 6AM with hot coffee and rum for workmen. 1/2d of coffee and 3 halfpennyworth of rum is the usual thing. Closes at 12.15 because the neighbourhood is deserted by midnight. Has one joint a day from which he serves himself and wife and 5 or 6 dinners. "I started this because it certainly increased my custom." Wife, potman, himself and one servant is the household.

Cellar below with beer and wine. Tubes running up from the casks to the beer machines above. Four bars upstairs, one generally taken by women, one salon bar, one bar that ranks socially with the women's bar as a convenience for those who don't want to meet one another and one public bar. Does not sell many sandwiches or pies, except at dinner time.

Has to drink with customers but has a concoction of tea to look like rum. "You could not possibly stand it if you drank spirits every time you drink with your customers."

Talk with Mr Clews in Clerkenwell

A great neighbourhood for women's drinking. Women take rum in cold weather and gin in hot. Dogs nose they also drink which is a compound of beer and gin. Won't have any noise in the house, it drives away trade. Gives the policeman on the beat a pot of ale about twice a week. Gives no money. Knows some who give nothing at all but not many. Just as well to be on the right side of the policeman because then he comes at once if he is wanted. Has been 5 years in the house. His father was a publican. Great thing to have a reputation for turning people out if they make a noise. His is one of the "women's houses" of Clerkenwell.

Coloured tiles at entry of the house, bars opening out of a long passage. This is the usual system in all newly-modelled pubs.

He complained of the amount he had to drink with his customers.

October 23

Talk with Mr [———————] , manager of the public house at the corner of Chapel St and Liverpool Rd. Has been a publican 20 years.

Chapel St is one of the cheapest market streets in London. "The second after Chrisp St in Poplar, so they say." Great many women turn in to the shop after marketing. Also many prostitutes come in here. "Crowds of them in the neighbourhood." Women's drinking on the increase. Thinks grocers' licences have much to answer for. Women put down spirits as tea. Men if anything drink rather less. Friday night very busy as well as Bank Holidays.

Gives 2/- a week regularly to the policeman. "It's a trade custom, everyone does, so I do." Says they (police) divide it up among themselves. He gives to one only. Police won't come at once if wanted unless they are given something, they can make themselves very disagreeable if they like. Thinks their services cheap at 2/- per week. About twice a month he calls them in to turn out drunkards. "It's too dangerous to give them drinks. You can only do that in the back streets, there it is usually done."

House depends for its main trade on a regular nucleus of customers but not so much as the two preceding ones. 'Casuals', i.e. passengers, come in here but every house has its regular set of customers, even if it does a large casual trade as well.

He employs two men and a potman besides himself. Bars ranged all round a hollow in which the barmen stand. Payments all put into a slot and change taken from a little wooden box with one side open and a row of trays with change. The sum in this box at one time should always be £5.10.0. The salon and private bars here would look straight across to the public bars if it were not for small revolving windows put to screen them off.

Does not like women as barmaids, "but you must have them where you have a 'city trade'". Says they are slower in serving and dawdle talking too much.

Thinks that children do sip a good deal when they come for beer. Is not allowed not to give sweets. "One of these Commissions decided it was illegitimate trade."

(B348-7)

dwellings, not better than PURPLE, in map PINK. On the southeast end of Hassard St is a large block of Waterlow Dwellings still building.

W through the Columbia Market, imposing, elaborate but empty, the shops round the inside of the market are used by a few cabinetmakers, costers won't come there. The coal market on the north side has likewise failed and been made into a swimming bath. S along Angela Gardens, roofed in and called a Potato Market, 2 men and a pile of potato sacks, "there's never been more business doing than you see today", said French.

W to a bare piece of waste ground called the 'Triangle', N into Crescent Place, which has two turnings west into Hackney Rd, 2-st, all alike, road in very bad repair, some books and china pots in windows, PINK in map but only just PINK, the northern most turning not quite so good and rather PURPLE.

E along Baroness Rd, late Westminster St, 3-st houses, tenanted by what French called a "booze up o' Saturday night class". PURPLE rather than PINK of map.

N up Diss St, 2-st, "You may mark this BLACK". But it is not so bad as Chambord St, he said, in map LIGHT BLUE, it looks more DARK BLUE, rough Irish, some prostitutes, but a working class. On the south side is Smith's Place, BLACK in map, 2-st, very poor, not worse than DARK BLUE, wooden wash hand stands standing out in the court, half made.

E along Willow Walk, narrow, windows dirty, broken, some prostitutes, coster class, a good deal of window mending done with brown paper, DARK BLUE to BLACK, in map LIGHT BLUE.

Across Diss St and E along Kings Place, 6 houses, 2-st, rough, DARK BLUE, in map LIGHT BLUE. The west end was blocked by firemen and engines, a warehouse being alight or just put out, no excitement but a crowd of children all well though poorly dressed. Up Diss St into Hackney Rd and S down Hassard Street, 2-st, Character PURPLE to PINK, in map PINK. W along Arline St, late Queen St, 2-st, thieves, windows broken, LIGHT BLUE to DARK BLUE, in map LIGHT BLUE, and N up Chapel St, 2-st, the same LIGHT BLUE to DARK BLUE. All these streets are troublesome to the police.

Across Hassard St and through Hassard Place to Ravenscroft St, 2-st, working class, mixed, PURPLE rather than PINK of map. Unfinished Waterlow Buildings at the southwest end.

E into a block of streets which are poor and always have been poor. Labourers of all kinds, all 2-st houses, litter of paper in the streets, such are Shipton St, LIGHT BLUE to DARK BLUE, Cadell St, narrow, LIGHT BLUE, Henrietta St, broader and therefore looks brighter, LIGHT BLUE, Nelson Place out of it on the east side, 16 houses, very poor and mixed, 2-st, LIGHT BLUE to DARK BLUE. Horatio St, LIGHT BLUE to PURPLE. Providence Yard, all cabinetmakers shops, cement paved (it is at the northwest end of Ezra St). S of Shipton St is Ezra St, late James St, 2-st, LIGHT BLUE to PURPLE and on the north side, Bath Grove, late Bull Court, 24 2-st houses, very badly paved roads, LIGHT BLUE as map, and Ropely St, LIGHT BLUE as map.

This is all a working class district. The west end round Diss St rather rougher than it was though nothing so bad as Chambord St. The rest is poor, by the look of the streets, always has been poor and always will be while the present houses stand.

The industries: cabinetmakers and costers. As to women's drink, French said he was sure it had increased but could give no reason for it except that it was no longer a shame to them to be seen entering a public house. He was equally sure that drinking among men had decreased.

Walk 30   B352-12

Tuesday 17th May 1898
George Duckworth with PC W.R. Ryeland

Starting at St George's Square out of the west side of Hoxton High Street

nearly opposite the Hoxton lunatic asylum. A messy square surrounded on north, west and south side by 4-st buildings, poor, rowdy, much trouble to police, haunt of Sunday gamblers who escape up the open staircases. Windows broken and patched, a few exceptions with tidy blinds, curtains, flower etc but the whole "worse than poor, compares with the worst end of Laburnum St." Is becoming worse, much bread lying about. DARK BLUE rather than LIGHT BLUE of map. On the south side is a passage called Mores Buildings, all cabinetmakers, shops, small men.

Grove Walk leads from St George's Square to Mundy St at the Hoxton St end of which on the north side are 5-st buildings called Stanley Houses, rather rough.

W into Hoxton Square, almost entirely given over to cabinet workers. The only living houses here are a Roman Catholic priory and an Anglican parsonage. At the northwest end is Austin's String factory. "Employs over 100 boys and is more like a father to them than an employer." All round are chair and couch frame makers, manufacturing upholsterers. One man calls himself a maker of 'Fancy tables, spittoons and footstools', others are marble workers, chair makers, spring makers, brook gilders and veneer cutters. The road atrociously paved, the reason being that neither the parish nor the trustees of the property wish to have the expense, "They are waiting for some accident which shall bring the whole question of jurisdiction before the courts." Ryeland said that the square belonged by special Act of Parliament to a body of trustees who liked to keep it for themselves. The parish on its own authority demolished some gates at the south end and repaved the street, saying that if the trustees would hand over the square to them they would maintain both it and the road as an open space. This the trustees (who are chosen from the surrounding houses) refused, well knowing it would mean a rise in rates but they added "You have pulled down our gates and repaved some of the road, you or no one shall repave the whole square". There the matter rests. A few houses at the southeast end of Hoxton Square, running into Hoxton High St, are poorer than the rest, PURPLE as map. The rest of Hoxton Square should be PINK (if coloured at all). S down Rufus St, all factories, in map LIGHT BLUE. The DARK BLUE spot between Rufus St and Coronet St is now all factories also.

N up Coronet St, 3-st, poor, houses west side only, the east side is all factories, rather noisy, LIGHT BLUE to DARK BLUE, in map LIGHT BLUE. The north end is taken up by the parish dust destructor, ligend, expulvere luxet vis, baths, Christian Institute. S into Hoxton Market. "Six years ago no policeman would have dared walk down it alone." 4-st buildings both on east and west sides. That on the east side was tenanted by a band of 'squatters' who would pay no rent, turned out by police, as was nearly the whole street. "Where they went, I don't know" said Ryeland. A better class is in now. A common lodging house is at the southeast corner. 'Is better than Laburnum St", now LIGHT BLUE rather than the BLACK of the map. The feelings of this neighbourhood were much touched in the hard winter of 1895 when police opened a subscription among themselves and themselves distributed the bread and soup tickets to the poor, whether notorious characters or not.

W along Boot Street {NB. the street immediately W of it is Charles St. and on the map reads 'Charles Boot St.'} "very shady quarter". Jubilee Chambers on the south side behind public house, the known resort of criminals and BLACK, rough, noisy, the whole DARK BLUE lined rather than DARK BLUE.

N up Pitfield St, market and shopping street, busy. E along Boot St into a court on the north side leading through into the west side of Hoxton Square, tenanted by small men, barrow makers, cabinetmakers and horse collar makers, LIGHT BLUE rather than DARK BLUE of map.

N up Pitfield St past Coronet St, only 3 habitations on the north side and workshops on the south side. E down Bowling Green Walk. South side taken up by the electric light works and the northwest end houses down. N up Foundry Walk (at the extreme east end of Bowling Green Walk) poor, quiet, flowers, 2-st, LIGHT BLUE as map. Like it are Royal Oak Walk, 2-st, narrow, flagged, Foundry Row, Foundry Place and Royal Oak Place. This last is the best and PURPLE rather than LIGHT BLUE. All poor, quiet, clean, "very old tenants", one old woman who thought we were about demolitions said she had been there 26 years, another had been in the same house 36 years. This is difficult of access and might have been a BLACK spot, but it is not.

N up Pitfield St and E along Ashford St, 3-st, 3 families to a house, 8 rooms and washhouse, no poor, clean blinds and windows, better than it used to be. On the Haberdashers' Co.'s Estates. Rents lately have fallen in, houses done up, rents raised and a better class have come in. Character PURPLE to PINK, in map PURPLE. N into

Aske St, 3-st, "all the north side have been let to new tenants in the last 12 months". Inhabitants employed in the City. Great demand for the houses, "All let before they were finished repairing." Same class as those living in Forston St and Napier St, better than Huntingdon St. At the east end are the Enfield Buildings, 6-st same class as the street. Fanshaw St, 2- and 5-st, like the rest, PURPLE to PINK. "The old tenants went further out." House taken by one family at 17/- and sublet, children, well booted, hatted, fed, with clean faces and pinafores.

N up St John's Rd and E along Pimlico Walk, 2-st, small shops, great thoroughfare for pedestrians, PURPLE as map except at east end opposite Kings North Place where it is LIGHT BLUE, 1-st. Kings North Place on the south side is 2-st, asphalted, rough, poor, rather noisy, LIGHT BLUE to DARK BLUE, in map DARK BLUE.

N into Britannia Gardens, rough poor, "belongs to Mrs Lane the proprietress of the Britannia Theatre", used to be recreation gardens behind the Theatre, now tenanted by a rough coster set, not criminal, piles of old packing cases, barrows and hens in the roadway, one barefoot child, DARK BLUE as map.

N into Myrtle St 3- and 3½-st, mixed, no criminals, "not so good as either Aske or Fanshaw Streets". PURPLE as map.

W across Pitfield St to Bevenden St, 3- and 2-st with basement, built 1802. Haberdashers' estate improvement, new set of tenants within the last 2 years, south side rather better than the north side, which, towards its west end has one or two mixed houses. Character, south side PINK, north PINK to PURPLE, in map both are PURPLE.

S of it is Haberdasher St, 3-st and basement, good, quiet, PINK, china pots in front windows, clean unbroken windows, white doorsteps, curtains good, all doors shut, PINK rather than the PURPLE of the map. S down Singleton St, only one house on west side, should be PINK both sides. Into Buttesland St, poorer than the foregoing but better than LIGHT BLUE of map, 3-st, mixed. Where the leases have fallen in the houses have been done up and a better class of tenants has come in. S into Great Chart St, 3½-st, "like Haberdasher St", PINK as map.

S down East Rd and E along Styman St, 2-st, poorer, all children booted, clean and well fed, factories on north side at the Bache's St end, character LIGHT BLUE to PURPLE, in map LIGHT BLUE, is poorer than Buttesland St.

S down Bache's St, only a few dwelling houses at the northeast end left, the rest have been replaced by large factories, PURPLE as map.

W along Craven St, the whole of the north side has been replaced by stables belonging to G. Patten, contractor. The south side is still rough and poor, 3-st, some prostitutes living here. There have been complaints of two houses on the east side of the turning into Brunswick Place being used as brothels.

E along Brunswick Place, 3- and 3½-st, shops on north side, dwellings on south and also a Board School, PINK as map. Into Charles Square, an old square, red-tiled

housetops, carved stone tablet let into house at southeast corner bears date 1771. John Newton the hymn-writer lived on the north side, square opened as a public space on Saturday last and full of children. German club at northeast corner, used to be a public house, shut by the police. Ryeland said the Germans who went there kept late hours, were noisy and did not live in the neighbourhood. Old sign of man and dog, coloured figures above doorway. Leverington Place out of the north side, poor, quiet, 2-st, 3 houses only, LIGHT BLUE to DARK BLUE, not coloured in map, children with holey shoes.

S along the east side of Charles Square and E along Charles St into Pitfield St. Charles St is poorer here, PURPLE rather than PINK of map. On south side of road is a turning through a swing door to four 2-st houses, poor, quiet, rent 7/-, LIGHT BLUE, not marked in map.

S down Pitfield St. W along Old St and N into the block of streets known as the Vinegar Ground, being behind Sarsons and Champions Vinegar factories, a rough block, but "better than it used to be". Must have been some mistake in map as it is marked PINK. The easternmost street of this block is Henson St, houses on west side only, factories on east, poor, mixed, PURPLE to LIGHT BLUE, Catherine St further west is a little better, PURPLE to LIGHT BLUE, Wilson St the same. Vincent St the same. Henrietta St and Staff St the same.

The north side of Catherine St is PINK, held by Champion men, "Bought by

Night spent at the Great Eastern Hotel. Proprietors Truman, Hanbury and Buxton the Brewers. Manager Mr Salter
25th March 1989

The Great Eastern Hotel is one of the largest public houses in the East End,. situated at the junction of East and West India Dock Roads. The Brewers bought it for (I think) £60,000. I had arranged to pass a night there with Noel Buxton but at the last moment he was prevented and I went alone.

Mr Salter the manager is a middle-sized puffy man of about 45 years who looks as if he drank too much. His wife is well dressed, capable looking and clean and much of the business management of the house must devolve upon her. Both she and his daughter (aged about 18-20) serve behind the saloon bar and one or the other of these three is always in the house. The house itself is 4-st and an attic. High, ugly. On the ground floor is the public house. On the first floor, lunching and dining rooms and on the second floor is the Billiard Room and banqueting rooms, on the third, bedrooms.

The public house does a large 'passing' trade with those on their way to and from the Docks. The Luncheon Room is used by petty officers, captains, agents and clerks and the bedrooms by ships captains.

{News clipping titled 'Public House Profits – Six Hundred Per Cent', cut from the Daily Chronicle, 9th May 1898}

The actual arrangement of the ground floor is as follows. In front is the 'four-ale' bar with two entrances. The bar itself juts out as a wedge into this bar and round it are ranged the other bars. Next, below the public bar is the women's bar. This finishes the front part of the house.

Leading from the back of the serving bar is a door through to the saloon bar which is quite apart from the front of the house. They serve in the front bars, two men helped now and then by Mr Salter. Barmaids (two maids and Miss Salter) helped by Mr Salter and occasionally by Mrs Salter.

In the Public Bar, men only are allowed. There are no seats. Near the window an empty barrel turned on end and used as a table. In the Women's Bar, glasses only and I think 'Special' whiskey only are served and no 'four-ale'.

The serving bar runs round inside the other bars and the counters are broken by the handles of beer pumps, or, inside on a level with the top of them, by taps for spirits. The fittings behind are all of zinc. The spirits fall by gravitation from barrels placed on a stage in the centre and at the back of the bar. These barrels are replenished by a pump to the spirit cellar below.

The front part of the house does a 'rough' trade. Sailors, prostitutes, dock labourers. No employer or tradesman would think of going to the public bar. But though the customers were rough, at no time was there much noise. As soon as voices were raised and the language became audible it was repressed. On the whole I was surprised at small amount of bad language, even when I listened for it. No children came to the bars. The jugs are served in a separate compartment at the back of the Saloon Bar.

This was a Friday night, very cold. Cutting northeast wind. The house was never full "Because it is so cold" said Mr Salter, "people will not leave their firesides after supper."

At closing time 12.30, there were 421 persons in the 'front', men and women, about 10 women, of the lowest class from Gill St opposite. The clock was placed 8 minutes on and so marked closing time before the hour. But the 53 gas jets were gradually put out between 12.18 and 12.30 and women and men finally made up their minds to quarters, put in small glass bottles, of gin and brandy to take away with them. No one was drunk. The women were treated by the men. At 12.30 the house was empty and the doors shut. Then began the washing and cleaning up for the morning.

At the back of the house there was a succession of tradesmen who looked in to say a word or two to Mr Salter and have a glass of 'bitter' or brandy and hot water. Three or 4 young men began horse play with one another and were nearly turned out in consequence. At one moment there was more row in the Saloon Bar than at any time of the evening in the front bars.

Upstairs there was a smoking concert of the employees of the Gaslight and Coke Company, their first, a very poor affair, presided over by a foreman. Patriotic songs of the bull dog pluck of Old England met with more favour than the rest, but no enthusiasm. About 50 men present, all gas workers, clean hands, collars, faces, greased hair, black coats for the occasion, all looking and feeling very uncomfortable.

The house opens at 5 in the morning. They professed to have forgotten to call me and I did not wake till 5.45. Getting light, the streets fairly full of men and boys going to work, very cold, comforters round necks, red noses, blue cheeks, hands in pockets. Streets fuller and pace quicker as the hands of the clock drew nearer 6. Downstairs very few people. "No one waiting for the doors to open this morning, it was too cold" said the barman. He refused to serve me hot coffee saying it was too bad in quality. Hardly anyone drank it even with rum (rum and coffee 2d). Four-ale in 'Bowlers' i.e. large glasses which hold nearly a pint but are charged as ½ pints in the public bar 'to encourage trade', rum and milk, and rum with hot and cold water were the drinks most in demand. Custom came and went. A few 'regulars' stayed 10 to 15 minutes, but most drank their glass, paid and went out again without a word except to name their drink. About 6.20 two women came in. One with four half-crowns in her hand, unfortunates, one Irish. The one with the money treated the rest both men and women. Very little conversation, the night and cold had pinched it out of them. The barman said it would not get busier till 8 when there was some demand for supper from those coming off night shifts and breakfast for those on day work. I went to bed again.

{Later in the day there is a good demand, except on Saturdays, for luncheons. Mr Salter calculates on serving 40 per day upstairs, ships captains, mates, officers etc. Saturday though quietest for lunch, is the busiest day for beer. He sells more moneys worth of spirits than of beer. His trade consists of a small regular nucleus and a large 'passing' trade.

He pays 5/- per month to each of 3 policemen, the night beat, day beat and fixed point. The fixed point is immediately outside his door.

At midday there is a brisk demand for bread and cheese. Trade is falling, Fewer ships etc. The best customers are German sailors, "they spend their money very freely but they are the roughest set of customers we have". A ship load has just gone. Mr Salter does not know whether to be glad or sorry.

As to the prostitutes "they will come and they do bring custom" but he thinks there are fewer of them than there used to be.}

(B352-3)

Champion to prevent Sarson from extending his factory." The south side of the road has been used for the extension of Champion's own factory.

The south end of all these streets is taken by 5-st buildings "a den of thieves and prostitutes". Vicious, assaults on police, "like Wilmer Gardens". I think the southern ends should all be DARK BLUE lined BLACK and the northern ends LIGHT BLUE rather than PINK. The north side of the west end of Catherine St alone remains PINK.

General remarks

Note the great betterment of Hoxton Market and of the Haberdasher Estate. The nearness to tramlines and buses makes the latter most suitable for those employed in the City. Hence when houses were done up and rents raised a new class came in and the "houses were let even before they were ready for habitation". Note also the extension of warehouses and factories which must have displaced large numbers of the population.

As to children fetching beer, Ryeland holds it in horror. It's not the profanity of the language used in the public house as the beastliness of it that he thinks so bad for the children. Thinks that if the women had to go themselves, some would go and stay but that more would go without to save themselves the trouble.

Walk 31

B352-13

Thursday 19th May 1898
George Duckworth with W. Ryeland

Starting at Pitmans Yard

which is south of the Police Station, on the west side of Kingsland Rd.

Old houses, 2-st and attic, a colony of watercress sellers, drunken, noisy, DARK BLUE as map. S along a passage into Eliza Place. 2-st, 2 rooms and washhouse, poor, respectable, clean, LIGHT BLUE to PURPLE, in map LIGHT BLUE. N up Sarah St, asphalted, 2-st, quiet, clean, change for the better, character LIGHT BLUE to PURPLE, in map LIGHT BLUE. Some cress sellers here.

S to Drysdale St, out of which on the south side is Dudley's Folly. 2-st, rent 6/- for 2 rooms and washhouse, very poor and dingy but fairly quiet, LIGHT BLUE to DARK BLUE, in map DARK BLUE. Along Drysdale St, the Kingsland Rd end and west as far as the public house at the corner of Drysdale Place is respectable. Men employed in the cabinet trade and sawmills on the south side of the street. But past the public house and west of Drysdale Place is a very rough set of 3-st houses on the south side, let in 1-roomed tenements. Drunken, "especially the women". Windows broken, patched, "like Wilmer Gardens", DARK BLUE lined BLACK rather than LIGHT BLUE of map.

N up Drysdale Place, 2-st. Built 1829 (old name Susannah Row), poor, all doors shut, window ledges and steps whitened, clean, flowers in windows. 8/- for 4 rooms and washhouse, LIGHT BLUE to PURPLE, in map LIGHT BLUE. The turning west of Dudley's Folly, out of the south side of Drysdale St is now all workshops (in map LIGHT BLUE). Houses burnt down 4 years ago and replaced by shops.

N up Hoxton High St and E to Hoxton Place. 7 houses on west side only, on the south side of the passage leading to it is the Municipal Soup Kitchen (the only one in London ?) opened 3 years ago. LIGHT BLUE, not coloured in map.

N of Hoxton Place is Windsor Place. 2-st, poor, respectable, front gardens, 3 rooms and washhouse, 6/6, old inhabitants, a great thoroughfare for policemen to and from their beats, LIGHT BLUE as map.

N up the High St. On the east side nearly opposite Pinlies Walk, is Henry's Place, DARK BLUE in map and still DARK BLUE. Drunken, criminal, rough, poor, a slum. One barefooted, ragged, dirty child. "A warm shop for policemen."

N again and E along White Hart Court into Wellington Street, 2-st, poor. "Some of the gambling fraternity live here" i.e. bookmakers touts. LIGHT BLUE as map.

N then E into Red Lion St. Houses on north side, Board School on south. Poor, noisy at times, asphalt paved, a poor women singing hymns, walking down the middle, begging. LIGHT BLUE as map. At the west end is a large showcard and box factory. Running north out of the west end are 6 houses with small front gardens, 2-st, children booted, well fed, rather dirty, LIGHT BLUE as map.

N and E along Huntingdon St, looks PINK at the east end and PURPLE to PINK at the west. E across Kingsland Rd and along Harwar St. S into Caesar St, 2-st, 6-roomed houses, let to two families, on the Long Estate. Whitish hard brick, asphalt paved, clean, quiet, windows clean and unbroken, "better than Windsor Terrace". "Under good supervision". LIGHT BLUE to PURPLE, in map LIGHT BLUE.

E then S into Long St, same class house as foregoing. North end poorer than south, tenanted by toy makers (homework). Some windows broken, poorer at the north than Caesar St.

E along Harwar St and S down St John's Terrace. 2-st, doors open, children with holey boots, though well fed. Birdcages in black pocket handkerchiefs at windows. Rough, poor and rowdy. DARK BLUE as map. E out of it into Hackney Rd is John St. "A degree better." DARK BLUE as map, 2-st.

S along the Hackney Rd. Out of the north side are Perrys Place, leading out of St John's Terrace, 2 houses only on north side. The south side is the back of the pawnbrokers, like St John's Terrace, DARK BLUE. S of it is Axe Place, 2-st, poor, respectable, front gardens, LIGHT BLUE as map. W along Union Street, small shops, PINK rather than PURPLE of map. N into Union Crescent. 25 houses, 2-st, old tenants, old unused pump in the middle. Hackney Rd Mission at the south end. PURPLE to PINK, in map PINK. Further west, and running from Union St northwards under the railway bridge, is Union Walk. All business premises, warehouses.

Back into Hackney Rd, and S. W along Cotton Gardens, poor, rough. The whole of the south side is now taken up by printing works, as is also one house (to be let as a warehouse) at the northwest end. The windows of the houses broken and stuffed with paper and rags. North side still DARK BLUE as map.

S into the Kingsland Rd, then N. On the east side of the road are Bernales Buildings, built 1807, entered under arch, poor, has improved, used to have Irish cockneys as tenants. 2-st and attic houses, LIGHT BLUE, not marked in map. North of it is Hudson's Court, backs on Cottons Gardens, but walled off from them. 2-st, old houses with red tile roofs. Wash hanging across fairly broad gravelled court. LIGHT BLUE.

{The court called Dyer's Alley and marked DARK BLUE in map, north of Caroline Place is now all workshops.}

Across to the west side of the Kingsland Rd, south of Wellington St is Caroline Place.

2-st, poor, very quiet and respectable. "The mother of 3 policemen and mother-in-law of two, lives here." 34 houses, flowers, great care of front gardens, fat cats, LIGHT BLUE to PURPLE, in map LIGHT BLUE. "Great proportion of the girls from here do work in connection with the mission in Basing Place." Basing Place, also quiet, rather better off than foregoing. Almshouses at the west end and Mission Chapel on north side. 2 police sergeants live here. "It is better than Caroline Place, which in turn is better than Windsor Terrace." The map gives all LIGHT BLUE. This should certainly be PURPLE. The Mission was originally connected with the old Hoxton Academy Church, which has now migrated to the New Tabernacle in Old St.
South of it, just beside the Police Station, is Basinghouse Yard, used to be an old coaching yard connected with the Mailcoach public house at its entrance. Stable with handsome overhanging roof still on north side. Few houses at west end (5), 2-st, used to be rough, now has a new class in and done up. Character PURPLE to PINK, in map DARK BLUE. China pots in windows, etc.

General remarks
Existence of small, quiet, old turnings and inhabitants of the Kingsland Rd.
Strawberries being sold off costers barrow in the Kingsland Rd, great pile of them, in good condition (from abroad). Did not see price but could not have been more than 6d per lb. This is May 19th!
Hackney Rd is inferior to the New North Rd as a shopping street. "It leads from one poor district to another."

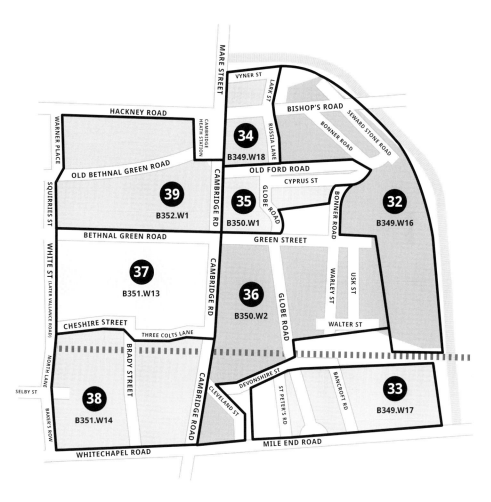

Walk 32 B349-16

Tuesday 28th December 1897
George Duckworth with Inspector Pearn
Inspector Pearn is of medium height, sturdy, dark moustache, has been 4 years in Bethnal Green as Divisional Inspector and was here as sergeant 10 years ago. Rather pompous but a good fellow.

Starting at Approach Road, which leads from Old Ford Road to Victoria Park

This is about the best street in Bethnal Green, PINK-barred rather than the PINK of the map. Houses 3½-st, 8 rooms, houses take in lodgers but are not inhabited by several families. In one of them lodge 9 or 10 police constables who pay 14/- or 15/- per week for their board and lodging. Robinson Rd on the north side is 2- and 2½-st respectable, PINK, not so good as the Approach Rd. Weston, the Superintendent of the J. Police Division lives in one of the houses. Bonner's Rd, the Wesleyan Chapel at the corner of the Approach Rd not PINK. The Bethnal Green workhouse and Dr Stephenson's Boys Home here, PINK as map. Kent's Brush Factory on the south side. "A large place, employing many women and girls, a good lot, tidily dressed. Messers Kent are very particular about their appearance and respectability" said Pearn. Waterloo Rd out of it, PINK as map, till it crosses Bishop's Rd, then PURPLE on the west side of the north end, houses 2½-, 3- and 2-st. Bishop's Rd, PINK as map, rather better on the north side than the south, several Jews living here, a few houses have turned the ground floor into workshops. Shops at the west end of the road. 3½-st, rents £40 to £50.

Then SE along Sewardstone Rd, 2-st, 6-roomed houses, PINK as map, rents 16/- and 20/- per week. At the entrance to the park are some larger 2½-st houses built in 1871, RED in character. St. James' Rd, 2½-st, PINK as map. Opposite is the London Hospital for Diseases of the Chest, "built here because of the sandy soil" said Pearn. Bandon Rd, also PINK as map. 2-st, 4 rooms and washhouse, 14 ft frontage, small gardens or yard behind, front parlour 10x10 ft bedrooms above, rather larger because they include the space taken by the passage below. Went into one of the houses which is occupied by a policeman and his wife who pay 10/- a week for it. He said he was very lucky to get it as all small houses were snapped up on the instant. The other houses in the street have 2 and 3 families in them and other rents are 11/6 and 12/- per week.

Then into the Old Ford Rd and westwards. Houses 2- and 2½-st, PURPLE as map. Some are BLUE, weavers houses with looms visible here and there. Old Ford Rd improves as it gets westwards.

S into Cranbrook St, houses 2-st, flush with the pavement, working class, some respectable, some not all. "A good mixture of thieves here." 2 and 3 families to each house, door posts shiny, litter of paper, orange peel, bread in the street, good many houses with looms in upper storeys, looks more LIGHT BLUE than PURPLE, none of it is PINK though the west end (marked PINK in the map) is rather better than the east. Alma Rd north of it contains a large proportion of weavers, "a very quiet and respectable set of men, but decreasing and their place being taken by less good" said Pearn. The west end of this road is PURPLE as map but the rest is not better than LIGHT BLUE.

Then S into a block of streets marked DARK BLUE and PURPLE on the map, all 2-st houses flush with the street, inhabited by a number of costers. Havelock Place at the east end of Cranbrook St, Cranbrook Rd, Harold St, Type St, Norton St, Sydney St. Of these Havelock Place looks better than the map, quiet, opposite Board School

LIGHT BLUE to PURPLE, Cranbrook Rd has two 2-st houses opposite the school which might be PINK as map but the rest is LIGHT BLUE, Harold St and Type St DARK BLUE as map, Sydney St perhaps PURPLE (as map) at the south end but DARK BLUE the rest of it. Great litter of orange peel, bread, potato parings, whelks, paper in all these streets. Hardly a single house had unbroken windows, all windows clean, all children (of whom there were a great number) booted but the majority hatless. Very rough and constant trouble to the police, said Pearn, many thieves, some house breakers. Pearn did not distinguish one as better than the other but gave all alike a bad character. The Baptist Chapel in Norton St "hardly touches any".

Then into Green St which is the shopping and market street of the district.

Then N into Ames St, shown PURPLE on map but now undoubtedly DARK BLUE, "You may mark this as bad as any of them" said Pearn. Most windows broken, some recently from the glass in the street. Many children, dirty but all looking well fed and booted. Paper, oranges, nuts, tins, bread, old straw hats in the street, many rough-looking lads, as passage leads past a beer house into Hersee Place, now DARK BLUE at the Ames St end, LIGHT BLUE the rest. "A rare lot of trouble to the police this place" said Pearn, map marks it PURPLE. 2-st, same litter as before. Tagg St, also PURPLE in map, but now as bad as the rest and DARK BLUE at the east end past the turning of Mace St, LIGHT BLUE the west end. Great mess in the street, rough women at the east end, and a thieves resort.

N up Mace St, better than the rest. The courts out of the west side marked DARK BLUE on the map look better, and not worse than LIGHT BLUE. Found a set of boys gambling with cards in one of them, is a great place for Sunday gambling, but the women at the doors of the houses in the courts looked distinctly a class above the Tagg St set. So did their houses. Football being played in Mace St. The house in Mace St dates from 1893.

Then S down Bonner St and into Usk St. 2-st, houses stand back with palinged gardens in font, LIGHT BLUE rather than PURPLE. On the east side of it at the north of the Victoria Cemetery is Prospect Place (on map DARK BLUE). Houses with fronts, open space of rope walk and the cemetery in front, looks less bad than Braemar and Moss Streets behind, 2½-st, costers living here and some thieves, perhaps DARK BLUE. Then into Braemar St, weavers top windows, not better than LIGHT BLUE (on map PURPLE), some new tenements at the west end. Collins Place, built 1862, looks better, LIGHT BLUE rather than the DARK BLUE of the map.

{Collins Place is known to the police as Collins Bunk}

Moss St, LIGHT to DARK BLUE, like Braemar, windows broken, wet ill-kept street, litter of paper etc, untidy women. Smart St a little better, a rowdy beer shop at the corner of Moss St has been shut up, costers. Out into Green St and then E to Preston St (DARK BLUE in map) but looks quieter and better, 2-st, flush with the pavement like the rest, LIGHT BLUE rather than DARK BLUE.

The passage between Collins Place and Green St is called Davis Place, 3-st, looks LIGHT BLUE rather than DARK.

Out into Green St and E to Palmer's Rd. One PINK house as map belonging to foremen of the large sawing mills, many wharves, paraffin etc down here.

General remarks

Inspector Pearn begun by saying that as far as he could see Bethnal Green was now what it had been 10 years ago. He said we had seen in this walk the best and worst parts i.e. Approach Rd ("Our West End") and the streets north and south of Green St which were equal to any of their bad spots. But though Bethnal Green as a whole may be the same he said "we have nowhere such violence leading to police casualties as we used to have" yet the streets north and south of Green St do seem to have changed for the worse, at any rate in appearance. The PURPLE of the map may have been due to the presence of more weavers than there are now, "A quiet respectable set of people", but every year these grow less in number. The only respectable-looking men in the street were one or two old men whom Pearn pointed out as weavers. The rest were of the coster class with neck clothes in place of collars.

Pearn spoke of the whole as a regular thieves' quarter. Much of the street litter was no doubt due to the Christmas festivities of the last few days, so were some of the broken windows but not many, the majority had been broken some days, many mended with brown paper etc. Pearn said they were broken normally and had nothing seasonal about them.

Bethnal Green, he said, remains the same because nobody goes except the weavers and no one comes. "It has no attractions, no railway depots to bring countrymen". Health good in spite of narrow ill-kempt streets because of sandy soil. Families live on from generation to generation almost always in the same house. The lodgers migrate from street to street but not the tenants. The house owners are mostly small owners living in one of their own houses themselves. Population increases but no one leaves if they can help it. Inhabitants form a great family party. He doesn't see why this district ever should change.

There is not a prostitute for hire in the place. "Walk down any hour of the night or day and I warrant you will never be accosted." But there is a great looseness of relations, and thousands who are living together unmarried as man and wife.

Men and women alike drink beer. Drunkenness is rather decreasing. We met 3 drunk women, mother, daughter and a friend, but not a single drunken man or boy. The beer houses are the roughest places. "They can't afford to be so independent as the public house." Beer houses have a certain fixed custom. Owner cannot therefore afford to offend by turning one of them out when he has had enough because all would follow and his trade be lost. "It is often really rather hard luck on the beer house keeper prosecuting him as if he had encouraged drunkenness."

Interview with Superintendent Weston at the Bethnal Green Police Station, chief of the J Division, 27th September 1897

Supt. Weston is a big fat man who has risen from the ranks. Very anxious to give all assistance possible, said that it was Sir Edward Bradford's special wish that the best men should be placed at Mr Booth's disposition.

With regard to the men who are publicans, "There are all sorts, you will generally find that the publican is of the same class as those he serves". The best men are in the largest houses, the largest houses are generally in the hands of the Brewers or companies who put men into them as their paid servants. In the case where a house is owned by a large company, you will find that the publican is of a class above those he serves, but these are practically the only exceptions to the rule stated above.

Mr Weston did not approve of the system of allowing companies to own houses. The licensee is by law supposed to be the man that has the chief interest in the business, lives in the house and manages it. Where a company holds many licenses, the "license is granted to a man of straw", while for rating purposes the actual conductor of the house is put forward. This leads to a great confusion. A year ago the police tried to make an enquiry as to the actual value of houses in order to help the rating authorities. But they were baffled. These big companies always manage to turn what seems a matter of common sense into a question of law. They pay the best lawyers, and that means that the police have to do so too and cases are dragged out at length. It was impossible to press home the charge of divided ownership, so they dropped it. It was hoped that the Licensing Commission would lead to a revision of the law "but they do not seem to be taking evidence on this point".

Although he disapproved of ownership by companies, Mr Weston admitted that the houses held in this way in his division were the best managed. The Tower licensing magistrates who grant the licenses in his division (i.e. the greater number of them) approve of plural ownership, saying that a man or company who has a great stake will not risk its existence by bad management, also, that a man who manages one house well will be the more likely to manage two houses well than an untried man.

The market value of houses has so much gone up in the last two or 3 years, that no house would stand being rated at its full market value. A house near the police station, he quoted as an example. Three years ago a man who paid £12,000 failed because the business was not large enough, since then it has been sold for £25,000. Rates in Bethnal Green are 6/- in the pound. Houses are now at a fictitious value. In Mr Weston's opinion, they have reached their high-water mark.

The small houses are the worst conducted and most difficult to deal with. "Say a man has £500 of his own, the brewer advances him £1000, this is the general thing, he must make it pay somehow or other." In order to pay, his customers must drink and be shielded from police interference. These men have a private room at the back into which they put drunk and disorderly and keep them there until they are sober. It is impossible for the police to enter into the private rooms of a man's house, even if they suspect that drunken men lie hidden there.

Brewers are very hard upon small men. He has known many a man ruined by spending all his own money on interest on the brewer's loan and when that was done, finding that the brewer sold the house over his head to a new man, so that he is turned out in the street, penniless.

There is not much harm in sending children to fetch beer. "Absolutely none in this district." "The language and atmosphere is no worse in a public house than what they hear at home. Besides, it would not prevent the children from frequenting the houses." "They look upon them as a sort of paradise." It is always to them that they are taken by their parents for a cake or sweets, they go there from babyhood upwards. To send them there to fetch a pint of beer is no demoralisation for them, or introduction to anything new and harmful. In better class districts, where parents do not frequent the public house it would probably be better not to send the children. Children always sip the beer they are sent to fetch. He has noticed it scores of times and often wonders that any of it reaches home, but he does not think they acquire their taste for beer in this way.

The number of licensed houses in the J Division has practically been stationary for a number of years. In point of fact it has slightly decreased. The exact decrease for London could be obtained at Scotland Yard. Every year the superintendents send it in, but it is not published.

For a policeman to be served with drink while on duty is a dire offence. 23 years ago, when he first entered the service, drunkenness was not thought much of, a constable was fined 5/- and that was all. Now it is very different, and for a man to be found drunk practically destroys all chance of his promotion. So stringent is the punishment that Mr Weston thinks constables rarely dare offend. Sometimes the publicans themselves complain. Only the other day, a publican in a large house was suspicious of a boy who had been sent to fetch a pint of beer. He told his little girl to follow the boy and see where the beer went to. The girl followed, saw that the boy put down the pot in a corner, and afterwards saw a policeman come up and take it. She reported to her father, her father reported to Mr Weston and now the man has been transferred to another part of London and his pay cut down.

Mr Weston does not think that the police are now paid money instead. Even to obtain a loan from a publican is a police offence. Publicans in small houses are more often local men than not. In larger houses they are men of more capital and come from a distance. It is easier for a man from a distance to start straight and to keep straight, he is not so tied by the claims of personal acquaintance with his customers.

It would be much easier to obtain convictions against houses and individuals if the magistrate took a more common sense view of drunkenness. It is not that they are afraid of having their decisions upset on appeal to quarter sessions. The justices of the peace who make up bench at quarter sessions are generally easy going retired gentlemen among whom you will not find more than one strong man. A stipendiary magistrate is generally a strong man and constant practice has given him a thorough knowledge of his business. Therefore it is not fear that restrains his granting convictions. It is rather the absence of any rule. Some say the publican must be told not to serve a drunken man and warned by the police as he enters the houses, while with others it is enough that the publican has been warned at the time his license is renewed. Between the two the drunken man escapes.

Again, magistrates will not accept the word of a constable that a man was drunk, they must have witnesses and witnesses are hard to find against a drunken man. In practice it comes down to the result that men are only taken up when drunk and disorderly, and disorderliness is the complaint on which they are convicted rather than drunkenness. Hence the police are deprived of the possibility of following up the case against the publican. The practice of the police is pretty well uniform as to the treatment of drunken persons, and Mr Weston referred me to the evidence of Supt. Smith given before the Licensing Commission.

Men serve behind the bar in all except showy neighbourhoods.

With regard to woman's drinking, there could hardly be any increase in Bethnal Green. It always had been and still was noted for it. Here they drink like the men, not as a relaxation but as necessity or habit. They are most of them working women and they go across to the public house, not to sit there and talk, but to take their half pint and then go back to their work again. In Chelsea and the Brompton Rd where Mr Weston was for many years on duty, you see better-dressed women turning in to the public house after their shopping. Here it is not so, and the fact that the lower classes of labourers' wives and daughters so largely frequent public houses, means that they are 'no class' for the wives and daughters of artisans or any who are respectably dressed and consider their position in society above that of labourers.

Mr Weston thinks there has been a decided increase in women's drinking in the West End but does not think it amounts to anything in the East. (He takes Bethnal Green as typical of the East). The increase in the West is not, as far as he knows, connected with the granting of grocers licenses.

{Mr Weston would like to see the number of licenses largely decreased.
1. Because there would be less trouble in police supervision.
2. Because there would be less temptation to drink, and therefore less drunkenness.}

He spoke highly of Flanagan, said he considered him the best police officer he had ever met. The only complaint against him was that he was "too opinionated". This made him very unpopular in one district, where a dead set was made against him by some of his fellow officers, an enquiry followed, Flanagan came out of it perfectly clean but the fact of there having been a row, somewhat unfairly, has stood in the way of his further promotion.

(B347-10)

Children in great numbers in the streets for their fortnight's Xmas holiday from the Board School. Nearly all well fed looking and healthy, all booted, girls generally worse dressed than the boys. Plenty of open space handy in Victoria Park and the Cemetery now taken over by LCC and made into a park. "Used to be an awful place, graves pulled to pieces and often the coffin edges showing."

No one doing any work. Day being observed as a general holiday by all the inhabitants except the shop keepers and publicans.

The better class from the PINK streets leave for the north side of the Victoria park.

There were a great number of small Xmas trees fully decked out with sugar plums and candles in the front windows, especially noticeable in the poorer streets, noticeable also the remarkable cleanliness, even polish of the windows everywhere.

Walk 33

Thursday 30th December 1897
George Duckworth with Inspector Pearn

Starting at the Globe Road Station on the Great Eastern Railway.

NE along Devonshire St, 2-and 3-st, 2 and 3 families to each house, houses built in 1851, a mixed street, some PINK, most PURPLE (as map), some LIGHT BLUE. By the side of the beer house on the south side of the street is a passage leading to 8 cottages marked BLACK on the map, each with 3 rooms, 1 upstairs and 2 down, 1 family in each house. "They wont allow more than one family in each of these houses" said a woman in the court, rent 5/9 a week. Inspector Pearn said that it was from courts like these that juvenile thieves came but he knew of no adult thieves living there, nor had the place a particularly bad reputation. Houses have been done up by the owner and repairs are still going on.

S down the Carlton Rd, 2-st, PINK to PURPLE, some houses not better than LIGHT BLUE, south end of the road better than the north, on map PINK. 2 families in each house, 2-st, 6-roomed houses. S past Leatherdale and Norfolk Streets equally 2-st and 2-familied, PINK halfway to the Globe Rd, then less good and PURPLE. Through Carlton Square, well kept by LCC, PINK as map. Into Holford and Colmar Streets, as map. Into Alderney St, not RED as map, many Jews, less good than the south end of Bancroft Rd and Grafton Rd, which are both PINK barred and RED at their southern ends, 2½- and 3½-st, 1 servant generally kept, mostly Jews, some single lodgers.

Then N up Bancroft Rd, the north end is older than the south end, 1842 as compared with 1854, 2 families to each house, PURPLE as map.

E into Moody St, PURPLE as map, working class, 1846. Into Buckeridge, Longnor and Bradwell Roads, a rough bit, many coal porters and labourers working on the G.E.R sidings, known to the police as Tiger Bay, difficult of approach as the only entry is through Moody St. Bradwell Rd is rather better in appearance than the rest. Pearn gave them all the same character. Public house at the corner of Longnor and Buckeridge Roads has been a great source of trouble by reason of illegal Sunday trading, crows always posted and alarm given before the police can get near. Pearn has surveyed them from underneath a railway truck and then made a dash but has never actually caught men actually in the house. All 2-st houses with 2 families in each, doorposts worn black and the bricks rubbed light by constant rubbing and leaning against them.

S down the Bancroft Rd and E along the Mile End Rd. Govey Place on the north side, not coloured on map, with four 3-st houses and 2 of 2-st. "Quite the lowest class here, occupying one room per family." Windows dirty, nearly every one cracked or patched with white or brown paper, rough, should be at least DARK BLUE. At the canal the Bethnal Green J Police Division ends, on its east side is the K or Bow Division.

W along the Mile End Rd. The first court on the north side of Grafton St is Mile End Place, quiet, respectable working class, 2-st houses built on both sides, palinged gardens in front. 6 policemen living here, well-dressed children, PINK to PURPLE in character. The next court westwards up a passage by the side of a public house is Grebe Court, it does not communicate with the next court as shown in map but is barricaded off from it, consists of eight 4-roomed cottages letting for 6/- per week. LIGHT BLUE as map. Next court is Driver's Court, LIGHT BLUE, costers, great heap of rubbish from the dug-out cellar under the 'buildings' at the entrance, ought to have been taken away "makes the place like a pigsty" said one woman, it has been there for 3 months and they say it will be 3 more before it is removed. 4-roomed houses here for 6/- per week. Then up into Frimley Place, DARK BLUE in map, is now better than it was, road has been repaved with granite blocks, about 6 houses on the southwest side are down, the rest are well done up. It is still poor and rather rough but not worse than LIGHT BLUE, the roughest characters have left. Into the Alderney Rd, a court lies between Frimley Place and Globe Rd, also improved, 8 cottages, called Alderney Place, built 1826, flush with passage, 4-roomed, looks more PURPLE than LIGHT BLUE, doorposts clean and windows, but some evidently poorer as shown by torn curtains.

N up the Globe Rd, on the east side of which, not shown on map, is a court entered along a passage, 5 cottages, called Ferriers Court, Very poor, LIGHT to DARK BLUE. Past the Leatherdale Rd, which at its west end is not better than LIGHT BLUE, but improves eastwards to PURPLE and then PINK. Caroline Place, shown on map but not coloured, is just south of Devonshire St, about 7 cottages on the north side of passage, 2-st, not better than LIGHT BLUE. The gardens in front are the backs of the Leatherdale Rd houses, a great many pigeons kept in them. "Pigeon flying is one of the sports of the locality."

W into Cephas St (formerly St Peter St). The houses at the east end have all the appearance of poverty, LIGHT BLUE. But once west of the church the road is PINK as map. Built 1855, houses let for 16/- or 17/- per week. Like it is St Peter's Rd, 2½- and 3-st. Like also Edward St and Nicholas Rd, 2½-st. Nicholas Rd on the east side of St Peter's Rd is distinctly less good and PURPLE rather than the PINK of the map.'

S into Willow St, respectable working class, street clean and well paved, many of the men employed in Charrington's brewery live here, but it is PURPLE rather than PINK. There is no opening into Stayner's Rd out of Willow St.

E into the Globe Rd, down a cul-de-sac called XX* Place, ten 2-st cottages, rather rough, PURPLE to LIGHT BLUE. stabling on the east side. Then into Stayner's Rd

*Note: This is to denote a new road, as yet unnamed.

out of Globe Rd, very rough, "a bad quarter, card sharpes, thieves, a few prostitutes here". Map marks it PINK. Some of the DARK BLUE and BLACK from Eagle Place and Frimley Place must have migrated here. A place for Sunday gambling, some houses do not look bad but the general colouring should be LIGHT BLUE lined with BLACK rather than PINK. The yellow bricks of the houses had been rubbed a lighter colour by the backs of loiterers.

Into the Mile End Rd, westwards past the Brewery is a court blocked at its north end by the Brewery buildings which the map marks as BLACK. Known as Eagle Place, 2-st, "perhaps a shade worse than Stayner's Rd", dark, rather narrow, better than it was, oil cloth in most of the passages. The west side belongs to the Paragon Theatre and the side entrance to the Theatre is at the northwest end. Some of the houses have been rebuilt and all repointed, character LIGHT to DARK BLUE.

General remarks
The dwellers in the PINK streets are chiefly the shop assistants from the Mile End Rd. There is a great demand for small houses. The amusements of the neighbourhood are pigeon flying, street gambling and music hall going. "All classes go to the Paragon and there is nothing they like better than an evening there."

Walk 34   B349-18
Date not given. Believed to be Friday 31ˢᵗ December 1897
George Duckworth with Inspector Pearn

Starting at the southwest corner of Old Ford Road
Mixed shops and dwellings, better at west than east end, some factories, a starch works, St Margaret's House for ladies at the east end of it in connection with Oxford Houses. Several employers with small shops who give a great deal of clothes and shoe work out to be done at home.

N up the Cambridge Rd, Patriot Square on the east side, 3½-st houses, quiet respectable, working class, PURPLE as map. W into Peel Grove, 2-st, as map. At a house on the southeast side took place the 'Bethnal Green Mystery', an old lady discovered with her skull broken, murder suspected but no murderer forthcoming, police theory that she fell downstairs, open verdict returned. It was suggested that she had been followed into the house and murdered by a thief who wanted the rents he supposed she had been collecting. She was a property owner and lived upon the proceeds of 2 or 3 houses in the neighbourhood. This theory was disproved by a witness who knew her well and said he was satisfied she had not been out because she always washed her face and hands before going out and evidently she had not done so on this day. Inspector Pearn had never been inside such a filthy vermin-infested house as hers. A large yard for building materials belonging to Glover's, a contractor in this street.

N up the Cambridge Rd past Palestine Place. This is all being demolished to make room for a large new Parish Infirmary. N to Parmiter St, 2-st houses, 2 families in each, respectable working class, PURPLE to PINK, 6-roomed houses letting at 15/- or 16/- per week, into Bishops Rd which has shops at its west end.

{Parmiters Almshouses (6 in number) here, supported by a charity founded in 1681}.

N up Mowlem St, 2-st cottages, flush with street, poor, LIGHT BLUE as map. A newish red church is on the east side, "it has been built sometime but only lately opened". Into Wadeson St, also 2-st, very poor especially at the southeast end, the outsides of the houses have been done up, dated 1889.

At the southwest end of Wadeson St is a passage leading through to Mare St (not shown on map) with about 15 2-st cottages, LIGHT BLUE, "poor but not rough".

Into Vyner St, a little better but hardly as good as PURPLE (except some houses at the west end), windows broken, flush with the pavement, backs on the canal, wood and china clay wharves.

S down Lark Row, 2-st, LIGHT BLUE to PURPLE, looks rather better than the other streets. "A few thieves living about here." 2 good houses at the north end bearing the date 1887, many children about, all booted and fairly clean. Down Russia Lane, it is respectable and PURPLE at the north end, 2-st houses, built 1852, some lately done up. Map gives it LIGHT BLUE. Lower down where there is a nursery marked on the map it is much worse. Here is a block of Quinn's buildings built by the same man as those in Pickering St, South Kensington. "Very rough, very poor, very noisy" said Pearn. Windows broken and dirty, curtains torn, 6 children looking out of one window high up, 2 rooms let at 5/- or 5/6. Opposite it are 3 courts. Ernest Place, eight 2-st cottages, LIGHT BLUE as map. Providence Place also LIGHT BLUE but with a better and cleaner lot of children playing in them.

Then into Old Ford Rd at this point looking PINK rather than the PURPLE of the map, 3½-st houses holding 3 families or 1 family and lodgers, substantially built, date 1814.

Here it began to rain heavily and we had to stop.

General remarks

Inspector Pearn thinks that sweets are never given now by publicans to children. The idea was that if the children were not given sweets they would not be so keen to go to fetch their parents beer. "But they have to go just the same and I can't see that it makes much difference whether they are given sweets or not." Nevertheless the order came from headquarters that it was an improper practice and so it was stopped.

Apropos of Quinn's buildings, Inspector Pearn thought that all statistics relating to deaths in buildings were one sided because as soon as any one was ill they were sent away to a hospital and not kept at home as they would be in a private house. In his opinion they are much more unhealthy than small houses and the danger of an epidemic spreading much greater. While the hospitals have room, he said, patients can be sent off and there is not much risk but supposing a general epidemic, and no room in the hospitals, then 'buildings' became a death trap to their inhabitants. Of the trades carried on in Bethnal Green he unhesitatingly put boot makers first as the largest drinkers.

Walk 35

B350-1

Monday 3rd January 1898
George Duckworth with Inspector Pearn

Starting at the southwest corner, N up Victoria Park Square

Formerly dwelling houses of a good class, now nearly all factories, boots, shoes, clothing. St Margaret's House connected with Oxford House is in this road, also Oxford Hall, a working man's club. 3-st houses, a few still used as dwelling places. No.30 to let, 6 rooms £35 rent. "You may add another quarter to this, i.e. £9 for rates and taxes" said Pearn.

E along Green St and S down the Globe Rd, PURPLE as map on the west side, 3½-st, houses used as dwellings or factories. On the east side, 2-st poorer, weaver's windows upstairs, many broken and patched, look LIGHT BLUE. On the west side are the Bethnal Green Barracks, now closed, moved to Woolwich, owing to opinion of authorities that you could never make decent soldiers of men drawn from the neighbourhood in the locality itself. "The Bethnal Green Militia used to consist of a greater set of scoundrels than you would easily find anywhere else." Sugar Loaf Walk running from Globe Rd to Victoria Park Square consists of a passage with a few fair 2-st houses, PURPLE, one a builder, another a file cutter. South of it is another passage leading to Burnham Square, dirty, ragged children but all booted, LIGHT BLUE, on map DARK BLUE, but Pearn said it was not worse than poor. So too Chester St, also DARK BLUE on map, and Chester Place, 3- and 2-st and Thurlow St, all poor working class, but well above Miso St, Collins Place and Ames St in character. "You will find a sprinkling of thieves as you will in even the most respectable streets about here, but that is not the regular employment of the inhabitants." Museum Buildings at the southwest end of Thurlow St and Green St are 4-st and have a rough type in them, for the most part let in sets of 2 and 3 rooms. The class of people in them is no worse than in the surrounding streets, many of the poor prefer buildings to a small house because a set of rooms in a large building is more of a castle to them than a house where there are lodgers, or another family above them. In buildings, he said, there is less interference of the family life of one family by its next door neighbour than there would be in a small house with one family on the ground floor and another above it.

Helen's Place, which is the turning out of Green St between Chester St and Victoria Park Square, looks still DARK BLUE, poorer, dirtier than the rest, costers buildings. E along Hartley St at the west end of which is a court known as North Passage, DARK BLUE on map. The south side of it is now down, and a new stable built up along-side of the demolition, north side still very poor, puddles, mud, costers barrows, loose stones, nearly every pane of windows broken. The few cottages on the north side could not look worse than they do. The west end of Hartley St is called North St, 2-st, LIGHT to DARK BLUE, children well dressed but windows broken and blinds dirty, some houses exceptions. Christmas trees covered with crackers, sweets, dolls and tinsel and candles, still in many windows. There is a passage, a continuation of North St behind Hartley St, about 9 cottages, 2-st, LIGHT BLUE as map. Cottages on the south side of the passage only. Houses outwardly in good repair.

Hartley St and the streets running north out of it i.e. Brierly, Gauber, Wharncliff, Hunslett and Stainsbury Streets are all 2-st LIGHT BLUE as map, working class, sprinkling of thieves, all have been done up, not lately, but still in good repair.

Many shoe makers, many weavers and a great many weavers houses. Metal on the streets not properly rolled in, has been kicked up and looks untidy. These streets are not quite so good as Royston St (PURPLE) but are almost PURPLE. The Mansion House Sanitary Aid Committee has been jogging the Sanitary Authorities and landlords in this quarter with good results, said Pearn. All houses 2-st and flush with the pavement. Cyprus St, PURPLE as map. Rents from placard of houses for sale. Nos. 86, 88, 96, 98, 100 Cyprus St bringing in a total rental of £105, ground rent £4, 2 leases of 51½ years, from 1850. Nos. 17 and 19 Cyprus St bringing in £65, 2 leases, leased from 1851, ground rent £2 landlord paying rates and taxes.

Out of Brierly St is a passage leading through to Park St and the Globe Rd, very poor, windows broken and dirty, doorposts black, bread and mess in the street, old tins, orange peel, etc. Map marks it LIGHT BLUE, but it looks worse. Pearn called it "low" and worse than the other streets.

General remarks

At the Bethnal Green station there are 177 policemen of whom 147 are constables. The proportion of police per head of population is probably greater in the west end than the east, said Pearn. "Here you have to look after people and there after property." There are no silver spoons in Bethnal Green to guard. Street rows, gambling, snatching, thieving are the chief offences. If a tradesman's cart disappears and with it all its parcels, tea, cheese etc. "you may pretty surely expect to find the cart standing unattended in a back street in Bethnal Green with its contents gone". The receivers of stolen goods are the small shops in the neighbourhood. You cannot convict them, "but if they were not, how could they afford to sell the tea and cheese they do as cheap as they do sell it?"

There are a large number of juvenile thieves. No thieves' schools here because there are very few lodging houses. "It is in the kitchens of the lodgings in Whitechapel that the thieves are taught." That is why you will never find an old thief who has not been a young one too. This he said was true in 19 cases out of 20. Old 'legs' are unmistakable if you have had any experience. "There is a look about a man who has been a convict that you don't see in other men." But it is difficult to say exactly in what it exists. Pearn was several years in Portsmouth dockyard and watched the convicts daily go out to their lunch. He has seen solicitors, clerks and navvies working side by side but he has not been able to tell the difference between them for they all looked alike. Besides their dress there is a look which they all get which they never lose.

From the Royston St quarter he said there had been migration of 40 or 50 families and weavers down to Essex. Alderman Evans used to have his factories here, has left London in fear of a union being started and built houses for these families who followed him willingly.

Note that in all the streets, especially the poorer ones there are signs of sanitary activity, paving, bricks repointed etc. Street sweeping might perhaps be more thorough than it is, and there would be work for a good many more dust carts than one sees going their rounds.

Pearn had been giving evidence about the Dixie St fire. Mother and children burnt, husband died same day in infirmary of consumption. All to be buried today. Pearn said it would be a curious sight. Funeral was by public subscription, the Vicar of St Bartholomew's having made an appeal. Dixie St is a passage with 2-st, 4-roomed houses on the south side of it only, DARK BLUE on the map in the middle of a very poor quarter. House completely gutted but neighbouring houses untouched.

Found funeral just starting, band played dead march preceded by a number of men and children. Roads blocked with people, day being observed as a general holiday. "Nothing very unusual in that because Monday generally is in these parts." 4 hearses with coffins, 4 mourning carriages, handkerchiefs with large black borders conspicuous in the hand of each of the mourners. plumed horses, mutes on foot with crepe bands round their hats, 2 hansom cabs, one with 2 women another with 2 men "probably publicans from the neighbourhood whose gossip after it will bring increased custom to their houses". 3 omnibuses, willing to take passengers to Plaistow (the burial place) and back for a shilling each, crammed, mostly women. Then a few carts but no costers carts. Respectful crowd. Hats lifted as hearses passed, greetings exchanged between the occupants of the mourning carriages and friends in the crowd, broad-bordered handkerchiefs fluttered at the windows. 30 policemen to keep order, but no attempt whatever at disorder. Procession at a foots pace down Somerford Rd (LIGHT BLUE as map) and then south along Cambridge Rd, trotting only when the Mile End Rd was reached. Everybody out in their Sunday clothes for the occasion, most women in bonnets, a few in shawls, men in caps, ties, black coats or brown, hardly a man or woman above 5 ft 4 in among them. Some bright patches of colour given by the hats of factory girls, colouring otherwise sombre but not black.

"It's wonderful what a lot they think of a funeral down here, there'll be many of them wishing they'd been burnt too to have such a turn out as this." A man may beat his wife and ill treat her so that she dies of it but if he gives her a good funeral he will be forgiven by the women of the neighbourhood who say, as Pearn has heard them say, "But he can't be so bad, poor man, look what a handsome burial he gave her." Even the poorest will pay £8 or £10 for a burial and then starve the week after.

MAP DESCRIPTIVE OF LONDON POVERTY, 1898-9
(IN 12 SHEETS)

THE STREETS ARE COLOURED ACCORDING TO THE GENERAL
CONDITION OF THE INHABITANTS, AS UNDER:-

Lowest class.
Vicious, semi-criminal

Mixed. Some comfortable others poor.

Very poor. casual.
Chronic want.

Fairly comfortable.
Good ordinary earnings.

Poor. 18s. to 21s. a week for a moderate family

Middle class.
Well-to-do.

Upper-middle and Upper classes. Wealthy.

A combination of colours–as dark blue and black, or pink and red

indicates that the street contains a fair proportion of each of the classes

represented by the respective colours.

The following sheets have been extracted for interest from the published maps.
They do not cover the whole area and they are at different scales.

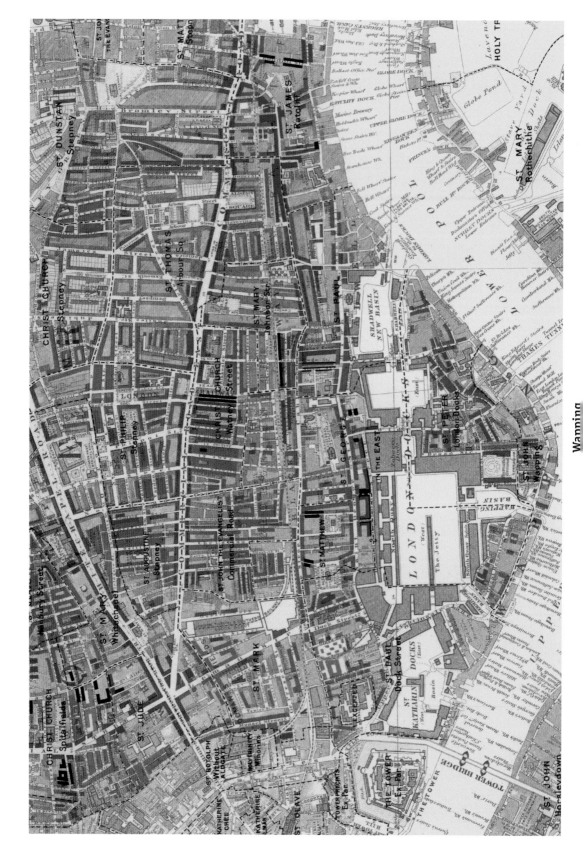

Wapping

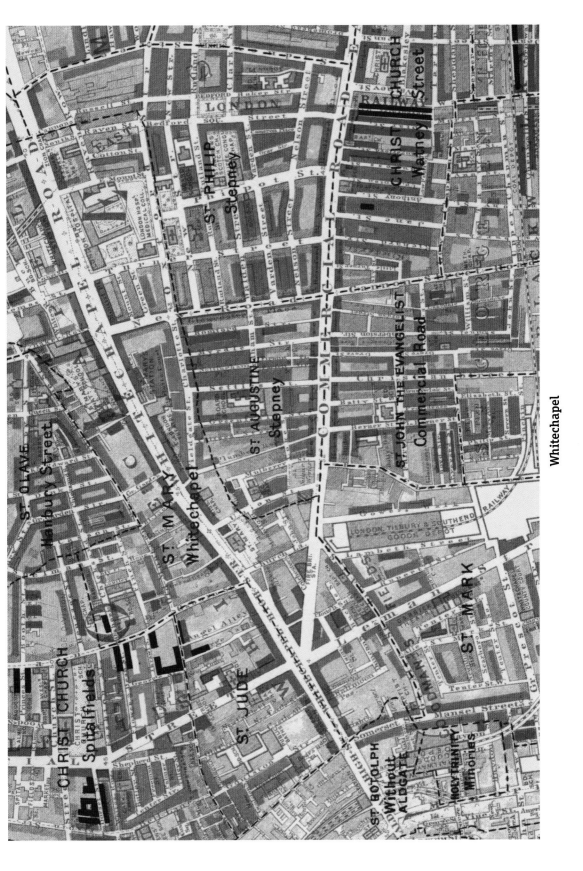

Whitechapel

Clerkenwell

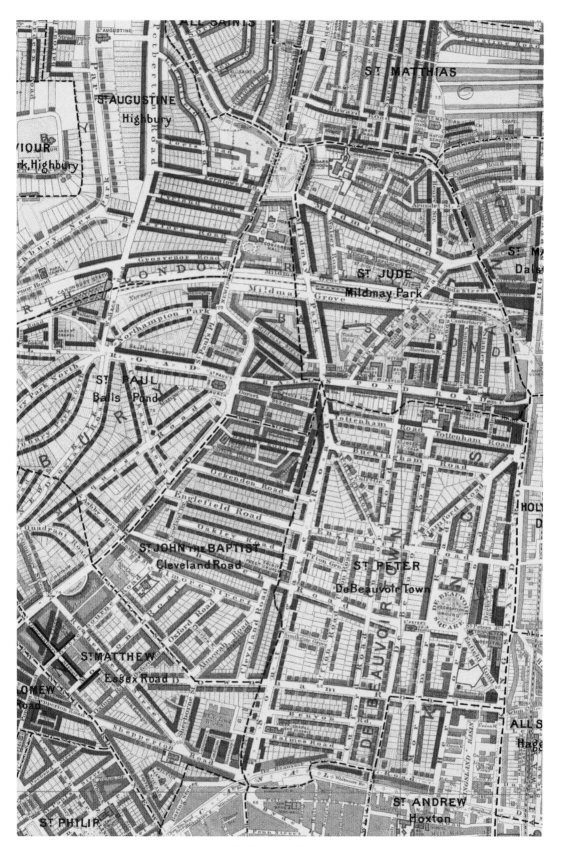

De Beauvoir Town

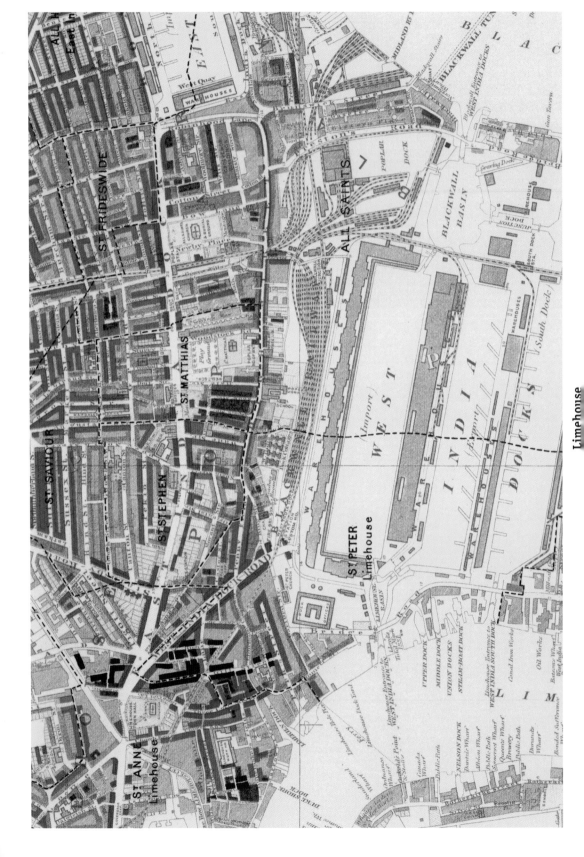

Limehouse

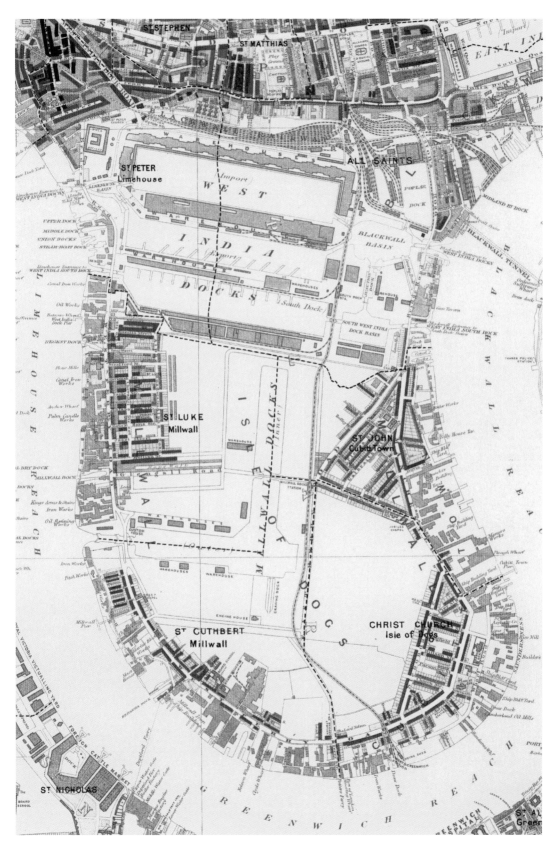

Isle Of Dogs

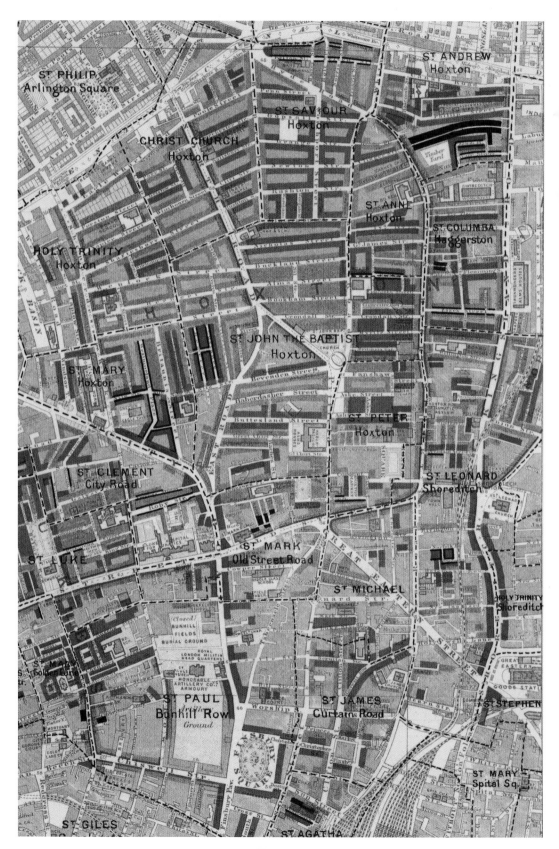

Hoxton

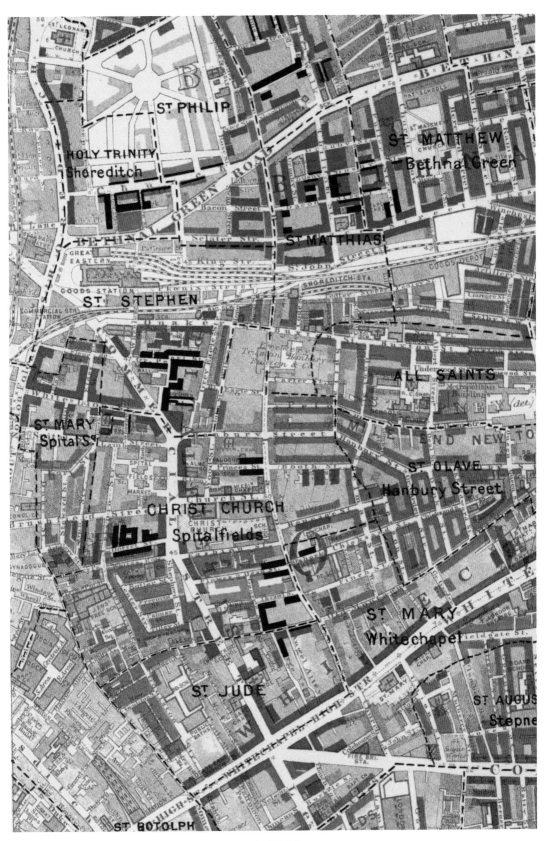

Spitalfields

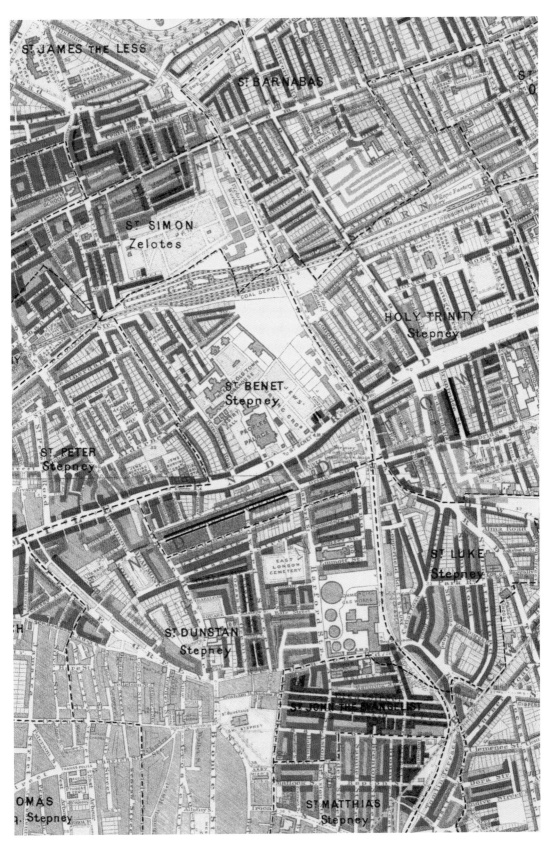

Stepney

'The Fenian Barracks'

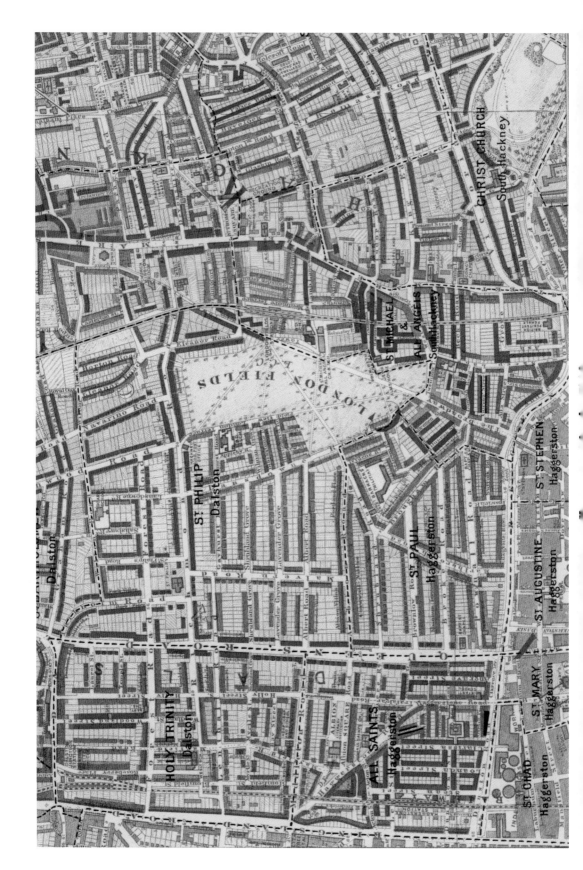

CHRIST CHURCH
South Hackney

ST. MICHAEL
&
ALL ANGELS
South Hackney

LONDON FIELDS

ST. PHILIP
Dalston

ST. PAUL
Haggerston

ST. STEPHEN
Haggerston

ST. AUGUSTINE
Haggerston

HOLY TRINITY
Dalston

ALL SAINTS
Haggerston

ST. MARY
Haggerston

ST. CHAD
Haggerston

Hackney & Homerton

S.THOMAS
THE APOSTLE

ANDREW

St.MATTHEW
Upper Clapton

ST. MICHAEL & ALL ANGELS
Stoke Newington Common

ST. JAMES
West Hackney

CHRIST CHURCH
Clapton

S.JAMES THE GREAT
Clapton

ALL SOULS
Clapton

WATER WORKS

EAST LONDON

FILTER BEDS

ALL SAINTS
Lower Clapton

St.PAUL
Lower Homerton

St. BARNABAS
Homerton

HACKNEY

ST. JOHN
Hackney

ST. MARK
Dalston

St.BARTHOLOMEW
Dalston

Walk 36

Tuesday 4th January 1898
George Duckworth with Subdivisional Inspector Pearn

Starting at the west end of Green Street

A market street, barrows and shops, rather poor class, small shop keepers living over their shops, not better than PINK (PINK-barred on map). Salvation Army lodging house on the north side, "takes in a very rough class". Beds 6d and 4d per night or 3/- and 2/- per week. Prices, good bacon 5d to 10d per lb. Fair mutton chops 4½d each. Cabbages 4d and 2d each. Sprouts 1d per lb, bowler hats (new) 2/6 and ladies crepe mourning bonnets 2/11. Some beef 2½d per lb. Large trade with women, hour midday.

S down Warley St, 2-st, PURPLE as map, 2 and 3 families in each house, carmen, porters, a good many broken windows, some thieves. "They don't always choose the worse streets to live in, they think they escape notice if they choose a fairly respectable street."

E into Usk St, 2-st, PURPLE in map but rather LIGHT BLUE, some ragged children. "Working class but quite 9/10 of them have been at the station for drunkenness." Walter St at the south of the Victoria park cemetery (now a playground and park) still DARK BLUE, one or two houses at the west end rather better, one window with books on table – mostly novels – others with Xmas trees, houses in bad repair. Swings etc for boys in graveled enclosure, in the part of the cemetery east of Walter St "a great resource for the rough lads of the district".

W into Morpeth St, better houses, built 1844, 2½-st. PURPLE as map. Knottisford St not quite so good. LIGHT BLUE. Tuscan St less good still, LIGHT to DARK BLUE, windows dirty and broken, 2-st. Bonwell S a mixture, 2½-st, some DARK BLUE, some LIGHT BLUE and some PURPLE. Butler St, 2-st, PURPLE to LIGHT BLUE. Up Baker St on the east side of which is Digby's Walk. Not coloured on map. 2-st, very rough, windows broken, doors open, doorposts black, great mess in the road. "Chiefly Vestry scavengers live here, and costers" should be DARK BLUE. Digby St with Vestry depot, LIGHT BLUE to PURPLE, 2-st. On the south side next to the beer house is a passage, Lansdell Place, 2-st, DARK BLUE, hatless ragged children, boots holey, messy narrow street, rough.

S along the Globe Rd into Portman Place, 2-st, 2 families, PURPLE. "25, 31, 33 Portman Place and 99 Cephas St producing £115.14.0, landlord paying rates and taxes" to be sold. Allas Rd running out of it, on map LIGHT BLUE, but now decidedly better. 6 houses on the southeast end, PINK and the rest PINK to PURPLE, "A decidedly respectable colony" said Pearn. By its position it might have been a slum, unapproachable, but instead of this the PINK has prevailed, books, flowers in china pots, etc in front windows, windows unbroken, curtains without holes. North St is the name given to west end of Portman Place.

W across Globe Rd and into Sceptre St, DARK BLUE at east end, LIGHT BLUE the rest, (PURPLE on map). "Rough and very poor" said Pearn. At the east end, south side, dirty children, one without shoes or stockings (the first I have seen in Bethnal Green). 2-st houses. Ann St also poor, LIGHT BLUE.

N up James St, some poor shops south end, a PURPLE to LIGHT BLUE street, no PINK in it now. On the east side of the road nearly opposite the turning into Essex Rd is St Anthony's Church, not marked on any map, though Pearn said it had been built at least 12 years. Essex St, 2-st, LIGHT BLUE (PURPLE in map). "Rough working class." Just to the north of West St, on the west side of James St, is a large bare space seen on map, tenanted by an old-iron dealer. "He was the only man in the district who said he would employ ticket-of-leave men when the police were making inquiries for the purpose. He never asks for a character from any of his men, has the very roughest working for him." Large yard piled with carloads of iron rubbish, pails, tin canisters, stampings etc. It is all pounded down into a compact mass and sold to ship owners as ballast. said Pearn.

W along Cornwall Rd, not better than PURPLE. At the southwest end (not coloured on map) is Cornwall Square, should be BLACK. "Mark it as bad as you like" said Pearn, "for it's as vicious and as bad as any place in Bethnal Green." A great source of trouble to the police. Haddock curers its inhabitants, many juvenile thieves. Though so bad it is a small place, belongs to the Commissioner of Police "who made us smile one day by sending down to say his tenants complained of constant row and absence of any police from the neighbourhood".

Along West St, 1824, PINK on map but does not look better than PURPLE, is not so good as Portman Place or Allas Rd, 2-st houses, flush with the street.

Hardy's Place, eight 2-st houses on the east side of West St not shown on map, is PURPLE to LIGHT BLUE. Children rather ragged and dirty. "Nos. 5, 6, 7, 8 Hardy's Place. Each with 4 rooms and a washhouse, rents amounting to £100, landlord paying rates and taxes, lease 4½ years, ground rent £10" to be sold.

W along Railway Place, LIGHT BLUE as map. Out of it on the north side is Entick St, PURPLE to LIGHT BLUE, 2-st houses flush with pavement. The convict who has just successfully escaped from Dartmoor came from this street. {Has since been captured, 20.1.98}. 2 families in each house, 2-st, built 1851, houses better on the east than the west side.

S along Cambridge Rd turning down a passage on the east side into King St, 2-st as map, like it is Doveton St. Into Devonshire St, this street is decidedly better than West St and should be PINK, except first at the west end and on the north side between the 2 blocks of almshouses, careful gardens in front, china pots in windows, etc.

S along Cleveland St, 2½-st , built 1846, PINK to PURPLE. On the west side, just north of Whitehead St is a court of 8 cottages, very narrow, flagged, called Coburg Place, LIGHT BLUE. Whitehead St, LIGHT BLUE as map, Macnamara's yard for postal vans by contract. "A poor set of houses and men", at the northwest end of the road. On the south side are 2 courts, Union Buildings on the east and Union Place on the west, both poor, LIGHT BLUE as map.

On the east side of Cleveland St, Bellevue Place, very respectable, entered under iron gates, dwellings of some of Charringtons men, 2-st. On the west side of Cleveland St lower down is a cul-de-sac, LIGHT BLUE on map but looks PURPLE, called Cleveland Grove.

Into the Mile End Rd and W turning up into Brunswick Place, BLACK on map, this has now disappeared, the whole place having been turned into Lead Glass and Varnish works, shut off by a stout door at the south end just past the public house.

N up Cambridge R, houses dated 1774 at southwest end and still older a little higher up. On the east side of the road are two very bad streets. Key St and Faith St, DARK BLUE on map and still at least DARK BLUE. 2-st, 2-roomed cottages letting at 5/- per week. At the southwest end of Key St is a 4-st model dwellings "very rough", windows nearly all broken, a rough set of boys playing at the bottom of the stairs.

General remarks

There seems to have been a general decline in the streets lying between Devonshire St on the south, Globe Rd on the east and Green St on the north and Cambridge Rd on the west. This has been partially compensated for by changes for the better in Devonshire St and Cullard St.

Great numbers of beer houses in the district. Great temptation to do Sunday trade and difficulty in catching them owing to their having crows posted to give the alarm. As to extra payments being received by police, Pearn at first said he knew nothing of them except those reported and authorised by the Commissioner. Payments for authorised duties amount he thinks to about 1/- per week each man in the course of the year. Every fortnight a man has a holiday and is generally allowed to spend it on extra duty at music halls etc. For this he is paid 5/-. The music hall pays 20/- and the remainder is pooled and divided among all the men at the end of the year equally. Call money, he said, was no more. Police are occasionally drafted off to other districts and are not therefore certain callers, so a race of professionals has taken their place and each morning at 4 AM you can see them going their rounds tapping at the windows with a long fishing rod. As to call-money being paid by publicans, he is not officially aware of the fact and if he were he would drop on the man and on the publican at once. "It may exist," he said "it may have taken the place of the beer which publicans used to give to the men just before closing time." Now publicans dare not risk their licenses. Pearn said that even were he to try and stop the practice of giving equivalents to a pot of beer per night, he thought he should fail. He admitted it was not a serious abuse but if he were aware of any instances he should at once put his foot down both on the policeman and the publican. He thought that beer houses in any case could hardly afford to pay every policeman that passed their door in the course of a week.

As to the complaints of convicts he protested vehemently that they were unfounded. He knows one working as a potman to a very respectable beer house keeper who has never even once suspected that his man reported himself every month at the police station.

Walk 37   B351-13

Monday 28th March 1898
George Duckworth with Inspector Barker

Inspector Barker is a middle-sized man, small moustache, very quiet, never speaks except when spoken to. Has been in the district 4 years, coming here from Paddington. Inspector Pearn who went round part of this, the J Division, in January last, has since been sent to Richmond as a mounted Inspector.

Starting at the Headquarters station in the Bethnal Green Road.
S down Pott St, 2-st, poor, toy horse and towel horse makers, many windows broken and patched, street very badly kept, LIGHT BLUE as map.

W along Lucas St, very poor, market bag makers, 2-st, weavers windows, LIGHT BLUE to DARK BLUE, in map LIGHT BLUE, to Fox St, 2-st, very poor, costers, LIGHT BLUE to DARK BLUE.

E then N up Pitt St, 2-st, narrower than the rest and more windows broken and patched with brown paper, costers, LIGHT BLUE to DARK BLUE, it certainly looks DARK BLUE. Barker said they were all a hard-working set of people who worked honestly for their living and got drunk on Saturday nights but are not troublesome to the police.

Into Bethnal Green Rd, then S down Gales Gardens. Houses extended nearly the whole way from Bethnal Green Rd to Birkbeck St on the west side, but only half way down on the east. The lower half of the east side is taken up by Carter Paterson's stable yards. Houses 3-st, road well paved, does not look so rough as Pitt St, fewer windows broken and patched, but is a rough street "like Collins Place". A few here from Boundary St. Some thieves, DARK BLUE to BLACK, in map DARK BLUE.

N into Bethnal Green Rd and S down Cambridge Rd, houses all shapes and sizes, PINK-barred as map. W along Birkbeck St, poor, quiet, LIGHT BLUE to PURPLE, in map LIGHT BLUE. S down Coventry St, there is a small nameless court out of the

southwest end, not marked in the map, 2-st, poor, LIGHT BLUE. E along Parliament St, part of which is DARK BLUE on map but Barker did not know it to be different from the rest, though poor, 2-st, all LIGHT BLUE. On the north side is Parliament Place, nine 2-st houses, some windows broken, curtains holey, doors open but carpeted with mats or linoleum, LIGHT BLUE, in map part is DARK BLUE.

W into Cambridge Rd then S, then E along 3 Colt Lane, 2-st, a little above the other streets but some windows broken and children dirty, PURPLE as map. N up Abingdon St, costers, one or two houses better but it is rather LIGHT BLUE than the PURPLE of the map. W along Glass St, 2-st, same LIGHT BLUE as map.

S down Coventry St, W along 3 Colt lane, N up Primrose St, the north end of which is blocked by Allen and Hanbury's chemical works, strong smell of Sanitas. Girls, a respectable set, just coming out of the works. Primrose St itself is rather better than the other streets, books and wax flowers in the windows, PURPLE rather than LIGHT BLUE. W and then S down Violet St, not coloured in map, poorer, 2-st, LIGHT BLUE, houses on east side only, the west side is the back of the Corfield St Buildings. Corfield St, Finnis St, Wilmot St and Ainslie St are all Waterlow Buildings, "The best class of Buildings in London" said Barker. Very ugly bow-windowed, 5-st, but well looked after and get a more respectable set than any of the neighbouring streets, mechanics, police "even from Commercial St", railway men, character PURPLE to

PINK. China pots, flowers, clean windows, none broken. In Corfield St are 43 blocks with 10 families in each. 22 blocks on the west side and 21 on the east. 7/6 to 9/6 for 3 and 4 rooms. No 1-roomed tenements. At the north end of Finnis St, Ainslie St runs east and meets Corfield St. Corfield St is continued north to the Bethnal Green Rd, having Buildings on its west side and the police station and yard on its east.

W along the Bethnal Green Rd and S down Seabright St. Houses on the west side 3-st, one storey having been added on their former top storey. Houses on the east side, 2-st, weavers windows, a few looms remaining but mostly become small cabinet makers workshops. "Men who make at home and sell to the large wholesale houses in Curtain Rd." This and the next street, Viaduct St, are a centre for home cabinet work and weaving. Both alike in character, both PURPLE, though Viaduct St in map is LIGHT BLUE. Barker said the last two years had been very prosperous, "No complaints of out of work," but that with a bad year both of the streets would fall below the line of poverty and become LIGHT BLUE. "The people do not save, they spend it all in drink." The two small turnings between Seabright St and Viaduct St are Viaduct Place and Weldon St, which latter has only one house at the east and one at the west end and none on the south side. All PURPLE in map. W into St Andrew St, like the rest, mixed, a few poor, PURPLE rather than LIGHT BLUE of map.

E along Cheshire St, 2- and 3-st, PURPLE rather than LIGHT BLUE of map on north side. S down Brady St and W along London St, houses on north side only, PURPLE as map. Court on north side, 5 houses with little wooden palinged front gardens, 2-st, not on map and nameless, PURPLE.

N up Mape St, 2-st, quiet, respectable, PURPLE as map. On west side is Kelsey St, 2-st, PURPLE as map, W along Sale St, the BLACK spot on the north side is down. {On the north side of Sale St, W of Hague St is Park Place, poorer, not marked in map, six 2-st houses, LIGHT BLUE.} Sale St itself is like the rest in character and appearance, PURPLE rather than PINK of map. Past Menotti St, 2-st, PURPLE as map and Hague St, PURPLE as map, to Vallance Rd. N turning E at Derbyshire St, 2-st, PURPLE as map, E past Hague St, on the south side is Hague Place, six 2-st houses, built 1822, very poor, rough looking, not in map, DARK BLUE. E to Mape St where Oxford House makes the northeast corner.

{On the west side of Menotti St is a court, 2-st, poor, called Manchester Buildings, "Don't call it a court guv'nor, it's a avenue" said one woman, children well fed fairly clean, LIGHT BLUE, not marked on map.}

W along Thomas' Passage, in map DARK BLUE, now stables on south side and backs and warehouses of Bethnal Green Rd shops on the north. At the extreme west end corner of Vallance Rd is a poor block of cottages, LIGHT BLUE rather than PURPLE of map. N into Bethnal Green Rd and E to the Police Station.

General remarks

This comprises the whole of St Andrew's (Rev. Eck's) parish. On the whole it looks better off than it used to be, probably on account of the good trade of the last 2 years. As to changes, Sale St is not so good as it was, from PINK to PURPLE, and Pitt St looks DARK BLUE rather than LIGHT BLUE. On the other hand the DARK BLUE of Thomas' Passage has disappeared, so has the BLACK bit north of Sale St and the streets of Waterlow Buildings look more PINK than PURPLE.

Industries: Boot, weaving, cabinet making, costering. For women, cardboard box-making.

The curse of the district is drink, said Barker. He has noticed a slight decrease in both sexes. "One sex drinks as much as the other here, and where the husband drinks, the wife generally drinks too."

There is no prostitution, "In neither of the 3 Music Halls would you be solicited". But there is much irregular intercourse and living together unmarried.

Walk 38   B351-14

Tuesday 29th March 1898
George Duckworth with Inspector Barker

Starting at E corner of Three Colts Lane and Cambridge Road

S down the Cambridge Rd, small shops, houses all shapes and sizes on west side, PINK-barred as map. W along Oxford St, 2-st, south side poor, LIGHT BLUE to PURPLE, windows broken, north side fairly well-to-do, PINK, neither coloured in map. Into Buckhurst St, built about 1845, working class, PURPLE to PINK, "in character, much like Corfield Buildings", respectable. The lower end is marked PINK in map, but is rather less good than the upper, now PURPLE all through.

S into Darling Row, which has 4-st buildings on its south side of which the easternmost block is less rough than the rest because the Jews are in, but the rest is very rough and DARK BLUE, not marked in map. Behind Buckhurst Row, small glass blowers furnaces and stables, a few houses on the southeast side. Crates of lamp chimneys outside the glass factories. "The glass blowers make very good money, but drink it all away, a good many of them in Bethnal Green but more north of the Bethnal Green Rd than south of it". LIGHT BLUE, not marked in map.

N up Coventry St, 2-st, 27 ft across from houses to houses, houses flush with the pavement, (27 ft seems to be a fair average width for a 2-st street), doors open, women rough looking. The street is rather rough, houses in fair outward repair, all LIGHT BLUE to PURPLE, Between Sommerford St and Octagon St is the best part, here it is PURPLE to PINK, in map the whole street except the north end is PURPLE.

N to Cudworth St, then W, at the extreme northeast end are saw mills and only 1 or 2 dwelling houses. Further west, houses on south side only, the north side being railway arches, tenanted by rag merchants and cats meat vendors, PURPLE to LIGHT BLUE, in map LIGHT BLUE.

S down Carlton Place, which is the same, into Barnsley St, respectable, better than the others "like Buckhurst St", clean and windows unbroken, PURPLE rather than LIGHT BLUE of map. Into Sommerford St, 2-st, poorer, rather rough, bread lying about, LIGHT BLUE as map. S down Fellbrigg St, 2-st, roadway in very bad repair, PURPLE to LIGHT BLUE, in map PURPLE. E into Octagon St, 2-st, LIGHT BLUE, in map PURPLE, windows broken, patched with brown paper, poor, rather rough "but not quite so rough as Pitt and Pott Streets".

Jane street, running north out of it is a little better, children hatless, holey stockings, PURPLE to LIGHT BLUE, in map PURPLE. E along Northampton St into Collingwood St, very rough, some houses on west side down. "More Irish here than in any of the neighbouring streets". 2-st, "quite as bad as Gale's Gardens". Same all the way through from Darling St to the railway bridge, DARK BLUE, in map PURPLE.

S down Fellbrigg St, great mess in street and windows broken, home tailoring, English, children with holey boots, LIGHT BLUE rather than PURPLE of map.

S across Darling Row into Cambridge Rd and W along Lisbon St, the whole of the south side has been taken by the extension of greengrocery back premises from Cambridge Rd and by Mann and Crossmans Brewery. The north side has the 4-st buildings, continued round from Darling Row, very rough, DARK BLUE. Here the disturbed DARK BLUE from the south side of the street seem simply to have moved across the road. S down Cambridge Rd, on the west side, the court marked DARK BLUE in map is now part of the brewery. W along the Whitechapel Rd, N up Brady St, E into Bath St. Brewery on south side, north side some small Jewish shops, PURPLE. N up Bath Place, 29 houses on east side only, with small wooden palinged uncared for front gardens, LIGHT BLUE as map.

Across Thomas's passage and up Pereira St, rough, roadway in very bad state, houses in fair outward condition though. The north end, said Barker, is rather better than the south in character, as DARK BLUE lined BLACK to DARK BLUE (the map marks the south end LIGHT BLUE). A turning east half way along east side of Pereira St leads into Little Collingwood St. This turning is of recent building, but inhabitants very poor and very rough, windows broken and stuffed with rags, some not stopped at all, blinds dirty, holey.

S down Little Collingwood St, narrow, 9 ft across road from house to house, 2-st, DARK BLUE rather than BLACK of map, all English, no prostitutes or bullies, inhabitants costers and fish curers. Some thieves and many juvenile thieves.

N up Pereira St (the northern end of Little Collingwood St is down) to Neath Place, BLACK in map. Houses have been and are still being rebuilt but the inhabitants are a little worse than those in Pereira St, so the east end may still remain BLACK. The end at the corner of Tapp St is down and a Mission Hall is to be built in its place. The west end (Brady St end) is better, "hard working poor", fish curers, hoop benders, LIGHT BLUE to DARK BLUE, rather than the BLACK of map.

E then S down Collingwood St, rough. Into Foster St, in map DARK BLUE, 2-st, bread in street, very rough, DARK BLUE lined BLACK, rather than the DARK BLUE of map, rough lads and a bookie at the north end taking their bets. Open doors, young girls not looking more than 16 years old at two of them, mothers, a labourer with bird cages done up in dark blue pocket handkerchief walking down street. N up Collingwood St and W along Cudworth St, 2-st, respectable. This and the north side of Barnsley St, making one block of houses, should all be PURPLE rather than the LIGHT BLUE of map.

Sommerford St houses being repainted and repointed. The houses on the south side of the west end of Sommerford St, 2-st, rather better, LIGHT BLUE to PURPLE. The south side of Barnsley St and the north side of Sommerford St all LIGHT BLUE as map.

S down Tapp St, houses on east side 3- and 2-st, PURPLE, families living on 1st floor look rather poorer than those on ground floor.

W along Neath Place, better this end than the other, LIGHT BLUE to DARK BLUE.

Across Brady St to Tent St, rough 2-st, windows broken and dirty, roadway fairly paved, DARK BLUE as map. At the west end is a turning with houses leading to Scott St, also DARK BLUE (not coloured in map). Scott St is DARK BLUE as map, roadway in bad state, mess and paper, behind it on the south side is Dixie St, 24 houses on south side only, paved court, very poor, on the north side are the backyards of Scott St separated from Dixie St by a wall of wooden bands. The top windows at the back of Scott St are long weavers windows.

S down Brady St and E into Eastman St, BLACK in map, now different, concrete pavement, 3-st dwellings on either side, poor but quiet, children out at elbows but well fed and markedly cleaner than in preceding streets, LIGHT BLUE.

On the east side of Brady St is Reuben St, houses on north side only, quiet, respectable, 2-st, LIGHT BLUE to PURPLE. South of it is Dagnalls Place, 2-st, looks rough though not much trouble to police. Woman with unfinished matchbox in her mouth, football going on in court, most doors open, young mothers, children well fed, the turning into Reuben St is boarded up. LIGHT BLUE to DARK BLUE. South of it is New Square, quiet, 18 houses, well cared for little gardens in front, 2-st, that at the east end had about 8 cages hung out on wall, character PURPLE, in map LIGHT BLUE. S down Brady St, PURPLE as map, small shops kept by Jews, at the southwest end below the manure works (now for sale) and the alms houses are large blocks of dwellings, "the 4 per cent Industrial Dwellings Company" tenanted wholly by Jews. Facing north are 13 blocks, and altogether there are 4 such, making 52 blocks, poor, respectable, quiet, LIGHT BLUE to PURPLE.

S to the Whitechapel Rd then W, on the north side is Nelsons Court, a very narrow entrance, 2-st houses, poor, but not rough, at the north end were two bookmakers apparently taking down bets from a respectably-dressed middle-aged woman, who moved away as we came up. Nelson Court runs into Winthrop St, it is not coloured on map. Winthrop St, 3- and 2-st houses, well paved. On the south side were formerly two brothels, one is still by the look of a woman standing at the doorway. The street is otherwise respectable, LIGHT BLUE to PURPLE.

S into Whitechapel Rd and SW, on the north side are Wood's Buildings, a turning leading over bridge over railway to the Board School in Buck's Row. The next is Court St, DARK BLUE in map, only 3 dwelling houses, small shops, PURPLE, leads to bridge over railway. W along Whitechapel Rd and N up Vallance Rd, on the east side all is down between Vallance Rd, Bucks Row and the Whitechapel Station, with the exception of the houses at the north corner of White's Row, now called Durward St. Durward St has one block of buildings at the west end next to Kearley and Tongues very large provision factory, and there are some houses between Thomas St and Queen Anne St, LIGHT BLUE to PURPLE, LIGHT BLUE in map. Further east is Sayders very large clothing factory, which employs a rough but respectable set of young women. They were skipping in the street as we passed. The houses are on the south side only, respectable PURPLE rather than LIGHT BLUE of map. At the entrance to the street by the Board School, took place the first Whitechapel murder. In front of the Board School between the warehouses and the underground railway is a wide open space, well paved with cobbles, "where the Jews assemble on Sunday and speechify".

N up Thomas St, PINK on west side, but less good on the east side, rather PURPLE than PINK. The Friends Burial Ground on the west side is a public garden with fair-sized plot of grass and asphalt square and sheds for shelter at the south end. The south end of Thomas St out of the Whitechapel Rd used to be of bad repute, brothel on east side and murder on west, but now well-to-do. The Tobacco Workers Club affiliated is on east side, in place of the brothel, and shops on the west, PINK as map.

N up Queen Anne St, 3-st, rough, children very ragged, some prostitutes, bread and bits of raw meat in the roadway, windows broken and dirty, all English, one woman called out "let us be guv'nor, don't pull the house down and turn us out". On the west side, not coloured in map, is a small court, hot potato can standing idle, narrow, DARK BLUE.

N up Thomas St, at the northwest corner 10 men waiting for the casual ward to open (it opens at 4, it was now 1.45PM). North end of Thomas St is a gate leading to private road, on the west side of which are 3 blocks of Dwellings called Blackwall Buildings, belonging to Blackwall Railway, decent class, PURPLE, at either end is a gateway which is shut at night. The furthest gate opens on to the stoneyard of the Whitechapel Union.

Interview with W. Weston, Superintendent of the J or Bethnal Green Division, at the police station in the Bethnal Green Road, 4th January 1898

Mr Weston is a big burly man who has risen from the ranks. Did not wish to be interviewed because he said his Inspector Pearn knew so much more about the district than he did.

As to the policy of fixed points, he said there were 7(?) in Bethnal Green but that in a rough poor district fixed points were giving way to short patrols. It is tiresome for a man to stand in one place or never to move more than 10 yards away from a given spot. The duty is disliked. It is more difficult to prevent men from talking to you and continuing to do so. Police are more open to temptation from bribes. Therefore he personally favours the short patrol, but he said it was a question of general policy, which he felt should more properly be answered from headquarters.

As to Buildings, he thinks that the builder or owner of large blocks who put in really strong caretakers and back them up, do more to humanise a rough neighbourhood than "all the churches, chapels and missions put together". "What that class want is discipline and a sense of orderliness introduced into their lives." All buildings have rules and if the caretaker enforces them properly, moral improvement should follow. "Once you get these people driven to cleanliness for their own sakes and not for the sake of cleanliness as an abstract virtue, you have won half the battle." They are driven to be clean for their own sakes, for they know that if they do not act up to a certain standard, they will be turned out and have to find a small house elsewhere, "a thing which is now very difficult". But on the other hand, where the rules of buildings are lax, "there are no worse places to be found". He mentioned as an instance of the latter Quinn's Buildings in Russia Lane.

Roughness, he said, was decreasing. Not rapidly, but he thought surely, even in Bethnal Green. "I am certain that it is if you take London as a whole." As to changes in Bethnal Green, "the bad places are not quite so bad, and the good not quite so good". It is harder for a bad place to become better, than for good place to become worse "because vice is more conservative than virtue".

He confirmed Inspector Pearn's statement that the proportion of police to population was greater in the west than in the east end. But he also said he could well manage with a few more than he had.

(B350-3)

W along Thomas St, the south side is poor, windows broken, PURPLE to LIGHT BLUE, in map PURPLE.

N up Vallance Rd, Jews, buildings and 1-st shops, PURPLE, wood paved as far as Underwood St. Turning E at Selby St, 2-st, doors open, PURPLE to LIGHT BLUE, like it is Arundel St, in map PINK. At the extreme east end of Selby St turning north is Waterloo Terrace, poorer, LIGHT BLUE, in map PURPLE. W along Artillery St and N up Vallance Rd, late Nottingham St, now PURPLE not PINK.

General remarks

Rough streets east and west of Brady St. No prostitutes and bullies as in Whitechapel, but thieves and rough class generally "will do anything from thieving and home breaking to shooting a policeman". A mixture here of cockney Irish.

Houses generally in good repair outwardly, but streets as a whole badly paved and ill kept. We passed two young men sweeping with a foreman to look after them standing doing nothing. The men swept very lazily "the Vestry employees get 24/ or 25/ a week but are a bye word in the neighbourhood".

As to publicans paying the police, Barker said it was never done, as the police would not dare accept the money. I told him I knew that it was done in other subdivisions and that the constant denial of the practice on the part of the police put me in a rather difficult position. He still persisted in saying he knew nothing of it.

Great many juvenile thieves in the neighbourhood, "especially young Jews, they are more cunning than the English", but he said you very seldom got an old Jew as a thief. With the Englishman, once a thief, always a thief.

Note flowers in windows of even the poorest streets, daffodils, primroses and hyacinths in small vases.

Walk 39   B352-1

Thursday 31st March 1898
George Duckworth with Inspector Barker

Starting at the south end of Camden Street late Ainsley Street

Very poor and rough, windows dirty, broken, blinds and curtains holey. Children ragged and dirty, boots holey. 2-st houses, costers, cabinet makers, DARK BLUE as map.

W along Grove St, 2-st. There is a passage up by Board School with one house LIGHT BLUE, leading west to Canrobert St where it broadens and has houses on south side only. 2-st built 1861. Windows look rough but Barker said only poor. LIGHT BLUE to DARK BLUE, in map DARK BLUE.

S down Cambridge St, ten 2-st houses, good outward repair, windows broken and ragged women, rough, DARK BLUE as map.

E into Jersey St late York St, looks a little less poor than Camden St but Barker said its character was the same. Rough class, DARK BLUE, in map LIGHT BLUE. W and S down Wolverley St, 2-st, poor, same character both sides of street, a shade better than the preceeding i.e. LIGHT BLUE, in map PURPLE. Daffodils and primroses in water in the windows of houses in many of these streets.

Into Bethnal Green Rd, very busy market street, not quite so busy looking as Brick Lane, but it is broader. Crowds of women round barrows shopping. N up Canrobert St, mixed, 2-st, weavers windows and a few looms remaining, poorer south of Grove St than north of it i.e. PURPLE. Houses north of it have been done up. Street better paved than most about here. Boot operatives. In map PINK.

Back into Bethnal Green Rd then W and N up Blythe St, 2-st, windows unbroken, in map LIGHT BLUE but it looks PURPLE. E into George Gardens, small 1-and 2-st cottages on either side of a passage. "Many of the inhabitants have been here 40 or 50 years. It is very difficult to get a house here." Quiet, respectable, poor, proud of their gardens which are "a picture in summer, you'd be surprised". One woman said she paid 5/- for 2 rooms and a washhouse and thought it would be impossible to find a nicer house, a better copper than hers or a pleasanter place to live in than George's Gardens. One man has a glass-house and goes in for market gardening. Inhabitants are woodyard men and cabinet makers. In map LIGHT BLUE, now rather PURPLE. It was washing day and gardens were filled with bed covers and clothes drying in the wind. Windows of houses generally full of flower pots or daffodils and primroses in water. 20 houses on the east side and 25 on the west.

W into Middle Walk. Same kind of place, rather poorer, LIGHT BLUE as map.

W into Mansford St. The west side has a Board School and dwellings and is respectable mixed class. The east side is poorer, one set of dwellings belonging to the East End Dwellings Co. is one of the roughest sets Barker knows anywhere. This set is on the east side. Like Gales Gardens and Pitt St, DARK BLUE, windows broken etc. 4-st. Lower down on the southeast side is a granary, no dwelling houses.

S into Bethnal Green Rd, W past the Red Church (St James 'the Great') now shut for repairs. "Used to marry anyone who came on Bank holidays for 7d but have not done so now for the last 2 or 3 years." N up Pollard Row, 2- and 3-st on east side, PURPLE as map, "great many chair and couch wood carvers living here, men who earn good money but drink it up fast".

{The houses on the west side of Pollard Row, N of the Adelaide Dispensary are decidedly poorer than the rest i.e. LIGHT BLUE.}

E along Florida St, small shops, LIGHT BLUE to PURPLE, LIGHT BLUE in map. N up Pollard St, 2- and 3-st, cabinet makers, mixed. 2 or 3 policemen living in the street. Built in 1846 (i.e. the 2-st houses on west side, the rest are newer). At the north end is Pearl Yard, nothing but cabinet makers shops, 33 of them, one above the other. W along Florida St to Squirries St, no LIGHT BLUE as map, houses both sides, 2-st, PURPLE. Between it and Pollard St is Norah St, Concrete passage, 2-st, respectable mechanics, like Corfield Buildings. PINK as map.

NW through Wellington Place, LIGHT BLUE in map, but now better, newish 2-st houses, PURPLE to PINK. Into Warner Place, 2½-st, PINK as map. E along Hackney Rd, and S down St Peter St, respectable, 2½-st, 36 ft across, fairly broad street. E along St Peter's Square, 2-st, and S down Nelson St all of the same class, PINK as map. Into Old Bethnal Green Rd, very mixed road, some PINK, some PURPLE, others LIGHT BLUE. Between Pollard St and Mansford St it is certainly PINK. The map marks it all equally PURPLE. N up Mansford St, late Rushmead St, 2-st, respectable, PINK as map. The court, LIGHT BLUE in map, on the west side is now all cabinet makers workshops. A good part of the southeast end, nearly up to Sheldon Place is taken up by new School Buildings.

N into Hackney Rd, then E, on the south side is a narrow passage leading to Northampton Cottages, ten 2-st cottages, poor but fair gardens in front and one old large tree, LIGHT BLUE as map. Back into the Hackney Rd, E to Teesdale St which has poor rough houses, broken windows, dirty, between the Hackney Rd and the Board School on the west side, LIGHT BLUE. The east side is 3- and 2-st mixed, the whole PURPLE rather than the PINK of the map. "Not so good as Mansford St," though the lower end is better than the north. On the east side is Claremont Place, houses on south side only. Poor not rough, not worse than LIGHT BLUE.

S and then W into Sheldon Place, well paved and quiet, 17 2-st houses, windows clean and unbroken, lately done up, PURPLE, in map LIGHT BLUE. S into Old Bethnal Green Rd and W. On the north side are Hammonds Gardens, nine 2-st houses, poor, quiet, flowers, bird cages abundant, LIGHT BLUE as map.

Then E and N up Canrobert St. Street wants mending, the north end is a cul-de-sac, bread in street, quiet, poor, bird cages, a beer house on its own, LIGHT BLUE to PURPLE, in map LIGHT BLUE. Catherine St running across it is like it, 2-st, LIGHT BLUE as map.

E to Temple St, "like Teesdale St", 2-st, PURPLE as map. N on the east side is Claremont St, houses on south side only. "Has a reputation for suicides", windows broken, dirty, rough, DARK BLUE as map. On the north side are new cabinet shops in place of the Baptist Chapel and all west of it is down.

E to Treadway St, which looks rather poorer and is LIGHT BLUE in map, 2-st. Barker said in character it was like Teesdale St. E to Minerva St, 2-st, like the rest, PURPLE, in map PINK. Houses letting at 10/- per week. Small general shop in middle of street. E along Centre St, 2-st, of which the south side is poorer than the north. South side LIGHT BLUE as map. North side PURPLE, map LIGHT BLUE. S down Matilda St, blinds clean and windows unbroken, respectable working class, PURPLE to LIGHT

BLUE, in map LIGHT BLUE. Felix Street, east of it, is rather poorer, PURPLE to LIGHT BLUE, in map LIGHT BLUE. W along Cambridge Circus, 2-st on south side, 3-st on north, LIGHT BLUE to PURPLE. That part of it east of Felix St is LIGHT BLUE.

N into Hackney Rd, then S down Clare St, 3-st tenements on west side only. The east side is taken up by railway arches which are used as stables, badly paved, rather rough. Rough women at doors, children hatless, dirty but well fed, LIGHT BLUE as map. S into Poyser St "a little better than Clare St", 2-, 3- and 5-st dwellings, LIGHT BLUE to PURPLE, in map LIGHT BLUE. The DARK BLUE spot at the south end is like the rest, LIGHT BLUE, five 2-st houses.

S down Cambridge Rd and W into Peacock St. The dark spot in the map is down but the road leads under the railway and then turns south with cottages on the west and north side only. Uncoloured in map, a rough place, like Gales Gardens, well paved, but doors open, windows broken, patched, dirty, children and women dirty and ragged. The turning that existed formerly by the east side of the railway arches is boarded up. Out into Cambridge Rd. S and turning E and S at Nant St, 3- and 2-st, PURPLE as map. Into the Bethnal Green Rd, westwards. On the north side is Hollybush Place, uncoloured in map, cabinet factory south end, above it 4 houses, respectable, PURPLE to PINK, front gardens.

W along Bethnal Green Rd and N up Hollybush Gardens, 3-st tenements, mixture of factories and houses, rather rough looking "but there are so few of them that we don't notice it as a rough place". LIGHT BLUE to DARK BLUE, LIGHT BLUE in map. The road is the same width all the way up to St Jude St, 2-st, broad road, 36 ft across, respectable, "like St Peter St", PINK as map. So is Middleton St, Clarkson St and Treadway St, all 2-st, PINK as map.

S down Punderson's Gardens, narrow, mixed. On the east side opposite the passage leading to Camden St is a very rough block of buildings which should be marked DARK BLUE, windows broken and rough men at the doors, the rest is PURPLE to LIGHT BLUE. On the west side of the street is a large clothing factory.

General remarks

In appearance this district is now less poor than the map would warrant, due probably to the good trade of the last few years. The improvement in the streets between Old Bethnal Green Rd and Hackney Rd may therefore only be temporary. The workers of the district are cabinet makers, who drink, glass blowers who drink, and costers who drink. "They make good enough money but none of them spend it well." Those employed both work and live in the neighbourhood and "few go out and very few come in search of employment". The roughest bit is that just opposite the Police Station, Camden St, Grove St and York St. "But roughness aint nothing now hanywhere in London to what it was when I first joint" said Inspector Webb inside the station.

Interview with Inspector Barker of the J or Bethnal Green Police Division at the Police Station, 5th May 1898

Inspector Barker is about 45 years of age. He has served over 20 years and is now within a year of retirement. Middle height, moustache, squash black felt hat. Not like a policeman to look at. Has been 4 years in the subdivision, is now a Subdivisional Inspector. Rather timorous.

As to juvenile thieves, there has been an increase in the charges of young Jew thieves, but a decrease amongst Protestants and Roman Catholics. The reason is that there is no Industrial School for Jews, and, as magistrates are unwilling to send boys under 14 to Reformatory schools they discharge them instead. The effect of discharging such boys is to leave them free to recommence thieving, which they do. In consequence the same boys come up time and again. The number of charges therefore increases but it does not necessarily mean that the number of Jew boys who adopt thieving as a profession is on the increase. Barker does not think that it is. The reason for the apparent decrease among Protestants and Roman Catholics is due to the Industrial Schools now in existence. There are now 400 children in the East End Industrial Schools.

[Note the above particulars were obtained by Inspector. Barker from Mr Hiscocks who is the School Board agent(!) for all the truant children of the East End districts, comprising Shoreditch, Hoxton, Haggerston, Bethnal Green, Bow, Bromley, Poplar, St George's in the East, Whitechapel].

As to adult thieves, Bethnal Green is, with Hoxton and Haggerston, one of the districts to which the police turn most naturally for the discovery of offenders and stolen goods. Very few adult thieves among Jews.

Drink on the whole decreasing both among men and women in Bethnal Green. He thinks it is still excessive but less than it used to be. Bank Holidays are the curses of the neighbourhood. Great trouble to the police. Bootmakers and cabinet makers observe the feast for a week. They save up before hand and then "go a buster".

Jews rarely get drunk. In 4 years he has only known two cases, both of women charged for being drunk and disorderly. Jew women as a rule lead happier lives than Gentile women, more respected by their husbands and more faithful. In Gentile families where one drinks you will generally find that the other does also. He has seen exceptions where the man or the wife were sober while the other drank but they were always exceptions.

Drunkenness begins about 17 years of age for males and 18-21 for females. "Very rare that you see a case under 16 and when it comes to under 20 it is only an exceptional outburst." Girls, he said, began when they first went out keeping company. Neither sex becomes a confirmed soaker until near 30, the women nearly always after marriage (i.e. the woman drunkard is probably a married woman).

There are he thinks too many licensed houses in the subdivision. Supposing that the numbers were halved it would have no effect upon those who meant to get drunk because they would go any distance, but the waverers would be saved from the exceeding temptation they have at present. Against this there is the increased danger of drunkenness in crowded places. If you had fewer places there would be less space and greater difficulty in distinguishing between those who had and those who had not already had more than was good for them. Nevertheless, he thought that even if the houses were reduced by one third there would be more than space enough and less temptation. He said he did not think anyone would be tempted to open a house in Bethnal Green even if free trade in houses was allowed.

The slum beer houses are the least reputable of the licensed houses. These are those with licenses previous to 1869 whose terms must be renewed unless there is anything against them. The Justices are attempting to get rid of them by refusing to grant new licenses except on the surrender of other licenses. Thus in Goldsmith's Row a new license has been granted with the provision that the house may only be opened after the surrender of two other licenses. The slum beer houses are cheaper to buy than any other houses and therefore the would-be owner of the new house is on the look out for two of them. In this way the justices hope to diminish their number.

Of prostitution there is none in Bethnal Green. Relations both before and after marriage often very loose, but no selling for hire.

The last 2 years have been very prosperous. No out of work nor want of food.

He does not believe any payment is made by publicans to the police.

(B352-5)

Barker said he thought that the Bethnal Green police subdivision was remarkable for the numbers of suicides and sudden deaths they had to enquire into. The first among adults and the second among children. Suicides followed on drinking bouts and quarrels between husbands and wives, sudden deaths from improper feeding.

The amount of drunkenness is still a sure sign of the amount of work in Bethnal Green so that "we are busiest when the people are at Bank Holiday season", they save up before, so that now there is a lull, but Barker thinks it is mounting and only means an outbreak at Easter time. Saints Monday is generally observed.

In the subdivision are 173 policemen all except 6 living out. "Most would rather be employed in the West than the East End."

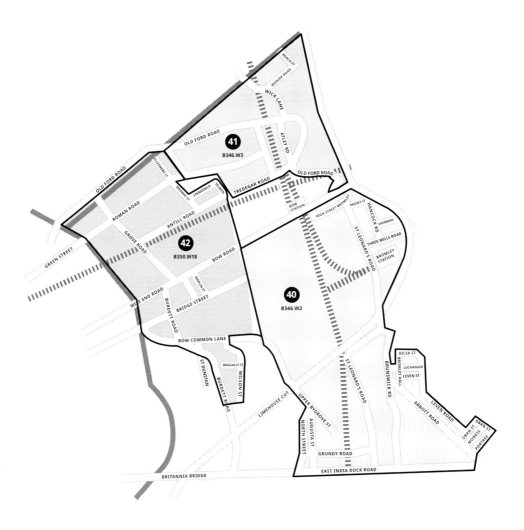

Walk 40
B346-2

Monday 31st May 1897
George Duckworth with Inspector Caleb Carter

Starting down the Campbell Road and into the Devons Road.

On the west of the Campbell Rd, Fairfoot Rd, Rounton Rd, Swaton Rd and Chiltern Rd, PINK in the map and inhabited by railway and policemen. Knapp Rd, PURPLE in the map, there has been some improvement but it is not nearly so respectable as the foregoing roads.

S of Knapp Rd are Fern St, Blackthorn St, Whitethorn Street and Sherwood St, on the west side of the Devons Rd, all BLUE streets, Blackthorn and Whitethorn being DARK BLUE. Inhabited by many Irish and workers in the Gas Works, a rough lot, given to drink and racing and betting. Whippet racing a favorite sport for Sundays on the Bow running ground. Whippets are dogs of the greyhound type, smaller than regular greyhounds and larger and faster than Italian Greyhounds. Blackthorn St is perhaps the worst street of this block. South of the Devons Rd are Glaucus, River and Weston Streets getting worse as they approach the Fenian Barracks. Weston St and Parring St both DARK BLUE.

The block of streets between Gale St and Furze St are the worst in the District, worse than in almost any district in London. Three policemen wounded there last week. This block sends more police to hospital than any other in London. "They are not human, they are wild beasts." You take a man or a woman, a rescue is always organised. They fling brick bats, iron, anything they can lay their hands on. All are Irish cockneys. Not an Englishman or a Scotchman would live among them. The group is known as the 'Fenian Barracks'. The streets have all the appearances of semi-vicious poverty. Hatless women, uncleaned doorsteps, two or three women drunk, shoeless and stockingless children in great numbers notwithstanding the fact that at 3.15 they should be in school. In Hawgood St a group of young men between 18 and 20 years of age playing pitch and toss. One older man of almost 25

to 30 years among them. Consternation at our appearance. Free fight to get out of the circle. Carter surprised at their having let us get so close. "What were the crows doing?" Crows being those put to watch and keep care. Eastward St, the roughest of this rough lot. All knew Carter by sight well. At the corner of Hawgood St the doors leading to a fat refinery. Not only are the inhabitants savage and think nothing of taking human life, the beasts are more terrifying. "You should come down here of an early summer morning, if possible after a shower of rain. Rats, not in twos or threes or in 10s or twentys, but in thousands and tens of thousands. The street will be covered with them, so will be the yard of the factory. Rats, not small rats but big and fat, the size of cats. You knock a flagstone with your boot and away they go with a rush and a hissing sound from their feet upon the pavements that will make your blood run cold. Most evenings or even during the day they will come up in search of water especially after a shower. Water is scarce in the drains in which they live. They will eat anything. A load of hams was condemned by the inspector as unfit for human food and brought down by barges to be boiled down for train oil. They arrived one evening, were unloaded and left till morning on the quay. In the morning nothing was left but brown husks with the outward appearance of hams. The rats had eaten out all that was inside." Carter saw them himself. What would happen if rat food ran short?

Then across the Cut over Stinkhouse Bridge down Guildford St into Chrisp St, a triangle bounded on the north by the Cut, on the east by the North London Railway and on the southwest by Upper North St, Bygrove St, Kerby St. Chrisp St runs down the centre of this group.

On the west of Chrisp St, Broomfield St, DARK BLUE in our map, but not so bad as the 'Barracks' which are also marked DARK BLUE. Perhaps there has been some improvement in Broomfield St, it did not look so bad as the barracks. Barchester St, LIGHT BLUE, is a better street than Broomfield. Brabazon St, PURPLE, still better, as is Ellesmere St. (The shades of difference in this block seem to be correct as regards themselves. It is only when we compare the DARK BLUE of Broomfield St with another DARK BLUE, such as Hawgood St, that you think that Broomfield St should be lighter or Hawgood St darker than they are marked.) Flint St still on the west of Chrisp St is the living place of prostitutes of the better class, who work the East India Dock Rd. Their customers are petty officers of ships, just as common sailors go to Jamaica Place so their superiors come to Flint St. The Duke of Suffolk Public House with a back entry into Northumberland St is recognised meeting place for these women who live in the neighbourhood, ie in Bygrove Street and Giraud St as well as in Flint St.

Bowen St, DARK BLUE, a short poor street with two beer houses and a small court Commodore Place. Barchester St, LIGHT BLUE, is a better street than Broomfield. Carmen, Charles and Cordelia Streets, not so poor, inhabited by dock labourers on fairly regular work. Some costers in Vesey St and Mary Place. Streets on the east side of Chrisp St, Morris, Fawes, Rifle, Cording, Milton as map. Then E through Grundy St turning N up the St Leonards Rd. On the west of St Leonards Rd, Church St, Ida St, Howard St, Lodore St. Ida St has 5 Public Houses, three of which are fully licensed, many rough women about and many women in the pubs. Monday is recognised as ladies day. In Carr St it is known as 'cowshed' day, poor women being known to their husbands and male neighbours as 'cows'. Monday is their drinking day because they have still a little pocket money left, they drink in the Public Houses which become in consequence 'cowsheds'.

On the SW side of St Leonards Rd, Cook, Follitt, Duffs Field, Gray, Tetley, Willis, Burcham, Tapley Streets. Tapley St, RED on map, is perhaps a little poorer and should be PURPLE. St Leonards Avenue north of it is a narrow street and poorer than Byron St which is an open street, though it has the same class of house.

Then E round Dewberry St and S down Brunswick Rd. Streets lying between St Leonards Rd and Brunswick Rd, a block of RED streets namely Joshua, Wilson, Andrew, Desart, Cawdor, Rowlett Streets. Of these Wilson St looks poorer than the PINK given to it. On the other hand Desart St (PURPLE) should be rather more PINK than PURPLE.

On the west side of the Brunswick Rd is the Abbotts Estate. The streets all beginning (from N to S) with the different letters of the alphabet and all the names are scotch. Going from N to S are Highland St, a fair street of a PURPLE BLUE. Glencoe, Findhorn, Eltrick, Dee, Culloden, Blair and Athole occupied by a very respectable class of poor employed in the Docks, or as lightermen, or foremen in the factories round about. These streets are all better, with the exception of Highland St, to the north than to the south ie the streets gradually tail off in character as you approach the East India Dock Rd. In Athole St are the headquarters of the North Metropolitan Tramways and of the London Gen Omnibus Co. and in the surrounding streets are many of the employees, stablemen, conductors, drivers etc.

Then down Athole St into Abbott Rd passing Aberfeldy and Benledi Streets, PURPLE as map. On the east of the Abbott Rd, a block of streets lying between Oban St and Abbott Rd, namely Portree St, Moness Rd and Oban St. Portree St and Oban St, PURPLE. Moness Rd, LIGHT BLUE. A poorer class come to Moness Rd because the rents are lower than in the other two streets. Rents are lower because the street is a lower level and houses used to be flooded. Things are better now and the sewers have been so improved that there is no longer any back flow. The north side of Oban St is LIGHT BLUE on our map but there is no perceptible outward difference between the north and the south sides.

Then NW up the Leven Rd, marked all DARK BLUE in our map. The south end may perhaps still be DARK BLUE, and there are a few mixed houses toward the centre. Higher up it is distinctly better, many house doors open, oil cloth and coconut mats in the entrance passages, flowers in the windows, decent curtains, sometimes a case of stuffed birds on the top of a book or two, all pointed to greater respectability, has the appearence of a street which is on the road upwards. At the north end is a large open waste which there is some talk of turning into a public garden. At present it is marshy and full of heaps of gravel, rubbish, etc but not fresh rubbish. Many gasworkers live in the Leven Rd.

{At the corner of Oban St is a public house which has been turned into a shirt factory. Every year a license is applied for and every year it is refused.}

Then up the Brunswick Rd with Zetland St, Galton, Wyvis, Venue and Uamvar Streets. Venue St is marked PURPLE but it is really better than the St Leonards Rd, also PURPLE but not quite so respectable as Uamvar St which we mark as RED. At the corner of Zetland St is the Bromley Hall Tavern which is a beer house only, a full license is refused every year.

On the east of the Brunswick Rd, Lochnagar and Spey Streets, both fair, and running between St Leonards Rd and Zetland St, Ailsa, Spey and Teviot Streets, all respectable, Teviot St being the best of them.

Then N over 4 Mills Bridge (known to the police as 3 Mills Bridge) and up St Leonards St. On the west of St Leonards St in a circle round St Andrews Church a group of BLUE and DARK BLUE streets namely Simpson St now called George St, Marnor St, Lingen St, rough streets, mixture of Irish. Devas St is the worst of them and has a very poor little nameless court out of it. These streets though poor and very rough, are not vicious in the same way as the Fenian Barracks. Donald St and Thomas St out of Devas St are also DARK BLUE. In Devas St were public houses with half open doors, women sitting drinking, with children of 3 or 4 years either on their laps or playing on the floor. Two small short streets, James St and Peter St on the east side of St Leonards St are LIGHT BLUE.

N again over the railway bridge and past the Bromley Station. On the west side a set of BLUE streets leading down to the Stepney Workhouse. Many of their occupants on their way there too. Powis and Stratfield Streets being a dark shade of LIGHT BLUE in character and Egleton Rd between them decidedly DARK BLUE (as map). Egleton Rd on the west and Hancock Rd on the east of St Leonards St are noted thieves' resorts. But all these streets bear a better police reputation than Devas St.

{22/IX/99. Great improvements in Egleton Rd. It now looks better than Powis Rd and if re-marked would be LIGHT BLUE}.

Three Mills Lane is PURPLE. Two houses on the north side are marked DARK BLUE and though they look worse than the rest of the road, don't look more than LIGHT BLUE. Maybe these two houses are brothels, Carter wasn't sure. Otis St, Jefferson, Washington and Sherman Streets are much of a muchness. Otis St and Jefferson St look fairly well "but they don't live up to their looks".

{Hinks Place, S of Jefferson St, poor cottages, LIGHT BLUE. Not marked in map}

In Washington St were many bare-headed women walking about. PURPLE in map but looks to be LIGHT BLUE. Franklin St and Priory St are the resorts of thieves. Both are probably DARK BLUE, we mark them LIGHT BLUE. Bruce Rd (PINK on map) is and has always been a respectable street.

Then N into the Bromley High St, past the Board School Manual Training School built on the site of a formerly well known common lodging house, which in its turn had been an old manor house with a valuable carved chimney piece. £100 was offered to, and refused by, the proprietor. When bought by the school board the chimney piece fell to the bid of a local dealer who sold it to the South Kensington Museum where it now is (according to Carter).

On the west side of the Bromley High St were two short streets leading down to the river, Amiel St and Amiel Terrace, with a bad reputation, jerry built, now all down, were not pulled down, but simply fell down of themselves.

Then W along the Bow Rd, several little courts on the south side, Garrity Court, DARK BLUE, Bakers Alley almost DARK BLUE, Bromley Yard, just small gardens, and behind the Police Station, Glebe Road inhabited by policemen and firemen, PINK.

At the corner of Garrity Court a common lodging house kept by a 'genius', a man who according to Carter has murdered several people in his time, by name Hume, well known and friendly with the police, well educated. We went in room on ground floor on the right, very untidy, the genius reclining, cloths, rags, papers all over the floor, no attempt at order. Mr Hume in his shirt sleeves, tall, enormously strong, grey hair and short grey beard, with arms the size of an ordinary man's leg, a very ill look in his eye, produced a whisky bottle from a cupboard, we refused and apparently displeased him. Carter rather uneasy had some difficulty in getting away, had to say we would look in again another day. Mr Hume belongs or says he does to an old Scotch family, has been well off in his time and consorted with gentlepeople, does not drink heavily himself, probably a touch of insanity somewhere, a very ugly customer. Back through Bakers' Alley into Bromley High St. Bromley High St is very rough throughout, marked PURPLE in our maps but must be more nearly DARK BLUE especially in the centre.

On the west side where the High St joins the Devons Rd, Back Alley and Stewarts Buildings, both should be BLACK, notorious brothels, and have been so for years. Here it was that Barrett who stole the silver ingots from the L&NWR hid.

General remarks

This district has many bad spots and a great many very poor streets. From the police point of view the 'Barracks' is the worst. This is a spot which, though not perhaps worse than other given spots if taken in bits, yet as a whole is consistently bad, and from its size very difficult to deal with. Small streets may be bad in themselves but they can be tackled. A large block is another thing altogether. Crows can be posted to give the alarm, then travel from house to house from within if chased. A cry of 'police' brings help from every house. The inhabitants hustle the police, they organize rescues, not the least bit of good anything less than 6 constables going down in case of a row if there is any prospect of having to haul off anyone to the police station.

Another obvious way (if not too expensive) of improving this group would be to run either Hawgood St or Eastwood St into Bow Common Lane. There is a bit of waste land now used for penny gaffs of a high reputation through which this road would pass. This would bring traffic down Gale St and Hawgood St to Stinkhouse bridge and cut the corner made by the Devons Rd and Bow Common Lane. For police purposes the convenience would be very great because they would be able to work the group from both ends.

Of the individual cockney Irish dweller in the Barracks, Carter had a poor opinion. Get him alone and he is a coward but let him and a pal get you alone and they think nothing of knocking you down and robbing you. Two or 3 of them will often wait to catch a single man on his way half drunk out of the public house.

Mr Bramham. Surveyor and Valuer to the assessment committee of the Hackney Union. 115 Bow Road. On an introduction from Mr Cox Young member of the above committee, 5th October 1897

Mr Bramham is a man over 50 years of age, pleasant and willing to give all the information in his power. He has plans with prices of all the licensed houses in Bow, Bromley, Mile End and Hackney. His list is not quite complete but on permission being given by the Assessment Committee he would be very glad to allow it to be used as a check on our map. But he is very busy till October 23rd, after which date he will be glad to give the matter his attention.

During the last 3 years houses have gone up enormously in value. It began by the loan of one million made to the Cannon Brewery by a Mr Calmont. With this money the brewery set to work to tie houses. The brewers looked on without minding until they found that their own trade was being touched and affected irrecoverably, then they set to work to buy also. Prices went up with a run. Then came the Death Duties Act and increased difficulties about the subdivision of property held by partners jointly for the purposes of taxation. So that Brewers found themselves at the same time wanting more money and a simpler method of reorganising their own personal property.

They turned their businesses into Companies in consequence. Mr Bramham gave as an example a public house in the parish of St John's Hackney. In 1892, this house with a lease of 49 years, at a rental of £105 per annum was bought in for £9,500. In 1895 £8,750 was stated to Mr Bramham as the price that had been paid for it. This year 1897, it has been resold for £23,000. Another house he mentioned as being sold in 1895 for £20,000 and resold this year for £32,000 in addition to which the buyer paid £4,000 in its redecoration and internal alteration. These are only two out of many instances Mr Bramham could give.

Public houses meet a real want, by some they are used as a refreshment house, by others as a club, by others as a place of business. The 'poney' glass or small half pint glass is the outcome of the use of public houses as places of business. "Come and take something" is the regular prelude to doing business with some people. Neither side wants to drink much but they want an office. They ask for a poney glass, they get their apology for drink and their office. The publican charges them the same for a 'poney' as for an ordinary half pint and so recoups himself for wear and tear of premises.

One man may not by law hold more than one license, but one man very often is the real proprietor of several houses. But the license is issued in the name of the manager or of his wife or his son.

He confirmed the evidence of others in saying that all classes became publicans and that the best men were found in the largest houses. And that one man who managed two houses well was more likely to see that 3 or four were well kept. He thought that the publican as a rule was a little above the generality of his customers socially, but at once gave instance of a man who found his clientele too rough for him and wanted to get men of his own grade into the house as customers and straightway proceeded to make things very uncomfortable for those below it. At the same time the higher the class of trade the more profitable the business.

The number of licensed houses is undoubtedly very large but "they must meet a want otherwise they would fail". Said that there were two policies that might be pursued. Either the numbers of houses should be increased and very great strictness be used with regard to them, or they should be decreased by making several houses in one district combine to buy out a few, recouping themselves in so doing by the increased trade that would result. In the first instance you would bring down prices and be able to regulate the rate at which they fell by the rate at which you granted increase. In the second you would increase the value of the houses that remained but at the same time reduce the number of temptations to drink. Some will hesitate to go at all when it is a question of going a hundred yards further. Wet weather is the worst for drink. Especially wet Mondays and Tuesdays when working men will make their wives give back to them some of the money they have given them for housekeeping.

With regard to the police, any policeman who looks as if he would like it is sure to get it, "there can be no question about that". Doubts if it amounts to very much but it would be better if it were not done. Publicans do it wherever they can because they know they will get help in turning out drunken men more easily if they do. A man who makes a noise drives away trade, therefore the publican is only too anxious to get rid of him. A policeman who takes drink is more likely to be near and to come quickly if he is called. "Well at any rate the publicans think so."

(B347-15)

Being Monday the district was alive with tallymen, insurance agents and rent collectors. Tallymen in dog carts, smart, some with a groom in livery and a pile of samples under the seat. Others on foot and calling for orders, some on bicycles. Others less smart driving a cart on which was piled furniture, mats etc. Bow District seems to be the paradise of tallymen. In the Campbell Rd they have their dwelling and in the neighbourhood they make their living. Young men, most of them, of a Jewish cast of countenence. There is hardly a thing they won't sell you. Always a bargain but always much dearer than you could buy it for in a shop. They run great risks of bad debts and "the live must pay for the dead".

Then there was the insurance agent with a business-like air, a brown or black billycock hat and a suit of dittos. The rent collectors nearly always had a top hat, an umbrella and an invariable black coat.

Pawn shops doing a fair business with women who were putting away their own and their husband's Sunday clothes. "One of the signs of a poor street is the pawnshop at the end of it." A pawnshop must be near its customers. "Pawnshops are used quite as much by the poor as a means of safety as a means of raising money." You know your clothes will not be either stolen or ill used while they are at your uncle's and it is worth paying something for this.

Walk 41   B346-3
Tuesday 1st June 1897
George Duckworth with Inspector Carter

Starting N up the Old Ford Road.
St Leonards Buildings at the corner of the Bow Rd and the Old Ford Rd with a very rough set of inhabitants. On the west of the Old Ford Rd, Clay Hall Rd, PURPLE in map, but with a bad reputation, is a BLUE PURPLE. Still it is better than Spring St (LIGHT BLUE). Further north are Blondin St, Douro St and Atley St, the first two being DARK BLUE.

On the east side of Old Ford Rd, Summer St, Spring St and Autumn St. Summer and Spring Streets are the resort of prostitutes of low class labourers. We mark them LIGHT BLUE, they have however a leaning towards a darker shade. Autumn St we mark PINK. Carter said it should be DARK BLUE and Iceland Row to the north of it, LIGHT BLUE. This district seems to have gone down a bit.

Then up to the Reformatory and into Wick Lane passing Maverton St to the west (PURPLE now, and marked PURPLE in the map) and round to the east down into a little block known as the Monier Rd district. A district quite by itself and keeping itself to itself. A policeman rarely seen here now that the powder barges on their way up to Eltham no longer here to be inspected. Formerly these barges lay off here and while the men went on shore to dinner, the police had to stand by to see that no one came near smoking pipes or with lighted matches. There is a Board School in Smeed Rd. The district is bound on the north by the Hertford Union Canal, on the east by the River Lea, on the south by an embankment and on the west by the railway. The map marks all the roads except Dace Rd, PURPLE. Dace Rd is PINK.

At the west end of the Monier Rd an open space, with penny gaffs and things for the amusement of the neighbourhood. There are many girls here employed in Birnbaums rubber factory. Wyke Rd is rather poorer than Monier Rd. Ripporth Rd of much the same character. The streets ended in open spaces leading on to the Canals. This is a spot which might easily become BLACK. Stanly wants the open spaces to be filled up. It is the right size, difficult of entrance and exit and close to the canal. Once the space between the canal and Roach Rd were filled up it would probably go rapidly down hill. A bit of garden along the canal, between the towing path and Roach Rd, anything that would prevent the roads from ending finally in a blank wall and encourage people to walk to the end of them and round them, might stop it. Now is the time if ever it is to be done.

Then back to Wick Lane and under the railway into Jodrell St and Parnell Rd. Jodrell St (being a PURPLE street if anything a shade better than the Wyke Rd), Lamp St, Parnell Rd and Candy St all PURPLE, inhabited by foot finishers and clickers. Locton St we mark PINK, but it is a roughish street and no better than the rest. Ruston St, PURPLE. Then down the Appian Rd, a very rough street, LIGHT BLUE in the map. Lefevre Rd and Janos Rd, PURPLE, much of a muchness.

Then W down the Roman Rd which is one of the great market streets in London. Things to be bought of every sort, even patent leather shoes. Some demands for quality as well as for cheapness. The streets on the north of the Roman Rd and lying between it and the Old Ford Rd are poorer and rougher than those on the south. We mark them (ie those on the north) nearly all LIGHT BLUE. This is a noted resort for housebreakers, who are generally men of intelligence and capable workmen. Often they are skilled carpenters or mechanics. On the south side are mostly PINK streets. Usher Rd we mark PURPLE but it looks to be LIGHT BLUE.

Beale Rd (LIGHT BLUE) in this district is a hot bed of socialists. They have a club in Ford St (many of the windows broken), and abound round about. Lansbury is their leader. Not such a bad chap, a rare talker, "all these socialist fellows are".

Then up St Stephens Rd into the Gesford Rd and W down Ford St. Many clothing works about. Women sewing at the doorsteps and gossiping. Halfway down on the west side is a group (DARK BLUE in the map) of much poorer cottages called Victoria Cottages. They are 2-roomed and set back to back and very poor. To Ford St generally Carter gave the same character as to the Ford Rd. We mark Ford St LIGHT BLUE and Ford Rd PURPLE.

T.B. Richards of the Ordnance Tavern, Barking Road, Canning Row, a man recommended by Mr Reeve of Messrs Truman's as having a special knowledge of the trade and being reliable, 26th October 1897

Mr Richards is a big man, looks more like a policeman than a publican. He is proprietor of the Ordnance Tavern having been advanced money by Truman's but works the house by means of a manager – he is therefore a sort of middleman manager. Before he came here he managed the Great Eastern Hotel for Truman's.

This is not such a big house as the Great Eastern but at the same time does a large trade. In 1891 when he was in the Great Eastern, his takings for a whole year were £17,300. He did, that is, a trade of £1,300 per month. As manager there he was paid £5 per week.

Here at the Ordnance Tavern he is overseer to his manager, does the accounts, is always about, but does not live on the place. Since then he has had as many as 6 houses under him but has disposed of them. Houses have risen so much in value that it has been more profitable to resell them than to trade in them. A short time ago two houses were bought by Charringtons, one, a smaller one than the Ordnance, for £44,000 and another, a freehold in the West India Dock Rd for £66,000. (This, I think, was the Aberfeldy Tavern). Mr Richards at the time of the sale tried to reckon what the house would be worth and priced it at £50,000; he cannot think it will be a successful venture at the higher price.

He had several reasons for the rise in prices.
1) The greater security felt by investors that there would be no temperance legislation for some time to come.
2) The amount of money seeking investment and much lower rate of interest that would be taken now than formerly.
3) The population was increasing but the number of licensed houses was decreasing slightly in total number and largely when considered in ration to the population.

With regard to reason 2, he said that he had had offers from bank managers for loans of money at 4%, a thing unheard of some years ago when the brewers were the only lenders to publicans. The outside public indeed are content with so much lower a rate of interest than brewers that in spite of the fact that breweries have been turned into companies and trebled their capital yet it is probable that the proportion of the publicans interest to the brewers interest in licensed houses is greater now than 10 years ago, i.e. that although brewers have been tying houses in every direction yet that the publicans themselves put into each house a larger sum than ever they did before.

The custom at the Ordnance is entirely working class whose tipple is beer. Friday and Saturday nights and Sundays between 1-3 are the busiest days of the week. On a Saturday evening he will often serve 4,000 persons. The household staff is 11 in number, one of whom is a general servant employed in housework, two are barmaids, two potmen, leaving 6 men to serve behind the bar in addition to the 2 women. "If you serve 4,000 men of a working population, you must serve a few who ought not to be served. They get near the window if they are too drunk to come to the bar and a pal passes a pot back to them. There is a policeman on point duty just outside and if he chose he could run each one of these men in as they come out. If the police made a set against you, they could ruin you certainly."

Mr Richards said he was still and always had been on very good terms with the police. They invite him to their dinner, send him excursion tickets to Yarmouth at the time of their annual outing, etc. He thinks they do their duty and are always policemen first and friends afterwards.

When he was an acting manager, he always gave 1/- per week to the man on the beat "for calling me in the morning". Now he gives nothing himself personally but thinks his manager probably does. He said it would be no good to pay the police to wink at any illegal proceedings such as allowing adulteration, for the public house was far too much under the public gaze. "You have always to remember the risk of anonymous complaints to headquarters without the knowledge of the men in the subdivison." This he implied is sufficient to prevent the payments by publicans ever from becoming so large as to be a public scandal. "It's quite certain you will never stop drinking by legislation, just as you will never stop betting."

Mr Richards had just engaged two private detectives to watch his house as he suspected a man of betting but had never been able to catch him. Today is the Cambridgeshire, rather than run any risks he had gone to the expense of these two men. He said it would not affect the amount of betting in any way but it might save him from having a man caught by the police in his house. He said that betting tipsters were no good to the custom of a house. The way they carry a betting in spite of his vigilance is this. The bookie knows his customers and only wants a place to meet them in, the bets are engaged by means of slips of paper. If you object the man rolls up the slip, walks to the gas and pretends he has only taken out the piece of paper to light his pipe. His urinal at the side of this house is also used for the exchange of wagers.

He said that, commercially speaking, it was much more profitable for him if the police did do their duty. It was no gain to him to serve drunken men, for it only got the house a rowdy character and drove away more business than it brought. For the same reason he did not want to have wafers round the door. But, as he could not help serving drunken men occasionally, he wished the police to recognise the spirit in which he did his work and therefore not to run them in. "This is why it is so important to be on the right side of them."

He said there was a good deal of betting in small sweetshops and that it was increasing, was inclined to deplore it "because there is less money left for beer". Women are taking to it as well as men, there are even women bookies.

His trade depends on the "connection of the house", as well as on casual passengers but much more in the former than the latter. "But a beer house depends a good deal more on a local connection than a 'public'."

During the day there is practically no drinking for pleasure, that begins in the evening. In the morning, midday, men come in for bread and cheese with their beer but no meat, "it would not pay". Women came on Mondays and Tuesdays. They generally drink gin neat, except when the weather is cold when they like hot water with it. Children don't sip, their parents are too careful that a full measure is brought home to them for that. They are not often given sweets now since the police orders against it. Language, if anything, better at the pub than at home.

He would say that women's drinking was not on the increase, i.e. not among women of the working class with whom he has to deal. This class is not affected by the grocers' licences. "A higher class go to them, they don't touch our trade."

Three years ago he heard of suppers being given to police inspectors but has not heard of anything lately. Police rules are much stricter than they used to be, testimonials are not approved of, concerts where tickets are taken by the neighbourhood for the good of police pensions and orphanage are more general now, but he said there is less indirect taxation of this kind than there used to be.

Mr Richards' manager here is paid 50/- per week. The wages of servants, barmen and potmen is charged to Mr Richards apart. Food is also allowed at the rate of 10/- per week per head, up to 8 persons and 8/- per head above that number. Drinks and cigars are allowed ad lib. House rent free. "So that the manager has really nothing but his own clothing to pay for."

Here the question of treatment by customers is not an important one. Sailors are the worst for it, West Enders and city men the next worst. Here it is purely working class. Mr Richards used always to accept a glass of gin with his customers and then help himself to plain water.

"A man earning 25/- a week down here would certainly keep 5/- of it himself for beer and tobacco."

(B348-11)

Hewlett St and Driffield St (PINK) are both better class streets.

The BLUE bit in North Bow is practically bounded on the north by the Old Ford Rd, on the east by Lefevre Rd, on the south by the Roman Rd and on the west by Hewlett Rd.

General remarks

The day of the week of this walk was a Tuesday. Hour between 2.30 and 4.

In the Old Ford district there were many insurance agents about, bowler-hatted and in suits of dittos. Many women at their doors, often at work on juvenile suits. The cats meat man was going his rounds and the cats who followed him looked rather lean, but not so lean as those in the 'Barracks' and the Devas Rd districts.

Old Ford and Hoxton are the home of housebreakers. Housebreakers seem to be a product of manual skill and liberal ideas. Old Ford also rejoiced in the possession of Receivers of the stolen goods, known to the police as Fences. One old man they were sure about but never could get enough evidence against. On he went from year to year, At last they obtained enough to 'pinch him', then he went and died and so escaped.

{This old man kept The 'Palm' public house at the corner of Palm St and Lessada St.} Bryant and May have a rough set of girls. there are 2,000 of them when they are busy. Rough and rowdy but not bad morally. They fight with their fists to settle their

differences, not in the factory for that is forbidden, but in the streets when they leave work in the evening. A ring is formed, they fight like men and are not interfered with by the Police.

The prostitutes living in Spring and Summer St ply for hire in the Old Ford Rd and the Roman Rd. There women satisfy the local demand, sailors don't come so far north. They generally take off their victims westwards to the brothels in Brantridge St (DARK BLUE in our map). Of all forms of prostitute the Polish Jewess is the worst. "They wont let you alone but follow you up and down the street and even catch hold of you." There are generally bullies known to the police as "Ponces" who live on their earnings. These men are more often foreigners than Englishmen and often themselves Polish Jews. "It's a curious thing about women like them, the more these men knock them about the more they like them." In the summer these men attend the races as betting men and in the winter live on the women.

Walk 42   B350-18
Thursday 20th January 1898
George Duckworth alone

Starting at the corner of Alma Road and Burdett Road
Alma Rd, 2-st, some more comfortable than others, very poor, LIGHT BLUE to DARK BLUE, in map LIGHT BLUE.

S to Salisbury St, 2-st, better, fair proportion of PINK, PURPLE to LIGHT BLUE, in map DARK BLUE.

S down Wilson St, 2-st, LIGHT BLUE to DARK BLUE, in map DARK BLUE.

W to Baggally St, 2-st, PURPLE, in map DARK BLUE.

W to Burdett St, no DARK BLUE. PINK.

N up Canal Rd, all PURPLE, mixed, in map unmarked and PINK.

E along Maidman, 2-st, unmarked to PURPLE.

S down Ewing, 2-st, unmarked to PINK.

W along Forester Road, unmarked to PINK.

N up Ewing, 2-st, unmarked to PINK.

W then S down Canal Rd, turning E at Bridge St, 2-st, PURPLE to PINK, narrower. In map PINK.

S down Single St, houses on the east side only, except at northwest end. PURPLE to PINK, in map PINK.

E along Bridge St, N up Edwardes Rd, 2½-st, some PINK, others very poor, there are houses on the southwest side, below Chapel not shewn in map. LIGHT BLUE to PURPLE, in map DARK BLUE.

E to Brantridge St, 2½-st, very poor. Windows broken, stuffed with rags, dirty, "used for all the girls who walk the Whitechapel Rd". DARK BLUE to LIGHT BLUE, in map DARK BLUE. W then N up Maplin St, 2½-st, mixed, PURPLE as map.

E along Bow Rd and S down Maritime St, PINK. Lockhart St, east of Maritime St, also PINK. Neither are shewn in map. They are in place of the London Maritime Institution, shewn in map.

N up Bow Common Lane and across Mile End Rd to Whitman Rd, PURPLE, in map LIGHT BLUE. N up, E along Longfellow, late Whitman Rd. 2-st, LIGHT BLUE as map.

E then N up Jupps Rd. Poor and very poor. LIGHT BLUE to DARK BLUE, in map LIGHT BLUE.

E then N up Clinton Rd, north end 2-st, PINK, in map PURPLE. To Ashcroft Rd, 2½-st, PINK as map.

N up Grove Rd and W at Burnside Rd, 2-st. Walls rubbed, some windows broken. PURPLE to PINK, in map PINK. N to Belhaven St, PINK as map.

N to Cordova St, PURPLE as map. There is no communication between the west ends of Cordova and Belhaven Streets as shewn in map. N to Hamilton Rd, PURPLE as map. The road takes a turn north at the west end. On the east side of this turn is a factory and two inhabited houses north of the factory. The east side of the northerly turn is not shewn in map.

N to Palm St, 2-st, PURPLE to LIGHT BLUE. In map LIGHT BLUE. Out of its north side runs Lessada St, 2 st, some very poor. LIGHT BLUE as map. Totty St, 2-st, LIGHT BLUE as map. N across the Roman Rd to Ashwell Rd and Gardener Rd, 2-st. Both better than Lessada and Totty Streets, PURPLE, in map LIGHT BLUE. E across Grove Rd to Kenilworth Rd, 2½-st, PUPRLE as map.

N to Chisenhale Rd. Houses all along the north side more PURPLE, otherwise as map. S down Ellesmere Rd, PINK as map. Built 1864. N up Auckland Rd, S down Vivian Rd, 2½ st, PURPLE to PINK, in map PURPLE. S across Roman Rd and down Conger Stt. 2-st, PURPLE, in map PINK. E along Olga St, 2-st, PURPLE, in map PINK, to Medway Rd, 2-st, PINK as map. N and W to Burgogne Rd, PINK to PURPLE, in map PINK. 2-st. W to Lanfranc Rd, PINK to PURPLE, in map PINK. W to Gernon Rd, PINK to PURPLE, in map PINK. S to Theydon Rd, PINK as map. S down Grove Rd and E at Medhurst, unmarked to PINK. S into Arbery Rd, 2-st, PINK, unmarked in map. S to Straham Rd, unmarked to PINK. S to Antill Rd, 2-st, PINK as map. E to Legal Rd, 2 st, PINK as map. Across Stanfield Rd, houses at the west end at south side only. PINK. Unmarked in map. E and S down Selwyn Rd. 2- and 2½-st, PINK as map.

General remarks

Note the betterment in the DARK BLUE patch south of Bow Common Lane and in Edwards St. Against this there is worsement in South Row though not sufficient to account for the displacement of all the former DARK BLUE. Brantridge St is the worst

of the lot. To the rooms here the women who walk the Mile End Rd bring home
their men.

North of the Great Eastern Railway and north of Bow Common Lane there are a
number of new streets which have tended to suck the PINK out of the surrounding
streets, but not very markedly.

Additional	From	To
Woodside Road	LIGHT BLUE	PURPLE
Copperfield Road	PINK	PURPLE
St Ann's Road	LIGHT BLUE	PURPLE
St Dunstan's Road	LIGHT BLUE	PURPLE
Kirk's Place	DARK BLUE	LIGHT BLUE
Georgina Place	DARK BLUE	LIGHT BLUE

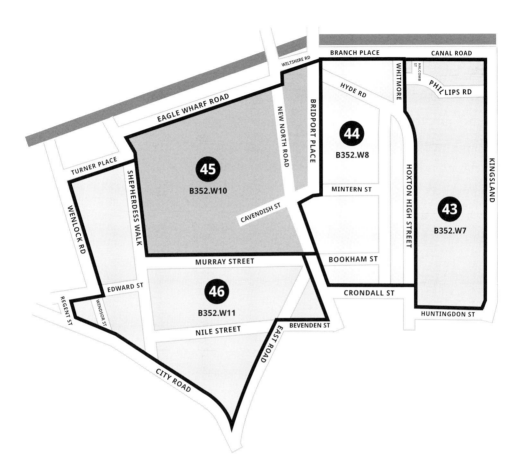

Walk 43   B352-7

Tuesday 10th May 1898
George Duckworth with constable W. Ryeland

Starting at the Police Station, N up the Kingsland Road

Then W at Huntingdon St, 3½-st, well cobble paved, artisans, clean windows, pots of flowers, rent £45 a year, tenants paying rates and taxes, 9-roomed houses, "about the best built houses in Hoxton", light yellow, hard, machine made brick, "of the same class as those streets to the east of the Caledonian Rd." About 25 years old, 3 and 4 families to each house, respectable, PURPLE to PINK, in map PURPLE. Used to belong to Mr Charles Deacon, former member of the London School Board. "He built and owned many streets round here and drove his carriage and pair." But he lost it all through drink. "Now he is a tramp about the streets and thankful if you will give him a crust of bread."

{At the east end of Huntingdon St (which looks better than the rest and decidedly PINK) are 2 houses on the north side which have always held notorious characters. "If ever a burglary on a big scale is planned, it is pretty safe to look here." The Muswell Hill Burglars were taken here. Two months ago £300 of stolen goods were found in another house two doors off.}

On the north side is Cross Street, only one dwelling house which is a chandlers shop on the west side, formerly called Sarah St.

W into Hoxton St, "one of the busiest market streets of London". Shops and costers barrows. Busiest on a Saturday night. All stalls cleared away by 11 on Sunday mornings. E along Essex St, 3½-st, outwardly like Huntingdon St, though doors open and more windows broken. A street with a bad reputation. Prostitutes, bullies, thieves and receivers of stolen goods. Being repaved with asphalt by the parish, tenements. "We always look for some bother here of a Saturday night". Is slightly better than Wilmer Gardens, in map LIGHT BLUE but should be LIGHT BLUE or DARK BLUE lined BLACK. At the east end on the north side is a cul-de-sac called Little Essex St, 3½-st, small, quiet, homework, no trouble, LIGHT BLUE to PURPLE, in map LIGHT BLUE.

N up Gifford St, 2- and 3-st, artisans, well paved, macadam, PURPLE to PINK. At the north end in the 2-st houses are many policemen. Date on houses 1830, rent 12/- per week. Running E between Gifford St and Kingsland Rd is Flemming Rd, 2-st, PINK to PURPLE, in map PURPLE. "Public house is a nuisance on Saturday nights with its concerts and friendly leads." The parish yard is in the street and the men employed by the parish, "a good set of men", live in the street, PURPLE as map. Further N is Hare Walk, no turning now out of it on north side (LIGHT BLUE in map). Covered by Bennett and Sheers Engineers and Coppersmiths factory. Just a few houses (LIGHT BLUE) at east end on south side. W along Tyssen St, 2-st, houses flush with pavement, inhabitants costers with barrows in Hoxton St, "too busy on Saturday nights to make a noise but apt to be troublesome on Sundays and Mondays when business is slack". LIGHT BLUE as map. S into Hare Walk, 2-st, narrow, looks quiet, but criminal "two or 3 men now away from here doing time", burglars, BLACK as map. S down Gifford St and W along Wilks Place, 2-st, narrow, 14 ft between house and house, 4 rooms, 9/6, labourers, poor, quiet, LIGHT BLUE rather than the DARK BLUE of map. Out of the south side is Wilks Court, 9 houses, used to be a rough place but is now quiet, LIGHT BLUE, in map DARK BLUE. Parish has had the court asphalt paved and the WC bought to the front of the house.

W along Wilks Place into Hoxton St. N then E down a cul-de-sac called Barton Court, BLACK in map and still BLACK, 2- and 3-st, windows broken and patched, mess, costers at far end, children several with bad eyes but well fed, gas burning in lamp in centre of court, bird cages hung up outside windows. Overcrowding here. In one house Ryeland found 7 in 2 small rooms on the top floor, 9 persons in 2, on the second floor and 6 in 2 rooms on the ground floor. One man nodded to Ryeland. "He has served several times" said R, "but he once saved my life here". Ryeland had been arresting a man in the court when a trolly was dropped from the first floor window on to R's head, he was stunned. This man prevented his fellows from kicking him when down. No exit from Barton Court into Wilks Place. N up Hoxton High St, fair meat 2d and 4d lb. Black crepe bonnets 4/11. Past the Hare public house which has a back entrance into Hare Walk, full of women, some with babies in arms, "a regular cowshed". "The increase in women's drinking has done much to counterbalance the decrease in the men's." Ryeland thinks that the blue ribbon movement has caused the change in the men's habits "but we don't get hold of the women". E into Steven's Mews, well kept stableyard, horse stalls and a few rooms where the owners live above. Used to be rough but is not now, it looks LIGHT BLUE. In one lives the best known poultry buyer in Hoxton, "a man who can't read or write but is one of the best known men in the London trade, does a wholesale West End business besides". Mark PURPLE, in map DARK BLUE.

N and E into Albert Mews, 2 houses only, rough, the rest is all factories and stables. Now cement paved and clean. Beer house at the corner known as the 'museum', all the freaks found by costers brought here and displayed in the front windows, odd shaped potatoes, carrots, animals etc. The mews behind is equally a depository of living freaks, donkeys with 5 legs, dogs etc. The two houses in Albert Mews still DARK BLUE as map. N then E into Harman St, 3½-st, same class of house and style of building as Huntingdon St, respectable, PURPLE to PINK, in map PINK.

N then E along Ely Place, a flag-paved passage, houses on either side, 2-st and 2-roomed, 77 houses in all, flags broken, mess, not criminal but poor, thriftless, women drink, two children bare footed, children happy, well fed, hatless, dirty, windows dirty, broken, DARK BLUE rather than the LIGHT BLUE of map, is private property.

{Ely Place, rather worse on south side than on north and worse on both sides west than east of the public house which has a back entrance on the north side. Decided to make south side DARK BLUE and leave north side LIGHT BLUE. {EA:ALB:GHD. Joint visit 16.XI.98}*

N then E down Lynedoch St, late Mary St, also private property, but rather better looked after than Ely Place. Paving good. Entered at either end through handsome iron gates, known in the neighbourhood as "the street with the beautiful gates". Property of an old maiden lady who takes a personal interest in it. "Last year she

*Note: EA–Ermest Aves, ALB–Arthur Baxter, GHD –George Duckworth

offered prizes for the house with best window box, the place was like a garden and became one of the sights of the district." Houses always well let, 3 rooms 7/6, 2-st houses, inhabitants small homeworkers, tailors and boot finishers, LIGHT BLUE to PURPLE, in map PURPLE.

N up Hoxton High St to a piece marked DARK BLUE in map, now covered by the Infirmary, called Land of Promise. A public house is at the south corner, at the north corner is the Board of Guardians office. It used to be a row of poor houses, promised by their late owner to the parish as a gift on his death. When he died his children refused to give it. The parish was annoyed and by way of revenge changed the name of the street to 'the Land of Promise'. Every passer-by asked why and heard the story which so disgusted the children that they agreed to make over the land as their father had promised. On the site of it is now the Infirmary attached to the Workhouse. Ryeland is a Temperance enthusiast and "the vicinity of the public house to the workhouse built upon a piece of ground called the 'Land of Promise' has often served me with a text at meetings." In the Infirmary, nurses are trained for work elsewhere.

N then E into Reeves' Place, 2-st, cobble paved, "the home of the aristocracy of the costers who ply their trade in the High St". The casual ward is at the east end of it. PURPLE rather than LIGHT BLUE of map. N then E into Nuttall Rd, usually called Kings Rd or Dirty Lane. Used to be filthy, now well paved, rough costers, six 2-st houses below level of street on north side like Ely Place. LIGHT BLUE to DARK BLUE, in map LIGHT BLUE.

E along Nuttall Rd, N up Louisa St, 2½-st, DARK BLUE lined BLACK as map. Watson Place, ditto. Nancy St worse, 3-st, should be BLACK. Into Ware St, 2½-st, LIGHT BLUE lined rather than PURPLE of map. This is a vicious quarter. Bullies, prostitutes working Liverpool St and Dalston Junction, thieves. Bread, tins, fish heads and mess in street. Crowds of dirty, holey-booted and pinafored, but well-fed children playing about the street. The home of flower sellers. Strong smell of flowers from one house, look down and saw the whole bottom floor of one house covered with tubs of narcissus. Houses fetch 14/- and those held in 1- and 2-roomed tenements 3/ and 4/- per room. A drunken rowdy set of inhabitants necessitating a fixed point policeman at the Kingsland Rd end of Ware St.

N up the High St past the Coster's Hall, vigorous, work like the Great Assembly Hall, "does much good". E into Wilmer Gardens, 3- and 2-st houses on the south side arranged on the flat system, 3 rooms to a floor, 3 families to a house, rents 6/6 to 7/- per floor, jerry built houses. Street has been built about 15 years. In map it is marked DARK BLUE lined BLACK but is now worse and should be BLACK. Deterioration due to immigration of thieves and housebreakers from Boundary St area. On the south side is a large common lodging house, originally built as model dwellings in 1893 by Alderman Beachcroft and still belonging to him though let by him to one James Shuttleworth who has turned the place into a lodging house, beds 4d and 6d per night, 2/- per week. "Takes in very shady characters and has helped to the worsement of the street." It failed as model dwellings.

N up Kingsland Rd and W along Phillips St, 2-st, PURPLE in map, a mixed street, some criminals and others respectable and fairly well-to-do. From this street came the Polish Jew connected with the Brick Lane murder of some months back. "The only foreign Jew I know of in the neighbourhood" said Ryeland. On the north side are 5 neglected looking 1-st almshouses. On the north side is Phillip Passage, late Albert Place, 3 cottages, poor, LIGHT BLUE rather than DARK BLUE of map. On the south side, almost opposite is Louisa Square, 6 houses, 2-st, LIGHT BLUE rather than DARK BLUE of map, and just west of it Little Louisa Square, 2 houses, also LIGHT BLUE. N up Halcomb St, 2-st, poor labourers "but a very steady class, have been here for a great many years, a stable population, no ebb and flow as in Phillip St". Rents 8/- for 5 rooms. Rents lower than in other streets because of old tenants, character LIGHT BLUE to PURPLE, in map LIGHT BLUE. Like it is Halcomb Place, late Albert Place, 1 family to a house.

N and E along Canal Rd. Wharves and men employed on them, PURPLE as map. Adelaide Place on south side just east of the Church has been taken over by the Church and used as a home for caretakers and dependants, 3 houses, 2-st, PURPLE. At the Kingsland Rd end of Canal Rd on the south side are 4 houses, poorer, LIGHT BLUE. S down Kingsland Rd and W along Mill Row, better than it used to be, poor, but not criminal, labourers and a number of rag, bottle and fat buyers and merchants, rather LIGHT BLUE than DARK BLUE of map. On the south side is Mill Court, two houses only, woodchoppers, LIGHT BLUE. At the extreme west end is Harland Square, quiet, with front gardens, well kept, PURPLE, in map DARK BLUE. Berry's Place, just west of the square is rather poorer, LIGHT BLUE to PURPLE, not coloured in map. That part of Mill Row which runs along the east side of Harland Square into Phillip St is like Mill Row of former days, 2-st, rough, DARK BLUE as map.

{Harland Square is tenanted by 1 family to each house. 3 rooms for 8/-, a fair general shop on east corner. Berry's Place looked very poor, so did Mill Row. {EA:ALB:GHD – Joint visit 16.XI.98.}*

General remarks

Note the good paving of the streets, contrast to Bethnal Green.

No Sunday Houses in the Subdivision, i.e. no public houses open for the use of travellers during prohibited hours. Greater sobriety among men. In the Hoxton

*Note: see page 195.

police subdivision out of 203 constables, 56 are now total abstainers, 15 years ago two were teetotallers.

Decrease in the number of pawnshops. In Hoxton High St there used to be 5 now there is only one "and he has hard work to make both ends meet". Ryeland thinks it is due to greater temperance among the men.

{N.B. There are 10 Pawnshops within a half mile area in Kingsland Rd and St John St but always 4 fewer than there used to be.}

Costers generally illiterate but "work their way up nevertheless", are wonderfully good buyers and sellers. Ryeland knows 3 or 4 who started with barrows and now have shops, "but they always take a shop in a market street, they would never stand the boredom and quiet of an ordinary road." As a class they make good money but spend it very freely.

Walk 44   B352-8

Thursday 12th May 1898
George Duckworth with police constable Ryeland

Starting at the east end of Crondall Street

"Not so good as Huntingdon St, but better than Essex St." The east end less good than the west, paper bag, stationery and cabinet factories on the south side, Hoxton High St end. On the north side behind is Gloucester Row, 4 houses, 2-st, no backs, small front gardens, poor, labouring class, quiet. Rent 7/- for 3 rooms and wash-house, character PURPLE to LIGHT BLUE, in map LIGHT BLUE. N up St John's Road, PINK as map, then PURPLE, small shops, a common lodging house on the west side between Alma and Bookham St. Beds 6d a night or 2/6 a week, or 5d a night and 2/3 per wk.

E along Bacchus Walk, 2-st, looks clean and is quiet, windows and blinds clean, doors shut, but the home of a fair proportion of criminals, housebreakers, a type of street almost peculiar to Hoxton. Inhabitants neither poor nor rowdy, but sportsmen who break the monotony of their ordinary work by an evening's housebreaking. In map LIGHT BLUE, but its real character would be more nearly represented by PURPLE with a line of BLACK. At the Hoxton St end about 6 houses are down for the extension of the Hoxton Brewery. The 'Bacchus' public house at the corner of the High St is the market house of the Hoxton Street Market. Twenty years ago it was sold for £3,000, two years ago the same house fetched £27,000.

S down Little John Street and into Upper John Street, look the same as Bacchus Walk but without criminals, windows unbroken, better class, labourers and skilled artisans, "better than Gloucester Row". Rent 12/ and 14/- for 5 and 6 rooms. Character PURPLE to LIGHT BLUE, in map LIGHT BLUE. N up Lower John St, six

MUSEUM OF LONDON

houses on west side only, built on flat principle, 2 floors, 3 rooms to a floor, on what was formerly gardens to St John's St. Not yet tenanted.

N into Great James St, 2-st, broad, clean, fairly good class of artisans, "no poor", rather poorer east than west end. "Much better than Crondall St." Character PURPLE to PINK, in map PURPLE.

S down Little James St, DARK BLUE in map, cobble paved, has a bad reputation. 'Houses seem to pass from one notorious character to another.' Murderers from here. To Turners Square, 2- and 3-st, poor, cement paved, LIGHT BLUE as map.

N up High St and W along Ivy Lane, 2-st, poor, rough, some criminals, doors open. Sir W. Besant lived in this street and took from it some of his characters in the 'Children of Gibeon', DARK BLUE as map, asphalt, well paved, birds cages tied up in pocket handkerchiefs.

N into Ivy St, slightly better, LIGHT BLUE as map, 2-st. The east end on the south side is down, a cul-de-sac, running east out of that part of Ivy Lane which runs into Ivy St, is called Stratford Place. 14 2-st, 2-roomed houses, rents 6/6 per week, rough, windows broken and patched. W into St John's St. From Ivy Lane to Newton St, St John's St is PINK rather than PURPLE of map. Shops and fair class houses. North of Newton St to Hyde Rd it is poorer and PURPLE as map.

E into Hemsworth St, rather better than Huntingdon St., fairly good backs, some police living here, no poor. 7-roomed houses, rents £32 per annum, PURPLE to PINK, in map PURPLE. North of it is Clinger Rd, 2-st, poorer, broad, doors shut, "a little better than Gloucester Row (LIGHT BLUE)". Character LIGHT BLUE to PURPLE, in map LIGHT BLUE.

N into Hobbs Place, 2-st, built 1850, poor, rough but getting better, "used to be a deal of trouble with drunken rowdyism, wife beating and quarrelling". Not so bad as Ivy Lane, LIGHT BLUE rather than DARK BLUE of map. The 5 houses on the north side at the east end are owned by the man who keeps a cats meat shop in one of them. He was formerly a cabman, teetotaller, saved money, bought these houses which are now tenanted by 4 cabmen (his sons I think), now he does a good business in the cats meat line.

Into Hoxton High St. At the northwest end is a court, now closed, called Vine Court, in map PINK, "used to be very rough and unsanitary". On the opposite side of the street are 3 small turnings. Smarts Buildings, 4 houses, 2-st, rough, though not quite so bad as Byng's Buildings, 3-roomed, rent 8/- per week, character LIGHT BLUE to DARK BLUE, in map DARK BLUE. S of it are Barrett's Buildings, 7 houses, very rough and rowdy, Irish cockneys, navvies, "they call themselves nowadays 'excavators'" said Ryeland. Have been there a great number of years, DARK BLUE, not coloured in map. South of it again are Byng's Buildings, "like Wilmer Gardens", rough, but not criminal, DARK BLUE, in map not coloured, mess, WCs being altered by order of parish. Advert. on walls 'To be sold Nos. 2, 3, 4, 8 & 9 Byng's Buildings – producing £122.19 per annum. Landlord paying rates and taxes.'

S down Hoxton High St, barrows allowed both sides on Saturdays but only on west side on other days. Some prices, Beefsteaks from 3d to 10d per lb. Scraps of meat 2d per lb. Good mutton chops 7½d. Good bacon 6d and 7d per lb. Starting at 3½d. Fair mutton chops 4½d each, shoulder of mutton 3½d lb. Potatoes 3lb for 2d. Cabbage 4lb for 2d. Haddocks 1½ and 2½d each. Bread 7d per 4lb loaf (N.B. Wheat now fetching 57/ to 60/- the quarter. Bread famine riots in Italy, war between Spain and America).

W along Ivy St and N just past the Board School up Ebenezer Place, houses on west side only, poor, LIGHT BLUE to PURPLE, not coloured in map. At the north corner is the Chapel where Lord Shaftesbury first started work among the costers. E along Hammond Square, no living houses.

S down High St and W into St George's Place, new houses, north side only. Is a continuation on a higher level of Gloucester Row, but walled off from it. Cement paved, 2-st houses, 5 rooms, 10/-, only 7 houses, PURPLE, in map LIGHT BLUE.

S down Hoxton St and W along Crondall St. W across St John's Rd. This part of Crondall St is poorer than the east end, 3-st houses, some overcrowding, no Jews, PURPLE rather than PINK of map. Up New North Rd and E into Bookham St, 2½-st, "a great deal better than Crondall St". In map PURPLE, but looks PINK. 2 families in most houses. North of it is Alma St, 2½-st, rather better than Bookham St, inhabited by artisans and clerks, warehousemen, typewriters etc. employed in the City. "A regular exodus every morning to the City both of men and women." 7-roomed houses, rent £37, streets want mending, clean blinds and china pots, doors shut, PINK as map. Buckland Street, "like Bookham St", 2½-st, quiet, PINK as map. North of it is Nicholas St, "the longest complete street in London without a turning and without a lamp post". The lamps are all on brackets from the houses, 2-st, rents 11/- a week, artisans, many with one family to a house, PURPLE as map.

North again is Mintern St, small shops at west end, 3- and 2½-st. On the south side is Mintern Mews, one living house only. The rest 25 workshops and mews. Cabinet makers. Width of street 39 ft from area railing to area railing, fairly typical of this group of streets. Out of it on the north side are Wareham and Wargate Streets, 2½-st, artisans, PURPLE to PINK, in map PURPLE. Similar also are Northport, Rushton, Newton, Grange and Penn Streets, all 2½-st, in character PURPLE to PINK, in map PURPLE. "All of these streets are a class above those on the east side of the Kingsland Rd", [i.e. Mansfield, Hows and Pearson Streets which are marked PINK in the map. At present all these streets look PINK, they may have been raised from PURPLEDOM by the good trade of the last year. In any case these streets are now a very PINKY PURPLE and the others a PURPLY PINK. Should their colours be changed? Mintern St, PURPLE, not PINK at south west end. Wareham St, PURPLE. Wargate St, PURPLE. Northport St, PURPLE. Rushton St, PURPLE. Grange St, PURPLE. Gopsall St, PINK. Bridport Place, PINK. Whitmore Rd, PINK,

Newton St, PURPLE. Penn St, PURPLE to PINK.

{A battle royal in these street between PINK and BLUE. "Getting worse" the verdict of a small general shop keeper and of a baker. The baker said it was due to the overflow of the 'Nile' i.e. the Nile St area. A good many houses in each street are aggressively PINK, while others are LIGHT BLUE and even DARK BLUE. The shop keeper complained that a 'rough' class was taking the place of those inhabitants that left. EA.ALB.GHD. 16.XI.98.}

N across Hyde Rd and up Harvey St, 2½-st. Highbury Presbyterian mission here. "Doing a splendid work." Poor, LIGHT BLUE as map.

W along Felton St, 2½-st, houses flush with pavement. Has gone down in character owing to immigrants from clearances in Central London. Not very poor, good mixture of criminals, LIGHT BLUE in map, now rather LIGHT BLUE lined BLACK.

N up Branch Place. Notorious, pickpockets, bus thieves, windows dingy, immigrants from Boundary St, worse than Felton St. Character DARK BLUE lined BLACK, in map LIGHT BLUE. '21 Branch Place to be sold, 6 rooms and scullery, yard, WC, let to weekly tenant at rentals accounting to 17/- per week of £44.4 per annum, landlord paying rates and taxes.' Doors closed "but more as a protection against prying eyes than a sign of respectability". Hutley Place, 2-st, criminal not rowdy, "a degree better than Wilmers Gardens", LIGHT BLUE lined BLACK rather than LIGHT BLUE of map. S down Holt Place (late Norris St), 3-st, a shade better, built 1820, LIGHT BLUE to PURPLE, in map LIGHT BLUE. Norris St, 2-st, LIGHT BLUE as map.

N to Kenning Terrace, facing canal, 2-st, troublesome, rough, criminal, windows broken, DARK BLUE lined BLACK rather than LIGHT BLUE of map. S down Whitmore Rd, small shops. W up Hyde Rd, shops, PINK as far as Northport St then PURPLE as map. Past Witham St, late Francis St, 2-st, being repaved, LIGHT BLUE as map.

General remarks

Ryeland said that as a whole the district had gone down. The rich had left, the poor were as poor and a rough class had come in. But the roughness of today was not to be compared to the roughness of 10 or 15 years ago. He can find no reason for the change. Education in his opinion makes good people better but bad ones worse. Therefore he did not think it was education that had softened the morals of the rough class.

He himself belongs to no particular religious body. "I refuse to tie myself down but try to help all equally." Between them all he gets many outings. Yesterday he was at Windsor and saw the Queen, tomorrow he goes with a Sunday School to the sea. He has two boys both learning to be cabinet makers. One 21 years of age, now making 30/- a week, the other 18 and earning 21/-. Both taught at the Shoreditch Technical School. "I paid three pounds or so in fees and they brought back more than £8 worth of prizes." He spoke highly of the moral teaching of the technical instructors. After one lesson they came home saying "What shall we do with our savings, dad?" He advised them to do as he had done and buy up small freeholds near Southend or Benfleet. Land that he bought some years ago for £20 he now refuses £100 for.

He lamented the Romish tendencies of the Church in the parish of Shoreditch. "In only two out of 23 Churches of the established Church can you find an Evangelical Service." The people do not like ceremonial, consequently Anglican churches are empty. "Those who are most successful and gather crowds both Sundays and weekdays are the Congregationalists and the Baptists, especially the latter."

Note the existence of streets neither poor nor rough but criminal, e.g. Bacchus Walk. The two off draught beer licenses, on St John's Rd and Hoxton High St both started as grocers, then had a wine and spirit license and now have a draught beer license.

Since they obtained the draught beer license they have given up the grocery business altogether and now confine themselves to wine, beer and spirits.

Note the good paving of the streets.

Walk 45   B352-10

Saturday 14ᵗʰ May 1898
George Duckworth with Constable W. Ryeland

Starting at the junction of Mintern Street and Bridport Place.

The DARK BLUE patch behind consists now of two houses only, each with 2 rooms and a washhouse and letting for 6/6 per week. The rest is given over to engineers shops, cowsheds and packing case dealers, "used to be very rough", now looks LIGHT BLUE, though Ryeland said it was not poor.

N into Rushton St, this end is not quite so good as that lying east of Bridport Place. 2-st, respectable, PURPLE as map. N up Bridport Place. 2½- and 3-st, PINK rather than PURPLE of map. "On a par with the best part of St John's Rd", said Ryeland. Tram down the middle, some shops and city men.

W along Clift St. 2-st, PURPLE as map. One or 2 poor. "Nos 12, 13, 14 producing £96.14. 19 years unexpired at £42." Advertised to be sold. N up New North Rd. Tram and bus lines, 3½-st shops built out to small front gardens. PINK-barred as map.

E along Salisbury St. 2-st, quiet, PURPLE as map. N and W along Dorchester St. 2-st. 1820-30 built streets. 2 families to each house. 5 rooms and wash-house. Rent 11/-. A few windows broken. Very like streets in Bethnal Green; cabinet workers, doors shut, fair repair, PURPLE as map. N and E along Poole St. Passing the drug mills at the east corner of the Bridge and New North Rd. 2-st. Poor, bad, rough, DARK BLUE rather than PURPLE of map. "Not quite so bad as Wilmer Gardens." But some criminals nevertheless, children dirty, holey boots.

N up Wickham St. 2-st. The east side has been taken by the umbrella and stick factory behind for its workers and is better than it used to be, PURPLE, the west side is still DARK BLUE as map. N into Wiltshire Row. West end all closed, has been condemned. The rest east of Wickham St 2-st, poor, and rather rough but do not look worse than the LIGHT BLUE of map.

S down Avebury St. The west side belongs to the stick factory spoken of above and is PURPLE. The east side is still DARK BLUE. On the east side of Avebury St is Devizes St. 2-st, DARK BLUE as map, birds in cages at windows, several criminals from here, one for painting chaffinches to look like canaries, the same man now doing 5 years for highway robbery.

S into Poole St, the west end of which is much worse than the east, Wickham St makes the dividing line. As DARK BLUE is to PURPLE. In map all PURPLE. In the same way the east end of Wiltshire Row is worse than the west and should be DARK BLUE rather than the LIGHT BLUE of map. Appearances point to a change about between the east side of Wickham St and the west side of Avebury St with the west end of Poole St and the east end of Wiltshire Row.

W along Eagle Wharf Rd. Factories on north side, small arms, bedsteads, bus yard, etc. 3½-st on south side, tenanted by a well-to-do regular set of men, chiefly engineers. PINK rather than PURPLE of map.

S down Cropley St. 2½-st, mixed. PURPLE to PINK, in map PURPLE. E along Parr St. 2½-st. Steady set, artisans, china pots, windows clean. PINK rather than PURPLE of map. Into Brackley St, the north end of which is poorer than the south and harbours a few criminals. "Much worse than Parr St." The north end should be LIGHT BLUE, the rest PURPLE as map.

S past Bristowe St. 2½-st and attic. 6 rooms and one above. "Rather poorer than Parr St." PURPLE as map. W into Wimbourne St. 2½-st, no poor, like Parr St. Good ordinary earnings, PINK rather than PURPLE of map. S down New North Rd and W along Shaftesbury St. 2½-st. Cabinet makers. Like Parr St. PINK as map.

S down Cropley St and E along Cavendish St. 2½- and 3-st. Gone down, poor, noisy, drunken, some criminals, "like Essex St but without the Essex St prostitutes". Windows dirty, broken and patched. DARK BLUE rather than PURPLE of map.

S down Sylvia St. 2- and 3-st, rough, poor, like Cavendish St. DARK BLUE, in map LIGHT BLUE. Into Wenlock St. Much better. 2½-st and attic. "Like Shaftesbury St", PINK rather than PURPLE of map. S down Evelyn St only 4 houses. Rest taken up by piano factory, etc. Into Herbert St, 3½- and 2½-st. West of Evelyn St the houses are of a better class. "Some servants kept." PINK-barred in this part. Houses let at £50 + rates and taxes, which would bring it up to about £70. East of Evelyn St, PINK as map.

S into Murray St. 2½-st, PINK as map. N and E into Witchhampton Street. 2½-st, quiet, narrower, slightly poorer. PURPLE as map. Along Shaftesbury St, PINK as map, to Shepherdess Walk. N then E along Napier St. 2½-st. "Better if anything than Shaftesbury St." PINK rather than PURPLE of map. Like it is Forston St, running parallel to the north of it. 2½-st. PINK. In map PURPLE.

N up Shepherdess Walk. 3½-st. PINK-barred as map. Into the west end of Eagle Wharf Rd, at the northwest corner is a common lodging house. Quiet, PURPLE, uncoloured in map. The south side is like the rest of the road and PINK rather than PURPLE of map. "No poor in this road." S down Shepherdess Walk as far as Wenlock St, then S down Trinity St, late Church St. Only 3 houses north of Herbert St, PINK rather than PURPLE. On the west side is Holy Trinity Church and vicarage.

General remarks

Note neighbouring improvements and worsements in Poole St and Wiltshire Row. Also the betterment of the district lying between Eagle Wharf Rd and Murray St, with the marked exception of Cavendish and Sylvia Streets and the north end of Brackley St. The general rise has been from PURPLE to PINK. No house work in these streets. "Men are regularly employed and would not be affected by a hard winter" said Ryeland.

As to the police receiving payment from publicans, Ryeland said he would rather not speak about it. "But it is less than it was." He said payments became general when the crusade against drink became strong in the police force, and said anyone could now get paid who wanted it. "You see we can completely change the character of the trade of a man's house if we want to by moving on the rough customers and showing them it is no place for them." He himself has always refused money from publicans, even when he was given a testimonial. "Though I lost about £70 by doing so." Call-money is a thing nearly of the past. He thinks cheapening of alarm clocks has had more to do with it than anything else. Some are still called and in one street Ryeland pointed out to me a string from the top window to the area which was used for the purpose, but more often by professionals than by the police. Strings to bells over beds, pea shooters against window panes, tapping with a fish rod are the means of awakening in general use.

Walk 46   B352-11

Monday 16th May 1898
George Duckworth with Police Constable Ryeland

Starting at the corner of Murray Street and East Road

S down East Rd. Shops. Fairly busy and well-to-do, Mr Kensit (of Protestment Alliance fame) has a stationery shop on the west side of the road, well-to-do, open books of the horrors of the Catholic confession and torture chamber with pictures.

W into Fairbank St. 3½-st, very respectable, 2 families to each house, some keep a general servant, rents £50 + rates and taxes, dismal but eminently respectable street. Clerks. Character PINK to PINK-barred, in map PINK.

W along Nile St and N up Allerton Rd. Poor, rather noisy with a streak of criminal, "though not so full as other streets nearby". Well paved, macadam, 2-st, 5-roomed houses, rent 12/- per week. 15 ft frontage, 27 ft from house to house across. LIGHT BLUE to LIGHT BLUE barred BLACK. In map LIGHT BLUE.

The next street west is Custance St. Rough, convicts, windows broken, bread and mess in street, was formerly a cul-de-sac, now parish has bought two houses in Murray

St and made an opening. Only open 2 months, a great convenience to the police, as they can now work the street from both ends. Worse than Branch Rd, DARK BLUE-barred as map. Like it is Marson St, 2-st. In map Marsham St DARK BLUE-barred, in map PURPLE. Also Moneyer St, 2-st, still a cul-de-sac. Macadam, fairly paved, but stones kicked up. Windows broken and patched, costers, bread and mess, overcrowding. "In one house I found a father, mother and 7 children in two rooms." DARK BLUE-barred instead of PURPLE of map.

Along Marson St, is Provost St, 2-st, "like Allerton St" with a streak of criminals but not very pronounced. At the corner a public house, full of men, sturdy looking, ages between 20 and 40. "Every one of them a thief or burglar" said Ryeland. LIGHT BLUE rather than PURPLE of map.

S into Nile St. Great changes here: the whole of the south side is down between East Rd and Provost St and also the east and west side of Provost Street below Ebenezer Place within 5 or 6 houses of the City Rd. Nile St itself gets worse as it goes west and the west end near Shepherdess Walk is as bad as Custance St. DARK BLUE-barred rather than PURPLE. The east end remains PURPLE, is a street market.

N up Chatham Avenue. Narrow, cement-paved, 4-st model dwellings, opened by

Prince of Wales in 1886. "One of the first attempts at the housing of the working classes." Belongs to the Bleyton Estate Charity under St Luke's parish. Before the dwellings used to be a rowdy street, the home of a rough class of Irish Cockney. Now 2 rooms let at 4/6 per week. 3 rooms for 6/-. "Baths, steam laundry and every modern convenience" at the southeast end of the street.

W along Nile St, N up Britannia St. 3-st north of Nile St much better than south of it, as Allerton St is to Custance St, i.e. LIGHT BLUE north end and DARK BLUE-barred south end. Both ends are DARK BLUE-barred in the map. The north end is better owing to leases having fallen in and a better class of tenants entering. Wellington Place is a small turning on the west side just south of Nile street, 6 houses only. Irish, drunken, rowdy, DARK BLUE as map.

W and N into Westmoreland Place. Like Britannia St. 3½-st. "Below Nile St it is as bad as Custance St", poor, rough, windows broken. Gets worse as you approach the City Rd, at the corner of Nile St (southeast side) is a coffee shop. "You may mark that as BLACK as you can."

E along Nile St and S down East Rd. On the west side is Mount St. 2-st, poor, but very respectable. 19 houses, south side lately done up and looks better than the north, LIGHT BLUE to PURPLE, in map LIGHT BLUE. Further south at the back of East Rd is a turning with workshops on the west side and 3½-st houses on the east. LIGHT BLUE to PURPLE, in map PURPLE.

Into City R, then N up the lower end of Westmoreland Place. DARK BLUE-barred. E into Collingwood St. 3-st. "Like Custance St", cobble paved, windows broken and patched. Large proportion of criminals. Not coloured in map. Now DARK BLUE-barred. Opposite on the east side of Britannia St is Ebenezer Place, of which the south side is down and the north side (DARK BLUE in map) wholly taken up by the red-brick building of St Mary's Church Hoxton.

Back into the City Rd, N up Shepherdess Walk. E past the south side of the famous Eagle Tavern (up and down the City Rd, in and out the Eagle, that's the way the money goes. Pop goes the weasel). Along Shepherdess Place, only one house now, tenanted by packing case makers and shops. PURPLE. In map DARK BLUE. Up Shepherdess Walk, W along Nile St. 2-, 2½- and 3-st, poor and criminal. From No.13 on the north side came Wright the burglar. S into Eagle Place. Houses closed and to be demolished. In map DARK BLUE. The Salvation Army tenure of the Gracian theatre is up next September and Ryeland thinks they mean to build a large police station and section house with married quarters at the southwest end of Nile St in its place.

N up Underwood St. Poor, quiet, 2-st, tenanted chiefly by workers in Barratt's confectionary works (on the north side of Underwood Row). Like it are Underwood Row and Underwood Place, the last named being rather better off as LIGHT BLUE to PURPLE. In map the whole is LIGHT BLUE.

N up Shepherdess Walk and W along Edward St. 2½-st. Very respectable. Regular men. Character PURPLE to PINK, rather than the LIGHT BLUE of map.

S down Windsor Terrace. 3½-st, good, broad street, 3 and 4 families to a home. Skilled artisans, children clean and well dressed. Character PURPLE to PINK, in map PURPLE. The front facing a space in front of the City Rd is asphalted. 4½-st, PINK as map. Behind Windsor Terrace on the east side is Wellesley St. Houses on west side only. 2-st, quiet, poor, children all booted, well dressed and clean. PURPLE to LIGHT BLUE, in map LIGHT BLUE.

W along City Rd and N up Regent St. The west side is all Bett's Lead Capsule Works, the east side is "like Edward St". 3½-st. Artisans employed in the neighbouring engineering and telegraph works. Character PURPLE to PINK, in map PINK. At the City Rd end of Regent St, is a milestone marking "One mile to the monument."

N up Wenlock Rd. 2½-st, poorer than either Windsor Terrace or Edward St. PURPLE rather than PINK of map.

W along Robert St, into Taylors St. Brewery extension here. Wenlock Brewery now takes up the whole space between Wenlock Rd, Robert St, Taylor St and Edward St. In Taylor St, south of Sturt St on the east side are now 3-st dwellings. Flat roof with iron railings round. Children booted and clean, character PURPLE to PINK, in map LIGHT BLUE. Taylor St north of Sturt St used to be called James St. This part is poorer, 2½-st, quiet, inhabitants employed in Esdailes Sawmills in the Wharf Rd, LIGHT BLUE as map.

N up Wenlock Rd and E along Turner's Place. 2-st, 2 families. The top family enters by separate staircase at the back of the house. Rents 8/-, 5/- and 4/6, for 'cottages and half houses'. Poor, quiet, not rough, narrow street, backs asphalted, LIGHT BLUE rather than DARK BLUE of map. Exit at the east end down steps, passage under house, up again into Shepherdess Walk.

General remarks

Note the improvement in the Nile St area. Some streets like Moneyer St and Westmoreland St and the west end of Nile St are worse but not sufficiently so to absorb all the displacement caused by demolitions. The district also between Shepherdess Walk and Wharf Rd is better than it used to be. The inhabitants here are employed locally. The men in the Engineering, Gutta-percha* and Cable Works (employing 400 hands) and sawmills, the women in the capsule works.

In Nile St we met a vestry man who said he was not sure whether the district was better or worse than it used to be. Certainly it is much less rough. But he complained that there had been so much sickness that the parish had had to hire a special wing of a hospital to accommodate its cases.

Great want of open spaces and playgrounds in this neighbourhood.

*Note: a substance made from Malayan rubber.

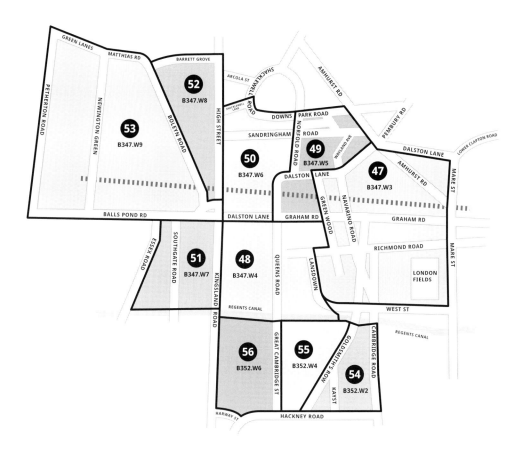

Walk 47
B347-3

Monday 30th August 1897
George Duckworth with Inspector Fitzgerald

Starting at the Hackney Station, North London Railway
S down Mare St and W along Graham Rd, RED to PINK as map, a few shops at eastern end, and a block of flats in place of the waste ground shown on ordnance map a little way down on the south side. Houses generally 3-st. Tram to Dalston starts at Mare St end. Behind it entered by the Penpoll Rd is Sylvester Rd, big dark houses with gardens at the back, built originally as dwelling houses. 4½- and 2½-st, many of which are now used as factories, boot etc. "Many railway people live here." S down Casterton St, PURPLE to PINK (map marks it PINK), a 2-st street. Gymnasium

on east side. Inhabited largely by labouring class working at the Hackney Furnishing Co. in Mare St. This company is owned by Mr Soegenberg, who on Saturday last (Aug. 28th) was elected a vestry man, Conservative. Pigwell Path, which runs out of the north end of Casterton St is now nearly built up. The map marks it LIGHT BLUE and calls it Grove Mews. It now looks PURPLE, the new little houses must have replaced former poorer cottages. It leads to Grove Passage, a very various street with two fully licensed houses at its north end. It also has 6 almshouses "for 6 poore widdowes of good life and conversation", founded 1666, rebuilt 1819. Also a common lodging house for men only, beds 6d per night. Also the Hackney Radical Club, a boot and shoe manufacturing and Jaffs confectionery works, which last are situated just behind the Town Hall. At the south end the grove becomes RED and respectable with a church mission room, it stops at Richmond Rd. Florefield Rd, the turning point out of Grove Passage, north of the mission room is much poorer. The map marks it PURPLE, it looks LIGHT BLUE. At the back of it are 4 very poor cottages almost DARK BLUE in looks. Houses in Florefield Rd are 2-st. "Some costers live here" especially at the west end at the bottom. There is a small general shop in the street. It is probable that the LIGHT BLUE inhabitants of Pigwell Path, who were crushed out by the new houses, have come to live down here. Tower St which is a continuation of Grove Passage on the south side of Richmond Rd, runs under the railway and has some poor LIGHT BLUE houses just on the south side of the railway arch but gets PURPLE and better lower down. The map marks the whole PURPLE, but just by the railway is distinctly poorer. Ellingfort, the turning at the south end, is still PINK as map. Collins' organ and piano works are at the east end. London Lane, though PINK in map, does not look quite so good. Mentmore Terrace also PINK. Houses 3½-st. Boot factories in the houses and at least 4 boot factors under the railway arches. Here and round Bethnal Green are the centres of the boot trade. Gransden and Fortesque Avenues, cement paved, gas lamps in centre, 2-st houses, respectable, take in lodgers, PINK. Lamb Lane, the north side looks poorer than south, as LIGHT BLUE is to PURPLE, map gives both as PURPLE. Sidworth and Bayford Streets both look PURPLE, map gives them as PINK. On the east side of Sidworth St is a cabinet makers factory. Rents in Bayford St for 5 rooms and scullery, 8/- per week. Helmsley St at the bottom of Sidworth St is poor, LIGHT BLUE. So is Helmsley Place, doors open, women at a machine working on babies slippers. Helmsley Terrace which faces on the Field is all boot and shoe factories, fancy and nursery shoes. They should be good dwelling places. They look now PURPLE rather than the PINK of the map.

Exmouth Place and Warburton Rd are two very poor streets. "Very rough characters live here", a litter of paper in the streets, cracked windows. They look DARK BLUE, the map gives them LIGHT BLUE. Triangle Rd and Triangle Place south out of the Warburton Rd are equally DARK BLUE. "Very rough and poor." "As rough and poor as we've got it." "Some no doubt live by their wits but I don't know any of them personally." "As bad as the streets behind the Fever Hospital in Homerton." said Fitzgerald. Their backs are small and crowded. Houses 2-st. Inhabitants costermongers and woodchoppers. In Warburton St was a notice that 12 freehold dwelling houses were to be sold bringing in £218.8.0 per annum. Let at 7/- per week. Landlord paying rates and taxes. These were 2-st houses.

S into West St whose north side the map gives as PINK and south as PURPLE. On the north side is a "manufacturer of coalboxes and bookshelves", a small maker. At the Triangle is a Registered lodging house with beds at 6d, 9d and 1/-. Six houses on the south side of West St were posted to be sold "bringing in £514 per annum". 3-st, flush with the pavement and unpleasant looking.

London Place opposite the bare asphalted end of London Fields is PURPLE now as map. Addis Brushworks here. Then along Twemlow Terrace at the south end of London Fields, small shops. The 'New Lansdowne Liberal and Radical Club' is here and there is a small DARK BLUE-looking terrace just before the public house at the corner of Broadway, not marked in the map.

Then N up Lansdowne Rd and London Field Terrace which is PINK as map. Richmond Rd RED as map. Lodgers usually taken in, front and back gardens, rents of 20/- per week. 3½-st to the houses.

N up Eleanor Rd across the Wilton Rd which has some medium shops at the east end. E into Navarino Rd which is rather better at the south than at the north end, as PINK is to RED, and Naverino Grove, PINK to PURPLE, which is a turning east out of the north end.

{Richmond Rd (best part) 2 houses. £385 each. 10 large rooms, bay windows, forecourts, long gardens. Rents £45 and £42. Lease nearly 50 years, ground rents £8 each. Navarino Rd. Dwelling houses. 10 rooms and scullery, good garden and stable. Let at £50 per annum. Lease about 60 years. Ground rent £8.5. Price £500}

And so out into Dalston Lane which has here 3-st bow-windowed houses of the type very common in the Brighton side streets, and good gardens front and back. Then S down the Spurstowe Terrace, which has some tenement houses and chimney sweeps, into Cottrill Rd and under the railway arch to Manor Place, both 2-st, PURPLE to PINK streets inhabited largely by railway employees.

General remarks

On the east side of the London Fields, i.e. the streets lying between London Fields and Mare St Hackney there are two gradual progressions. From good to bad as one goes from north to south. Graham Rd at the top is a mixture of RED and PINK. Pigwell Path, PURPLE and Florefield Row, BLUE. The BLUE is broken here by the RED respectability of Richmond Rd and the first progression ends and the second begins.

Then there is Richmond Row, RED, the streets about Gransden Ave. a PURPLY PINK and those round Warburton St BLUE.

On the west side of London Fields, there is only the Richmond Rd progression, i.e. Richmond Rd, RED, Gayhurst, PINK, Blackstone St BLUE.

It is strange that there should be so much poverty in the neighbourhood of a fine open space like London Fields. The Fields themselves seem to feel the influence of their surroundings and although they have been for some years under the County Council are still rather a dreary waste. The grass is coarse and tussocky. There are no shrubberies, no flowers, the only trees are long lines of aspen poplars. Very few children were playing on them. The lower end has been asphalted but only adds to the general appearance of bareness.

The industries are bootmaking (principal), piano and cabinet making, and costers and woodcutters in the poor streets. Women seem to be employed more in the shoe and slipper line than anything else.

The large gardens behind so many of the houses have tempted manufacturers to start in their own homes and then to build out behind as soon as they become large employers. In this way many factories are quite hidden away and their fronts look like ordinary dwelling houses were it not that their front doors are generally open and in at the ground floor windows one can see piles of cardboard boxes.

Walk 48   B347-4
Thursday 2nd September 1897
George Duckworth with Inspector Flanagan

Inspector Flanagan has been 5 years in this district as Inspector. He has 1½ years more service and then retires. He is a tall man, grey haired, delicate gentlemanly looking, none of the robust rotundity of the ordinary police inspector, looks more like an American on tour. Soft brown hat, purply brown coat, grey eyes, very short hair, clean shaven except for a fair moustache turning grey. Is a native of the North of Ireland.

Starting at the Dalston Police Station
First S down Holly St, a PURPLE to PINK street, the map marks it all PINK. Rents 11/6 for a whole house.Some of the police force lodge there. Turning out of it on the east side are Laurel and Temple Streets, also PURPLE to PINK, Temple St being the poorer of the two. A small general shop is at the corner of Temple and Holly Streets. Then across Forest Rd which is better off, as map, PINK-barred with red. Some good trees in the front gardens. 2-st houses, Bow windows on the south side. Small fronts. The

east end of the road is better than the west. All houses look a little neglected, but solid, as if the houses were better than their inhabitants.

S again into the Richmond Rd, as map, RED. It is better at its east end than at its west end. Houses 2-st. Lenthall Rd also improves at its east end, the west end of it harbours some doubtful characters. Houses 2-st.

On the west side of the south end of Holly St are Myrtle St, PINK as map. Some houses detached, good gardens behind, 2-st. Bay St is poorer, looks more PURPLE than PINK. Shrubland Grove on the east side is as Myrtle St.

Across Middleton Rd, a 2½-st street with front gardens and also good back gardens, PINK as map. Here Holly St is called Trafalgar Rd. Again S into Albion Square, good 2½-st houses round it, but a very badly kept square. No gates, no flowers, only mud heaps and trenches dug by street boys who were playing in them. 40 or 50 year old trees, remnants of former care and a delapidated iron railing round were the only things to show it had once been cared for. Albion Hall, a literary institute and swimming baths, is now closed. Dances were once formerly given there and the baths open. Now the institute has lost its licenses owing to the character of the dances given, and the swimming bath is also closed. It adds to the ill-kemptness of the spot.

Then out into Haggerston Rd, past the end of Acton St, a poor 2-st, PURPLE to LIGHT BLUE street. E into Livermere Rd, 2-st houses with good gardens behind, containing 5 rooms with a washhouse in the back kitchen. Let at 14/- to 14/8 per house per week. Nearly all take in lodgers. Old-fashioned houses with ornamental capitals to the pillars holding up the lintel over the front doors. So into the Queens Rd, a fine broad Road of detached and semi-detached houses. Big trees in the front gardens. Some houses let out in tenements. Dated 1844. "Houses better than the people." They seem to have been built for a different class than now occupies them, retired tradesmen or Germans should be their occupiers.

Then N along the Queens Rd passing a large new Board School on the west side of the street at the corner of Albion Rd.

Then E down Albert Rd whose houses are of yellow brick and 2½-st, with iron rails raised on a low wall round rather badly kept fronts, the back gardens are large. Up Malvern Rd which is as map PINK-barred with RED like Albert Rd, past Lavender, Shrubland and Gayhurst Roads, all 2-st PINK roads, quite clean and bare, a milk cart here and there and 2 men calling shrimps the only signs of life (4 PM). All the houses have good gardens.

Then N across the Richmond Rd into St Phillip's Road which is RED as map. 3-st on the north side and 2½-st on the south, fronts with trees, houses dated 1861. Across the Forest Rd, which is like it, bare clean, empty, into Wilton Rd which here has a small florist garden on the north side. (The owner of this garden keeps a flower shop in Dalston Lane). Then W into Parkholme Rd. This is on the Cecil Rhodes estate and has been recently improved, i.e. the old houses pulled down and new red brick ones set up instead. The new houses allow a little more front garden but take a corresponding amount off the back. They are only on the west side at present. They are 2-st, with ornamental fronts, terracotta pots at the entrance steps with small alves in them. Window boxes with ornamental tiles, china pots, very large and very ugly on tables in the front windows and lace curtains over the windows both up and downstairs.

Then E again down the Wilton Rd out of the south of which are Salisbury and Lansdowne Roads, both about the same, PINK in colour.

Down S along the Lansdowne Rd to the LIGHT BLUE patch on the west side of the London Fields. Wilman, Blackstone, Blanchard, New and Blanch Streets, a poor block, 2-st houses with small backs. No front gardens, houses flush with the pavement. Built of hard yellow brick. Coloured and worn shiny about 4 ft up on either side of the door. Plaster worn away between the brick edges at corners.

Then W along Shrubland Rd which is rather poor at the east end. Behind No. 70 is a cabinet factory. Close to it are the works of Belotti's, the plate glass levellers and silverers, and on the tongue made by the junction of Albion and Shrubland Roads is Dunmo Ellis and Hill's piano factory. On the south side is a corregated iron congregational chapel, pastor Rev. J. L Udall. The houses are for the most part semi-detached. Date of building 1844.

Then SE down Brougham Rd past the end of Marlborough Rd which has the same shops and looks no better than PURPLE though the map marks it PINK. Brougham Rd has small railinged ill-cared-for fronts, 2-st, working class, PURPLE, map marks it PINK. Brownlow Rd on the west side is 2½-st on the south side and here looks PINK. On the north side the 2-st houses are poor and look more like LIGHT BLUE. The map makes no difference. Broke Rd lower down on the west side of Brougham Rd also looks no better than PURPLE, many children here coming home from school (4.55 PM), nor does Pownall Rd, also a 2-st street.

Then into the Broadway, a market street, with barrows and a rather poor class of shops, it looks no better than PURPLE. Its shops would be used by the poor in Duncan St and Duncan Rd and also by the poor block on the west side of London Fields. Duncan St running northwest out of the Broadway is a very poor rough street, houses 2-st, DARK BLUE in character as map, some broken windows about, a sweet shop in the middle of it, litter of paper in the streets and many children. Doors generally open and women at them holding babies, two empty barrows in the street, Costers are its inhabitants. The top of the street is taken up by 'Hope Cottage' a 3-st house with a large front, now a tenement but evidently originally built for other uses, a wooden balcony supported from the ground runs round the first story.

{Though rough, Flanagan said he did not consider Duncan St so bad as Duncan Rd on the east side of the Broadway}

Here Duncan St narrows and takes a turn and goes past a red-brick building which is the St Paul's mission church. Down the road came a slatternly girl of about 18, slipshod, with large holes in her stockings carrying a baby, many pieces of sodden bread were lying about the street. The road has more respectable houses at its north end. Suddenly it touches Trederwen Rd which is quite respectable, PINK in map but really more PURPLE, a quiet street, inhabited by men working in boot factories. Houses 2-st, bow-windowed on both stories.

Then E to London Fields and S turning W again into Hamburg St, perhaps LIGHT BLUE as map, certainly no worse. The City of Dublin Bottling Co. have offices here

and also Smith and Darridge Boot factory. Note that the west end of Hamburg St does not run into Duncan St, the way is stopped by the mission chapel which is wrongly placed in the map. Bremen St running SE out of Hamburg St is also LIGHT BLUE, houses 2- and 2½-st, old fashioned with windows something like this on the ground floor, good backs but lower than the road, many pigeons kept by the inhabitants. Character LIGHT BLUE to PURPLE.

Then W up Brougham Rd, along Albion Rd and into the west end of Middleton Rd where there are a good many mantle machinists employed. Then N along Bloomfield St, 2-st houses, rather poor, PURPLE, some prostitutes known to live here. No.2 Lenthall Rd, at the corner of Bloomfield St is a dancing place, well conducted. Then down steps looking along a row of 2-st houses which have a passage and low wall between them and the railway. LIGHT BLUE in character. Flanagan said its inhabitants were rough. Then into Roseberry Place. railway people, 2-st, good gardens but more PURPLE than PINK, and into Woodland St, PURPLE, working class, 2-st, the map marks it PINK. 2 Woodland St at the north end is a notorious brothel. It is of a lower and rougher class than that at 36 Mayfield Rd.

On the east side a sweet shop kept by a middle-aged woman, Rose by name. Flanagan said she was in the habit of "going on the spree" about once a year. She drinks a drop too much and takes up with chance men who fleece her. Last year a man borrowed about £20 off her and she never got it back. This year another man has tried to do the same. He went off to Yarmouth and sent to her for the money. She replied that she was sending it but having her suspicions she asked the police to meet him as he came to fetch it. So he was caught. How does such a woman have £20 to spare out of the pennies and farthings spent by the children on sweets? Flanagan says he knows of no other allowance made to her. As far as he knows she is and always has been a respectable woman except for her annual sprees.

Between Roseberry Place and Woodland St is Mayfield Rd. No.36 at the south end is a brothel kept by "the notorious Bella Freeman". This Mrs Freeman, said Flanagan, used to keep brothels in Stepney and Leicester Square and she still has one in the City. From Stepney she was turned out by the efforts of Charrington & Co. She charges a good price, has everything very comfortable and not only has women living with her but keeps rooms for those who bring women with them. Her women work Liverpool St and the City.

This neighbourhood has a bad reputation for brothels and kept women. The district is quiet and very quickly reached from the City, rents not excessive and houses good.

General remarks

There are only two poor spots in this district and they are both in the SE corner near London Fields. The rest is well-to-do, the houses well built, the roads broad, the gardens large and the soil gravel. The houses indeed are better than their inhabitants. It is distinctly an unfashionable neighbourhood and that may perhaps partly account for the fact that so many go to West Kensington or Leyton, much further away, instead of coming north to Dalston, which is reached from the centre of the City in 9 or 13 minutes as the train is express or not. As the suburbs get filled up there will probably be a return to this neighbourhood.

The streets near Dalston Junction have the unenviable reputation spoken of above of harbouring prostitutes, but this is not sufficient to keep people away from the whole neighbourhood.

Kingsland Rd which is a first-rate market street is the shopping place of the neighbourhood. There are not many Jews though they abound on the north side of Dalston Lane.

The public houses are large and do a very good jug and bottle trade. They all look bright and clean as during the last two years there has been a regular epidemic of buying and selling and refurbishing old houses. They are largely used as clubs by the male inhabitants who turn in there of an evening to talk and smoke and read the daily papers which are regularly taken in. These houses have not much of a casual trade and there are seldom many in them before evening.

Flanagan has not remarked that men engaged in the boot and shoe trade drink more than others (Fitzgerald says they do) but he has noticed that women drink more than they used. Perhaps it is because they earn more. They have no shame at entering a public house for that is where they generally go to drink and he did not think that the granting of grocers licenses had anything to do with the increase. Male heads of families allow their wives a fixed sum for household expenses, anything they can save out of this they can spend how and where they like. This is true both of the working class and the middle class above them, so that there is no need to ask the grocer to put down so many bottles of beer as so much coffee in order to hoodwink the husband, as is sometimes asserted.

Walk 49   B347-5

Friday 3rd September 1897
George Duckworth with Inspector Flanagan

Starting at Dalston Police station

Along Dalston Lane to the Graham Rd down which the tram runs to Mare St, Hackney. Graham Rd is a PINK and RED road inhabited by respectable City clerks, houses 2½-st. Up Dalston Lane and into Ritson Rd on its east side with Stannard Rd south out of it, both quiet and respectable, PINK and RED charactered 2-st houses.

Then E along the Graham Rd which has Clifton Grove on its north side and Massie Rd, Fassett Square and Fassett Rd, PINK to RED in character. Fassett Square is very well kept and tidy with beds of bright geraniums and some trees about 50 years old. Houses 2- and 2½-st.

Then N up Greenwood Rd into Dalston Lane, PINK and RED as map. Greenwood Rd is RED, large houses for the district of 3½-st. Across to Wayland Avenue which runs between Dalston Lane and the Sandringham Rd. There is a large public house at the corner of Wayland Avenue and Dalston Lane which has been shut for 6 months, its license was taken away for harbouring prostitutes. The police prosecuted and obtained a conviction. Three doors off it was a notorious brothel, since closed also. The public house is kept clean and smart as its owner is anxious to sell it.

Just opposite is the Refuge for Fallen Females, a kind of rescue home which has had a peculiar effect on the district. The superiors of the home try to get places for the inmates as soon as they have been sufficiently reclaimed, they generally get them taken on in the neighbourhood. "Their new employers take advantage of their having been unfortunates to give them as low wages as possible with the result that they are often driven to the streets again." Not only this but the general servant of the neighbourhood has the reputation of being a very queer kind of girl. "It is a monstrous shame" said Flanagan.

Running E out of Wayland Avenue is Sigdon Rd, PINK and RED, as map, 2½-st street, dull houses with china pots in front windows, steps up to front door, an ornamental iron railing on a low brick wall round the small front garden. Nearly all take lodgers who may be either families or single men in furnished or unfurnished apartments. Women are rarely taken up as lodgers by outsiders unless they come with written characters. One general servant suffices for the housework. The wife of the house generally does the cooking.

Then across Sandringham Rd into Ferncliff Rd also PINK and RED and 2½-st, out of which on the west side runs Mountford Rd, a quiet and respectable street, PINK and RED in character. All are dwelling houses apparently but in one and in the garden behind there are 100 women employed in making bead trimmings.

Then S down the Norfolk Rd across which runs the Montague Rd where many Jews live, and so back again into the Dalston Lane which has some shops and a row of 3-st houses dated 1792.

General remarks

This is a small well-to-do district. Its only peculiarity is its general servants. This walk completes our District 13.

Walk 50   B347-6

Tuesday 7th September 1897
George Duckworth with Inspector Flanagan

Starting at the Dalston Police Station

There is a block of LIGHT BLUE with some DARK BLUE at the back of the police station. In Tyssen Passage there are 37 2-st cottages whose inhabitants are rough and troublesome. Many costers. LIGHT BLUE as map. Behind it there is a bare space where rubbish has been shot for a great many years. Its owner wants to let it as building land but the vestry wont allow it until the rubbish is all cleared. The rubbish is now as high as the top of the garden walls of the passage cottages so it is improbable that it will ever be built upon unless the vestry relents. From time to time Sangers circus pitches there and the round entrenchment made for the ring is clearly visible. Hartwell St which runs into the west end of the passage has also poor cottages. Tyssen St out of the east end of the passage is like it in character. Dyssel St out of Bath Row (which joins the northern end of Tyssen and Dyssel Streets and is of a rather better class than either of them) is a 2-st street paved right across, there is a common lodging house in it, inhabitants poor, rough, bare legged and ragged children playing about. The Atlas mineral water factory is at the south end of it!

Then N along Dalston Lane past Charles St, on the west side just before crossing the railway, LIGHT BLUE in character. Ridley St runs west on the north side of the railway. A few houses 2½-st on the south side, let at 15/- per week. Lodgers usual. Further along the houses stop and their place is taken by a wall along the top of the railway embankment with aspen poplar trees growing up behind it. The south side of the road is not paved. On the north side, there are good houses, PINK in character as map with good backs. One or two of these backs are taken up by L.G. Omnibus Co.'s stables and confectionery works. Then N again up St Mark's Rd a good road sloping uphill to the north. St Mark's Church with a chiming clock, ivy covered, in a large green is on the east side of the road. Many Jews living here. Two organ builders (established 1832 and 1860) have their works at the north end. Colverstone Crescent and Montague Rd on the west and east side of St Mark's Rd also harbour many Jews. Houses 3½-st. Small front gardens with shrubs. Streets bare, wide, clean. No flowers. Further N is Sandringham Rd PINK to RED like the other roads round here. Between the backs of Sandringham Rd and St Mark's Rd runs a lane between low walls leading to Gold Beater's skin factory. Over the walls the back gardens were easily seen. In many of them was the weekly wash hung out to dry and slaveys sweeping carpets, in one, a little Jewboy of about 11 years pitching halfpence by himself. In none of them were there any signs of care and order or flowers. Most kept a dog which howled at our approach.

Down's Park Rd, 2½-st, PINK to RED in character has Eyre and Spottiswoodes printing works at its west end. At its east end where it runs into Amhurst Rd there are some shops and trees on the pavement. At the north corner is the big house and garden of a very prosperous local doctor, Doctor Daley, and at the south corner (No. 183 Amhurst Rd) is the Salvation Army home for the unfortunates and discharged female prisoners. Amhurst Rd at this point is very broad and prosperous, almost YELLOW, 4-st detached houses on its east side, trees in front gardens, and many with their own carriage drive.

Abersham Rd, S out of Down's Park Rd, 2½-st, bow windows on lower story (*see Notes*), front gardens, PINK in character. Map marks it PINK-barred with RED.

Up Norfolk Rd, which has small houses on its west side but large old gardens behind them in one of which is a very fine old mulberry tree. On the east side are the ordinary 2½-st, PINK character houses, with 18 ft frontage, bow-windows on the lower story (*see Notes*), green or white venetian blinds to the windows or shutters and lace curtains. Trimmed privet hedges in front shut off from the pavement by iron spear-head railings. At the north end of the street is a German orphanage founded in 1879.

S into Shacklewell Lane, where there is a large, well-kept green under the Hackney Vestry with old-fashioned houses round it and large gardens behind them, especially Grove House on the south side belonging to Dr Lyle. Round the green was driving a Jew smoking a cigar with his wife by his side, a servant in livery with cockade in his hat behind. Flanagan recognized him as a small tally tailor whom he had known when he was stationed as a constable in the Whitechapel Division.

Then W along Arcola St, which is a poor but respectable working class street, LIGHT BLUE, map marks it as PURPLE. Dunn St on its south side has a few houses but is chiefly made up of the ends of the Shacklewell Lane gardens. On the north side of Arcola St is a court entered by an iron gate not marked on map, known as Miller's Avenue. Not long built but badly built by one Miller "a friend of the Vestry clerks". 2-st, a thieves' resort. Opposite the end of it on the south side of Arcola St is a respectable-looking coffee house with a "good pull-up for carmen" in large letters across the window, which is in reality a well-known but low-class brothel.

Then into the High St, on the west side of which are new red-brick mansions built on what were formerly the front gardens of old houses as can be seen from the old houses and gardens still remaining a little higher up. The flats all have let well but the shops are still empty though they have been there already 2 years. On the other side of the road are shops, but some of them have shut up. It seems a bad district for shop keepers, the probability being that the class of shops attempted was too good for the class of tenant living in the immediate neighbourhood.

Alvington Crescent on the east side of the High St runs rather downhill, a dark street, at its north corner a laundry, collars 6d per dozen. Shirts 3½d to 4d each, Cuffs 1d per pair. Fronts 1d, were the charges printed in the window. The houses are 3½- and 2½-st, 18 ft frontage.

Then down the High St, on the east side of which running south out of the Sandringham Rd, is Birkbeck Rd, which is mostly workshops. The New Dalston Synagogue at one end. At the south end down steps is Winchester Place. 3 poor cottages, LIGHT BLUE, but well-kept gardens.

The High St is a street of shops with costers' barrows in front who do a good trade. One barrow kept by a man and his wife who live behind the police station was selling tomatoes, medium quality English at 3d, per lb. Small hard pears at 1½d, Sweetwater foreign grapes at 4d, golden pippin apples 3d plums 3d, blackberries 4d, fair mushrooms 5d, filberts 4d. The man in shirt sleeves rolled up. The woman in a fine hat with black ostrich feathers and a red blouse with spangles on it. On a shellfish barrow were crabs at 3d, 6d and 8d according to size.

Further down on the east side is Abbott Rd, a 2-st street running east and then turning north at right angles into a cul-de-sac. Nearly all its inhabitants are costers. The houses 2-st, LIGHT BLUE as map. The turning north is paved across. Two boys racing iron hoops against another running barefooted down the middle of it. Houses back on the railway but are open behind. They have a 9 ft frontage and let for 8/- or 9/- per week. No. 18 Abbott St is a dwelling house licensed to sell British wines off the premises, a very old license, a remnant of former times. Except for the notice over the door there is no outward appearance of anything being sold there. Out of Abbott St at its east end is a little open court known as Tranquil Place, as poor as Abbott St but more refined with creepers over the houses and flowers in the fronts.

General remarks

The three poor spots in this neighbourhood are 1) That behind the police station. 2) That near Arcola St 3) That off the southeast end of the High St before you come to Dalston Junction. Of these only the second is really vicious.

The houses known as Miller's Avenue are new and let to a bad class of tenants, there is a low brothel in Arcola St just opposite. The landlord, a Mr Miller, local auctioneer and estate agent is not well spoken of.

The rest of the district is a noted Jews' dwelling place. It is the intermediate stage on their march from Whitechapel to Hampstead. According to Flanagan the Jews are disliked by everybody but can get on in spite of it. Landlords dislike them because they fill every hole and corner of their houses with lodgers, then they are dirty and they take no care of their gardens, added to this they don't seem to patronise the local shopkeepers. Further they stay at home of an evening and don't use the public houses as clubs.

Walk 51 B347-7

Thursday 9th September and Monday 13th September 1897
George Duckworth with Inspector Flanagan

Starting at the Dalston Junction

W along the Ball's Pond Rd as far as the Essex Rd. The Essex Rd is a wide road with trams down it, shops on the east side and dwelling houses on the west. The shops are of a substantial class at the north end. At the south Flanagan said there was a street marked with costers and street barrows but not so much frequented as the Kingsland High St. Eastwards out of the Essex Rd is Dorset St, 2-st, poor, LIGHT BLUE in character as map. Houses flush with the pavement, small back gardens. Two general shops in the street and a large tin box factory which takes up 5 of the dwelling houses on the southwest end of the street. Many girls of a rough class employed here. The firm's name is Jahucks.

S down Cross St into Orchard St, also LIGHT BLUE as map but rather better than preceding, the street broader and better kept. Houses flush with pavement, 2-st on south side but with small front garden with wooden railings on the north. Some of these fronts were bare or untidy, others full of flowers, dahlias, cornflowers, tobacco plants in blossom.

E into Wall St, better still, PURPLE as map. Some children under school age playing about. No.7 at the south end is a brothel, not of the very lowest class, but the women there are very noisy and disorderly. Houses all 2-st. Baxter Rd out of the west side of Wall St is a working class street. 2½-st with 6 stone steps leading up to each front door, white lace curtains to the windows, both upstairs and downstairs. All take in lodgers. PURPLE as map. Norfolk Rd looks much the same, the map marks it PINK. Its houses have small back gardens in which newly-washed clothes were drying. Over the walls you caught sight of the heads of sunflowers and hollyhocks.

Then down Baxter Grove, at the bottom of which are 6 small cottages, three of which on the east side are 1-st, while the 3 on the west are 2-st. No room here for a garden but several plants and creeping Jennies in pots. It is a cul-de-sac, paved across. Very much out of the way. LIGHT BLUE as map. At the corner of Baxter Grove and Wall St is a beer house kept by a woman. "What you don't very often hear of." Down Wall St and into the Ockendon Rd. RED as map. Its inhabitants were for the most part still out of town and the houses in the hands of the builders and painters. 3½-st with small green fronts and good back gardens. At the corner of the Essex Rd "Jays" the big Regent Street mourning warehouse have an ordinary popshop. "Advances made to any amount."

Into the Essex Rd as far as Englefield Rd. Semi-detached 3½-st houses. RED as map. A richer class here. "Some even occupy the whole house themselves." "Some are city solicitors." There is a common lodging house next to the public house at the corner of Englefield Rd and Essex Rd. Church Rd looks the same as the foregoing. The map marks it PINK barred with RED. Houses 3½-st. Good gardens and trees behind. Crowland Terrace, Oakley Rd, are also much like it. Houses old and well-built. Many notices in the window of "apartments for a single gentleman". One of the inhabitants announces himself on a brass plate as a "lecturer at the Polytechnic and People's Place". Fine trees about.

Then E into the Southgate Rd. The streets on either side of it are known as the 'Overtown Estate'. Flanagan could not say more about it than this. There are trams running down the Southgate Rd. The houses stand back from the road, are 3-st and have good gardens. RED as map.

Ufton Grove between Southgate and Ufton Roads has rather smaller houses – PINK as map. Ufton Rd is broad and bare and well kept. The milkman going his rounds the only sign of life.

N into the Englefield Rd which tails off to PINK as map at its east end. Houses 2½-st inhabited by many builders and prudential agents. Good gardens, sunflowers, hollyhocks, chrysanthemums, golden rod, tobacco plants in flower. Trees chick, limes and elders.

Ardleigh Rd running northwest out of Eaglefield Rd is PINK barred with RED as map. Culford Rd, though marked the same, does not look better than PINK. At the triangle apex made by Ardleigh and Culford Roads is the Sussex hotel, a large, old-fashioned public house owned by Whitheads. With its dancing licence and assembly rooms it is more characteristic of what the neighbourhood was than of what it is. But even now it is used as a club and the neighbourhood goes there with its wives and daughters to the variety of entertainments and dances given in its assembly rooms. There are flowerboxes above the doorway and at the windows of the first floor and a small railing in green also bright with daisies and geraniums in front of the house. It is more like a county town hotel than a hand-on public house. The Culford Rd is clean and bare with small fronts and large backs. Builders plates on the doors. Only the east side of the road has a pavement. The west is still a gravel footpath. No Jews in this neighbourhood.

Then on down the Mortimer Rd to de Beauvoir Square (pronounced locally 'de Bover Square'). Two factories are built into the large back gardens of the Mortimer Rd. One belonging to a straw-hat maker. The other an artificial flower makers

employing about 60 girls. Flanagan thought the hat maker employed about 25 but
was not sure. De Beauvoir Square is surrounded by old-fashioned looking stone-
built houses with odd-shaped windowpanes. They looked good enough houses but
Flanagan had been surprised at the poorness of the inhabitants and the insides once
when he had occasion to visit a house on the west side. The west side has good large
gardens and should be the better side. The east has practically none and backs on
the PURPLE Derby Rd. The houses about here look as if they had been the habitation
of the "lean annuitants" of whom Charles Lamb speaks as living in the "suburban
northerly retreats of Dalston and Shaklewell".
Church Rd is typical of the whole of de Beauvoir town. 2½-st semi-detached yellow-
brick, slate-roofed houses, with long gardens behind. The level of the gardens is
rather lower than that of the street. The house shown in the sketch is at the corner

of Ufton Rd and Church Rd at the northeast corner of Church Rd. PINK barred with
RED in looks as map. Southgate Grove out of the Ufton Rd is PINK, 2½-st as map.
Across the Downham Rd which is as map on the west and (PINK barred with RED)
but gets worse as it goes eastward. The north side of the east end is certainly not
better than PURPLE. The map marks it the same as the rest.
Then S down the Culford Rd into Benyon Rd, PINK in character. 2½-st, good fronts.
No Jews. Into Balmes Rd which is much the same, houses flat-roofed and so into
de Beauvoir Crescent, which is not so good in the character of its inhabitants. The
houses on the south side which the map marks PURPLE, are much the same as the
rest marked PINK. All of them look PURPLE. Then eastwards across the south end
of de Beauvoir Rd to look into the patch of DARK BLUE shown in the map next the
canal. It is known as Bankstock Buildings and consists of 16 houses, entrance from

de Beauvoir Rd under an archway, a poor clean court with one gas lamp standing out on brackets from the wall. Houses 2-st, flush with the court, 4 houses had flowerpots with flowers on the first-floor windowsills. The doors were shut. (This was Monday afternoon, 4 PM). No women about. The backyards of the northern side form the south side of the end of de Beauvoir Crescent (not marked on map). In nearly every one of them was a flowerbox. Then into the Mortimer Rd. 7-roomed houses and washhouse and WC. Numbers two and 4 to be sold. "Let for £85.16 per annum, landlord paying rates and taxes."

E again into Hertford Rd. PURPLE as map. Rather lower in character than de Beauvoir Crescent. There are a whiting works and a large dust contractors wharf and works (Crane by name) on the east side. The north end of Hertford Rd is better. Small houses. 2 windows opening down to ground. In character like the rest of De Beauvoir town. The houses on the west side are 2-st, many of the inhabitants work at Cranes. Eight of the houses bringing in £282.2.0 placarded for sale.

Then E along the Downham Rd, which at this point is decidedly poorer than the west end, and then across Kingsland Rd into Acton St on into east side. 2-st houses, PURPLE as map. Gatti's Chocolate works here. Under the railway bridge and northwards up a dark passage leading to Staten Buildings which is the triangular BLUE patch shown on the map. Factories are on the south and west sides. The class above costers living here. Houses 2-st, well-clothed children playing. Flowers in pots at the windows, some litter in the street. Curtains to windows.

Then again into Haggerston Rd and up into Frederick Place which lies on the west side of the railway. The map marks it DARK BLUE lined with BLACK. It consists of 17 houses, 2-st, of which the 3 northern ones have small front gardens, kept with flowers. Some broken windows. Inhabitants no trouble to the police. Passage asphalted. It does not look any worse than LIGHT BLUE. Flanagan had never heard of any brothels being there.

Then into the Kingsland Rd. A shopping street, not so active at the south as at the north end. On the west side are shops and some dwelling houses with long front gardens. The shops, where they exist, have been built out on these. The road is broad and has very wide sidewalks, not paved all over, like Mile End waste though not so broad. Saturday is the great marketing night. There are costers barrows down this end but not nearly so many as out the north end in the High St. Some years ago the vestry ordered all the costers away from the High St southwards to the waste, but business was not so good and one by one they have gone north again and no one has said a word against it. This is a repetition of the experience of the shops in the Poplar High St. Barrows bring buyers both for themselves and for the adjoining shops.

Then W into the Tottenham Rd. Marked PINK in map, but looking no better than PURPLE. Houses 2-st with very well-kept wooden pailinged front gardens full of flowers. There are poorer streets northwards out of it eg. Bently Rd, 2- and 3-st and Tottenham Square, which looks LIGHT BLUE, has a rough common lodging house in it. Bed 6d per night and 2/6 per week. The Kingsland Gospel Mission is here. Number 102 Tottenham Rd is a brothel of a bad class frequented by the women who work the Dalston Junction and neighbourhood.

General remarks

De Beauvoir Town has seen better days. Small houses and large gardens are its features. It is a residential neighbourhood though here and there factories have been built into the back gardens. A great number of small jobbing builders also live there. Generally speaking its inhabitants tend to get poorer as they approach the Ball's Pond Rd on the north and the canal on the south.

The district is singularly free of Jews. Flanagan said he did not know of any. "The people will not neighbour with Jews and Jews will not intermarry with Christians."

Speaking of women's drinking, Flanagan said that the King's Arms in the High St was the 'cowshed' par excellence of the district. It is an old established house and has been lately done up. This was confirmed by a Mr Gong, one of the guardians for the parish, who has a perambulator shop nearly opposite. He said, "11 AM and 6 and 8 PM were the great hours for women's drinking. All classes go in." No one seems in the least to mind being seen. Their tipple is gin. He has watched a butcher's stall just opposite and noticed that every buyer of a joint was taken off there for a drink. Monday is the chief cowshed day. Sometimes in a poor street you will hear an old woman say to a young married woman. "Come along my dear, you just put your husband's clothes away, he will never find it out, besides every one does it. You will take them out again, when you get your money from him on Saturday." That is how the women of the lower classes begin drinking. As factory girls they don't indulge themselves at all regularly this way.

In the lower middle classes, he thinks, the drinking habit is started in the courting days. A young man now always takes his young woman into a public house, so does the young married man. Young married couples will often spend many hours of the evening at the public house, it is dull at home but bright and amusing out. The taste is acquired, which afterwards becomes a habit.

Walk 52

Thursday 16ᵗʰ September 1897
George Duckworth with Inspector James Flanagan

Starting at Dalston Junction

W across High St into Kingsland Grove. Some old houses. PURPLE to PINK. N past Elizabeth Buildings, which now stand in a patch shown in the map as LIGHT BLUE. They are a block of 4-st dwellings on the northeast side of the grove, built about 5 years ago and inhabited by a poor working class. PURPLE to LIGHT BLUE. Frederick Place, just by, is poor also, LIGHT BLUE, cottages built 1826, front gardens with flowers. Sutton Place, also poor, drunken costers. The Lord Clyde Coffee House at the corner has been a noted brothel for years. Bradbury St, 3-st, a street of shops, middle class, owners living above them. Gillett St, the next street north on the east side of Boleyn Rd, 3-st, poor, rough houses, generally sub-let, LIGHT BLUE as map. Boleyn Rd. 2-st and PURPLE in character. Streets run uphill to the north. John Campbell Rd. 3-st. PINK as map. Coffee works at the west end. Castle St not so good as former, though PINK in map. 2-st on south side. PURPLE. Wolsey Grove. 2-st, poor, rough, though not badly kept. Wash hung across it to dry. LIGHT BLUE. Boleyn Rd here is rather poorer. 2-st on west side. Dr Ridge's food factory on the east side. Then up Shellgrove Rd which rises a little uphill. Looks PINK, map marks it PURPLE as it does Millard and Hayling Roads. The houses are 2-st with low windows on the ground floor, painted china flower pots on the table in the front window, lace curtains; small front railings from the road by an iron rail on a low wall, small backs. The milk going round in a hand-cart at 4d per quart. Trumans Rd is rather poorer at the west than at the east end. 2-st. PINK. Prudential agent's plate on one of the doors. At the southeast end is the low wall of the long gardens belonging to the houses in High St, a mulberry tree in one. At the northeast end is Salcombe Rd with a block of 'mansions' built in what correspond to the gardens on the south side of Trumans Rd. 4-st red brick.

Out into the High St whose shops will not let on either side of the road and N to Barrett Grove on the west side, houses like those in Shellgrove Rd, belonging to small owners, dressmakers' plates on some doors and sometimes a privet hedge inside the railings in front. Like Barrett Grove is Pellerin Rd, just to the south of the west end, PINK.

Walk 53

Thursday 16th September 1897
George Duckworth with Inspector Flanagan

Starting from the junction of Boleyn and Mathias Road

Elton (late Prince Down). 2-st houses flush with the pavement. Doors open, 5 women gossiping bare headed, bare arms, aprons, at one door. Very few flower pots, a general shop with goods at prices between 7d and 10d per lb. 'Selected' eggs 12@ 1/-, butter 1/-. Suffolk Place which is further up hill is a little better on its west side, LIGHT BLUE as map. Pretty gardens at the back of the east side, hedges of scarlet runners between each, a wash-house and closet built out behind each house. Sunflowers, nasturtiums and chrysanthemums in blossom and children playing. At the end of it on the north side Woodville Rd. Garden villas, a poor 2-st row of houses, off the main street full of tousely-haired women and babies.

Coach and Horses Passage, 2-st very poor houses, with well-kept gardens, boarded off from Mayville Grove. Mathias Rd has a mixed set of houses, on the whole very poor street. Mayville Street is better though jerry-built bow windows on ground floor, 2½-st, PINK, and Woodville Grove also PINK, a row of 50-or-60-year-old poplars on the west side of the street which has no houses but only the walls of the back gardens to the houses in Mildmay Rd.

Then E along the Mildmay Rd to King Henry St (on the north side) at the corner of which street (Arundel Street) is a public house new done up. Flanagan has watched it, never sees any customers or only a few and wonders how it continues. It was empty as we passed (about 4 PM). Arundel Grove. 2-st, LIGHT BLUE to PURPLE, bare-armed, bare-headed women gossiping in groups.

Arragon Terrace 2- and 3-st, PURPLE to LIGHT BLUE all round here is poor and very poor. Again into the Mildmay Rd which has houses of 3½-st on its north side and 2-st on the south, front gardens, PINK to RED in character, many Jews on its north end.

NW into Newington Green. Very well kept, flowers, and grass like a billiard table, old-fashioned houses all round, shops on west side; on the south side the hunting lodges of King Henry VIII with an underground passage (reputed) to Anne Boleyn's house, a handsome, gabled, red brick house on the west side of the Green. There used to be an open space at the back, now the China Inland Mission buildings and the Jews synagogue occupy it.

Then NW up Green Lanes, mansions, built 1892, 4-st with shops below (steaks good 9d and 10d, tomatoes 6d, apples 3d). Much building has been going on in the neighbourhood. In Green Lanes four different builders live next door to one another. At corner of the turning into the Leconfield Rd is a low old-fashioned public house only 2-st high with 5 separate entrances.

Then into the Petherton Rd, down the middle of which runs the "New river". The river can be seen just by the Wesleyan chapel (Rev. R. Dixon) where it emerges. The Petherton Rd is a very broad road. 2 rows of small plane trees down the middle, a very favourite road for cyclists and would be cyclists. Shops on its east side all closed it being early closing day for the district. Dwelling houses on the west side – many lodgers, city men. Canonbury Station is at the south end of the road. Leconfield Rd running south out of it. PINK 2½-st, many Jews. Poets Rd. like Leconfield, like Ferntower, 2½- to 3½-st, PINK to RED. Pyrland Rd 3½-st. Bows on ground floor windows, RED. Beresford Rd broad clean road, empty, 3½-st houses with the front sloping away to give light to the area windows. Yellow brick. Grosvenor Rd like the rest. No 67 which is typical of the other houses is 'to let'. Estimated rental £55, 52 years unexpired lease, 2 attics 4 bed 2 dressing rooms, dining, drawing, breakfast rooms, kitchen, scullery, lavatory 2 WCs etc, garden at back with pleasant outlook. Then down Wallace Rd and across the railway. There is a nursery garden still here, as map. Northampton Park. RED as map, semi-detached houses. 3-st with very good gardens. Northampton Grove at the top end is poorer, PURPLE as map. Pontifex's boiler works here. St Paul's Rd which is the name given to the west end of Ball's Pond Rd, semi-detached houses on south side. On north side 3½-st 18 ft frontages houses like Wilton Place Knightsbridge.

Then up St Paul's Place, 3½-st not quite so good as St Paul's Rd. Compton St running out of it, PINK as map. N up the Essex Rd past Mildmay St PURPLE as map, to Mildmay Avenue. This the map marks DARK BLUE lined with BLACK. Now it looks no worse than LIGHT BLUE. Flanagan knew nothing against it, the houses on the north side have come down and their places been taken by a yard of the London Parcels delivery company, and also by an engineering and electrical firm.

Then SE down Mildmay St into Mildmay Park. Houses 3½-st, gardens behind dwelling houses but some have factories (one a shirt factory) built into gardens behind. Trams up the middle of the road. The Wesleyan chapel at the south end is very well attended. Mildmay Grove has good houses 3½-st, 18 ft frontage, RED as map.

N up Wolsey Rd and into Queen Margaret's Grove. PINK as map. 2½-st and E to St Jude St, houses 2-st on south side and 2½-st on north, PURPLE as map. King Henry Rd good plain 3-st houses.

Then S down Kingsbury Rd, houses 2½-st. Jews Burial ground on west side. Map marks this and the neighbouring streets PINK but they do not look better than PURPLE. Hawthorn St looks decidedly poor. 2-st houses some with Virginian creepers up them, "not particularly rough". At the back of it is the cluster of Almshouses which with the Jews Burial ground, nearly fill the triangle made by Kingsbury Rd on the west, King Henry's Walk on the northwest and Ball's Pond Rd on the south (Metropolitan Benefit Society's, Bookbinders, Cutlers, Dyers, Bricklayers, Asylums).

Past Canterbury and Stanley Roads, PINK as map. So into Balls Pond Rd, a shopping but not a market road, many private houses on the south side.

General remarks

The poor bits in this district are the block of streets behind the High St lying between it and Mildmay Rd and an isolated bit between Mildmay Grove and Ball's Pond Rd.

Walk 54   B352-2

Friday 1st April 1898
George Duckworth with Inspector Barker

Starting at the east corner of Hackney Road

N up Cambridge Rd, W past public house into Hare Passage, late Cambridge Place. Changes here, no passage is marked in map underneath the railway arch as now. Only two dwellings houses, 2-st, on east side south of this turning, poor, not rough, LIGHT BLUE, in map both sides are DARK BLUE and part PURPLE. No houses now on west side, the brewery extensions have taken up space formerly occupied by dwellings.

N to the canal and W along Crescent Cottages, 2-st, mechanics, windows clean, unbroken, flowers, books, china pots in windows. One house tenanted by a master glass blower, PURPLE to PINK, in map LIGHT BLUE.

S into The Oval, bare, uncared-for square, stones. Shaton Chapel built 1873 (H. Myerson pastor) on the west side, character PURPLE to PINK, in map PURPLE. Between the Chapel and the Hackney Rd it is rather better, i.e. PINK. On the southwest side is a turning, LIGHT BLUE in map, also PURPLE to PINK, not LIGHT BLUE. Quiet, respectable, fairly well-to-do.

W along Hackney Rd and N into Marian St, 2½-st, "roughish", but no windows broken, windows full of flowers, PURPLE to LIGHT BLUE, in map LIGHT BLUE. At southwest end are 4 houses belonging to Lee & Co, the large draper at the west corner of Hackney Rd and Marian St, where the assistants sleep.

Back into Hackney Rd then N up Pritchard's Rd. E and N up Emma St, 2-st, poor and fairly rough, houses on west side only, children ragged but clean and well fed, some windows patched, street being repaved with cobbles. Character LIGHT BLUE to DARK BLUE, in map LIGHT BLUE. Gas workers living here.

N to Marian Square, 2½-st, square shows signs of being well cared for spasmodically, beds and paths well laid out and planted but covered with weeds. 'The inhabitants look after it themselves." Some fairly well-to-do, the west side is PINK in appearance, better than the rest which is PURPLE to LIGHT BLUE, "Some master limeworkers here". In map the whole is LIGHT BLUE.

N up Pritchard's Rd to Ada Place, Wharf Rd, 2½-st, rough, bread and mess in the street, DARK BLUE, in map LIGHT BLUE, wood wharves at the south and north ends backing on to the canal.

S down Pritchard's Rd, a mixed road, at the north end shops, at the south 2-st houses, "like the Old Bethnal Green Road in character". It looks PINK as far south as Caroline Place, then there are broken windows and it is no better than PURPLE.

N into Goldsmith's Row. This is a continuation of the Broadway which leads to London Fields, a busy shopping street trying to be a regular market street but not officially recognised as such. Barrows and stalls allowed by the police to remain so long as they do not congest traffic too much. The north end of the road is very narrow. The west end is new, 2-st and attic, shops on ground floor, PINK as map. On its east side is a passage, un-named, consisting only of cabinet makers workshops. South of it is Oakley Place, LIGHT BLUE as map, well paved, poor, respectable, cabyard at east end windows patched.

S then W into Dinmont St, 2-st, mixed, furniture makers, furniture being carted off on a coster's barrow. Some windows broken, PURPLE to LIGHT BLUE, in map PURPLE, "not quite so good as Pritchard's Rd". At the north end on the east side are workshops, the west side leads to Queen Caroline Place. Old small 2-st houses with wooden palinged strips of garden in front, built 1821, LIGHT BLUE as map, leading to Old Caroline Place, more gardens, one or two 1-st houses, workshops at west end, poor, LIGHT BLUE, not coloured in map.

W into Goldsmith's Square, great changes here, a new LCC playground on the south side in place of the DARK BLUE of the map. On the north side, eleven new, 2-st houses, inhabitants now fairly respectable, mixed, PURPLE. The playground is divided into two, the eastern half being gravelled with swings, bars, giant stride etc. for children, the western half more of a garden with grass, flower beds and asphalt paths. On the west side of it, fronting on Goldsmith's Row is a row of dwellings put up by LCC when the old places were demolished "but quite a different class came into them. The old ones had a job to find houses, they most of them settled into the neighbouring streets".

S down Kay St, 2-st, same character both sides, map gives the west side LIGHT BLUE, and the east PINK. Some broken windows, now both sides PURPLE. At the north end is the 'United Radical Club', founded 1883, affiliated. "A curse to the district, men stay drinking there till 3 or 4 in the morning."

E along Teale St, built 1854, 2-st, mess in street, all rough, windows dirty, broken and patched. Children very ragged and boots holey. 6 houses in a court on north side not marked in map DARK BLUE, and in another court further east on north side, 4 1-st houses, also DARK BLUE, and a collection of six thin and very mangy cats. In map this is all PURPLE. S down Gillman St, 2-st, windows broken, also DARK

BLUE, in map LIGHT BLUE, into Hill St, 3-st on south side, 2-st on north, LIGHT BLUE as map. "Poor but fairly decent." W past Seabright Music Hall and N up Gloucester St, 2-st, "just a trifle better", LIGHT BLUE to DARK BLUE, mixed, in map PURPLE. S down Kay St into the Hackney Rd.

General remarks
Note effect of clearances on the neighbouring streets, the betterment of Goldsmith's Row and the worsement of Teale, Gloucester and Gillman Streets.

Walk 55   B352-4
Tuesday 3rd May 1898
George Duckworth with Inspector Barker

Starting at the south end of Boston Street
Which runs out of the north side of the Hackney Rd, 2-st, poor, hard working people. Some windows broken and patched but clean, well paved, "better than it used to be". No trouble to the police, PURPLE rather than the LIGHT BLUE of map. Out of it on the southwest side is Essex Place, 25 houses, 2-st, 2 families to each, cement paved court, poorer than Boston St, windows broken, children dirty, LIGHT BLUE, as map, inhabitants costers.

W along Hackney Rd which is in the intermediate stage between a living and a shopping street. Some houses standing back with long front gardens between them and the road and used as residences, others used as workshops, and others with the front gardens built over to reach the main road as 1-st shops.

N up Tuilerie St, 2-st, inhabitants bootmakers and cabinet makers, a row of small cabinet shops down a passage out of the northwest end rented by weekly tenants i.e. one or more small masters working orders already given. Character PINK to PURPLE, in map PINK. W along Hackney Rd past an 'off' license. Advertisement in window, Mild Ale 4d, Bitter 4d, India Pale Ale 6d, Stout 6d, Porter 3d. These seem to be the usual prices.

N up York St. Joinery works southwest end, 2-st, clean curtains, PINK china pots in front windows, houses of the 1820–30 type, broad road, 42 ft across, PINK in map. Like it are Dunloe St, 2-st and Busk Street and Holms St running between Great Cambridge St and Tuilerie St.

S into Hackney Rd and N up Great Cambridge St, PINK-barred as map as far as Dunloe St, 3½-st, but not better than PINK north of it, broad cobble paved, 3-st on west and 2-st on east side. E along Edith St, 2-st, mixed, gasworkers, like Boston St, doors shut and door posts clean, some windows broken. Looks PURPLE rather than the LIGHT BLUE of map.

N up Great Cambridge St and E along Whiston St and N up Bath Place. Houses on east side only, rough, poor, 2-st, gasworkers and woodchoppers, DARK BLUE as map. W along Alfred Terrace, DARK BLUE as map, children dirty, ragged, boots very holey, rough, all well fed. S down Cester St, late Gloucester St, also DARK BLUE as map. E along Whiston St, PURPLE in map but not better than LIGHT BLUE to DARK BLUE, "worse than Boston St", no thieves or prostitutes, "a trifle but only a trifle better than Bath Place". S down Nicoll St, 2-st, LIGHT BLUE to DARK BLUE, in map DARK BLUE, but does not look worse than LIGHT BLUE, houses east side only. Into Dove Row, DARK BLUE lined BLACK in map, but "not a criminal street, drunkenness on Saturday evenings and some assaults", like Whiston St, poor, better than Bath Place, LIGHT BLUE. Barker knows of no reputed thieves living there.

S down Boston St, 2-st, PINK in map but no better than PURPLE, women bare armed, hatless, standing at open doors. Some windows broken, in character the same as the south end.

E along Audrey St and S down Maidstone St, "like Whiston and Dove Row", LIGHT BLUE as map, some bread about, children dirty and well fed, hatless, is a cul-de-sac, 2-st. Houses above Audrey St on east side newly done up with rather a better class in them, in character PURPLE.

N into Dove Row, E then S down Moye St, new houses, all very respectable, 2 families in each, cement paved road. Inhabitants of the same class as those in Busk St and neighbourhood, in map LIGHT BLUE, now PURPLE to PINK.

N up Hay St, 2-st, rough, DARK BLUE as map. Out of the northeast end of Moye St is a court, not marked in map, newly done up, called Nelsons Place, 2-st houses, mess and children with dirty faces, character LIGHT BLUE, quiet, no trouble to police. At the corner of Moye St and York Place is a public house which had a large bill 'The only free house in the neighbourhood.'

W along Whiston St and N up Jacobin (late James) St, character LIGHT BLUE, in map there is some DARK BLUE. Then to Nicoll St, 2-st, broad street, poor not rough, not so bad as Bath Place, LIGHT BLUE, in map DARK BLUE. At the northwest end fronting the canal is Waterloo Place, one 3-st house on the canal bank looks rough, broken windows but Barker said no, all LIGHT BLUE, in map DARK BLUE. It is boarded off from Alfred Terrace.

E along Park Place, 2- and 3-st houses, mixed, poor, "better than Whiston St and Dove Row", open space between the houses and the canal, character LIGHT BLUE to PURPLE, in map LIGHT BLUE. E and S down Charles St, "not rough", now LIGHT BLUE, in map DARK BLUE, 2-st houses.

E into Goldsmith's Row, shopping street, north end very narrow, only room for one cart at a time, a stream of men, boot operatives, going over the canal bridge to their work in Hackney. On the west side is a block of model dwellings in place of the

Goldsmith's Almshouses, windows very dirty, look grimy, 5-st, "3 rooms for 8/- and 8/6. 2 rooms and scullery for 6/6 to 7/-". Character of the buildings PURPLE, the rest of the street PINK, not coloured in map.

General remarks

This bit seems to have improved. Neighbourhood of the gas works accounts for what roughness there is. No prostitution, nor known thieves. Some months ago it was noted for pistol gangs of boys aged 14-17, a girl was wounded and the sentences passed very heavy. Since then there has been no trouble.

Rough streets are Dove Row, Whiston St, Maidstone St and the upper end of Moye St, all LIGHT BLUE to DARK BLUE in character but none of them so bad as Bath Place. Roughness here means drink on Saturday nights and consequent assaults.

Rents, from an advertisement of a sale, Nos. 6, 7, 8, 9 Manchester Buildings, Menotti St, Bethnal Green, producing £53.6.29, Dove Row, producing £52.68 and 70 Boston St producing £46.16 (2-st houses). (All Freehold). 37 Collingwood St producing £23.8 (copyhold). 123 Boston St, 10¼yrs unexpired, free from ground rent and let at £28.12.

Tip cat the almost universal game of the school boys in the streets.

Walk 56 B352-6

Monday 9th May 1898

George Duckworth with Police Constable W.R. Ryeland of the Hoxton Subdivision of the G or Finsbury Division of the metropolitan police.

Ryeland is a man between 40 and 45. Has been 20 years in the police force. Always in Hoxton. Was on the GWR before joining. Brown short beard and moustache, teetotaller, pay 34/- per week, rather over medium height, black soft felt hat. Knows district well. Offends a little by his self conscious righteousness but is really good, I think.

Starting at the south end of Great Cambridge Street

N then W along Dunloe St, 2- and 3-st, a mixed street, cabinet makers, well paved, cobbles, character west of Great Cambridge St PURPLE, LIGHT BLUE, PINK, in map PINK. N up Brunswick St, 3-st, average of 3 families to each house, yellow brick houses of 1820–30 type, 19/- per week for whole house, inhabitants cabinet and shoemakers, character PURPLE to PINK, in map PINK. Kent St running out of it is like it, in map PURPLE. Looks a little poorer than Brunswick, children clean, well booted, hatted and fed, no rags, women at doors gossiping over a perambulator, wives of artisans. Not the class that would sit on the doorstep. At the west end the cabinet factory had overflowed into the road and there was a selection of half finished wardrobes on the pavement.

S down Scawfell St, 2-st, inhabitants north of Dunloe St mostly cabinet makers, south of it are boot finishers, riveters etc. 2 families to each house. 5 rooms and wash-house, small backs, rents 16/- per week. Road well paved, houses let to respectable landlords, not rackrented. Back again to Brunswick St, on the west side of which opposite St Mary's Church, are almshouses with gardens in front. The houses north and south of the gardens are called Brunswick Square, not so good as Brunswick St, doors open on south side where houses want doing up, 2-st, PURPLE to PINK, in map PINK. The churchyard has been taken over by the parish and turned into a recreation ground.

N up Laburnum St, that part east of Brunswick St is 2-st, 4 rooms and wash-house for 12/6 per week. Six policemen living here, the rest cabinet makers, one family to a house, PINK rather than PURPLE of map. This is the respectable end of Laburnum St. S down Great Cambridge St, 3-st on west side, let out in tenements, less good than the east side, PURPLE to PINK, in map PINK-barred.

S into Hackney Rd, 3½-st north side, tenanted chiefly by builders, shoemakers and cabinet makers, some with front gardens running to the main road, others built over. N up Weymouth Terrace, 3½-st south of Dunloe St and 2½-st north of it. 3½-st houses letting for £45 a year paying rates and taxes, inhabitants carvers, goldleaf beaters, bed frame makers etc. North end houses with 5 rooms and wash-house and fair backs, 40 ft in length, letting for 10/- per week.

N past Francis St on the east, very few houses, all PINK now, no LIGHT BLUE as map. Across Mansfield Street, 2½-st tenements east of Weymouth Terrace, birdcages round windows, PURPLE as map.

W along Laburnum St, 3½-st. Half the houses between Weymouth Terrace and Shap St belong to an absent landlord and the other half to a resident landlord. The eastern half belongs to the absentee, houses let in 1-roomed tenements, 3/- per week for back rooms, 4/- for front rooms. Inhabitants tailors, boot finishers and matchbox makers. Windows broken and patched. 8-roomed houses, children ragged, boots holey, well fed, hatless, trouble to the police, drunk, rowdy not criminal. The absentee's property is DARK BLUE, in map PURPLE. The resident landlord's is obviously better and though poor, looks between LIGHT BLUE and PURPLE, in map PURPLE. At the west end corner of the Kingsland Rd is the Britannia Public House, "One of the most important in the neighbourhood" and the largest seen this morning. "Sold a few months ago for £12,000."

S down the Kingsland Rd, cobble paved, trams and omnibuses, small retail businesses and factories, small shops, 3-st. E into Mansfield St, 2½-st, PINK as map. On the south side a little west of the railway bridge is Mansfield Court, entered down six stone steps leading to passage under a house, opening on to two cottages at the back, poor, tenanted by labourers, quiet, not shown in map, LIGHT BLUE. Mansfield St itself has good houses, 7 rooms and wash-house with good gardens at the back, police living here, competition to get houses when vacant, rent 16/- per week.

S into Hows Street, 2½-st, rather better east than west of Shap St. All artisans, PURPLE to PINK, in map PINK. Some immigration here from the west side of Kingsland Rd, "When one or two rough families do get in it is wonderful how quick the better inhabitants turn out." Street not so good as it used to be.

E to Fellows St, 2-st, broad, shoe and cabinet makers, macadam road, good, 38 ft across from house to house, PINK as map, rents 16/- for 5 rooms and wash-house.

W to Appleby St, rather narrower, 2-st, rents 11/- for 5 rooms, "used to be 8/- 7 or 8 years ago". Formerly poor, in map LIGHT BLUE, used to give trouble to police. When rents fell in, houses were done up and rents raised. In consequence the old inhabitants moved out. Belongs to part of the Maria Pearson estate, tenants artisans, present character PURPLE to PINK. W along Pearson St, as map PINK, cobble paved, rents average 14/- for 5 and 6 rooms. Across Shap St, 2-st, "like Appleby St", artisans, one family to each house, 11/- for 5 rooms, used to be 8/-, PURPLE as map. Further west is Ormsby St, 2-st, 1 family, PURPLE as map. The west side of the south end is taken up by the L&NW railway Shoreditch goods and coal station.

W to Maria St, rougher, drunken, rowdy, pitch and toss going on among a group of young men of about 18 to 20 years. Houses 2- and 3-st. Carmen working at the coal sheds earn good money, "more rough than poor". On the whole PURPLE as map though far less good from a police point of view than Ormsby or Appleby or Shap Streets.

On the north side of Pearson St is York Row, 2-st, houses recently done up, built for 2 families, carmen and bricklayers, PURPLE rather than PINK of map. "Same character as Maria St." 5 rooms and wash-house for 16/- per wk. Very small backs. On the south side is a turning running down behind the Almshouses called Elizabeth Place, nine 2-st houses, plaster covered, outwardly in bad repair, "tenanted by marble polishers, a season trade therefore uncertain and poor", but quiet, respectable, windows clean, flower pot, PURPLE rather than the LIGHT BLUE of map.

S down Kingsland Rd then E along Harwar St, small shops and houses with workshops behind them, 2-st. PINK as map. Out of the north side is Harriet Square a cul-de-sac, rather narrow, road being repaired, "rather worse than Maria St." LIGHT BLUE as map.

Into the Hackney Rd then N into Nichol's Square, 2½-st houses, only one entrance, almost monopolised by policemen, members of the City police, of the Hoxton, Bethnal Green and Whitechapel Subdivisions live here. Met Sergeant French of the H Division going into one of the houses. Plaster fronts, 2 families to most of the houses, rents 17/-.

General police questions with regards to the Dalston Subdivision of the J Division. Talk with Inspector Flanangan at the Dalston Police Station, Dalston Lane, 21st September 1897

The Dalston police Subdivision is bounded on the south by the Regent's Canal, on the west by the Southgate Rd, Church Rd, Essex Rd, St Paul's Rd, Wallace Rd and the Petherton Rd, on the north by Green Lanes, Barretts Grove, Arcola St, Shacklewell Rd and the Amhurst Rd, on the east by Dalston Lane, Greenwood Rd, London Fields and the Broadway.

With respect to Public Houses, a man, before he is granted a license, has to put in an application to the police and state who he is and where he lives and what he has been doing. He has further to procure two references as to character. This done, the police go to the two referees and take their testimony. Naturally they have to accept what the two say even though they may have their own suspicions that the would be publican is not so desirable a person as he is made out to be. Undoubtedly, Flanagan said, undesirable people do become publicans, because they are able to square their referees before the police see them. (But is questionable whether it would be better to place any more power in the hands of the police by allowing their own judgement as to an application fitness. G.H.D.)

Every class of man becomes a publican. The better sort, as a rule, to the fully licensed houses, the rougher to the beer houses. There are regular transfer days for licenses. If a man takes a house before one of these days he has to apply to a magistrate for a protective license. Then he is said to be 'under protection'. At transfer day he applies for a full license and if his conduct has been satisfactory meanwhile, he is allowed the magistrates certificate without which he cannot obtain an excise license. The excise license is obtained from the Inland Revenue and is a permit to sell.

The value of public houses has gone up greatly of late years. It is a mystery now how they pay their way when one considers the prices for them. Flanagan put the extremes in this division for a fully licensed houses as lying between £40,000 and £5,000 or £6,000. An example of a house worth the first is the [space left blank] at the corner of Kingsland Rd and Dalston Lane. A house lately sold for between £6,000 and £7,000 is at the corner of the Forest Rd and Queen's Rd. The test of the worth of a house is the amount of beer and spirits sold. Lately the prices of houses has been so high that men with local knowledge have made it their business to buy houses, 'work them up' and then sell them to the Brewers or anyone else who will buy them. There is one 'Dyke' who is known for this in the district. He it was who first had the house mentioned above at the corner of Forest Rd and Queen's Rd. Then he sold it to a local newsvendor. The newsvendor has just broken and the house been resold for £6–£7000. The bankrupt has returned to his newspapers. There was no reason for the newsvendor failing, he was a local man and knew his neighbourhood. There is some knavery in working up a house, but Flanagan did not know in what it consisted. Carter in Poplar spoke once or twice of men pouring away beer into the drains in order to show a large consumption. The greater the consumption the greater the capital value of the house.

Women's drinking has certainly increased whereas men's has, if anything, diminished. Men drink beer, but women more often drink spirits. It is beer upon which the working man gets drunk. Factory girls drink but it is more often the young married women and middle-aged women who indulge too much. It is in these latter that Flanagan has noticed the increase, not by any means only among the poor. "It is noticeable among what would be the 'middle class' of a district like this." They have no shame at going into a public house either during or after their shopping. Between 4 and 6 of an afternoon are their hours. Grocers licenses have not had much to do with it because it is away from home that the women indulge. In this district there is nothing in the allegation that women buy spirits and charge them as groceries to their husband accounts. "Why should they? It is the immediate stimulus that they want and they have no shame at going into a public house." The houses known popularly as 'cow sheds' in the Dalston Subdivision are 1) The King's Arms on the east side of the Kingsland High St just a little north of Dalston Lane. 2) The Bull just opposite it which is now being rebuilt. 3) The Tyssen Arms in the Dalston Lane opposite the north end of the Mayfield Rd. The first two are in the market centre of the district and the third not far off it. The Tyssen Arms is not doing quite so well as it used and its owners are anxious to sell for £17,000.

Flanagan sees no harm in children being sent to fetch beer. It is not the children who sip the beer when they come out but the women. He has over and over again noticed this. Since 1894, by a police order from headquarters, it has been an indictable offence to give children sweets when they come to fetch the family beer away. He warns each publican of this as he gets his license and has had only one case of it since he has been here. Speaking generally the beer houses are chief offenders in this way, the keeper of a public house dare not do it. It means so much to them to have their license endorsed. Not that licenses are often endorsed. Magistrates are very chary of doing it. An endorsement always means an appeal now-a-days. Appeals go before quarter sessions who may veto a magistrate's decision. Magistrates don't like this at all, especially at the hands of quarter sessional magistrates. Quarter session magistrates "are a very pettifogging body".

There are three sets of licensing magistrates in the Dalston Subdivision. 1) The Tower body. 2) The Stoke Newington body. 3) The Highbury body. The Tower magistrates will allow a publican to hold more than one license, saying that a man who has many will be more careful that they are looked after because damage to one will naturally affect the reputation of the lot in their eyes when they have to consider the renewals. And they argue that a man who has already two or 3 well-kept houses is more likely to see that a forth or fifth is also well kept than a new man altogether. The Highbury body says no, "no man shall have more than one house under his care because no man can properly look after more than one house". The result being that there is a deal of hard swearing among would-be publicans in the division and men of straw are put up to take the oath. "With respect to this swearing business there seems to be nowhere any notion of morality among publicans." The Stoke Newington body does not care, has no principle or rule on the matter at all.

With regard to the receipt of drink by constables on duty, it is an offence that is very severely punished and if a man is caught red-handed his character is damaged for ever. He is fined a week's pay and his chance of promotion or at any rate of being drafted into the Reserve is practically nil. Nevertheless it is pretty generally done though not so much in this district as in others. Men have even complained to him that the publicans won't serve them when they ask them to. "I know I am considered a pretty hard nail by publicans but it works for the best in the end. I warn them when they first start that they will have no mercy if they offend, and if they do offend it's no mercy that they get at my hands." A man who has had his two half pints at closing time is brisk enough for an hour or two, but after that he gets drowsy, he is no longer properly fit. "A custom has grown up in this district in consequence. The publican gives the man 1/- or two shillings per week instead, which at any rate leaves him with his wits about him. The publicans will pay something in the same way that they always give a cigar or a packet of tobacco to any constable whom they have summoned to eject a drunken man. I have told them often that the police are bound to come for nothing, but they prefer to do it." The publicans are human and the police are human.

The street walkers (women) don't give anything to the police. They are for the most part too poor a class. But the brothels do. The only large sums that are given come from the bawdy houses. The police could institute proceedings against such places if they liked but they have orders from headquarters not to do so. Others may prosecute, then they will watch the house if requested and may be summoned as witness, but they won't take the initiative.

(The good things that come in this way seem to be evenly distributed amongst the force because later on Flanagan stated that no man was allowed to be on one beat for more than one month at a time, nor allowed to come on the same beat again within a twelve month.)

Betting is not largely carried on in the Public Houses. The betting men are known by sight and when they see them about, the police can pretty well tell which houses are the offenders. Prosecutions against them are generally the result of orders from headquarters. Complaint is made by anonymous letters, that is the general thing in complaints of this class, and "curiously enough they are nearly always sent direct to Scotland Yard so that our orders to prosecute or watch come from there in the first instance". Then there is a fair amount of betting in the streets, generally between the hours of 12 and 2, i.e. the dinner hour. A magistrate can only impose a fine of £5 and that is not heavy enough to deter. One man has already been convicted three times this year. He stands at the corner of Dalston Lane behind the police station. Last time he said "What's the good of carrying me off to fine me £5, you know well enough that it's not me but my gov'ner that pays and I shall be at it again, but what I do mind is the indignity of your leading me through the streets between two officers, couldn't you manage it in the evening or down a back way?"

"You must change the people a bit before you stop betting" said Flanagan. "Police orders won't do it."

Very little is now done in the way of waking men up of a morning. "More's the pity, it's a very nice little bit of business that is gone." Night watchmen or men who make it their business are now employed instead. Why? "Well, I think it's the fault of giving beer to the police about closing time, they get drowsy and forget to call men." The public houses have lost their confidence in the police as earlycallers.

Undoubtedly there might be more complaints and convictions for serving drunken men than there are. But is a difficult thing to be sure of. A man is almost always allowed to go home without interference even though drunk, if he can manage it either by himself or with the help of a friend. But he must not make too much noise or be disorderly and collect a crowd in doing so. Then you may run your man in for being drunk and get him convicted, but it is very hard to get evidence that he has been served while actually drunk. Those in the bar at the same time are very unwilling to give it. Besides, a man may be right enough inside and not aware he has had too much until he gets into the air outside. Asked whether having to be up early at the police court the next morning has anything to do with police unwillingness, Flanagan said it certainly had because a man on a night beat would lose some hours of his proper sleep while attending to the case. {vid. Sir J. Bridges evidence before the Licensing Commission.}

It is also inconvenient to his superiors to have a man away from his duty very often for he has to attend several mornings at the court. The constable uses his discretion about running-in drunken men and complaints against publicans, a little more on the negative side than perhaps he should do.

The railway from Dalston to Broad St was made 33 years ago. Before that (how long before he did not know) there was a line between Chalk Farm and Poplar with a station at Ridley Rd. When the new line was made, the Ridley Rd station was abolished, turned into a coal depot as it is now, and the Dalston Junction set up in its present place.

(B347-11)

General remarks

Ryeland said the district had gone down in the last 10 years in so far that the richer people had left and were leaving. This year the greater poverty was not so visible because it had been such a prosperous year for trade, no frost and a brisk demand. This was also the opinion of the school board visitor whom we met on his rounds. They both said it was the better off among the artisans who moved most easily and were first to take advantage of cheap fare and rapid locomotion. Thus the better element does not attempt to resist the incoming of those who have been crowded out from poorer districts and as a result central London tends to become poorer.

The special changes in the working classes noticed by Ryeland are decrease in drink among men but increase among women and greater love of holidays in all classes. He did not know why women drink more than they used to do, not owing to grocers licenses here because there are so few of them, but said they certainly had now lost any shame of entering a public house. Women he said never drink singly so that the evil spreads more quickly than among men.

Industries of the district are boot making and cabinet making. Ryeland pointed out bits of furniture known technically as 'balloons' i.e. chairs and 'tripe' which are all goods veneered with deal backs.

Roads generally broad, well paved and kept and houses with the exception of some in Laburnum St and Elizabeth St, outwardly in good repair. Yellow brick houses.

In the Hoxton Subdivision are 6 inspectors, 18 sergeants, 202 constables. (Some of whom live in a section house, "But all would rather live out if they could").

The extreme values of licensed houses seen in this walk were £12,000 for the Britannia P.H. in Kingsland Rd and £120 for a beer house in Dunloe St.

10
HACKNEY & HOMERTON

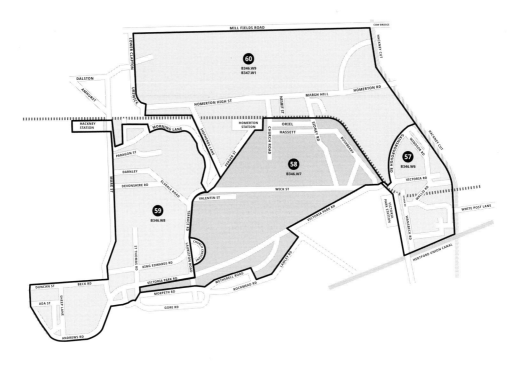

Walk 57

B346-6

Thursday 22nd July 1897
George Duckworth with Inspector Fitzgerald

Fitzgerald is a man of medium height, age between 35 and 40. Round faced, rubicund, brown hair, moustache. A bit of a blarney. Has been in the district 3 years but does not know it particularly well. He is an Irishman from somewhere near Dublin. Widower. Wife died 4 weeks ago after an operation. "A beautiful operation, a 40lb tumour was taken away, but she never recovered consciousness." Lives in the Newick Rd at the junction of Upper with Lower Clapton Rd. Is a lodger with a housekeeper to take care of him.

Officially he is a district Sub-Inspector to the J Division under Superintendent Weston whose headquarters are at the Bethnal Green Police Station in the Bethnal Green Rd not far from its junction with the Cambridge Rd. Superintendent Weston is medium height, short grey hair and beard. Very large. Has risen from the ranks. A Superintendent is the highest post that any man who has been an ordinary constable can rise to. Salary £400 or £450 a year. A groom and 2 horses allowed. A month or 6 weeks holiday. (These data are from Fitzgerald). Fitzgerald would rather that men from the ranks should not rise to such high positions, "they know just a little too much", but he hopes to do the same himself.

Weston was very friendly to me and placed Fitzgerald entirely at my disposition, "for any hour either of the day or of the night."

Gainsborough Road is still PURPLE as in our maps. Four of its houses are occupied by the clergy and lady helpers belonging to the mission whose church and large red classrooms and Hall are on the southwest corner of the road. The west side of Gainsborough Rd is only partially built on (by Gaytons Vinegar factory) the rest is open on to the Hackney Marshes. Its inhabitants are clerks, warehousemen and men employed in business in the city.

Then SE down Osborne Rd. We mark it PURPLE but it is not so well off as Gainsborough Rd. Many of the houses take in lodgers.

SW into Daintry St. Wesleyan chapel making the corner of Daintry and Mallard Streets. Character same as Osborne Rd. S down Chapman Rd, the north end of which we mark DARK BLUE lined with BLACK. It is about the worst-looking street in the district. Worse than Felsted St because it has two sides. Doors open. "No brothels there now though there used to be" said Fitzgerald.

Then along the Victoria Rd, on the north side of which is Mallard St. Fitzgerald gave Mallard St the same character as the Chapman Rd but it looks better. We mark it LIGHT BLUE and it looks LIGHT BLUE. There is a Salvation Army hall halfway down the east side of it.

{Victoria Rd is a BLUE to PURPLE road with several shops at the west end of it}

Then S down Montague Terrace. Rather better. Gardens in front. Foremens houses. Then into Felstead St. A very poor street. Is better than Chapman Rd because it only has one side. The north side is dwelling houses, the south side Ingrams Rubber factory, with an open space palinged in, taking up more up more than half the road. Houses badly built. Stopped up cracks noticeable, women and children at the open doors. A man selling the 'Duchess novelettes' in the street, 1d each. He found one customer.

E into Prince Edward Rd which looks LIGHT BLUE at its southern end, map marks it as PURPLE. On the west side is Montague Rd, we mark it PURPLE. Fitzgerald said its inhabitants, both men and women, were employed, the men as scavengers on the dust shoot in Hackney Marshes, the women in the jam or rubber factories. All are very poor. Some difference in character shown by the state of the different gardens. A few might still be PURPLE but not many.

Further N two DARK BLUE streets namely Percy St and Homfray St. Percy looked the better of the two. Both are less disreputable than Felstead Rd. Children at most of the doors, which were open. Only one child was shoeless.

Up the Osborne Rd into Gainsborough Rd and E to Plover St, a respectable street with an ill-kept open space giving on the Hackney Cut on its east side. At the south end of this space is a gipsy's camping ground. Then cut into Windsor Rd which looked much poorer at its southern than its north end. Windows broken and patched in the south but snug-looking bow-windowed houses in the north. Trees planted on either side of the road.

Wallis St, opposite Clarke Nicholls and Coombs jam and sweet factory. We mark a little patch of PINK here. It is more PURPLE than PINK in spite of a respectable row of cottages called 'Clarnico Cottages', probably belonging to the factory, one of whose specialities is 'Clarnico' jelly tablets.

Under the Railway Bridge, W up Whitepost Lane which we mark PINK. It is a street of poor shops and looks hardly PURPLE now and by no means PINK. Fitzgerald gave it a rough and rowdy character so much so that a fixed point policeman is placed at the Victoria Park end of it. Running N out of Whitepost Lane are Suther St a respectable poor street, Chapman Rd which becomes PURPLE as it passes under the railway bridge and has a congregational mission chapel, and Bower Rd, which is also PURPLE.

S of Whitepost Lane is a block of PURPLE streets, some, I think are, very nearly LIGHT BLUE. Of these Wansbeck Rd is fairly PURPLE, it has some allotment gardens at the south end on the west side between the railway and the cut. Trego St is PURPLE to LIGHT BLUE. Girls and boys with grottos sitting on the pavement at either end of it and asking for pence. Allanmouth St is rather better, houses with plants in front windows of the respectable stiff evergreen sort and more grottos on the pavement. The doors of its houses were shut. Kelday Rd which was not built at the time of our map, looks PURPLE. Behind it is a waste space full of brickbats and rubbish. At the east end of the road there is a small factory in course of building. Camboss St looks PURPLE like the other streets though we mark it LIGHT BLUE. Davey St, also marked LIGHT BLUE, is still LIGHT BLUE and decidedly poorer than the rest. Rothbury Rd is PURPLE.

General remarks

The whole district is very poor and looks as if it were likely to become poorer instead of better as the houses become older and less habitable. The neighbourhood: jam, xylonite, rubber factories, provides work for women and boys but not for men or only a comparatively small number of men. The boys become earners at an early age but are turned off at 16 or 17 when they want more money. Then they do nothing or trust to odd jobs or work as scavengers on the dust shoot. The home therefore is supported by women and children in most instances, the men having every encouragement, owing to want of work and want of training, to be a loafer. In spite of this it cannot be said that there is a vicious look about the district. Chapman Rd is the only exception and *pace* Fitzgerald, Chapman Rd still looks vicious. The openness of the surroundings give an airiness to the rest and the number of flowers in the windows and gardens a brightness which makes the place in summer look rather more comfortably off than I think it really is.

That part of the district where *a priori*, one would have expected the greatest amount of poverty, namely the triangle enclosed on two sides by the branching North London Railway, with the Hertford Union Canal as its base is, on the contrary the most comfortable. This fact is probably due to the allotments in the Wansbeck Rd, which encourage the settlement in the neighbourhood of a steadier class of man. It is a pity that the waste at the back of the Kelday Rd between it and the canal is not also turned into allotments or a garden. Once these open spaces are built over, this district will possess all the advantages of the most vicious with difficulty of approach, presence of a canal etc. The steady men will leave and their place be taken by the rougher elements in Hackney Wick lying north of the railway, of which there are plenty.

Of Hackney Wick itself Fitzgerald said "It's so rough we don't go down there often". It was a fine afternoon, between 2 and 4. Many children about, all except one wearing boots or shoes. Many grottos in the course of erection built of shells and bits of crockery and stone. The children ask you to "remember the grotto" and hold out a shell for pence. What is the origin of it? Why especially at this time of year?

There are no places of amusement in the District. The Eton mission has a working men's club. In Hackney Wick there is a fully licensed large public house on the corner of Victoria Rd and the Gainsborough Rd. There is one on and off beer license and 7 off beer licenses. In the triangle already mentioned there are 2 full licenses, 2 on and off and 2 off licenses.

Walk 58   B346-7

Friday 23rd July 1897
George Duckworth with Inspector Fitzgerald

Starting along the Wick Road

which is a poor street and though marked PURPLE is probably inclined to BLUE, and then SW down Victoria Park Rd. On the north of Victoria Park Rd are Homer St a poor BLUE street, very like a Hackney Wick street inhabited by costers. Street littered with paper and rubbish, doors open. No children about (2.15PM). Street nearly empty except for a 'catch em a live oh' man selling sticky papers covered with flies.

The next street westwards is Brookfield St, very respectable with a Primitive Methodist Chapel (Rev. J. W. Coad). The houses have good gardens and front gardens with trees. Map marks it as PINK barred with RED. Then Dagmar Road, also respectable, tenanted by shopkeepers living away from their shops. Not so rich as the inhabitants of Brookfield Rd. Lodgers usual. Annis Rd as Dagmar Rd. Some shoemakers. A bat and lawn tennis manufacturer at the southern end. Christie and Harrowgate Roads are much the same. Plates on the doors showing that some of the inhabitants are insurance agents, dressmakers, builders. Most of the houses take in lodgers.

Gascoyne Rd which faces SW over Hackney Common is a good deal better. Some large square houses. We mark it RED, in point of income the inhabitants must verge on YELLOW. Mostly retired shop keepers said Fitzgerald. Trimmed lawns and greenhouses visible at the back.

Then SW down Cawley Rd which looks southwest over Victoria Park. Small, smug houses. Respectable, well cared for, probably the abode of any dissenters. W into Rockmead Rd, RED, like Cawley Rd. N into Wetherall Rd which is rather poorer. Its west end is decidedly poorer and we mark it LIGHT BLUE. It looks to be a LIGHT BLUE verging on PURPLE. Half way down on the north side is a congregational chapel of corrugated iron. Pastor the Rev. G. Snashall. Behind Wetherall Rd is the Jews Cemetery.

On westwards across the Lauriston Rd to Morpeth Rd which the map marks BLUE. It looks better than this though there are 2 laundries and a boot factory in it and running out of it two streets of a doubtful reputation. The first Connor St we don't mark at all. It has no roadway for carts but is an asphalted passage, turning sharply at right angles into the Lauriston Rd. Probably the abode of prostitutes. There is a large public house at the corner of the Lauriston Rd. The second, Victoria Grove, which we mark DARK BLUE. It has a bad name. Fitzgerald spoke of its inhabitants as idle and drunken. Some are prostitutes who seek a living in the Victoria Park. There are however not many women of this kind in the park. The County Council is very sharp on them and there are none like those in Hyde Park. Albert Grove, another cul-de-sac out of Morpeth Rd, is still and is marked in the map LIGHT BLUE. It is better than Victoria Grove. (Note that all this bit looks rather vicious, though Fitzgerald would not admit it. He was very reticent on these questions and had apparently received some warning from his superiors on the subject.)

Then N up the St Thomas' Rd passing the Gore Rd. All the houses opposite the Park are going up in character. The park is so much better kept now that it is under the LCC that it is more like a garden than a park. Consequently the houses which look on to it have a pleasanter outlook. The Jews have been the first to recognise this and there has been a large influx of them into the neighbourhood. The west side of St Thomas' Rd looks rather better than the east but both might be marked RED. The map marks them PINK.

{Gore Rd. 2 houses, 9 rooms and scullery, 2 WCs, both stabling and coach house, producing £104. Lease about 56 years at £14 on the whole. Price £1150}

Then E into the Victoria Park Rd, which at this point is full of good houses and some institutions, e.g. a college of music and a school and almshouses. Out of the south side of Victoria Rd run two cul-de-sacs Cornwall Rd and Derby Rd, both PINK roads, Derby being a little inclined to PURPLE.

Then S down Lauriston Rd to look into Rutland Rd, also PINK with Hollidges ink factory tucked away at the west end of it. Ruthven St is a cul-de-sac on the opposite side of Lauriston Rd, has only 10 houses, character PINK to PURPLE.

Then E along Victoria Park Rd which at this point is poorer than further west. It is poorer than we mark it with shops of a PURPLE character. On its south side, Shafton and Minson Streets, both PINK, Minson looking rather better than Shafton St.

Then N up the Banbury Rd at the southwest corner of which is a fancy boot-box manufacturer. On the east side is the large garden of the French Hospital for poor and aged Huguenots or others of good family. On the east side is Southborough Rd, RED, 3-st houses with front gardens. Comfortable and respectable. Further north is Penshurst Rd. Not so well off, character PINK to RED, inhabitants fairly well-to-do, nearly all businessmen or foremen. Some enquiry agents aand commercial travellers live here. Edenbridge Rd, houses of 2½-st i.e. the basement is half below and half above the level of the front garden and has two stories (*see Notes*) above it. Character PINK to RED. Groombridge Rd is a 3-st road, houses rented out at £1 per week for the whole house. RED in character as marked on our map.

Then N up Church Crescent. Looks RED, we mark it PINK lined with RED. On the north side are Monger's Almshouses founded by Mr Monger with very pretty garden in front. Phloxes, hollyhocks and cornflowers in flower. Meynell Rd, a newish street of 2-st houses all alike with red-brick fronts, faces south over Hackney Common.

Then N up the Terrace Rd, the west side of which is poorer than the east. The west side looks PURPLE and the east PINK. The map gives both sides PINK and PINK lined with RED. Out of Terrace Rd on the east is Valentine Rd, PINK as map, and out of Valentine Rd, Bishop, Poole and Queen Anne Roads, all PINK roads of 2½-st though the west side of Queen Anne Rd is 3-st.

Then E along the Bentham Rd crossing Kenton Rd which is PINK to PURPLE, map marks it PINK. Its north end is better than its south end. The houses are 2-st. Bentham Rd looks PURPLE, map marks it as PINK. 2- and 3-st houses. Some men working in Berger Colour Factory live here. On the south side of the Bentham Rd are Brampton, Bradstcok and Gloucester Roads, which run into the Cassland Rd. Brampton and Gloucester are PINK in character as map. Bradstock more PURPLE than PINK which the map gives it, inhabited by labouring class of a good sort.

Then through Hedgers St and Grove into the Wick Rd. Hedgers St is bare and PURPLE in character. Hedgers Grove is LIGHT BLUE decidedly and is marked so in

Talk with Subdivisional Inspector Fitzgerald of the Hackney Subdivision of the J. Police Division, 29th September 1897

Policeman's beats vary in extent from taking 10 minutes to cover them to two hours. Every beat is measured up and each policeman on a beat is supposed to be continually walking at the rate of 2½ miles an hour. Each policeman is on duty 8 hours a day, in two periods of 4 hours with an interval of 4 hours.

Fixed points are placed so that no inhabitant may have to go more than a reasonable distance in search of a policeman. Every householder is informed of the locality of these fixed points. In the outlying districts fixed points are on from 9AM to 1AM, i.e. 16 hours. In the West End they may be on for the whole 24 hours. A fixed point is supposed never to move out of sight of his point. In the Hackney and Victoria Park Subdivisions there are four night patrols, from 5PM to 1AM.

1. Wells Street and Morning Lane.
2. Mare Street.
3. Chatsworth Road and High Street Homerton.
4. Lea Bridge Road and Clapton Road.

Night patrols are men put on in special districts in which people either stay up late or are especially noisy.

In a big street like Mare Street Hackney there are two beats and two fixed points. Point duty is on from 9AM to 1AM, i.e. 16 hours.

That is four different men on duty.

A comes on 9 - 1PM	C comes on 9 - 1PM
B comes on 1 - 5	D comes on 1 - 5
A comes on 5 - 9	C comes on 5 - 9
B comes on 9 - 1AM	D comes on 9 - 1

In addition to them there are two beats who are walking all the time. These beats abut on Mare St, i.e. a part of Mare St is a part of each beat. The beats are continued day and night, thus during the 24 hours there are 6 different men passing through the street on their beats. At night there is one evening patrol who does his duty straight off. In all there are therefore 11 different officers employed in Mare St during the 24 hours.

He does not believe any officer on duty takes beer from the publican. Sir Charles Warren in 1886 first started the crusade against drunkenness amongst policemen. Before that it was a common thing to have seven charges a week. Seven charges a year would now be above the mark. Every year the superintendents are stricter and there is less mercy shown offenders. A policeman hardly dare take a drink while on duty, it is not worth the risk. As to taking drink at closing time that is not the time when he would do it if he did it at all, there are too many about and people are not so friendly with the police that they hesitate to report a man. There may be a few who will take a pint but they are soon found out and dismissed. Fitzgerald strongly disapproves of policemen being given anything, whether beer or money. "It is against orders." He does not believe constables are given money instead of beer. "Most of them would not stoop to accept it." A case of money being given has never come up before his notice. [Fitzgerald was very uncomfortable during these questions which may have been natural nervousness, but rather gave the impression that he was putting his estimate of police integrity too high.] The class of men who have become policemen in the last 10 years has also risen so that in addition to there being greater danger in the acceptance of drinks there is less likelihood of the men wanting to have them.

The prices of public houses in Hackney have about reached their limit. The highest price actually given that he had heard of was £40,000 for the house in Blurton Rd. Some of the houses in Mare St would probably fetch more if they ever came into the market but they are handed down from father to son. Examples, The Britannia near the Town Hall and the Amhurst Arms at the end of the Amhurst Rd opposite the Hackney Station. The latter is held by one Hymes, the son of a great betting man. No betting is done in the house. "Hymes is too big a man to do things in such a paltry way." Besides it is not worth the risk. The house is too good a property, he estimated it at £60,000 and then said he was sure Hymes would not take even such a price. The trade there is very paying. So many passengers. It is at the end of the Amhurst Rd, opposite the Hackney Station and in the middle of a crowded thoroughfare.

There are no brothels in Hackney. There were two, one in Navarino Rd and another in Morning Lane. But they both disappeared on a notice from the Vestry to the landlord and from the landlord to the tenants. They may have gone elsewhere but he knew nothing of it.

"The extraordinary earnings of constables are so insignificant that they may be disregarded." They are always said to take money from loose women but they never do. They would not stoop to it. Nothing is received from brothels because there are none. Nothing is received from early risers for the business has completely passed out of the policeman's hands. Now it is a regular calling and he knew a man when he was in Deptford who used to make 30/- a week from it for 3 hours work a day, i.e. from 3 or 3.30AM to 6AM. He dates the disappearance of this source of income to the time when so many extra constables were necessary for the maintenance of order in Trafalgar Square. At that time in the outlying districts many beats were combined. Policemen could not get round them in time to call the early risers and they had to find someone else.

Fitzgerald is opposed to the sending of children to fetch beer, he would never let a child of his do it.

Drunken men are allowed to get home if they can do so quietly by themselves or with the help of friends. Drunkenness is a very difficult question. A man goes into a house who is obviously drunk outside, he gets to the counter without being noticed, there he keeps himself steady by holding on the ledge underneath the bar. The publican can't tell if he is drunk enough not to be served, serves him and if he is run in for doing so suffers great injustice for what was really not his fault.

Fitzgerald is not a teetotaller but he has never taken a glass of anything or accepted a penny of money while in uniform throughout his whole police career.

Prices vary more from department to department in a public house than they do between house and house. It is the object of the publican to separate his customers as far as possible into their social grades. That is why there are so many divisions. Social grade is roughly gauged by ability to pay, but quality as well as price is considered so that different articles are sold at the saloon bar than are at the public bar and not the same thing at a higher price. At the saloon bar you will only get 'Special' whiskey at 3d per glass. At the public bar you ask for whiskey and you are given a 'two' of 'Scotch' or 'Irish', the whiskey is not so good but it costs 2d instead of 3d. If you want better at the public bar you must ask for it especially.

The usual prices for beer are 2d a glass for bitter, i.e. a half pint. 1½d a glass for mild and bitter, known technically as 'Old Six' because it costs 6d a pot. [A pot holds 2 pints.] 1d a glass of pale ale, the ale that is known as 'four' ale because it costs 4d a quart.

As to ex-convicts, the police never tell employers. Their orders are against it. The convict always allege that it is done but it is a libel.

(B347-12)

map. This is a very bare little bit after the other streets. No trees or front gardens. The Wick Rd is so marked and looks PURPLE throughout, even a little worse than PURPLE in places.

Then N up the Sidney Rd on the east side of which are Bushberry, Benn, Bartripp and Cowdry Streets, inhabited by labouring classes. PURPLE to LIGHT BLUE in character. The north end of Bartripp St, which is called Bushberry Rd, is rather better than the south but it is worse than the PINK which we mark it. It is no better than PURPLE. These streets have 2-st houses of 7 rooms each, inhabited generally by 2 families and rented out at 15/- per week for the whole house. On the west side of the Sidney Rd are Oriel, Hassett and Ballence Roads mainly inhabited by the labouring classes. Ballance Rd, which the map marks PURPLE, looks if anything better than Hassett which we mark PINK. Hassett Rd has a London City Mission station at its west end. Houses all 2-st.

W down Hassett Rd into Church Rd and N to Homerton Station, turning thence SW down the Berger Rd which takes its name from Berger's oil and colour factory close by. Church Rd looks PINK to PURPLE. It has shops and a chapel. Out of Berger Rd on the east side are Marlow Rd, very poor. Doubtful characters living here said Fitzgerald. The street looks LIGHT to DARK BLUE in character. The map marks it PURPLE but it must have gone down since then. Digby Rd and Daley St likewise marked PURPLE are very poor, inhabited by workers in Bergers factory, a rough lot, unskilled with a great capacity for drink, said Fitzgerald. Anderson St, marked in map LIGHT BLUE is very poor and still LIGHT BLUE in character. On the north side is Shepherds Lane, a long narrow passage, "a low rough quarter" said Fitzgerald.

General remarks

There are practically 3 distinct strata in this district. The poor (PURPLE and LIGHT BLUE) bit lying between the North London Railway and the Wick Rd. The steady working class, PINK, between the Wick Rd and Hackney Common. And the comfortable, commercial, both active and retired, round Victoria Park, Hackney Downs and the Lauriston Rd. The steady upward trend of the scale of respectability only receives a check at one spot and that spot is in the best part of all, namely the Morpeth Rd bit, which lies just behind the Gore Rd.

As to drink, Fitzgerald said there had been a great improvement on the last 10 years due to church and temperance work, but I don't think his words carry much weight. The worst people in the district for the drink , he said, were the boot makers and the labourers in Berger's factory.

{Note. The north end of the district seems rather to have gone down in character while the south has rather gone up.}

Walk 59   B346-8

Saturday 24th July 1897
George Duckworth with Inspector Fitzgerald

Starting from Hackney (NLR) Station.

A fine, hot sunny afternoon with a fresh breeze. Time 2PM. Just down Mare St on the east side, opposite Sylvester Rd is a waste bit of land. Very dirty, paper, rags, debris of all sorts lying about. It is used as a gaff, swings and steam roundabouts are set up there from time to time. By the look of it one had just left. A little lower down still on the east side is a narrow opening into Chalgrove Rd and Morning Lane.

{Off Morning Lane, 3 houses in thorough repair, each with 5 rooms and wash-house, let at 8/6 per week, lease 80 years. Ground rent £3.10 each. Price £450}

Chalgrove Rd we mark DARK BLUE and Morning Lane, PURPLE. Chalgrove Rd is still DARK BLUE though the houses don't look bad. They are 2-st with 5 rooms. Fitzgerald gave it a very rough character. 2 or 3 families in each house. The abode of prostitutes and street hawkers. The street is ill kept, much paper lying about and many children. From its appearance it would seem that very few carts ever went down it, but it had not the gloomy and degraded look of the Carr St District. Morning Lane in which Chalgrove Rd begins and ends is a market street and has shops all along it. Jackson's Buildings, character PURPLE to LIGHT BLUE, are here. Homerton Terrace on the south side of Morning Lane in which St Luke's Church is still PURPLE, a quiet street down which carts seldom go. Stevens Avenue out of it is a new 2-st street, PURPLE in character.

Then back into Morning Lane, a little E, and then S down Woolpack Place. This is a small block of poor and very poor streets, all marked LIGHT BLUE in our map but there is some DARK BLUE there as well. Ribstone and Hockley Streets running east out of Woolpack Place look to be DARK to LIGHT BLUE. In Woolpack Place 6 children were sitting on the ground round a pie dish shelling peas for their Sunday dinner. Out E into Morning Lane which is a little better off this end than its west end but is still PURPLE. This end was formerly called Water Lane. The houses here have good gardens behind.

S down Morning Lane, passing Durham Grove on the west side, a PURPLE street, and then turning W down Retreat Place, which is so called because at its west end is a retreat for old ladies, the "Widows of Protestant dissenting ministers professing Calvinistic principles". It was founded in 1812 by one Sam Robinson for 12 widows, and belongs to the parish. Here again are good gardens. The character of the inhabitants is PINK as marked in the map.

S again past a LIGHT BLUE block of streets, Arthur, Brunswick and Margaret Streets. They are inhabited by a respectable working class and the LIGHT BLUE is of a PURPLE character.

Then SE into Well's St which is a market street. The street itself all up for wood paving. A very heavy red wood, looking like mahogany being piled at either side of the street. Butchers chopping up joints ready for the evening sale, some housewives buying already. The green grocers shops and fruit stalls very bright. Heaps of brilliant blood-red currants, dusty-looking black currants and gooseberries. A background of potatoes, tomatoes and greengages and pale yellow lemons. The orchard mission and Sunday School carried on by J. R. Richards is just here.

Then NW into Elsdale St. The first little turning to the N is Orchard St by the Board

School, the second is Mead Place which, though the map gives it PURPLE, looks rather poorer. Darnley Rd the continuation of Elsdale Rd westwards, is a comfortable RED road, same as map. Then N into Chatham Place, a RED-looking road (map, PINK barred with RED) past the Unitarian Chapel and Hackney Free School, which latter is shut. This block of streets whose general character is PURPLE to LIGHT BLUE has a peculiarly large number of institutions. Within the boundaries of Morning Lane (N), Well's St (E), Elsdale St (S) and Chatham Place (W), there are 2 Board Schools, i.e. Morning Lane and Orchard St, St Luke's Church, a congregational Chapel and School, Ram's School, Unitarian Chapel and School and an asylum for the widows of dissenting ministers.

Then W into Paragon Rd, RED and PINK.

{Paragon Rd. 9-roomed residences 2 at £34. 2 at £30. Lease 76½ years from March 1863. Ground rent £5 each. Price £1,150}

N into Stockmar Rd, PINK as map, a street with 2½-st houses with gardens in front and behind, inhabited by working classes.

{Look up a DARK BLUE street lying between Stockmar Rd and Chalgrove Rd. This is Fox's Lane, all DARK BLUE on west side gone, only small patch on east left.}

Trelawney Rd, marked PINK in map, is really more PURPLE. Largely inhabited by conductors, cab drivers and postmen. 6-roomed houses letting at 15/- per week. Then come several courts between Paragon Rd and Mare St, marked in the map DARK BLUE and called Jerusalem Passage. They look LIGHT to DARK BLUE in parts and even PURPLE. Formerly, Fitzgerald said, prostitutes lived here. At the north end used to be a tripe factory. Fitzgerald did not know if it still existed or no, but it probably does to judge from the swarm of flies round the doors.

Then S down Mare St past Devonshire St and up a small turning to the east called Lyme Grove which has Young's Assembly Rooms, a well-conducted dancing establishment, Barretts Coppering Works and Pikes large boot factory on its northern side and backs of St Thomas' Square on the south.

Then along past Baker's Almshouses with a triangle of green in front of them and gardens full of sunflowers, hollyhocks etc., into the Devonshire Rd past Conrad and Rayner Streets which look PINK to PURPLE.

E into Well St which on the opposite side at the corner of the Cassland Rd has the Sanctuary of the 'Zoee perisson' society written up in large letters.

Then come a block of BLUE streets lying between Well St and the Frampton Park Rd, of which Eton Place was and is still LIGHT BLUE and leads to Priory Place and a nest of odd courts inhabited by a poor working class. The north end is a cul-de-sac. Lower down are two very old wooden houses, most doors open, many children, bits of bread lying about. Man selling kippers from a barrow, children building grottos. Two cats, one of which was very lean and ill favoured. Queens Court looks DARK BLUE but many flowers at windows and bits of garden in front.

Then into Well St again and N up Palace Rd which the map marks DARK BLUE. The doors were open here too and many children and much paper littered about the street. A man with a costers barrow drawn by a pony was crying "good cabbages at two a penny". At the north end of the street just where Cross St begins, was a disorderly house. It still looks very much like one, Fitzgerald professed ignorance as to whether it was so or not. Just here was a boy with a hokey pokey stall (*see Notes*). The next street, Havelock St, is marked PURPLE in the map. It is better than Palace Rd but not so much better as all that, LIGHT BLUE looks more like its colour. Then across the Frampton Park Rd, whose north end looks rather better than the south and whose colour is PINK (as map), into Glaskin Rd which looks as the map marks it, i.e. PINK barred with RED, but in which Fitzgerald had been told by a colleague who lives there there has been a great improvement during the last 15 years. At the bottom of Glaskin Rd is the mark of the 4 mile radius.

Then into Well St and E to Percy Rd on the south side. Percy Rd is marked LIGHT BLUE, it is a cul-de-sac. At the southwest end are the Percy Road Schools. One of its inhabitants is a night coffee stall keeper and his coffee stall was standing outside his door. About half way down is a very large block of granite in the middle of the road. None of the neighbours knew why it was there. It always had been ever since they could remember. It looks as though it marked some boundary but nothing is engraved on it. Fitzgerald made special enquiries from the town clerks but could discover nothing. From this point downwards half the road is barred off from the rest by post and rails. Percy Rd is a very respectable LIGHT BLUE by appearances. Balcorne St, the next street on the east side of Percy St is better than Percy St. Houses built in 1852. The works of a fancy box manufacturer are here. Like Holcroft Rd, turning north out of it, Balcorne St seems to vary between PURPLE and PINK. The map marks them both PINK.

Then S down Lauriston Rd into King Edward's Rd, a very prosperous road. All the roads round here are fat and well-looking. Life in them must be very dull and respectable.

{King Edward's Rd. 9 rooms and scullery. 43 years lease. Ground rent £5.15.0. Price £450}

Speldhurst Rd looks PINK. Southborough the same. Handley Rd RED. St Agnes Terrace leading to one of the gates of the Victoria Park, decidedly RED. All this bit has been going up in character. The map marks St Agnes Terrace and Gore Rd PINK but they are well above this now. Many Jews have come to live in this quarter.

Then along W out of Gore Rd into North St, marked PURPLE in the map. The canal runs along at the back of it. Along its south side which we mark DARK BLUE, looks much like the rest which is LIGHT BLUE to PURPLE in character. "No prostitutes" said Fitzgerald.

Out into Mare St and E along Victoria Park Rd and up Gotha St, the first turning on the north side, a street varying from PINK to RED. 2½-st. Up into Fremont St, also PINK to RED, at the corner of which is the Jewish home for incurables. Holmbrook St also PINK to RED.

Out into King Edward's Rd. N up Shore Rd, a prosperous, RED and Jewy road. W down Tudor Rd which is PINK barred with RED in the map but looks rather poorer. There are good gardens.

{Tudor Rd. Semi-detached dwelling. 9 rooms and scullery. Let at £36. Lease 34 years. Ground rent £4.10. Good repair. Price £310}

N up Tudor Grove, PURPLE in the map and PURPLE now. Houses built in 1867. In it is a labour home, 'The Tailoring Department of the London Society for promoting Christianity among the Jews'.

Into Well St opposite Tudor Grove is Weston St. LIGHT BLUE as map with Saxony Cottages which look more like DARK BLUE. Then W. Opposite the end of Mare St is a DARK BLUE court, which is still DARK BLUE. It is known to the police as the 'Rookery'

Then quite S again to the canal, turning W along Andrews Rd which looks PURPLE to LIGHT BLUE and not PINK as in map.

Talk with the Rev. St C. Donaldson, vicar of St Mary's Hackney Wick. The Eton Mission, 28 Gainsborough Rd, 30th September 1897

Mr Donaldson was in bed having just had his knee cap sewn up the result of a bicycle accident. His sister, Mrs Lawley, wife of the incoming rector of Hackney was with him.

In Hackney Wick proper (i.e. north of the G.E.R.) there are 7 off beer licenses and only one full license and one on and off beer license. It was to find out the effect of this 'off-license' policy, that I went to see him.

"There is just as much drinking whatever the license as far as I can see." If a man cannot drink on the premises then he drinks on the opposite side of the road 'off' them. The law may be that the man may not drink within sight of the off-licensed house which supplied but the law is not enforced. Very few policemen come down here, but even if those who do come tried to enforce the law they would find it impossible to do so. Police practise can only be just a little ahead of the morality of the district. "In all they do to suppress rowdiness they must have the moral support of the better class of the neighbours if they are to be successful." Public opinion here does not distinguish between drinking 5 or 50 yards away from the beer house. The police are really wise in acting as they do, they would soon find out how weak they were if they came into conflict with the neighbourhood on a question like this. The people would find it out too and there would be an end of all respect for their authority.

The regular soaker i.e. the man who 'blobs' (the slang word for drinking) for 10 days or a fortnight on end without eating any solids does not spend the whole of his time in the public house, at least very few of them do. What he drinks he drinks at the pub, but your genuine man (i.e. your out-and-out soaker) does not sit long over it and when he has had enough he goes back home again, as soon as he is ready for more he goes back again.

Asked as to his practice with regard to confession he said that he approved of it in certain cases and practised it but always as an exception and never as a rule. "The whole spirit and teaching of the Church of England is against it. My rule is not to do it except in special cases." There are certain people who go on day to day bottling up their grievances and sorrows and becoming bitter and hardened and at the same time confirmed in evil living merely because there is an outlet for their feelings. It is taking a load off such people's minds to allow them to confess. "I have known several people to lead new lives after solemn confession, people with whom it had been impossible to touch in any other way." It is because there is no general practice of confession that so many go over to Rome. "After all the Church must give the people what they want." But he implied that the means of confession should only be given to those that asked and not upon the initiative of the priest. Confession is of most use among women, more than among men. and among boys of about 17 and 18. "I can't say that many boys came to me but I think it would be helpful for them if they did." Those who most use it are women and it is especially valuable to middle-aged women between 40 and 50. "I do not approve of it for children though a great many do especially of the younger clergy." Mr Donaldson recognised all the dangers of the practice but said that he had become convinced that in certain cases there was nothing that did equally well and that the people wanted it.

Here Mrs Lawley (who has been married about a year) broke in "Let the clergy confess men if they like but let them give over the women to women. You clergy seem to think you are always priests and forget that you are also men." The answer was that women won't confess to women so that it is as good as denying it to them altogether to lay down that as a law. As I went away he said "But mind you if Mr Booth is going to publish any statistics about confession in his book he will bring a regular hornets' nest about his ears and we all shall be for having a pot shot at him, but it will be mighty interesting."

Asked as to the acceptance of drinks by policemen, "They would be more than human if they did not take them, there is a pressure on them on every side. Everyone likes to be on the right side of the policeman and the first thing that strikes a man is to offer him a drink. But it is not much and does not lead to neglect of duty though it would be better undoubtedly if they did refuse them."

The noisiest public house is that at the corner of the Victoria Rd and Gainsborough Rd but he cannot say it is badly kept. The noisiness is more the result of the character of the people than of the conduct of the publican.

It requires a man with peculiar qualities to be a centre of evil. A man generally drinks for the enjoyment of it or because he has nothing better to do. Nearly all the harm he does, he does to himself. The disease does not become contagious until it reaches women. One drunken woman in a street will set the whole of the women in the street drinking. Somehow women are born with the persuasive qualities necessary to make others follow in their steps. One thing, they will not drink alone, a man will, certainly he does not mind drinking alone. Sociability is one of these qualities. A woman is so often talking with her neighbours, if she drinks, they go with her.

In this district he has not noticed much improvement or worsement. He has been here 6 years. People tell him the men are rather better and the women distinctly worse. "I don't know why the women should be worse than they were but it is no wonder that they are as bad as they are." Worry is what they suffer from. A woman never knows whether she will have her money at the end of the week. Anxiety is constant. In consequence you are getting a race of women with hereditary tendencies to endure stupidity, unresistingly. Rest and hope are what they want. Drunkenness dulls the sense of present evil and gives a rosiness to what is to come. That is why they drink. But he did not know why it is now that they have especially taken to drink rather than before. "Perhaps it is a fashion." This is a district of wastrel women. Women who have learnt drinking in the smart bars further West. One or two of these settling here are enough to set the fashion.

Speaking generally of the character of men and boys in Hackney Wick he said that lack of the power of concentration of mind was their greatest failing. They never could talk about the same thing for 5 minutes together no matter what the subject. A person, to succeed, must meet them on their own ground. It is useless to claim their attention for the whole of one sermon or set of sermons on one matter. They tire of it at once and don't attend. The tit-bits style of information is what they will listen to and every now and then something will stick. "It is no good for a person to come down here and sit at home and read books." His estimate as to the amount drunk by a steady artisan was 2 pots i.e. 2 quarts per day. They drink 'four-ale' i.e. 4d per pot, which makes 8d per day.

(B347-13)

N up Sheep Lane which is LIGHT and DARK BLUE in character. On the west side of the street are many small workshops, shoe, cabinet etc. and the street is inhabited by shoemakers, cabinetmakers and costers. On the west side of Sheep Lane is Ada St, LIGHT to DARK BLUE in character. Street inhabited by some wood choppers. The St Michael's and All Angels mission house on the south side is shut and looks disreputable. In Antwerp St, marked LIGHT BLUE on the map, Fitzgerald said there was as much drinking as in any other street in the J division. Antwerp St looks rough. It turns south out of Ada St.

Up Sheep Lane again to Goring St, another very rough street. Looks more DARK BLUE than LIGHT BLUE. It is a thieves' resort. Half way down on the south side is a common lodging house with beds for 2d and 4d. Duncan Rd and Duncan Square, also DARK BLUE. Streets littered with rubbish. The north end of Sheep Lane has some very poor cottages, very small and very poor. 4 or 6 of them I think, but all with bits of front garden and sunflowers.

Then E into Beck Rd which is a much better road, PINK TO PURPLE in character. At one window was a man at tea with his children. The man an artisan in appearance reading the Daily Chronicle, in his shirt sleeves. From the opposite side of the street sounds of a piano very much out of tune. A news boy running along the pavement and shouting the Star and Latest Winners. But no buyers as far as I could see. Then back into Mare St.

General remarks

The only really DARK BLUE quarters, i.e. several streets or courts of similar character in a group together, in all this district are 1) the streets round Palace Rd and 2) those between the Broadway and Sheep Lane, i.e. Duncan, Goring, Ada, Antwerp Streets. In the first of these the poverty is of a sturdy character. And it is only in the Ada St. bit that it is really unrelieved and grimy.

The rest of the district has an old-fashioned air, easy going and independent. The Jews have taken the best places. Mare St, the chief thoroughfare, is typical of the whole with its shops large and small, its houses which often stand back from the main road and have a bit of a drive and garden in front, and its chapels. Everywhere, even on a sunny day like this, the soberness of the general colouring was noticeable. The only bright bits were provided by the fruit stalls. Everywhere also, except in the Ada St quarter, was there a sense of openness, airiness and breathing space.

Walk 60

B346-9

Monday 26th July 1897
George Duckworth with Inspector Fitzgerald

Starting from Homerton Station

E down Homerton High St to Nesbit Place which has a block of model dwellings and some small factories of tables and pianofortes. Children were making a grotto in the street. Further E into Nesbit St which the map marks as DARK BLUE lined with BLACK. From Fitzgerald's account it would perhaps be DARK BLUE but not BLACK. It is evidently poor, many children and costers' barrows about (2.40PM). Two families in each house. Houses 2-st. "Prostitutes used to live here but do not now and it was never a notorious place" said Fitzgerald. One or two houses were noticeable for torn blinds and broken windows. The houses have 7 rooms and are let for 13/- to 14/- per week. They have yards rather than gardens at the back of them.

{Miss Paul says "four rooms and scullery 6/6 single rooms 2/-"}

Being Monday there were straw-hatted rent collectors all about. All the children had boots, some employed in setting up a grotto. Tranby Place on the north side of Homerton High St, opposite Nesbit Rd, is decidedly DARK BLUE. The map marks the west side of it DARK BLUE and the east side DARK BLUE lined with BLACK. Fitzgerald did not distinguish between the two sides. Many children in the court, the wash of the court being hung across from one window to the other, but no bare-legged children. Crozier Terrace the next street eastward is DARK BLUE still as the map gives it. Its inhabitants are common labourers. The men work at the dust shoot in the marshes and the women go out charring at 2/6 per day or go out to do/take in washing. Houses 2-st. Another rent collector going his rounds. Copersale Rd on the north side of the High St looks PURPLE rather than PINK. Pickles Buildings on the south side next to the workhouse, LIGHT BLUE. Glyn Rd on the north side is a PURPLE to PINK street, the map marks it PINK. It is a long 2-st bow-windowed street. All the houses alike with little gardens and little trees in front. Rentals of 16/- per week. Most of the houses take in lodgers. Roding Rd, PURPLE to PINK in character. Its male inhabitants mostly work in the city. "They are men of small income who go to work in a BLACK coat."

Then came a block of newly-made or half-made streets round the Sidney Rd Board School. They are on the top of the hill, which goes down into the Hackney Marshes. Chevet St, Swinnerton St, road hardly made or very badly kept. No pavement. 2-st houses, PURPLE in character. Women throwing slops into the street. Kemey's St next to the Board School, better cleaner, PINK. Tynte St on the south side of Board School, made up of the large airy factory of the Crown Perfumery Company, a strong smell of scent in the air. Mabley St still in the course of building.

Then N up the Glyn Rd and past the Glyn Road Board School. The name of the road running round the school is Chelmer Rd, instead of Kesteven as map. On the east side is Ashenden Rd with a newspaper shop at the corner. Road not properly made. No pavement. Pincey Rd behind it backs on the marshes. PURPLE to PINK in character, all 2-st houses with green or yellow venetian blinds and white curtains. N with Clifden Rd on the west side which is PINK, Dunlace Rd, the next road, being equally PINK. This is a good situation, on the top of the hill, it is a new district and has grown up since the last 3 years. All the houses much about the same. "The original tenants are the present tenants" said Fitzgerald, "for they are not people who move much." Glenarm and Blurton Roads on the crest of the hill at the Glyn Rd end are PINK also. Redwald Rd which runs down the hill on the east side is not quite so good as the foregoing. Those at the top of the hill are better than those at the bottom and Glyn Rd follows the same rule and gets poorer as it runs down hill at the north end. Rushmore Rd is rather better on its north side than on its south, when it has crossed the Glyn Rd. The north side remains PINK almost right down the hill. The south side becomes PURPLE sooner. There is a working man's club (All Souls and All Saints) in it, a newspaper shop and a good baker.

Then E into a block of PURPLE streets lying at the bottom of the hill between Glyn Rd and the Hackney Marshes. Of which Overbury St looks a PURPLY PINK, Pedro St, a distinct PURPLE. All Saints St a red-brick church is in this road and there is some open, unbuilt space opposite it. The houses have small gardens behind but the impression left is that Pedro St is on the road to squalidity. McLaren St which is a turning south out of Rushmore Rd is the same as Pedro St to all appearances though the map marks it LIGHT BLUE. Carlton, Mandeville and Rock Streets are much the same, a PURPLE with a tinge of BLUE. Rock Rd is unfinished and has a gipsy's encampment on the marshes in front of it. Carlton Rd has a chapel at the end of it. Etropol Rd, a new 2-st street ending in the marsh. The corner shop selling papers, sweets and toys. Maiwand Rd, the next street northwards is PURPLE too. All this bit is low-lying and unhealthy. "There is much sickness down here," said Fitzgerald. There must be some BLUE about because he gave it a rough character and said it had a good many thieves though not juvenile thieves.

Then on to Cow Bridge where many boys were bathing in the ditch on the other side of the cut. A policeman came up and at the sight of him the boys cut and ran, hurrying away without any clothes so near houses, that is why the policeman was there.

Then into Millfields Rd and up the hill westwards. The houses in the road are PURPLE to LIGHT BLUE in character. The South Millfields, which is the name of the large open space opposite, is rough and not taken care of. Many horses were on it. Fitzgerald said the LCC would probably soon take it over as an open space. When they do the Millfield Rd will go up in character. Oswald St out of Millfields Rd looked PURPLE as map and Chippendale St which feels the rise of the hill, decidedly better with its small houses and trimmed shrubs in front. Sewdley St, PINK with a tinge of PURPLE like Chippendale. Elderfield Rd is a long road running west out of Glyn Rd, across Chatsworth Rd and curling south up the hill. It gets better as it goes up hill. Houses are 2- or 2½-st. Note that the gardens behind most of these houses are a good deal lower than the level of the road.

The Chatsworth Rd which runs nearly north and south from the Homerton High St on the south to the South Millfields on the north is one of the chief shopping streets of the district. After it passes the Fever Hospital it becomes narrow and is called Brooksby's Walk but up to that point it is a broad road full of a fair class of shops, not so good as those in the Roman Rd but what may be called PINK shops. The houses are 3-st.

{On Saturdays there are stalls on both sides of the road. This day gooseberries were selling in the greengrocers shops at 2d and 1d per lb, greengages (fair) at 4d, red currants 3d, lettuces at 1d and 2d each according to size. There were some good stationers shops selling newspapers and good bakers at the corners.}

Then into Powerscroft Rd from its north end. PINK to RED in character, "All small city people here." All the neighbourhood has this "small city people" character. Thus Almack Rd, also PINK with fair gardens, very respectable, though many of the houses have two families in them, and Saratoga Rd, 3-st and Colenso Rd 2½-st, a bare, dull and respectable street with generally a grown-up daughter sitting with needlework in her lap in the front bow window just behind or at one side of the usual evergreen plant in an ornamental china pot. Some piano strumming. Then into the Millfields Rd, which at this end is nearly the top of the hill. Houses 3-st with bad backs but respectable fronts overlooking a private cricket ground. New roads and houses being built on north side of the road above the cricket ground which will destroy the amenities of the street. It is now RED in character. Newspaper shop at the corner of Saratoga and Millfields Roads.

Behind Saratoga Rd are roads not marked in the map. "New within the last 7 years." Elmcroft Rd, with the remains of a country hedge on its east side, PINK to RED in character, and Hilsea St, a 2-st street, also PINK. Atherden Rd, the same, only partially paved. The west end of the Rushmore Rd comes in here and there are 3 or 4 shops. 1) selling ices and sweets. 2) Selling vegetables, tomatoes 2d per lb (Italian), lemons and small pears also 2d per lb, gooseberries 3d. 3) A bootmaker and dress repairer combined. 4) The Elgin cash groceries stores.

Mayola Rd, a continuation westwards of Almack Rd, is RED like the rest. Then into Linscott Rd which has the central building of the Salvation Army, "The Congress Hall", which blocks up the east end of the street. The road is 3-st. "Chiefly occupied by Salvationists". There were several walking about in strange Egyptian and Indian dresses. "The district is the stronghold of the Army". "The Salvationists have drummed all the best people away" said Fitzgerald. The west ends of the Blurton Rd and the Median and Powerscroft Roads all look RED in character. We mark the Blurton Rd PURPLE, it looks better than this. The rents in these streets are 20/- to 24/-. The 'Priory Tavern' which is one of the few licensed houses in the district is at the corner of the Blurton Rd and the Elderfield Rd. It is large, does a good business and was sold for £40,000 6 or 8 months ago.

Then S down the Elderfield Rd, E along the Clifden Rd and S into Brooksby's Walk, past the Fever Hospital. Opposite the wall of the Fever Hospital is the Clapton Park working man's club. A little lower down is the Grove Mission Room, in connection with the Clapton Park Congregational Chapel. On the Chapel notice board was "Articles of clothing are on sale every Thursday morning from 11-1."

Turning W out of Brooksby's Walk is a block of very poor streets. We mark them DARK BLUE lined with BLACK. Of these Holmbrook St is still very rough and low, its inhabitants, wood-choppers, bone gatherers and bottle merchants. Some of the men are employed on the Dust Shoot. The houses are 2-st. Many children were about in the street. Women talking with babies at the open doors. Carts tipped up against the pavement. Litter of paper. Some slatternly girls. "No brothels now but there used to be." But it looked as though there might be still especially in Belshaw St which is the same as Holmbrook St, poorer if anything. Fitzgerald said "Prostitutes certainly bring no man here." 3 families in the houses, which are rented at 8/- per week, Church Terrace we mark LIGHT BLUE but looks like the rest. Houses are all 2-st. The west end boundary of this block is College Lane which has one or two better houses but consists for the most part of the ends of the other streets. Over the walls you can see the gardens of Holmbrook St and The Grove. The Grove we mark PURPLE and it is certainly better than the rest. Sunflowers and scarlet runners in its gardens. But across the partition wall old clothes were the only flowers.

Then W past two LIGHT BLUE streets, College St and Homerton Row. Homerton Row seems to be the name of Cross St in map. Johns St the next LIGHT BLUE street (in map) looks worse. Fitzgerald gave it the same character as Holmbrook St. Fenn St, the next westwards which the map marks PINK at its north end and DARK BLUE at its south, runs into Homerton High St under an arch. The north end is occupied by a cow keeper, children running about but all booted. It still looks DARK BLUE and not PINK even at the north end.

The north side of Homerton Row are Templar Rd, a PURPLE road as map, "inhabited largely by cabmen and by train drivers and conductors". Churchill Rd, the next road west looks nearly the same as Templar Rd, rather better if anything. Map marks it PINK. It is 2-st. Houses with 7 rooms rented at 12/- to 14/- per week. Halidon St, the next westwards, is a good clean street with plane trees in front gardens. The Homerton Row Baptist Chapel founded in 1822 is at its southern end. Homerton Row. Here at its west end has 6 houses which look PURPLE in character, well built but of an Artisan style. Four of them have beds of French beans in their front gardens and one of them, a fine show of hollyhocks.

At the corner of Homerton Row and the High St is a fine looking old-fashioned house with trees in front of it called 'Eagle House'. Two years ago it was turned into a common lodging house and now beds are to be had at 4d and 6d. Isabella Rd on the south side is PINK now as formerly. Opposite the Truant Board School is Sutton Place, which ends in St John's Church Yard, a place with good houses and good gardens. St John's Church Rd, the next road to the north is like it. It is an old fashioned quiet corner this.*

College Avenue is better on the south side than on the north – as RED is to PINK. At the corner of the Urswick Rd and College Avenue is 'Rams Episcopal chapel Infants school'. Turning out of it on the north side is Lesbia Avenue with one of the London General omnibus stations.

SW into Portland Place and N to look into the Median Rd which at this extreme end of it has shops and looks PURPLE. Portland Place is the road joining Mare St

*Note: Notebook B346 ends here and the walk continues in B347.

Interview with Mr T. Cox, manager of 5 public houses at the Penbury Arms in Hackney, Amhurst Rd, 10th November 1897

Mr Cox has dark brown hair, beard and whiskers, is about 50 years of age, middle height. His father, grandfather and great-grandfather were publicans and his son is going to be one.

He has 5 houses under him. 1) Pembury Arms, Amhurst Road, 2) The Unicorn at the Junction of the Commercial Street and Shoreditch, 3) one in Tottenham, 4) one in Denmark Hill, 5) one in Homerton(?).

Mr Cox said that the old-fashioned publican was a man of the past, with his white apron, long clay pipe and his habit of drinking with his customers. Now you have a different class of manager – a capitalist. A better class. He thinks that houses never were so well managed as now.

At the Pembury Arms there are 7 bars. Two of which are reserved for men only. One is for jugs and bottles. Women are never allowed in the men's compartments, not even wives of customers.

His chief custom is from the residential class of the neighbourhood, clerks and city people, who come home, have their supper, then take a turn out of doors and come in to meet their friends at the Pembury Arms. With some houses the main trade is done with passengers. "It depends of the kind of district you are in."

It is most important that your house should be conducted respectably. Therefore you must serve no drunken man. His potman fetches the police and he turns out anyone they see has had too much. He sends for the police in preference to letting his potman turn them out because of the remarks that would be made. "Look at him turning a man out and treating a man like that after he has made him drunk." The police are not always near. He has tried for years to get a point placed opposite his door but unsuccessfully. The Commissioner always says he cannot spare any more men.

Every week he pays 1/- per week to the police as "call money". Nominally it is for calling the servant just before 6 o'clock. This house opens at 7. His house in Shoreditch at 5.30.

The potman is now called "porter" in better class houses, pots are seldom used now. Glasses are becoming more and more universal, the reason being that where you have women at the bar, you can't prevent them from having favourites and it used to be their habit to give nearly a pint to such as these at the price of half a pint. Men too when they asked for a half pint always liked to have it served them in a pint and insisted on full measure. With a glass you serve 1/2 a pint just, which both you and your customer can judge of before you hand it to him.

Those to whom most harm is done in public houses are the servant girls sent to fetch beer, not the children. In his houses he now has a separate compartment for jugs and bottles so as to prevent this source of annoyance. Children sip, he has often noticed it. He never gives sweets. Considers it unfair trading but has lost the custom of many children by doing so. "A child will go 100 yard further for their parents' beer if they will get a sweet by so doing." He did not think that the gift of sweets stopped the habit of sipping.

Houses have gone up enormously and still are going up. Thinks many of them cannot pay at the present prices. "They are getting more and more into the hands of brewers." They are worth more than they can give a return on now because of their prospective monopoly value. No new licenses are granted. Population increases and with it the demand for beer.

He has noticed no increase in women's drinking with regard to treatment by customers. Mr Cox, when he served behind the counter, always refused to accept drinks. People were offended at first but rather glad of it later. They gave a preference to the house where they knew they would not have to stand a drink to the publican.

(B348-16)

and the Clapton Rd. The train lines run along it. Good houses and large gardens on the south side in one of which lives a Miss Wilks, a lady doctor who has come to live there. She is not looked on with a favourable eye by the police because they are afraid she may cut into the practice of their divisional doctor, an old man, very popular with them, who lives there.

S down the Urswick Rd which has the factory of a 'Feather Duster' on the east side. He remakes mattresses. Down the Isabella Rd already mentioned into Mehetabel Rd which looks PURPLE, though the map makes it PINK. The next street eastwards which the map calls 'Balls Buildings' is now called Link St, is also worse than the map. Fitzgerald said it was poor and rough. It looks LIGHT to DARK BLUE.

Then along Homerton High St which has on its south side Marian St, Taylors Buildings, Bridge St, Shepherds Lane, Rosina St, Digby and Sedgewick Streets. Homerton High St is a street of shops and factories. Many of the houses having been solid dwelling places formerly. The old house is seen behind the newish shops which is built out on the old front garden. Some of the houses are dated 1776. The present shops are neither good nor bad in appearance. The whole still has an old-fashioned village look.

{The British Xylonite Factory is in the High St. Xylonite is very flammable being a species of gun cotton. The company has its own fire brigade. Even when alight they will allow no outside brigade to enter. The men were leaving work as we passed. Lighting their pipes at a flaring gas flame coming out of the outside wall.}

Marian St is on the map LIGHT BLUE but it is worse than this. Prostitutes live there. It is a cul-de-sac. There is a small general shop at its northeast end. "It's as low we have 'em." Taylors Buildings, also a cul-de-sac with a large house at the bottom of it led up to by a flight of stone steps. 2 carved stone lions, one very rough, as if someone had started to build a house and had been stopped by cost or death from finishing it. Now it is inhabited by many families. All poor, noisy and rough, many children. The upper sides of the street are occupied by dining table and cabinet makers. Shepherd's Lane has houses along its east side only. Very poor. Prostitutes here. Taylor's Maravilla Cocoa works at the north end.The map marks the Northern and southern ends LIGHT BLUE but the centre PINK and PURPLE. It is BLUE that has prevailed over the rest.

Rosina St, the turning up some steps east out of Shepherd's Lane, ends in the blank wall of Abbott's factory. The map marks it LIGHT BLUE. It varies from LIGHT to DARK, more DARK probably than LIGHT. Abbott's are the large coal merchants and dust removal contractors and the men in the street, those that are not costers on their own account are employed by them. They are a rough lot, all Abbott's men. "One day at work and two days drink is about their character." Digby Rd, PURPLE to LIGHT BLUE. Opposite the end of it is a large building and garden of the Homerton Congregational College. Building closed and garden running to waste. Sedgewick St is rough and poor and has a little general shop of its own half way down the east side.

General remarks

The day was fine and cool with occasional showers. It was a Monday and therefore many rent collectors were on their rounds. Women were not noticeable in the Public Houses. Homerton and Clapton have no "Cowshed" day. As to the character of the neighbourhood, in shape it is a rough square bounded on the south by the North London Railway, on the east by the Hackney Marshes, on the north by Millfields Rd and on the west by the Lower Clapton Rd. In character the east and south sides are PURPLE to BLUE, the centre is PINK and the west corner is RED. The extreme northeast backing on the marshes is PURPLE to LIGHT BLUE, going down in character and now more blue than PURPLE. an unhealthy district and likely to become worse. Pedro, McLaren, Oswald, Mandeville, Mainwand and Etropol Streets come within it.

The block south of the Fever Hospital is DARK BLUE and was DARK BLUE 10 years ago. St Barnabas Church with its large church yard has had no apparant influence on it, although Belshawe St, the worst of the group, nearly touches it. South of the Homerton High St again, between it and the railway is a poor bit which seems to have got worse rather than better. There is more BLUE in it now than the map shows. Up on the hill on either side of the Chatsworth Rd is a regular PINK district, Men of small incomes "who go to their work in the city in a black coat", shop assistants, clerks etc. who have married and settled down and have hard work to make both ends meet. It is a regular Salvation Army district and the Army has its headquarters there. About the Clapton Rd further west there is greater comfort.

(As to the religious influences, one would expect the Church of England to be the most active body in the northeast, the RCs to have many adherents in the south, the Salvation Army in the centre and the Nonconformists in the northwest. Whether this is so or not, exception being made for the Salvationists, I do not know.)

Interview with the Rev. the Hon. A. Lawley, now rector of St John's Hackney, for 10 years vicar of St Andrew's Bethnal Green, 28th Janaury 1898

He is a tall man, pale, ascetic face. No nonsense about him, is married to a sister of Donaldson (of Hackney Wick), he was in the running for the Bishopric of Stepney (lately given to Winnington-Ingram). These 3 have always worked in together. He is about forty years of age. It is two years I think since he was in Bethnal Green, which he left by reason of ill-health, brought on by overwork.

Under him at St Andrews were 4 or at times 5 curates, all living in the same house. When he first came to the parish, the staff consisted of a vicar and 2 married curates living outside the parish and a certain number of ladies who came down from the West End to help during the London season. Two married curates were given livings in the curatory soon after his arrival, the West End ladies were told that it would be better if they did not come at all. After that he chose 5 from the numbers who offered themselves. "There is never any difficulty about getting good curates in the East End, all keen men, my difficulty lay in keeping them back. Here in Hackney, I have rather to urge them on."

In Bethnal Green the limits of the parish were strictly territorial. In Hackney they are more congregational. "People have an extraordinary affection for the parish church here and will come from great distances to have themselves or their children baptised, married or buried in it."

At Bethnal Green the parish was strictly divided up for visiting purposes, each curate and himself had a district allotted to them, under each curate there was a district visitor. All complaints passed in the first instance to the curate and then to himself as a court of appeal. Every Monday morning they met together and after a prayer compared notes. Relief was allotted according to needs and means. Only one exception, whenever the district nurse recommended expensive foods for the sick they were always granted whatever the cost.

He attaches great importance to Sunday schools, mothers' meetings and district visiting. "District visiting is the unique heritage of the Church of England." Has never been able to understand why the dissenters don't visit, but they don't. Once or twice he has been sent for by dying noncons. "Why don't you send for your own minister?" "Oh, he's only good in the pulpit" was the answer.

Mothers' meetings, he said, may be as demoralising as anything in the parish but they may be the reverse. He has seen a whole district in Bethnal Green civilised and he believes mainly through the mothers' meeting. It was a district of free family fights. Always a row between warlike mothers. In 3 years this was altered. "But you must choose carefully those who are to lead them. Never ask mothers to come, let them come because they want to."

Sunday schools are more useful to the teachers than to the taught. Their real value is to the teacher. Sense of responsibility, esprit de corps, visible way of helping the church – all encouraged and hence encouragement given to "that most important body of all, the church nucleus". He prefers it to the Dupanloup* system, "unless you happen to have a Dupanloup man among you, but it's the man not the system that makes the difference". He teaches his teachers and then lets them teach the children. Children sent partly to be got out of the way, partly tradition, partly hope of treats and prizes, partly to learn. Prizes he stopped at once and so were treats unless the parents would provide for the journey money. Result at first a falling off but afterwards increased respect felt for school and increased attendance. In Bethnal Green he has 1,000 at Sunday school. Here in Hackney, in a parish twice the size, he has only 500. Last Sunday he told Superintendent he was going to stop all prize giving at Sunday school in Hackney. "But they will all go to the Wesleyans and Baptists. Let them go. I won't have children bribed to come to school. There are many better ways of spending £20 here in a parish with a debt of £3,000 on its school than prize books."

The great leakage occurs after Sunday school age. "To continue at Sunday school is to dub yourself a child." Children of 14 won't do this. It is not that they would rather not but that they wish to show outwardly that they had ceased to be children, that is the main reason why they leave. For a long time he could hit on no remedy. Then he tried refusing admittance to Sunday school at 14 years of age. "They were turned out, never mind how much they wanted to stay." And he started a Sunday class, the same thing as they had left but with a different name which was consistent with their dignity and proclaimed their age and was successful. "It is in little ways that you make a great organization successful."

His plan now is to make sure of a small number who shall remain permanently faithful to the church, "know the reasons for her existence and the why and wherefore of everything she does". This nucleus is the hub of the church life in a parish. Like a corporation, it never dies and when once properly

*Note: Felix Dupanloup (1802–78) was a charismatic bishop of Orleans who became prominent in education and French religous life.

started, is independent of a charge of a minister. The personal influence of a minister may be enormous, often is, but the reaction is the greater when he leaves. "What he has to do is to see that those who are not so likely to leave as himself, are the conducts of right thinking and right living to the congregation rather than the minister himself." He said that the clergy should feel their congregation in this way indirectly rather than directly. He admitted one great difficulty, i.e. that the church nucleus were the better men in a poor parish and for that very reason were more likely than not to move out of it as soon as they could afford to, but he was sure that the principle was the right one. "Begin small." After 20 years experience he is sure this is the only true road to success. As to large congregations the easiest way to get them is to get up a controversy with your neighbour. "Crowds will come to hear one person attack another." The next best way is to denounce your congregation, blood and thunder. But he approves of neither. The most popular part of the service, he said, is always the sermon and in practise he has found the most successful of his own sermons to be a course of teaching upon the Lord's prayer or catechism. "The reasons for everything is what they wanted to know in Bethnal Green."

"The first condition of success in a working class district is to work hard. Nothing will ever persuade the working man that the clergy are not paid out of the rates." He can't conceive how they ever got that idea, but there it is and though he has argued it with them again and again, it is no good and it is a fact that every parson must accept. But they do not mind paying if they see the parson really working. "Ingram, for instance, the working men would willingly subsidize." For this reason he thinks that a working man if he had his choice would choose to be a dissenter rather than a church man, for dissenters pay for results, which are forthcoming because if they were not, payment would cease. But dissent is expensive. Again the church service was constructed for instructed people. Working men don't understand it at first and for that reason dislike it. "The church in a working class district is handicapped by her service until the congregation has been trained to it by sermons."

Every religious man he said is a target in the workshop. Much is expected of him if he "gets religion". "But I don't think it amounts to actual persecution unless the man is a fanatic and you will generally find that it is the religious man who is entrusted with the shops club and sick funds." This he has seen several times. In Bethnal Green he said he thought the church had never quite got over the way in which it was started. "Irrespective of need or preparation of audience, churches were dumped down by acts of Parliament." Instead of by living agents the church in Bethnal Green was started by bricks and mortar. He said this mistake had often been made by the church and ascribed a great part of the success of the 'Romans' to their consistent following of the plan of creating a need and then making people pay themselves for the means of its satisfaction.

He hates Dissent, though he has many good friends among dissenters. It seems to him abominable that in the church of all places there should be difference. Twenty years ago he thinks that the "piety of the nation" was really with the dissenters. Now, since the Anglican revival, it is with the established church. "Nonconformists are too political, this has been their ruin, on a platform they are well enough, but in organization and real influence on private life and action they are nowhere." He complained of their unwillingness to show the records of relief given or of members of mothers' meetings so as to prevent overlapping. Also of their want of method in treatment of the poor. "In hard winters they have the money but no idea of those to whom it should be given. Then it is that they come to us."

Then he spoke of the devotedness of the members of the Salvation Army but said they had never "caught on" in Bethnal Green. At first they met with hostility and they prospered under persecution, when that ceased, they failed. He criticised their methods. In the roughest and most criminal of the streets in his Bethnal Green parish – Gales Gardens – he has seen two Salvation lasses singing and going into the houses. They were good looking and the treatment they met with was brutal. Thought it was wicked to expose girls in this way. Another man he knew, "one of the best and earnest of men" was literally starved out of the Army. He had given up his trade to work for them, for pay he only had what he could get, in Bethnal Green he could not get enough to pay for his daily bread. Finally, he was very ill, he sent for Lawley and in the end was taken in by a Church Convalescent Home.

The worst streets in the St Andrew's parish are Gales Gardens next to the railway (DARK BLUE in map) and Pitt St (LIGHT BLUE). Pott St (LIGHT BLUE) is nearly but not quite so bad. The BLACK spot in Sales St has been pulled down. Parliament St (DARK BLUE) is still bad. The worst characters are the rough thieves. There is not betterment as yet, the clearances in Boundary St prevented that, some of the roughest characters came hence to Gales Gardens and Parliament St.

Crowding is now greater than it used to be. Buildings enable more people to live on an acre than formerly. Even with the poorer families there used

to be a regular migration to Plaistow or Ilford in the summer and a return
for the winter. This is not done now because of the uncertainty of finding a
room again. He thinks that life in Buildings may make for improvement if the
Superintendent is strong and the managers careful. "If not, they are a hell."
In places like Gales Gardens the male inhabitants as a rule go to the country
to brickfields in summer. The weavers were a respectable set of men but
"cramped in body and mind, caring for nothing except their work". He spoke of
them as "curious cantankerous and warped". It is the case of an industry where
the work is too absorbing, where body and mind are bent to the loom only,
where outside interests have no entry, where every person whether political or
religious is judged by his possible affect on the weaving trade to the exclusion
of all other considerations.

Drink among both men and women shows a slight tendency to improvement. "In Bethnal Green it never has been a shame to any woman to enter a
public house." He was astonished therefore the other day to overhear in the
street at Hackney a woman saying she hoped she should never be brought so
low as to enter a public house. It showed the difference between the two places.

Of prostitution for hire there was none as far as he knew in St Andrew's
parish, much looseness of relations and some marrying within the prohibited
degrees, especially of the deceased wife's sister. But he said among the very
poor there was a strict code of outward decency which could not be violated
with impunity. Cited the case of a coster who had started living with a woman
who had nursed his wife during her last illness, as soon as the wife had died. The
whole street felt outraged and the pair were forcibly ejected and had to go and
live elsewhere. In this case the cohabitation with the woman during the wife's
illness had been condoned.

On the whole he thinks the police do their duty well though "there are queer
ones amongst them as there must be among any large body of men". Said
he thought police unaccountably stupid at times. Case of murder in Bethnal
Green clergy and all knew the murderer. Detectives came from headquarters
etc, but never found him out. He knows one or two very well but he has never
been able to obtain from any one of them an admission of payments made
to them irregularly, even though he knew that all the big shops in the Bethnal
Green Road paid regularly 1/- a week to the man on the beat, the same was
paid by publicans. "But it is nothing large enough to be a scandal and is done
more that they should do their duty than they should neglect it." "The pressure
put upon them to accept payment is very great." He did know of 2 or 3 who

refused it, "but they were only two or three" and when a policeman was called in to stop family rows the regular thing was to offer 2 or 3d and it was always taken. Personally as a vicar he never offered anything to them but he is sure that his school superintendent did so. They lose their tempers occasionally and run lads in for being drunk and disorderly because they laugh at them in the street. One lad he knew about and gave evidence in the police court in his favour to the complete upsetting of the police evidence. Then he has seen them being handed drink after closing time. "But the abuses were not serious and are getting less than they used to be."

As to health, Bethnal Green is on sand and healthy but the public authorities are "sloshy", they prefer to employ 24 men rather than 3 machine sweepers and time and again he has seen the men sitting on their brooms until someone in authority has appeared when they would start sweeping vigorously. The employment of men is a form of patronage which the Board are too weak and need to be willing to give up.

As to confession. The great mistake that has been made is to regard it as something secret. "The prayer book allows it, not as 'must' or 'ought' but as 'may'". It should be a medicine but not a food, an aid to independence and not a pauperizer. It should not be in the hands of young curates. If people ask for it, give them but let them understand that it is something exceptional.

Here the bell rung for lunch. Lawley said there was a great deal more he should like to say about confession. He wished that the reasons for it, its existence and its justification could be stated openly, not hidden nor glossed over as some tried to do.

He said that every religious worker, churchman or dissenter was feeling the competition of outside attractions. More difficult now to lead simple lives. Amusements, bicycles, education, political interest, etc. In consequence Church was giving and would give up as much as possible of her social work and in future stick to religion only.

When he started at Bethnal Green, he was not hostile but lukewarm towards C.O.S.* This is one of the things he regrets. Experience brought wisdom. Is convinced theirs is the real way of dealing with poverty. As soon as he was convinced he joined their committee and for the future will always back them strongly.

(B350-10)

*Note: Charity Organisation's Society, founded 1869 to regulate christian charity and make decisions about who should receive aid and how.

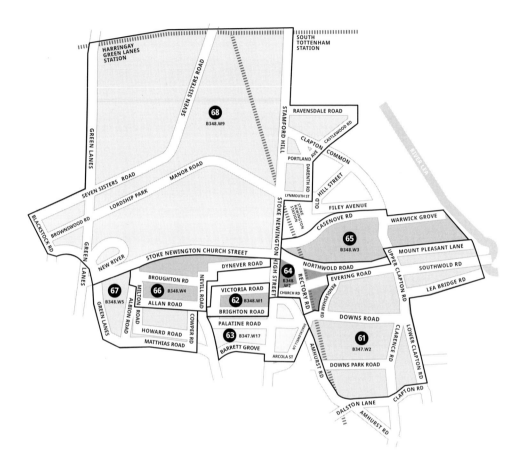

Walk 61   B347-2
Tuesday 27th July 1897
George Duckworth with Inspector Fitzgerald

Starting at the G.E.R. Clapton Station

Southwold Rd runs downhill to the North Mill Fields from Clapton Station. So it does in character. The west end being RED and the east PINK to PURPLE. The next street eastwards is Comberton Rd, RED and respectable. The next, Aveley Rd, not quite so good, PINK. All the houses in these streets have 2- or 2½-st and there is plenty of air and open space about.

Then up the Theydon Rd which is PURPLE. All houses are tenements holding 2 or 3 families. The gardens at the back are a good deal lower than the road. On the west side of Theydon Rd, Detmold and Inver Roads, both PINK to PURPLE in character. 2-st houses. Small bow windows and front gardens. Further E is Mundford Rd, poorer, PURPLE. Dudlington Rd, tenement houses, pretty fronts but backs on a much lower level. Middlesex St , poor riverside street, LIGHT BLUE.

Then along the Lea Bridge Rd, which separates North from South Millfields, W into the Clapton Rd, there turning N to look into Beecholme, Prout and Cassimer Roads. Beecholme Rd is PINK. Prout Rd, 2-st houses, little bow windows. The west end is LIGHT BLUE and decidedly poorer. Out of it is a court, LIGHT BLUE, whose inhabitants sweep chimneys and take in washing. Cassimer Terrace looks like a retired working class road, a PURPLY PINK. Many tramway men live round about here.

Then up the Clapton Rd to Clapton Station and a little further N the roads on the west side being Brooke Rd, RED to PINK, "nearly all take in lodgers," Ickburgh Rd, RED, very comfortable, mostly business people the inhabitants. There is a private house at the east end of the Brooke Rd, the house itself being in the Clapton Rd, with a very large kitchen garden of its own. Evering Rd, another comfortable RED road that does not take in lodgers, green front gardens with prim privet hedges and broad clean, empty roads on which several young ladies were learning to bicycle. Walsingham Rd not quite so good, PINK. Kenninghall Rd, RED.

Running S out of Kenninghall Rd is the London Rd, PINK. It has shops on its east side. Its houses are better at the south end where it approaches Hackney Downs, than at the north. They are for the most part 3-st.

Then E along Cross Rd, PINK, running out of which are Avenue Rd, PINK, good gardens, and Oakfield Rd, more comfortable than the preceding, RED. Some houses with wooden gates and a short carriage drive.

Further E is Nightingale Rd, Love Lane, Ferron Rd, Charnock Rd and Heyworth Rd, all of 2- or 3-st houses and PINK to RED in character, with clean and quiet roads and fair gardens. Then into the Downs Rd which runs along the north side of Hackney Downs. There are good houses here but not such good ones as on the south side. The Downs themselves are managed by the LCC. They are bare green and open. In the middle is an attempt at landscape gardening and a few flowers. Also a band stand where a band plays twice a week. Queen's Down Rd bounds the east side of the Downs. E along the Down's Rd is Powell Rd, PINK and RED and rather better than Cricketfield Rd on the south side. Clarence Rd, the next road eastwards is a road of fair shops. It is the direct continuation of Mare St, Hackney and could make the shortest way for the trams into Upper Clapton Rd, but they have preferred to turn off along Portland Place and then go up the Lower Clapton Rd.

Then into the Lower Clapton Rd and up to the Thistlewaite Rd on the east side. Respectable houses. Trees on pavement look about 10 years old. The next street south is Newick Rd where Fitzgerald himself lives as a lodger. The inhabitants of this street are, he says, commercial travellers and men in the shipping business. The houses are let on 99 year leases and nearly all belong to owners. They are 2-st with bow windows top and bottom. Their price is £480 for a single and £680 for a double-fronted house, ground rent £6 per annum. Young trees on the pavement in front.

The Lower Clapton Rd at this point is an old-fashioned, broad, country-looking street, flanked by a mixture of shops and dwelling houses. There is in it a pond full of water with a Notice Board in the middle of it "This site to be let for building purposes". Many doctors live in the Clapton Rd. Driving up the middle of it was a clergy man in a low pony cart.

S past Atherden Rd and Laura Place, RED. The Goulton Rd, a RED to PINK road. Fitzgerald knows 3 of its inhabitants, "One keeps a fish shop in Mare St and two are retired publicans." The houses have good gardens "beautiful backs".

Then along Portland Place. Before you come to it on the west side is Clapton Passage, PINK, leading to Clapton Square also PINK. There are a good many houses to be let in Clapton Square and they look rather past their prime. Opposite the end of Clapton Passage is the Clapton Park Congregational Chapel, known to the neighbourhood as the 'Round Chapel'. On the north side of Portland Place are many linen drapers shops. On the south side large dwelling houses, and below it are more shops. Small green apples in the green grocers shops at 3d per lb, red currants 3d, cherries 6d, tomatoes 2d and plums at 1½d.

Then N a little way up Clarence Rd on the west side of which is Clarence Terrace, very poor, DARK BLUE, the map gives it LIGHT BLUE. The Clarence Rd at the lower end looks PURPLE and the houses have workshops in their back gardens. Clarence Terrace leads into Orchard Place which looks PURPLE to LIGHT BLUE, which in turn leads to Pembury Grove. A better street, PINK, 3-st houses, taking in lodgers, with a Methodists Free Church (Rev. E Goode) halfway down on the north side.

W into Pembury Rd, RED, Bodney Rd, PINK to RED. Andre Rd, just under the railway, consists of railway arches where there are farriers, stables and fibrous works. The east end of the Amhurst Rd varies between PINK and RED. more RED than PINK. The inhabitants usually take in lodgers. Manor Place running south out of it looks PINK to RED as map. Further along the Amhurst Rd on the north side are Kenmure and Brett Roads, both PINK. Kenmure Rd with 2-st houses consisting of 6 rooms and a scullery and letting for 17/- per week and Brett Rd a large block of tenements 5/6 at the top and 8/6 at the bottom for 4 rooms and a scullery. Kenmure Avenue, which runs south out of the east end of Kenmure Rd looks LIGHT BLUE, and Aspland Grove on the south side of Amhurst Rd looks PINK to PURPLE. The map marks it all PINK. At the corner of the Amhurst Rd and Mare St is a large public house kept by one Hines (?). He is a great betting man and is said to make more money that way than by selling spirits.

General remarks

The whole of the district is well-to-do, and varies from RED to PINK in character. There are only two spots which are BLUE. One is in the northeast corner near the river which is PURPLE to LIGHT BLUE and another in the south in the angle made by the Clapton Rd and Dalston Lane. With these exceptions there are really no poor. There is much open space that is public such as the Hackney Downs and Millfields and much that is private in the gardens attached to almost every house.

Walk 62   B348-1

Monday 11th October 1897
George Duckworth with sub divisional Inspector Frank Thorpe of the N Division.

Out of Cressington Road into the Wordsworth Road

Along the west ends of Prince George and Princess May and Wiesbaden Roads. At the bottom of the Wiesbaden Rd is still a fairly large waste space. N past the South Hornsey Public Elementary Schools which are under the County of Middlesex and not under the London School Board because Hornsey refuses to be amalgamated with its surroundings. Along the Wordsworth Rd which has shops at its northwest end and into the Nevill Rd. PURPLE. A mixture of shops and dwelling houses. Some model dwellings. Allan Rd, running west out of it, is a street of poor class shops.

Brighton Rd running W into the High St is one of the ordinary 2-st streets. Bows on ground floor. Fair backs. 8-roomed houses and a scullery. PINK. Let for £34. 12 chimneys between two houses = 6 rooms each plus four with 2 rooms and 2 kitchens behind.

Then comes Walford Rd. 3-st. Two or 3 families generally in each house. Rents £40. A few occupied by one family only.

Gordon Rd. 3½-st. Maynards confectionary factory at the northeast end using buildings which were formerly a brewery. Running north out of it are Arthur, Gainsborough, Warwick Roads. 3-st. PINK. Victoria Rd is like them. Houses 2½- and 3-st. Holding 2 and 3 families as a rule.

Into Victoria Grove West and Victoria Grove. Houses here are older and have larger gardens. Mostly 1 family and a lodger. Of the square box shape. PURPLE.

Shipway and Chalmer Terraces are also PURPLE. Labouring class. 2-st. The south side of the Victoria Rd here is made of the large gardens to the High St houses, one of which is a nursery garden. All to be built over as soon as the rents fall in.

Walk 63

Monday 11th October 1897

George Duckworth with Inspector F Thorpe of the N Division.

Thorpe has been 21 years in the service. Ten years ago he was stationed in this Division. After that he went as a sergeant to Clerkenwell. Now he has been here three years as an Inspector. He is a round podgy man of medium height, moustache, pleasant, good-humoured face and voice.

Starting at the police station in the High Street

Then a little way S turning E at Church Rd, here are the National Schools built 1837. PINK in character. Houses rented at £32 a year. Running N out of it are Glading Terrace and Leswin Rd, roads of 2-st houses with bow windows on the ground floor. PINK. tenanted by City people, clerks, warehousemen. Two families in most of the houses. Rents £30 to £32 for a whole house. No house to be had under a 12 months tenancy and some held under a 3 years agreement. Tenants pay rates and taxes. Evering Rd runs northeast out of the Church Rd to Clapton Rd. Character PINK-barred with RED. Houses 3-st with fronts. Gets better as it goes eastwards, is a better street than Leswin Rd.

Then S along the Rectory Rd. Many old houses. Rents £45. Old fashioned wooden palings round front gardens. Semi-detached. RED. Running W out of it are Sydner Rd. PINK, 2-st. Poplars in front gardens, nearly whole length of south side of street. Asphalt pavements. Bare, empty, clean street. Very small backs to the houses. Rents £32 to £34. Foulden Rd has better backs, 2½-st. Rents £36. Low iron rails on low brick wall round fronts. At its west end rents are higher, £40 to £45 and houses larger, 3- and 3½-st. Farleigh Rd, PINK, 2½-st, blocks of houses the corner one of each being larger than the rest. Rectory Rd, there are shops on the west side of the lower end. At the corner of the Rectory Rd and Amhurst Rd is a large brick building with a boy in buttons at the entrance, the 'Amhurst Club', patronised by the locality, is a social club. Subs 2 guineas per annum. Amhurst Road, houses 3½-st. RED. Rents £48 to £50. Not more than one family in the majority of houses.

NW along the Amhurst Rd and into the Newington High St, a busy road "and becoming busier every year." Traffic never ceases. All night there are carts from the market gardens around Enfield.

S past the Foulden and Farleigh Roads, then W along the Wellington Rd, an old street, houses all shapes and sizes, mostly with two families. Street was better than it is now. Now mostly artisans, PURPLE, but large gardens and remnants of many flowers. Many houses built on the square packing case shape with windows at regular intervals, dated 1847. The road itself is narrow, rents £26 to £30. In it the Wellington Road Hall, to let, lately tenanted by Salvationists. Trees on either side of the road. Somerford Grove further south is much like it. Trees along both sides of the road which was paved for the first time this year. Semi-detached 2- and 2½-st houses. One small 2-st house on the north side of the street was sold this year, 22 years still to run, and fetched £200. The 4 mile circle notice is on one of the lamp posts.

Into the Newington High St again, on the west side of which is a block of new streets marked by a blank in the map. 10 years ago when Thorpe was last here it was a field used for grazing purposes. Palatine Rd, 2-st, bow window on ground floor. £34 rent. This is the oldest street of the block. Prince George St, 2-st, 7-roomed houses letting at £34. In this street Thorpe himself lives. House not worth the rent "but people like new houses". At the east end on the north side are 4 houses laid bare by the County Council because they had been built up beyond the pavement, i.e. they came too far forward. Builder and owner refused to pull them down, so County Council paved off the outer wall and made them level with the street. PINK. Wiesbaden Rd, the next southward is the same as Prince George St except that the houses have a bathroom. Built only 2 or 3 years ago. Rents the same because rooms are slightly smaller to make space for the bath. Coloured tiles let into the side of the entrance porch. Princess May Rd, like the foregoing but the houses at the west end are not yet finished building. All these have very small backs. 17 ft allowed only between one house and the next i.e. each has only 8.5 ft of yard at the back.

{Many Jews of the lower class living in Prince George and Princess May Streets.}

Then E across the High St and into Arcola St past Millers Buildings turning N into Dunn St, PURPLE to LIGHT BLUE in character. 2-st, large gardens, two with glasshouses in them, flowers and clothes lines. Like it is Middle St, with wooden palinged fronts. Children coming out of school. All booted and particularly clean looking. Inhabitants of street are costers and labourers. Women engaged in laundries, several standing about gossiping, bare armed, in white aprons, bare headed. Street no trouble to the police. Thorpe put earnings of the men at 18/- to 20/- a week. Hindle St like the others, 2-st. All these streets might easily become a bad slum, but are probably saved from it by the large Board School at the north end of Dunn and Hindle Streets, which has steps leading down into each of them. "A very good school." Headmaster exercises great influence on the children who come from the neighbourhood and through them on their parents. Then out into Shacklewell Rd, which has a mixture of new and old houses. The newer 2½-st houses on the east side are dated 1866. On the north side of it is Shacklewell Row, a narrow, 2-st street, houses flush with the pavement. Occupied by a better class of labourer than Dunn and Middle Streets. St Barnabas Mission room on the east side. 'The Merchant Taylor's School Mission, 1893'. Rev. A. J. Ellerton, 307 Amhurst Rd. Out of the north end of Shacklewell Row into Seal St, which with Perch St and April St were built between 1881 and 1885. Each house consists of two flats with a parlour, bedroom, kitchen with range and scullery, WC. Ground floor 8/- and 7/6 per week. First floor

Invalid Asylum – Stoke Newington

7/6 and 8/-. "Combining the advantages of a model dwelling with the privacy of a small house" as a notice said. The top floor has a separate entrance to the yard by steps running down behind. All these streets are PURPLE in character.

Then W across High St Stoke Newington and down Barrett Grove, PINK except for No.4 which is a model dwelling and PURPLE to LIGHT BLUE in character, 20 to 30 families in this one house. Cressington Rd out of it, PINK, 2-st, 2 families in each.

Walk 64   B348-2

Tuesday 12th October 1897
George Duckworth with Inspector Thorpe

Starting at the Police Station in Stoke Newington High Street
S and then E along the Church Rd past the West Hackney Church. Rev. Mr Jukes. "Church a very popular one, it is always full. Last Sunday the harvest festival there was a regular struggle to get in." Along the Evering Rd, which is still RED as map. S down the Maury Rd, this end of it is PINK, map marks it red. "2-st, 8 rooms and 2 kitchens in each house, rent £36. Shops at the south end of it. Then SW along the Rendlesham Rd, here 2-st, PINK.

Then NW up Landfield St into the block of streets Ottaway St, Mellington St, Landfield St, Heatherley St, and Stellman St. Known as 'Navvies Island', 'Tiger's Bay, 'Spike's Island' or 'Myrtle Grove'. Why 'Myrtle Grove'? "Oh an aristocratic name given sarcastic like." This is the roughest quarter of the district but much better than it used to be. Its inhabitants are low-bred English, none are Irish, of no particular occupation. Some are labourers, very few earn a regular wage. Some of the women wash, but most of them "you had better judge for yourself" said the policeman on the beat. It used to be the resort of ex-convicts, now there are none, they have moved to the Tewkesbury Estate in South Tottenham, especially the St Anne's Rd. There is only one 'licensed' man in the neighbourhood and he is a reformed character. "It is a foul libel that the police give information to employers." Well, but it is sometimes done because I certainly know of at least one case. "That must have been where the employer asked of the local police whether any of his men were on a ticket-of-leave, then it might be done."

There is no public entry into 'Navvies Island' except through Rendlesham Rd. There is only a wooden boarding between the lower end of Benthal Rd and Stellman St but the ground between the hoarding and the street is private property. It could be a great advantage to the Island if this were opened but not to Benthall Rd. The backs of two houses in Ottaway Rd back upon Jenner Rd from which the police have a right of entry into the district. The public may do so on payment of 1d as they go through. Twelve years ago the landlords in the Island wished to raise the tone of the inhabitants. One of them invited the police to go and live there rent free and at the same time offered them a right of way through his back yard. They accepted. Six of them are now living in the Island. Rents are still much cheaper than anywhere else but the district has improved so greatly that instead of asking no rent the landlords now demand 7/6 per week. Since Jubilee this has been raised 6d which makes 8/- for 4 rooms and 2 kitchens. houses 2-st, flush with the pavement, narrow backs. There is a good deal of pitch and toss. Police have orders to stop it, every now and then they make a raid but the 'crows' at the corner always give warning. "Besides what's the good of it, with a lot of trouble you may get half a dozen fellows fined 5/-, they pay or go to prison, and then come back and start again." What about the police having been caught gambling themselves? "Not in my time." He has been here 3 years. But evidently there is some truth in the Rev Joyce's statement that four had been caught.

The landlords of the 'Island' he thinks are small men. The largest owner has 8 houses. Ottaway St is marked the best of the lot, on the map, i.e. PURPLE. It does not look it. Landfield St is the best according to the police, and looks it. The backs to the houses are larger and rents higher i.e. 10/- per week for the same amount of room as in the rest of the houses. Mellington St which the police call 'Middle' St is the worst but hardly looks as poor as Ottaway St because it has small railinged fronts. Heatherley St consists of the end of the other streets on its south side. On its north side are the Rendlesham Rooms, a mission place with an announcement of a meeting for the 'band of Christian police' and Jenners Mews a ramshackle stabling place for horses and carts. Stellman St has 8 shops and a beer shop. "The shopping place of the district."

The inhabitants give no trouble to the police. All the children about were booted and looked healthy. All the houses 2-st. Landfield St PURPLE and the rest an improving LIGHT BLUE is about the character of the district. Not more than 2 charges from here have been entered at the police court during the last 3 years.

Then NW along the Brooke Rd. PINK-barred with RED. Lodgers usual. 2-st on the north side, rent £36. 3½-st on the south, rent £40. The Reighton Rd on the north side, 3-st, rents £34. 2 inspectors live here. Two or 3 years ago rents were £30, 15 years ago the houses would not let at all. Rents are going up all round. "Anything will let or sell in Stoke Newington now". Character PINK to RED. Norcott Rd, 2-st, 7-roomed houses. 2 rooms in front, 3 at the back and 2 kitchens. Maury Rd the same. So too is Benthall Rd.

Then N up the west side of Stoke Newington Common. Some new and some old houses, the new built in 1882 and the old in 1788. They are called Sanford Terrace, map marks them PURPLE but they are better than this, PINK barred with RED, probably their character has bettered since the LCC took over Stoke Newington Common. Sanford Lane is decidedly poorer. LIGHT BLUE to PURPLE, 2-st houses, 2 families in each. Smalley Rd has 2- and 3-st. Neighbourhood improving. Houses on the east side being done up, evidently by contract, 6 men on 6 ladders working on 6 houses, belonging to one owner. Rents £28 to £30, 4 rooms with 2 at the back. Clevedon St, 2-st, PURPLE as map. Union St, which is DARK BLUE on the map has gone, its place being taken by tenements, built for a better class than lived there before. These are not yet finished. Bull Alley, a 'crow' at the end of it shouts down 'Bull Alley' as we appear. Costers its inhabitants, a remnant of labourers houses built for the poor behind the High St when Newington was a country village, each with little gardens in front. Bowling Green St has also disappeared. There are a great many tenements and model buildings about here. Gibson St on the north, entered under an Iron Gateway with a cemented court, consists entirely of 4-st model dwellings built by 'the Metropolitan Association for improving the dwellings of the Industrious classes', rents 5/- to 6/9 per week.' Fairy St is now called Garnham St and has been run right into the High St. At the High St end is the 'Jolly Butchers' public house with a picture on the side-wall in coloured tiles of the Duchess of Devonshire buying a vote for Fox with a kiss. Lawrence Terrace, behind, has 3-st tenements, inhabited by a poor LIGHT BLUE class, built in 1887 belonging to the owner of the public house.

Then down the High St on the west side of which there are 3 or 4 small courts with low 2-st houses, remnants of a former time, inhabited by costers for the most part who ply their trade in the High St. The first of these is Chapel Court, 2-st, 5 houses, LIGHT BLUE. Then Pawnbrokers Alley, now called Kynaston Avenue, 6 houses with good front gardens and remnants of a fine show of dahlias, very well kept. Mason's Court, rather lower down, looks very poor, costers' children playing, all booted. Another court lower down nearly opposite the end of Union Rd called White Hart Court, entered by a very narrow passage past a butchers shop which is built entirely of wood, also LIGHT BLUE. Only 7 houses, the passage not more than 3 ft wide and opening on a flagged court.

{There is another similar court between Mason's and White Hart Court, called Rochester Place.}

Turning W into the Victoria Grove and up another cul-de-sac on its north side past the Methodist free church, called Hamilton Place. 9 small 2-st houses, roadway full of chickens, LIGHT BLUE.

On the east side of the High St are a set of 2-st streets, Leswin Rd, Bayston Rd, Darville Rd which are more PINK than RED in appearance. One of Maynard's confectionery factories is in Leswin Rd. Tyssen Rd, Union Rd, John's Rd are equally 2-st and PINK.

General remarks

The general character of that part of Stoke Newington included in these two walks with Inspector Thorpe is PINK barred with RED. The inhabitants of the houses are probably better off than those in the PINK district to the west of the Chatsworth Rd but very few of them are sole occupiers of their houses. Single lodgers usual. One general servant is kept in the larger houses. Male heads of families or lodgers all turn out in the morning to go to the City to their work, "You may meet regular droves of them any morning between 8 and 9AM". Stoke Newington is very healthy and has a great reputation. Nearly all the houses are small, "it is very seldom that you will find any one of them empty." Thorpe knows by experience, as he knows the rents of the neighbourhood, because he has lately had great difficulty in finding one for himself. "You would have thought that where there are so many you would have been certain to find one without difficulty, but you don't. Anything will let or sell in Stoke Newington."

The typical house of the neighbourhood is 6-roomed. two on the ground floor, two on the first floor and 2 kitchens, built one over the other out at the back, then there is one scullery and one WC which are at the back and for the common use by both upstairs and downstairs. In front of the house is a small green front with an evergreen hedge and an iron rail on the top of a low brick parapet which separates it from the street, behind there is a fair back garden.

No part of the district gives any trouble to the police. The poorest bits are 1) the

Talk with Supt. Macfadden, of the North or Islington Division at the Police Station Stoke Newington High St, 25th October 1897

He is a Scotchman and very cautious speaker.

He deplored the great increase in values of licensed houses. A licence is practically never endorsed. Magistrates chary of doing it unless the offence is very serious indeed, result it is never done. "When a stroke of the pen can rob a man of £20,000, you will naturally hesitate, it's only human nature."

On the other hand, he said, it seems unfair that by granting a licence, you should increase the value of one man's property by thousands while you leave his neighbour who paid the very same amount at the outset with his plot worth only hundreds.

Does not like to give a decided opinion, has always refused to do so to the Licensing Justices, but is inclined to think that a great increase in the number of licences would do no harm. "Don't do away with the preliminary enquiries as to a man's character but when you've got that grant him a licence without more ado." This, he said, would have the additional advantage of reducing values, a magistrate would not hesitate to endorse a license worth but £50.

As to women's drinking, it has increased but he doubted whether grocers' licenses had helped it. "I know it's always said that they have, but I never have come across actual proofs. If a woman is inclined to drink, she will have it whether she can get it from a grocer or no."

As to Sunday drinking, the Manor House is their great Sunday house. Its owner has 2 men at the door to find out whether customers are bona fide travellers or not. (One of them is a pensioned ex-police sergeant who gets 7/6 per day for the job.) In his opinion it is kept in a very orderly way. The beer house about 20 yards down is not open during prohibited hours. Why? "I think it is because the Sunday travellers drink spirits and not beer, it is not far enough out for them to drink because they are really thirsty. Then Sunday is a holiday and the custom everywhere is to have something extra good." He thought that the interests of the public would be better served by having several houses open on Sunday round Finsbury Park, but could not say that he had any complaint to make with the service of the Manor House Tavern in itself.

"You may argue all these questions about drink and licenses up and down and at the end of it have no decided opinion on the question." He mentioned the difficulty caused by the varying influence of alcohol on individuals. With many men, who have been drinking, no effects are apparent until they are fully 100 yards away from the licensed house, then they suddenly become unmistakeably drunk.

(B348-8)

stokenewingtonhistory.com

group of streets behind Somerford Grove Board School, 2) Navvies Island. 3) the small piece at the northwest corner of Stoke Newington Common, which is now largely in course of rebuilding. 4) The small courts off the west side of the Stoke Newington High St.

Outside of the High St there are remarkably few public houses. Thorpe strongly disapproves of any but children of the working class being sent for beer. "With the children of labourers it does not much matter, they don't hear any language different from what they are accustomed to at home, but with my class it is different" and he never would send a child of his. He has noticed however, that children of his class are sent, for he has often watched them go. "Children don't generally sip the beer but women do." Children when told to fetch beer choose the house naturally where they are given sweets. Publicans are not allowed to give them and the police have orders to prosecute where it is done. "Some of the agitators got hold of headquarters and had that order passed." If children did sip, sweets would if anything tend to prevent them doing so. Said he did not think sweets were often given, at that moment out came a little girl with a jug, from the public house next to the police station, and her mouth evidently full of them.

Women's drinking he is sure has increased. "The increase of grocers licenses must have helped it. Then women seem to have minded going into public houses. They have more leisure time at home, no clothes to make because clothes can be had better made and as cheap when bought ready-made, in addition to which they are taken out much more than they used to be, further, public houses are more attractive." "But Clerkenwell where I last was is the real spot for women's drinking. You never saw anything like it." He was there six years. At the beginning of his time all the cases of drunkenness were men (practically all); at the end of it four out of every 6 were women.

Walk 65   B348-3

Thursday 14th October 1897
George Duckworth with Inspector Thorpe

Starting at the Police Station

Up past the Stoke Newington Common and into the Northwold Rd at the St Michael and All Angel's Church. Fountayne Rd, RED, 2½-st, bow windows and gables on both floors. Mostly tenanted by one family only. 8 to 9 rooms per house. Rents £40 to £45. One general servant the usual thing, but sometimes two. Northwold Rd, a mixed road. Some old houses on the south side waiting for their leases to fall in. When that happens they are to be replaced by the new 2-st gabled houses which are a feature of the neighbourhood already. Durleston and Geldeston Roads are built on this principle. The old cottages which were before them were 2-st dating from 1828. They are all built by a builder Osment who has his workshops on what was formerly Frederick St. Sovereign Lane, on the south side is quite new, not yet paved. All these streets are becoming PINK or PINK and RED.

Then N into Winsdale Rd, PURPLE, working class, where Osment's men live. Into Rossington St which runs through the middle of a poor LIGHT BLUE block of streets. Poor but respectable, no trouble to the police. Houses generally 2-st with 4 rooms and a scullery. Rossington St itself is PURPLE, long strips of garden behind and evidently a great care for flowers. The gardens of these old and poor houses are much larger than those of the modern 2-st street. The older the house the larger the garden is generally true. Caroline St, LIGHT BLUE. Caroline Passage, 1-st cottages. Conduit St LIGHT BLUE to PURPLE.

Into High St Upper Clapton, shops taking the place of the old houses that used to line both sides of the road. District going down in so far that the rich are not so rich as they used to be. But a good many pheasants and partridges for sale in the shops. Then E along Mount Pleasant Lane, 2-st houses, RED. An ink factory built in the garden of an old house on the south side and the house itself used as offices. Muston Rd and Sach Rd, built in the garden of Sir William Birt's old house (the general manager of the G.E.R.). On the south side of Mount Pleasant Lane is Comberton Rd, the west side of which is the garden wall of an old house, one of the few that still remain. Comberton Rd runs downhill.

Then down the hill on to a waste bit of land on the east side of the railway lying between the railway and the river. This was first a brickfield, and then a rubbish heap, now it is to be built on, 800 houses. Thorpe thinks it belongs to Mr Buttens who lives in Stamford Hill and is the owner of the Craven Park Estate.

On the south side of this waste (which is not marshy like the other side of the river because the rubbish has raised its level) is a poor block. Theydon, Mundford and Dudlington Roads, many tenements built in 1885 with gardens much lower than the street. They remind one of the poor district on the south east side of the Millfields, just across the way, PURPLE to LIGHT BLUE, labourers.

Then NE over the waste, under the GER railway arches and up Baker's Hill, at the bottom of which is Connell's dying, cleaning, washing factory, employing a number of girls from the neighbourhood. A good class, they were all coming out to dinner, some taking it on the open green on the south side of Baker's Hill. Nearly all had their front hair done up in metal hair curlers.

N of Baker's Hill, which has a few 2-st houses and is PURPLE, is a block of very poor lanes rather than streets which run down the hill from Mount Pleasant Lane to the river. District known as High Hill Ferry. The streets are Elizabeth Place, Lea Place, Retreat Place and Cottages, Orchard Hill. All very poor but respectable. Inhabitants, costers and poor labourers. Two beer houses and one large tavern, the 'Robin Hood'. "They exist on a trade among bona fide travellers, many are not bona fide at all, they come merely for a drink." Thorpe wishes that the houses could be closed altogether on Sundays or at any rate only allowed to open from 1 to 3 PM. Men when accused of not being travellers give wrong addresses, you can't disprove them. It is dangerous to run them in because every now and then one may be telling the truth. Orchard Hill and Elizabeth Place look the poorest of the streets here.

Then up the Harrington Hill and into Mount Pleasant Lane. At the top of the hill is a beer house. Two policemen at its door, one of whom had no business there and had been drinking. "Fairly caught" said Thorpe. On the west side of the lane is the Springfield Park estate, gradually being cut into by 2½-st houses with an attic, RED in character. Remnants of large old trees, Old gardens and old houses still about. The new houses are tenanted by one family only, rented at £36.

Then W along the Warwick Rd, large old, double-fronted, ugly, yellow brick houses, each with a carriage sweep of their own. Trees on either side of the road. 3-st. Rented at £80 to £90. Too good for the neighbourhood as it is now. Cazenove Rd has equally large houses at its east end which become semi-detached at the west end. The old will soon have to give way. Geldeston Rd is creeping up the Northwold Rd with the houses that modern occupiers want. Twelve to 14 years ago there was a barrier at the end of Osbaldeston Rd and Cazenove Rd and all to the north of it were fields. Now there are Chardmore, Foxburg, Filey and Osbaldeston Roads, some all red brick and some a mixture of red and yellow brick. 2½-st gabled houses. Generally one family in each.

Number 66 Cazenove Rd, which is typical of the houses on the western portion of the road, is to be let. 6 bedrooms, 1 dressing, 3 reception. 97 years lease from December 25th 1877. Ground rent £13, gravelled front approach held in common with number 64.

General remarks

The 3 poor spots in this walk are 1) Rossington St district. 2) Detmold Rd district. 3) High Hill Ferry. Nothing vicious, only very poor. "You may say that brutality is a thing of the past in London, any rows we have now have none of the roughness of former days."

The rich are leaving the district, so are the poor. The first in search of the green fields they used to find here, the second to Walthamstow where houses are cheaper and fares to London by the G.E.R only 2d. Their places are taken by a middle class who, if they have a family, rent a whole house at £30 to £35 and let off some of the rooms. The houses are all built for two families, 2 rooms and a kitchen on the ground floor, 2 rooms and a kitchen on the first floor and a common scullery and WC out behind. The garden belongs to the tenant of the whole house. "If you have children you practically must take a whole house. None will take a man and wife with encumbrances." Tenants may leave at a weeks notice but the landlady has to agree to remain in the house for a twelve month.

Police very rarely drink. Everywhere they do so much less than formerly. In the outskirts of London it is less usual than in the centre. "A crowded district with rough beer houses is where you will find that the police are offered and accept most." Said he used himself always to have his half pint of an evening when he was a constable but ever since he has been an inspector he has made it his practice not to drink away from his own home, where he takes regularly a glass at dinner and another at supper. He has never heard here of the police taking money in these parts instead of beer. Why the publicans offer beer and money is when they have frequent occasion for police services in turning out drunken men etc. Here the neighbourhood is respectable, they very seldom have to send for the police, therefore they don't put temptation in the constables' way.

The best way to get a new license nowadays is to start with one for wine and spirits, these are granted very freely. Next time offer to give this up for an 'off' beer license. As often as not you will be allowed to. After that there is more difficulty but from an 'off' beer you may get an 'on and off' and in the end obtain a full license. But an application for a full license right away is sure to be rejected. Thorpe attends the licensing courts regularly. Both the Vestry and the teetotallers regularly oppose any new licenses. but the Vestry will probably be less keen about it in time. "The saving on funeral rates is so large owing to the extra rates they are getting from the public houses that they will be loth to do so."

Walk 66   B348-4

Monday 18th October 1897
George Duckworth with Inspector Thorpe
This district looks PINK and clerical but is inhabited more by artisans than clerks.

Dynevor Road

2- and 2½-st, 6- and 8-roomed (including 2 kitchens), lodgers usual. PINK. Chesholm Rd running north out of it is like it. Broughton Rd running west out of the south end of Dynevor Rd. N out of the Broughton Rd are Oldfield, Harcombe, Woodland and Sandbrook Roads: all 2-st roads, inhabited by skilled artisans and shop assistants from the High St. These houses were let at £26 to £28 four or 5 years ago. They now fetch £30.
Then N along the Oldfield Rd into Reynarton Rd, which is also 2-st. PURPLE to PINK. Some shops out of it on the north side are Defoe, Brodia, Berkley and Dumont Roads. All of the same, 2-st, class PINK to PURPLE.
Then up Rersley St into Church St which with High St are the two shopping streets of the district. Out of Church St are on the south side, Lancall St, PINK to PURPLE, 2-and 3-st houses and nearly opposite on the north side, Summerhouse St, 2½-st of the same character.
Then W along Church St. The streets running north out of it are all poorer the nearer they get to it. i.e. poorer at their southern extremities. Bouven's St, 2- and 3-st, PINK. Park St, PURPLE as its southern end, some 3-st tenements let out by floors. Then S down Marton Rd into Painsthorpe, Aresome Roads, working class. PURPLE. 2-st, with small backs. Then back into Church St again. There is a small triangular block at the south end of Lordship Rd, occupied entirely by a public house, at the back of which the police 30 years ago had a lock-up. The southern end of Lordship Rd is PURPLE. Barn St, the next street westwards is a poor street, 2-st, PURPLE to LIGHT BLUE. No trouble to the police, all the children with boots on.
Falcon Court, on the south side of Church St nearly opposite Barn St, is still poorer.

Entered down a passage at the court end of which is a very offensive open dust heap. In the passage also is the urinal of a public house. Character of court, LIGHT to DARK BLUE. Further west on the north side is Edwards Lane. Now poor. An old house at the bottom west end has now been turning into six 3-st houses let out by floors. PURPLE.

At the west end of Church St some very pretty old houses between the free library and the church. At No.7 used to live Mr Baxter the coroner for North London. There are two churches at the west end of the street. 'Old St Mary's' on the north side with a country-like churchyard and a red-tiled roof and 'New St Mary's' on the south side, of stone with a great spire and slate roof. (Mr Stephen, father of Mr Stephen, who was father of Sir James Stephen (underseeing for the colonies) and therefore great-grandfather of Leslie Stephen, is with his brother buried here. This Mr Stephen was always in financial difficulties, had been imprisoned for debt and lived in Stoke Newington because it was then considered one of the cheapest places to live in near London.)

Then S down the Albion Rd, wood paved, the bus route between Stoke Newington and Victoria. 3-st. Formerly inhabited by one family only but now lodgers are usual, artisans at the northern end. Character PURPLE to PINK to RED. Hawkslea Rd on the east side is 3-st PURPLE to PINK.

Then E along the Broughton Rd. S down Londesborough Rd, past St Faith's Church, a monstrous monument of yellow-brick ugliness. Houses 3-st. PINK. Through the Knebworth Rd, 2½-st, PURPLE, and through Victoria Rd, up Chalmers' Place and so into the back entry to the yard behind the police station.

General remarks

On the whole this an artisan district. Artisans who live in 6-and 8-roomed houses and let off 2 rooms. Houses generally 2-st, 15 ft frontage, letting for £30 to £34. Flowers in pots usual in the ground floor front window, but the flowerpots not so often put in painted china outside-pots, as in more clerical districts.

The only poor portions are the courts and little streets off Church St. None of them give any trouble to the police.

As regards publicans and police, Thorpe said that it was certainly to the advantage of a policeman, if he was invited to have his beer, that a house should be badly conducted. "If it was not badly conducted, he would not be given drink." But it is practically impossible for anything of this kind to go on in a main thoroughfare. Too many people are passing for it to be worth the risk. The danger of taking drink now is such that whereas 15 years ago not one policeman in 100 was a teetotalitarian, now he put the average proportion as 1 in 5.

There are not many tallymen living in the district but they do a deal of business in the neighbourhood. They come up here from Bow. "It's their power of talk."

Wives left at home all day, dull, along comes a tallyman with an oily tongue, they like a gossip and don't have the chance of seeing many men, so they talk and then buy.

Walk 67   B348-5

Tuesday 19th October 1897
George Duckworth with Inspector Thorpe

Starting along Allan Road

which is a road of rather inferior shops and public houses. Going W from Cowper Rd, which is an artisan PINK to PURPLE street, there is a cul-de-sac on the north side called Lenard Place. Very poor. Wood choppers. 2-st. LIGHT to DARK BLUE. No trouble to the police. On the south side of Allan Rd is Spenser Rd. 2-st. Houses rented at £30 to £32. Then come two roads running between Albion Grove on the north end and Howard Rd on the south, Shakespeare and Milton Roads. Both of which are better at their north than at their southern ends. 2- to 3½-st, PINK to PURPLE. Milton Rd was built in 1852. All the houses about here were built about 50 years ago.

Then down Milton St to Howard Rd. PURPLE. Working class. Some 3rd rate shops. 3 public houses and 2 beer houses, these last an almost sure sign that there are some poor streets in the neighbourhood. In the south side of the road opposite the end of Shakespeare Rd is Thomas' Place leading to Philip St and thence to Watson St. The first two are very poor. Labourers. LIGHT to DARK BLUE. No trouble to the police. Children booted but in ragged clothes. Watson Street has a rough character but is not so poor. Some 3-st houses inhabited by respectable people at the west end. "They came in before the neighbourhood went down, they are the owners of their houses and would move if it were not so expensive to do so. They own one or two houses about here and so don't like to be far off but if it were not for these two reasons, they would not stay." A coal cart here going its rounds, coal ½ per cwt.

At the east end of Howard Rd with its south end blocked by the west end of St Matthias Church is Goldsmith Square. 2½- and 3½-st. PINK to PURPLE.

Then W along Matthias Rd, which has shops on its north side. Rather poor and decidedly poor dwelling houses on its south side (these back on Garden Cottages), PURPLE to LIGHT BLUE). Past Hornsey Place. 10 houses, 2½-st. PURPLE. Along the north side of Newington Green, where is the Mildmay Radical. "A club that's kept in very good order." Thorpe thinks that to some men clubs do a good deal of harm, men who might have been kept out of it if it had not been for clubs. There are not a great many of them, he said, but he knows some who stay in the public house until

Inspector Thresher retired after 26 years service in the London police corps, of which 12 years service spent in Whitechapel.

He keeps a sweet stuff shop now in the Upper Clapton Rd. Address: Swanley House, The Pond, Upper Clapton Rd. Thresher is a man of about 50 years of age. A teetotaller and has been all his life. Has left the force now 3 years.

He knows very little of the neighbourhood. He has now made his house and was, like the active police, unwilling to say anything that could be construed as unfavourable to the force.

As to indirect earnings, he said they were practically nil, "if they were divided among the whole force, I don't believe they would amount to ½d per head per month". There used to be call money for waking men and shops in the morning but this has gradually become a business of itself and each district now has its own early callers. The loss to the police has been a gradual thing. Began well before the Trafalgar Square days. Fact is that every now and then there was a case to be run in and that meant that a whole batch of men had to be left uncalled, customers were dissatisfied and so cast about for some more certain means of being woken. He fancies that some publicans still pay call money, though he said it was quite exceptional that they should pay anything at all.

Policemen sometimes get treated to beer but this is less common than it used to be. Public houses are so much more strictly kept. There is so much money at stake in them that it is not worth the publicans' while to run any risks. Beer houses are more likely to offer beer than publics. He admitted that any man who looked as if he would not mind a drink would get it. He has seen potmen bring it round to the constable in the urinal at the side of the public. But policemen are a more sober lot than they used to be.

Children do sip the beer they are sent to fetch, but this is not the origin of their liking for beer. This dates back to early infancy while they were yet in their mothers' arms. Mothers drink stout in order to increase the supply of milk in the breast but often help the baby straight from the pintpot from which they help themselves.

There is a good deal of betting about. The difference between betting here and in Whitechapel is that here it goes on in the streets but in Whitechapel in the clubs.

(B348-17)

closing time when, instead of going home, they go across to the Club where "the enough they have had becomes too much."

Then along Green Lanes, on the north side of which are Winston Rd with Lavell and Reedholm Streets, out of it on the east side. All 2-st, artisan, PINK to PURPLE streets. Venetian blinds, lace curtains, flowerpots. Frontage of 15 ft. So too is Lidfield Rd. Aden Grove, 2½- to 3½-st, is rather better, PINK. Springdale Rd better still, PINK barred with RED. 2½- to 3½-st. Many take in lodgers. Like it is Burma Rd.

Aden Terrace. Alongside of which the new river runs, is RED. At the corner here is the Wesleyan Chapel which Flanagan mentioned as being well attended. Thorpe said "very large congregations, every service crowded, which is most unusual."

Statham Grove at the corner of Church St and Green Lanes. 3½-st, PINK-barred.

Then E along Church St, which has many large houses with large gardens, two or 3 of which are schools. Then S down Clissold Rd. RED. Some take in lodgers.

General remarks

The poor district here is that which lies between Howard Rd and Matthias Rd. It belongs in character to that which is south of it – Garden Cottages, etc.

Thorpe says they have no trouble in the district. There no thieves. "Both thieves and 'fences' live in Hoxton, they come out here to do a bit of business occasionally but don't live here."

The only people of whom there is any complaint now are the Socialists. They have come up here from Bow and try to hold meetings. But the neighbourhood won't stand them and are constantly complaining to the police to turn them out. Thorpe in consequence has attended meetings, but has never heard anything indictable spoken and they are not disorderly.

There never was such a place as Stoke Newington for doctors. Especially the middle class bit of it. None of them walk. The poorest drive a gig. Next above them hire a single-horse open Victoria. Above these there are a few in pair-horse Victorias. "It's a very paying neighbourhood for doctors though it is the healthiest district in London."

Walk 68   B348-9

Thursday 21st October 1897

Inspector Thorpe had corns on his feet so George Duckworth went round this district on a bicycle and then went over the streets with him on the map afterwards. There is a marked absence of public houses and poor streets. Olinda Rd at the north east corner of Stamford Hill is the only exception.

Starting at the southern end of Stamford Hill

N as far as Chapel Rd then E up Old Hill St, countrified with shops at its east end, RED. So are Stamford Grove East and Stamford Grove West out of it. Out on to Clapton Common, the west side of which is better than the east. On the west side are 4½-st houses, mews at the back, red-tiled old houses letting at from £80 to £100 per annum, occupied by one family only. Character RED to YELLOW.

Then W to the streets lying between the Common and Stamford Hill. Braydon, new houses, 7-roomed, £40 to £45 rent, no basement in front, gardens rather lower than the street which allows for an extra room behind in the basement. Built 1894. Like it are Firsby Rd, Kyverdale Rd with a large depot of the North Met. Tramways Co. stables for horses and cars, Darenth Rd, which rather better at the north end than the south (as RED to PINK) and Portland Avenue.

Out at the north east side of Clapton Common and down the Castlewood Rd, out of which run the Rookwood, Leabourne and Moundfield Roads. Ground runs downhill to the east. Houses built 1877. 3½-st, PINK to RED. Built before the modern demand for small houses such as those in Braydon and Darenth Roads and therefore not so well occupied. Much open space, houses stop suddenly, bricks and iron lathes sticking out from their sides – London's ragged edges. Remains of hedges, ditches and trees. Football grounds on the west and north sides of the Board School. Distant view over canal and filtering beds to the Essex Hills. Behind the

houses on the east side of Clapton Common are still green fields. Like the above is Ravensdale Rd.

{The elaborate Agapemonite Church is at the end of the Rookwood Rd.}

Then past the Board School into Baileys Lane and W along Olinda Rd. The easternmost end of the street is LIGHT BLUE, but it gradually and visibly improves as it runs uphill to the west. Many tramsmen, car washers, horsekeepers, etc. living here. Also 3 ticket-of-leave men.

Then N into South Tottenham as far as the Railway Station along the High Rd which has a new unfinished look. Some old shops tenanted, and some new empty. On the west side of the road are the Crescent, 2-st, built 1877, PURPLE and Sherboro' Rd also PURPLE. On the east side are a set of new streets, Ferndale, Lealand and Gladesmore Roads, PURPLE to PINK in character, 2½-st, the half storey (see Notes) being an attic. Poor clerks here, low ground rent but close to station. Many houses still building.

Then to lunch.

Starting afterwards at the southwest corner of Clissold Park, Highbury New Park, YELLOW. A large corner house to be let with fair-sized garden and summerhouse. Box room, 6 bedrooms, bath room and lavatory, passenger lift to hall, drawing room and morning rooms, conservatory. Inner and outer entrance halls, pantry, lavatory, breakfast or billiard room and domestic offices. estimated rental value £130. 52 years unexpired lease. £18 ground rent.

Then W along the Highbury Quadrant the south side of which is YELLOW, semi-detached houses with good gardens. On the north side are 2½-st row of houses of a lower class, PINK barred with RED, which are like the houses on the north side of the Riversdale Rd. Those on the south side of Riversdale Rd and the streets off it are lower again. 2-st, PINK to PURPLE, Canning, Wyatt and Herrick Streets.

Then into the Blackstock Rd which is a second rate shopping street. The streets behind it, Finsbury Park Rd, Wilberforce Rd and Queens Rd get better as they get further away from it. PINK to RED. Lodgers in the less good streets. The Queens Rd is 2-st. Some double-fronted houses, runs rather up hill towards the park. Front and back gardens, a few 3-st on west side. Single-fronted semi-detached houses fetching £75. City men and retired tradesmen. Digby, Brownswood and Kings Roads out of the east side of Queens Rd are RED but not quite so good as the main road. Then E into Allerton Rd and Queen Elizabeth's Walk. 2-and 3-st, 6 and 7 rooms, RED but not so good as Queens Rd.

N along Lordship Rd, detached houses with carriage sweeps, RED at the southern or lower end but YELLOW once above the filter beds. Into Woodberry Down, YELLOW, detached houses, carriages, menservants, hot houses. Fishing allowed in the river, a member of the police force caught an 18 lb pike there this year. Bethune Road at the east end of Woodberry Down is RED, 2-st, many of them to let. Seven Sisters

Rd, YELLOW, houses standing in their own grounds. Woodberry Grove, RED. 2- and 3-st, fine view to the north.

Then down the hill along the east side of Finsbury Park to Hermitage Rd, built in 1883, which begins RED at its west end and then gradually becomes worse ending PURPLE. At its east end are open fields with dust heaps, cows, horses and gipsys. Vale Rd 2-st, PURPLE. Eade Rd newer, 2-st and an attic, PINK.

Along Eade Rd, E to Amhurst Park, YELLOW to RED. The streets off it Cranwich, Bergholt. Denver, Darley Road are RED. So too are Eastbank and Westbank, 2-st and an attic, 1 family.

On the east side of the railway are Northfield, Linthorpe, Glaserton and Wilderton Roads, all RED though Northfield Rd is rather better than the others. They are modern gabled houses, faced with red brick. Dunsmure Rd has some shops at its west end, character RED barred with PINK, some furnished lodgers. Houses look better than the former roads but it is a main thoroughfare and more noise so rents are rather lower and company not so select.

Between Lordship Rd and the railway are Fairholt, St Andrew's, Paget, St Kilda, Heathland and Grangecourt Roads, 2-st RED and RED-barred. Manor Rd rather better but RED. Bethune Rd at the south end has flats with 2 families to each house. Then down the Bouverie Rd, RED-barred and PINK, some unfurnished apartments.

General remarks

A very comfortable district, many City solicitors to judge from the brass plates on the front garden gates. No public houses. 'Furnished' apartments are generally let by better class families than 'unfurnished'.

Notes

The following notes mainly refer to street name changes and errors by George Duckworth in his directions. You will be able to tell how deeply engaged Mike became with the minutiae of the maps!

Throughout this volume:
Where text appears in brackets {like this} it has been copied from a left hand page. The great bulk of text is contained in the right hand pages of the notebooks.
Wherever there is a ? in the text it is Duckworth's.
Duckworth describes the levels in a house as 'story' and 'stories' throughout the text

Walk 1 (B346 Walk 4)
p.21   Turner St is now Turner's Rd. Thomas St is now Thomas Rd.

Walk 2 (B346 Walk 1)
p.28   Woodstock Rd is now Woodstock Terrace. Penny Fields is now one word.
p.29   Duckworth error. There is no Alpha St. Alpha Rd, then and now, runs parallel and to the east of West Ferry Rd. Then and now it runs south to Mellish St. At its northern end the street it met was Manilla St now called Strafford St.
p.29   Tooke Street. No such street now, only The Tooke Arms pub near junction of Strafford St and West Ferry Rd. Gaverick St is now Gaverick Mews. Duckworth says 'Ferry Rd, now called Powis Rd' but that name didn't last. Glengall Rd is now Glengall Grove.
p.30   Prestage St is now Prestage Way.
p.31   Montague Place is now Mountague Place. Newby Place and Grove Villas, were demolished in 1931–2 as part of the rebuilding of Poplar Baths .The remainder of the area was badly damaged by bombing during the Second World War and the buildings were subsequently cleared.

p.31   Woodstock Place is now Woodstock Terrace.
p.32   "A few courts on the north side of King St". The Booth map shows it as King St but Ming St now leads from Dingle Gardens to West India Dock Rd.

Walk 3 (B350 Walk 12)
p.37-9   GHD has an interesting encounter with the Metropolitan Police Commissioner Sir Edward Bradford "on my way to the station". He does not say which station nor whether he was about to begin or had just finished his walk. The Station could be Shadwell Railway Station which he might have used to go to or from home and which was about 8 blocks directly west of Albert Square. This might involve walking beside the railway line on its north side but more likely turning left out of Albert Square after a swift half at the Old Vic to Commercial Rd East, going seven blocks to Sutton St East where he would turn left and go five blocks down to the train station. He might, instead, have been referring to the police station though probably not to the fire station immediately east of it. These

two stations are between Juniper St and Carriage Way north and south and King David Lane and Hardinge St west and east. Getting there from Albert Square would involve walking three blocks to Hardinge St, turn left and then seven blocks to Juniper St.

Walk 4 (B350 Walk 15)
p.40   Duckworth should have made clear that Green Bank, Love Lane, Lowder St/York Place, Watts St/Calvert St and Chandler St are all parallel and that Raymond Place (not St) goes N from Green Bank to Watts/Calvert where it changes name to Meeting House Alley which continues N to Chandler St.

Walk 5 (B351 Walk 2)
p.44   Princes Square is now Swedenborg Gardens.
p.46   Duckworth error. He says 'then S down New Gravel Lane'. He must mean Old Gravel Lane. New is east of Old and not in the scope of this walk. Redman's Rd must be Redmead Lane.

Walk 9 (B351 w1)
p.56   Glasshouse St is now John Fisher St.
p.58   St George's St is now The Highway. Neptune St is now Wellclose St.

Walk 10 (B351 Walk 4)
p.60   Duckworth error. "W along Leman St" would be impossible. Must mean Swan St into the Minories.

Walk 12 (351 Walk 3)
p.66   Greenfield St is now Greenfield Rd. Parfelt Place is now Parfelt St.
p.66   Duckworth has the walk proceeding between Fieldgate St and Nottingham Place both shown clearly on the map

with Charlotte St clearly shown between them but no sign of a Charlotte Court. Not every street or court is shown in the maps but even so we think Duckworth has mistakenly called Charlotte St Charlotte Court.

Walk 15 (B351 Walk 9)
p.77   Underwood St is now Rd.
p.82   Duckworth says the east end of Chicksand St is called Osborn Place. The Booth map shows that he should have said the west end.

Walk 17 (B350 Walk 6)
p.86   Oxford St is now Stepney Way.
p.88   Various spellings of what is now Diggon St. Duckworth spells it Diggins St, but the Booth map says Diggons St.

Walk 18 (B350 Walk 7)
p.89   Heath St is now Head St.
p.91   Duckworth error. "E into Jamaica St" but Jamaica St is the western boundary of this walk so it should be "W into Jamaica St".

Walk 20 (B350 Walk 11)
p.94   Whitehorse St is now Whitehorse Rd. Ben Jonson's Rd is now Ben Jonson Rd.
p.95   Salmons Lane is now Salmon Lane.
p.96   York Rd is now Yorkshire Rd.

Walk 21 (B353 Walk 2)
p.99   Tilney Place is now Tilney Court.

Walk 23 (B353 Walk 4)
p.106   Duckworth talks about "Mitchell St, late Richmond St" but the Booth map shows both streets adjacently. Mitchell St is immediately east of Helmet Row and St Luke's Church and Richmond St is immediately to the right of them.

Walk 24 (B353 Walk 5)
p.108   Fusee chain making dates back to
1660 in London and is generally credited
to Gruet of Geneva for their use in clocks
and watches. Tools were simple, consisting
of punches and dies, hammers and anvils.
It was a time-consuming process requiring
good hand-eye coordination in candlelit
conditions.

Walk 28 (B351 Walk 11)
p.126   Winbolt St is now Wimbolt St.

Walk 34 (B349 Walk 18)
p.151   Date not given but educated guess
makes it 31/12/1897. It is the only walk
not given a date by Duckworth but the
circumstantial evidence overwhelming
points to this walk being on either New
Year's Eve 1897 or New Year's Day 1898
between B349-17 and B350-1.There were
four other walks in the western part of
Bethnal Green area. All were with police
officers other than Inspector Pearn and
they all took place in early March 1898.
Inspector Pearn walked with Duckworth
five times: on Dec 28 and 30 and Jan 3 and
4, and this one.

Walk 35 (B350 Walk 1)
p.153   Duckworth error. "E along Green
St and S down the Globe Rd" but looking at
the map it makes sense only to go north not
south. In the 1930s, Green St was merged
into the Roman Rd.
p.156   Cambridge Rd has been Cambridge
Heath since 1938.

Walk 36 (B350, Walk 2)
p.157   Green St has been part of Roman
Rd since 1932.

Walk 37 (B351 Walk 13)
p.162   Originally what are now two
parallel roads running south off Bethnal
Green Rd between the police station and
the railway line was all called Pitt Street.
As the Booth map shows, by the time of
Duckworth's visit in 1898 the left hand
western upright had been renamed Pott
Street.

Walk 38 (B351 Walk 14)
p.164   Duckworth error: "S down
Fellbrigg St, E along Northampton St
into Collingwood St" but this is not
possible. Northampton's west end meets
Collingwood and goes no further.
Must mean W because going E along
Northampton takes the walker away from
Collingwood.

Walk 41 (B346 Walk 3)
p.185   Duckworth error. "Then back to
Wick Lane and under the railway into
Jodrell St and Parnell Rd". In current A-Z
we have Jodrell Rd not Jodrell St coming
off Parnell Rd on its east side going in a
NE direction parallel and close to Hertford
Union Canal. Lefevre Rd is now Lefevre
Walk.
p.185   After some years as a Liberal agent
George Lansbury joined in 1892 the Social
Democratic Federation, which later became
affiliated to the Labour Party. Under his
leadership the Labour Party in Poplar
gained widespread notoriety. The policy
he followed, which came to be known as
'Poplarism,' was severely criticised, and
in 1921 he and other councillors went to
prison for refusing to collect rates. He
entered national politics in 1895 when he
contested Walworth as an SDF candidate
for Parliament. He polled only 207 votes.
At the General Election of December 1910,

he won Bow and Bromley, holding the seat until 1912.

p.189   Suits of dittos – The mid-19th century saw the introduction of a type of suit that would become the dominant form of Western men's clothing of the next century. The ditto suit, as it was called, featured a jacket, vest, and trousers made from the same fabric. Also called the sack suit, the new style was characterized by a loose-fitting jacket which hung straight from the shoulders with no seam or fitting at the waist. The ditto suit was a fairly informal type of dress clothing, and it was generally worn for business, travel, or street wear.

Walk 42 (B350 Walk 18)
p.190   Duckworth indicated no accompanying police officer in his notes for this walk which accounts for the lack of the usual extra commentary. It is mainly a list of streets visited with his allocation of a Booth colour for each.

Walk 44 (B352 Walk 8)
p.199   Sir Walter Besant (1836–1901), was a novelist and historian. William Henry Besant was his brother, and another brother, Frank, was the husband of Annie Besant.

Walk 45 (B352 Walk 10)
p.204   Evelyn St is now Evelyn Walk.

Walk 46 (B352 Walk 11)
p.207   Duckworth error: "N up Shepherdess Walk, W along Nile St. S into Eagle Place." It is not possible to go W along Nile St at that point, i.e. crossing Shepherdess Walk to the west, because Nile St ends at Shepherdess Walk. No sign on map of Eagle Place.

Walk 48 (B347 Walk 4)
p.214   "Wilman, Blackstone, Blanchard, New and Blanch Streets" implies that all five are "Streets" but according to the Booth map they are not all called "Street". Wilman is Wilman Grove; Blackstone is Blackstone Rd; Blanchard is Blanchard Rd; New is New St; Blanch has been cut in half by the map designer. Unlike all the others it has nothing after "Blanch". It may well have been Blanchard Row or Passage or indeed Street. This would follow a pattern of street naming in Booth's day when there were often pairs of adjoining or close streets with the same main name and different transit names . "Blanch" meets Blanchard Rd at a T-junction.

Walk 50 (B347 Walk 6)
p.220   Duckworth introduces Abbott Rd but then calls it Abbott St. The 2015 A-Z shows an Abbot St just north of the junction of Kingsland High St and Dalston Lane.

Walk 57 (B346 Walk 6)
p.243   Duckworth writes "The south side Ingrams Rubber factory, with an open space palinged-in" which takes up more than half the road. This is not very clear but we think he means the open space has palings (fencing).
p.243   Duckworth error. "Further N two DARK BLUE streets namely Percy St and Homfray St." The Booth map very clearly calls it Percy Terrace.
p.244   Clarke Nicholls and Coombs jam and sweet factory had extensive premises in the area. They were established in 1872, as a sweet manufacturer – mint creams, butterscotch, caramels, and chocolates etc., including their 'Clarnico' jelly tablets.

p.244   Suther St is clearly Suthers St in the Booth map.

Walk 58 (B346 Walk 7)

p.245   It is often difficult to decipher Duckworth's writing, especially with names. For example, "The next street westwards is Brookfield St, very respectable with a Primitive Methodist Chapel (Rev. J.W. Coad)." Coad seems plausible but it could be Grad.

A few paragraphs later "North into Wetherall Rd … Half way down on the north side is a congregational chapel of corrugated iron. Pastor the Rev. G. Snashall." Marshall would be a more English name and Duckworth's vicar certainly ends with "-shall" but it looks more like "Snashall".

Walk 59 (B346 Walk 8)

p.254   'O che poco' (Oh how little! As in 'how cheap'). Hokey Pokey was 'a vulgar name for ice cream' (James Joyce) – poor quality with questionable ingredients in unsanitary conditions, often offered as 'penny licks'.

p.255   "N up Shore Rd, a prosperous, red and Jewry road." The word 'Jewry' or 'Jewy' appears to be an adjective describing the street. It is not the name of a street as, for example, Jewry Road. All the streets he mentions for the first time are underlined. This is not.

Walk 64 (B348 Walk 2)

p.285   Amir Dotan of stokenewingtonhistory.com supplied us with a good copy of a photo marked on the internet "Suffragettes outside Stoke Newington Railway Station 1899". Thanks to a query from Amir we know they were suffragists if they were indeed waiting for the train in 1899. Mrs Pankhurst didn't invent the suffragettes until 1903 while Millicent Fawcett's suffragists had been going for 20 years or so.

Three Colts

There are a variety of roadways in East London with Three Colt in their names. They are:

Three Colt St in Limehouse which goes south from Commercial Rd East just before it becomes East India Dock Rd. Duckworth says this one has "more brothels, streets and courts very crowded and narrow." (p.20; p.24).

In Bethnal Green Three Colt Lane is the section of the B135 between Bethnal Green Railway Station and Cambridge Heath Rd, referred to as Three Colts Lane by Duckworth (p.163 + p.141 map; p.161).

Three Colt Corner is immediately east of Grimsby St, an L-shaped road between Brick Lane and Cheshire St (p.118).

In some cases Duckworth uses the plural but in the maps it is always singular as in Three Colt.

Index